CURRICULUM PLANNING
FOR BETTER TEACHING AND LEARNING

4TH EDITION
CURRICULUM PLANNING
FOR BETTER TEACHING AND LEARNING

J. Galen Saylor
University of Nebraska

William M. Alexander
University of Florida

Arthur J. Lewis
University of Florida

Holt, Rinehart and Winston, Inc.
Fort Worth   Chicago   San Francisco   Philadelphia
Montreal   Toronto   London   Sydney

Library of Congress Cataloging in Publication Data

Saylor, John Galen, 1902–
  Curriculum planning for better teaching and
learning.
  Edition for 1974 published under title: Planning
curriculum for schools.
  Includes bibliographies and index.
  1. Curriculum planning—United States. I. Alex-
ander, William Marvin, 1912–   joint author.
II. Lewis, Arthur J., 1919–   joint author.
III. Title.
LB1570.S29   1981   375'.001   80-20764
ISBN 0-03-048761-7

PREFACE

Curriculum Planning for Better Teaching and Learning is a guide for planning the curriculum for any educational program serving the learning needs of people. It is intended to be a basic text for students engaged in professional study of the scope and nature of curriculum and its planning, and a reference for all persons who participate professionally in planning educational programs in any setting. This book is comprehensive in its treatment, presenting models of the process of planning and analyzing the factors and steps involved.

Curriculum planning, by its very nature, constitutes choices—choices among social aims, social theories, and psychological systems leading to choices from among a variety of ways to organize education. The choices made are based on values; curriculum development is full of values and valuing. We recognize that a commitment to values is a necessity for all curricular activity. This book retains the characteristic feature of earlier editions by presenting alternative choices without advancing a doctrinaire position. Hence, we have cited a large body of literature, often presenting different points of view, on many of the topics treated. Readers are encouraged to draw on many sources, including those cited, in formulating their own values and concepts about the nature of education, developing their personal models of the process of curriculum planning, and proceeding with the job at hand. We believe that the concepts and recommendations presented in this book provide an adequate base, both as to the scope and nature of the curriculum and the processes to be used in its planning, for students and specialists to develop further their competencies in the most important of all professional responsibilities.

Curriculum Planning for Better Teaching and Learning differs from earlier editions of this book, as well as from most other curriculum books, in two important ways. First, the book is based on a recognition that schooling and education are not synonymous; that is, education includes but is broader than schooling. Second, the book is oriented toward the utilization of future forecasts in curriculum planning.

The principles of curriculum planning described and illustrated in this book apply to the development of educational programs in any setting. Thus this book provides assistance to curriculum planners whether they are working in schools, colleges, museums, television studios, computer centers, religious organizations, voluntary groups, business and industry, or in any other education-related activity. Further, the book provides specific suggestions to enable various educational agencies to cooperatively plan comprehensive and lifelong educational programs.

The future orientation of the book reflects, in part, the experiences of the newest author. For the past five years, grants from the Florida Department of Education have enabled him to study social, economic, and technological trends and their impact on education. This resulting knowledge has influenced the content of several chapters. Chapter 8, "Curriculum Planning and the Future," makes explicit the way in which curriculum planners may develop their own interpretations of future forecasts and use these interpretations in planning educational programs. The possibilities and problems associated with developing a network of learning systems are explored in Chapter 8.

A distinctive hallmark of earlier editions of this book has been its valuable historic perspective on curriculum planning. This edition maintains this tradition. Thus the book epitomizes what we believe to be the ideal mode of progress for education—to move forward with one foot planted firmly in the past and the other stepping into the future.

The organization of this book follows that of its predecessor volume because this is our conception of the elements of the curriculum and its planning. However, each chapter has been completely revised to include research and other pertinent publications of the intervening years and to give full consideration to current curriculum developments—for example, minimum competency testing and mainstreaming.

Chapter 1 provides historical perspective on several curriculum issues and presents a basic framework for curriculum planning. General principles to guide in the process of planning together with practical applications are included in Chapter 2. Effective curriculum plans are based on data regarding society, learners, nature of knowledge, and concepts from behavioral sciences. Chapter 3 includes some of these data and suggests additional sources.

Chapter 4 describes procedures to follow in specifying educational goals, subgoals, and objectives. Five different types of curriculum designs are described in Chapter 5. There, as throughout the book, the importance of making appropriate choices of design based on values and to achieve different purposes is emphasized. Similarly in Chapter 6, a variety of instructional models is presented and their use is related to possible curriculum designs. Chapter 7 presents alternative approaches to a continuing aspect of curriculum planning—evaluation. Chapter 8 relates forecasts of the future to curriculum development.

We are indebted to our students, colleagues, and former teachers for helping us to learn about curriculum. We are especially indebted to Hollis L. Caswell, whose contributions to the theories and practices of curriculum planning over many years constitute the basis for valid and forward-looking planning in the future.

We dedicate this book to all of those who have the privilege of planning opportunities for learning in any setting. Our hope is that insights gained from this book will result in superior programs of education.

Lincoln, Nebraska   J. Galen Saylor
Gainesville, Florida   William M. Alexander
Gainesville, Florida   Arthur J. Lewis

September 1980

CONTENTS

ONE
...
CURRICULUM PLANNING
..
an overview
.

This is a book about planning educational experiences; education is defined as an orderly, deliberate, and sustained effort to transmit or develop knowledge, concepts, skills, attitudes, or habits. Education takes place in a variety of settings and through the efforts of many different individuals. Schools and universities constitute one obvious source of education. But other settings provide orderly, deliberate, and sustained efforts to transmit or develop knowledge, concepts, skills, attitudes, or habits. For example, education takes place in religious schools, in youth organizations such as Boy Scouts and Girl Scouts, in museums, through radio and television, in homes, and in many industries. As the need for education increases in the future, more individuals will be involved in planning educational experiences in an increased variety of settings. The value of the educational experience depends in large part upon the quality of the opportunities for learning that are planned and provided.

The purpose of this book is to help individuals who plan learning opportunities. The book is based on the assumption that schooling and education are not synonymous; schooling is but one, albeit an important one, of the elements of a total system of education. This assumption distinguishes this curriculum publication from others in two important ways. First, the text is written to assist individuals and groups as they plan learning opportunities in any setting. The value of the principles developed in this book has been demonstrated for school settings. These principles can also be used in designing educational programs for other educational settings. Because previous writing on curriculum has focused on schools, illustrations drawn from schools will predominate. Second, the book shows how curriculum plans for a group of learners in one setting may be related to educational experiences provided for the same learners in other aspects of their educational environment. Ways to integrate different elements in any given learner's system are emphasized in the book.

This book presents no single, simple formula for curriculum planning. Any such presentation would be a dangerous oversimplification of a complex field. We will instead review various concepts of curriculum and its planning, explain and illustrate some principles and practices we consider especially relevant, and leave to readers the development and application of their own formulas for use in particular curriculum planning situations.

This chapter is an overview of the field of curriculum planning and an introduction to the book. Alternative concepts of the curriculum are presented together with some basic considations in planning a curriculum. In this publication, the curriculum is viewed both as a conceptual scheme and as the changing, living happening it can be and is in the school and community of real people. Similarly, curriculum planning is viewed both as the system it can be and as the combination of operations, however inadequate and unrealistic, it is in actual educational settings.

CONCEPTS OF THE CURRICULUM

Since education is an orderly and deliberate effort, some plan is needed to guide this effort. The term *curriculum* generally refers to this plan. The way in which curriculum is defined reflects value judgments regarding the nature of education. The definition used also influences how curriculum will be planned and utilized.

The authors of the many books and other publications on curriculum that have appeared since the first in 1918, Bobbitt's *The Curriculum,*[1] have usually presented a particular conception of the curriculum. Many of these conceptions have contained similar elements, if not phraseology, and some efforts at their classification have been made. Lewis and Miel identified definitions of curriculum in the following categories: course of study, intended learning outcomes, intended opportunities for engagement, learning opportunities provided, learner's actual engagements, and learner's actual experiences. They defined curriculum as "a set of intentions about opportunities for engagement of persons-to-be-educated with other persons and with things (all bearers of information, processes, techniques, and values) in certain arrangements of time and space."[2] Tanner and Tanner traced the history of curriculum definitions showing that "curriculum has been variously defined as: 1) the cumulative tradition of organized knowledge; 2) modes of thought; 3) race experience; 4) guided experience; 5) a planned learning environment; 6) cognitive/affective content and process; 7) an instructional plan; 8) instructional ends or outcomes; and 9) a technological system of production."[3]

Our own analysis of past and present concepts of the curriculum benefits from and relates to those just cited but employs somewhat different categories.

[1]Franklin Bobbitt, *The Curriculum* (Boston: Houghton Mifflin Company, 1918).
[2]Arthur J. Lewis and Alice Miel, *Supervision for Improved Instruction: New Challenges, New Responses* (Belmont, Calif.: Wadsworth Publishing Company, Inc., 1972), p. 27.
[3]Daniel Tanner and Laurel N. Tanner, *Curriculum Development: Theory into Practice,* 2nd ed. (New York: Macmillan Publishing Co., Inc., 1980), p. 36.

The Curriculum as Subjects and Subject Matter

Historically and currently, the dominant concept of the curriculum is that of subjects and subject matter therein to be taught by teachers and learned by students. In high schools and colleges, the term *curriculum* has been and still is widely used to refer to the set of subjects or courses offered, and also to those required or recommended or grouped for other purposes; thus, such terms as the *college preparatory curriculum, science curriculum,* and *premedical curriculum* are commonly used. In curriculum terminology, *program of studies* is more properly used in these connections.

Despite efforts for over a half century to achieve broader and different curriculum foci, the concept of curriculum as subject matter persists as the basis of the dominant curriculum design (see Chapter 5). It was central to and emphasized by the wave of curriculum development in the subject fields that began in the 1950s and was stimulated by the Russian advance into outer space and subsequent pressure to improve American education.

The concept of the curriculum as subjects and subject matter has been reflected in a plethora of theories relating to principles for selection, sequence, and grade placement of subject matter. Comprehensive statements of the theory underlying curriculum planning for a subject curriculum are of relatively recent origin, perhaps because the process was so long unchallenged and in a general sense is well known. Curriculum planning for a subject curriculum follows a fairly common formula:

1. Use expert judgment (based on various social and educational factors) to determine what subjects to teach.
2. Use some criterion (difficulty, interest, sequence, for example) to select the subject matter for particular populations (grouped, for example, by state, district, age, or grade) and subjects.
3. Plan and implement appropriate methods of instruction to ensure mastery of the subject matter selected.

Even with the more sophisticated theories and processes now available, we reject as inadequate any conception of the curriculum which confines education to the fields of organized knowledge. Earlier, when subject planning and materials development were less well done than they are today, curriculum theorizing generally tended to be focused on moving away from the subject design.

The Curriculum as Experiences

The concept of the curriculum as the experiences of the learner, including those utilizing organized subject matter, was introduced in early curriculum publications. Caswell and Campbell embraced the experiences concept of the curriculum as they observed the sterility of instruction based on textbooks and courses of study outlining subject matter. In their popular *Curriculum Development* (1935), they gave this concept wide exposure, holding the school curriculum "to be composed of all the experiences children have under the guidance of teachers."[4] Many subsequent publications utilized similar definitions.

The discrepancy between the planned curriculum and the experienced curriculum continues. Goodlad, after visiting hundreds of classrooms, identified four curriculums: *formal curriculum* (as set forth by the state and local school boards); *perceived curriculum* (what teachers say they are trying to do); *observed curriculum* (what observers see when present in the classroom); and *experiential curriculum* (what the students are perceiving and reacting to).[5] This disparity between the formal or perceived curriculum and the observed or experiential curriculum is symptomatic of separating means and ends in education. The ends in education are responses to the question, "What shall be taught?" while the means of education are responses to the question, "How shall it be taught?" When means are separated from ends, the curriculum experienced may vary from the curriculum planned.

An earlier edition of this book (1966) used a definition Lewis and Miel classified with Caswell's as "something actualized." Our intent, however, is to emphasize the curriculum *as a plan* rather than as a record or even an observation of learning opportunities; but along with Caswell and others, we reject concepts of the curriculum that focus solely on subjects or objectives. For the curriculum to have the vitality Caswell and Campbell and subsequent authors sought, the curriculum plan must be based on consideration of "all elements in the experience of the learner,"[6] so that means and ends are consistent.

The issue posed by this concept has to do with the relation of planning ends and means. Seeing the curriculum as a plan, we would place our concept of the curriculum in the classification by Lewis and Miel as "something intended," but we believe that the intention should include both ends and means. Certainly means and ends (that is, instructional strategies and curriculum objectives) need at some points to be considered separately. And in a particular curriculum planning situation it is to be expected that objectives, designs, instruction, and evaluation will at points be studied and planned separately. But the relation is so inextricable that

[4]Hollis L. Caswell and Doak S. Campbell, *Curriculum Development* (New York: American Book Company, 1935), p. 69.
[5]Harold Shane Interviews John Goodlad, "A Preview of Schooling in America," *Phi Delta Kappan, 60* (September 1978): 48.
[6]Caswell and Campbell, p. 69.

we find it inadvisable—indeed, virtually impossible—to plan curriculum and instruction separately as though they were really discrete.

The Curriculum as Objectives

Early efforts at curriculum improvement made much use of aims and objectives as bases for curriculum planning. The scientific-management approach used in business and industry at the turn of this century encouraged Bobbitt to apply scientific principles to the curriculum field.[7] By applying such procedures, Bobbitt determined curriculum objectives based on skills and knowledge needed by adults. Bobbitt defined curriculum as "that series of things which children and youth must do and experience by way of developing ability to do the things well that make up the affairs of adult life. . . ."[8]

Tyler[9] contributed a model that systematized this approach through the Eight-Year Study of school–college relations and his later publications. Instruction tended to be subsumed under curriculum, although the phrase *curriculum and instruction* was commonly employed to include both curriculum designs and instructional strategies. However, methods courses tended to remain apart from curriculum courses in teacher education and certification. A series of research studies in instruction paralleled the search for new curriculum content beginning in the 1950s, and many writers began to separate more definitely the study of curriculum and the study of instruction. One result was a definition of curriculum as consisting solely of objectives or ends and instruction as the means of their attainment. This view of the curriculum was clearly stated by Johnson:

> Curriculum is concerned not with what students will *do* in the learning situation, but with what they will learn (or be able to do) as a consequence of what they do. Curriculum is concerned with what results, not with what happens. And it stands in an anticipatory relationship to the learning process, not in a reportorial relationship, after the fact. It deals with expectations or intentions, and, more specifically, with the learning outcomes intended to be achieved through instruction, that is, through the experiences provided, through what happens and what learners do.[10]

The concept of the curriculum as objectives to be achieved has had a profound impact on education. It provides the rationale for competency-based education, which has historically served as the model for vocational

[7]See Raymond Callahan, *Education and the Cult of Efficiency* (Chicago: University of Chicago, 1962), Chapters 2 and 4.
[8]Bobbitt, p. 42.
[9]Ralph Tyler, *Basic Principles of Curriculum and Instruction* (Chicago: University of Chicago Press, 1949).
[10]Mauritz Johnson, "Appropriate Research Directions in Curriculum and Instruction," *Curriculum Theory Network,* 6 (Winter 1970–1971): 25.

education. The competency-based model is being used in many professional schools and is being legislated in several states for K–12 programs. (See Chapter 5 for further discussion.)

The Curriculum as Planned Opportunities for Learning

Three conceptions of the curriculum have been considered: subject matter, experiences, and objectives. Clearly all three play a role in education—subject matter provides the knowledge core of education, learners have experiences, and stating objectives is important for many curriculum plans. However, to limit our definition of curriculum to any one of these three conceptions would restrict thinking and block consideration of important alternatives.

An adequate definition of curriculum should encompass subject matter, experience, and objectives. The definition should also provide for a plan or set of intentions, since we regard curriculum as anticipatory or intended. A curriculum plan includes specific plans (really subplans) for whatever learning opportunities are anticipated. It is focused on, but not confined to, aims and objectives, and it includes those elements identified later in this chapter as curriculum design, implementation (that is, instruction), and evaluation, which are essential to consideration and use of the plan for a specific population. The curriculum plan should minimize the dangers of separating means and ends.

Our definition of curriculum needs to be broad enough to cover learners of any age learning in any setting. The important role of the learner in the planning phase as well as the implementation phase of education should be recognized. Tyler emphasized the importance of learner participation when he commented on changes he would make in the four basic curriculum questions he posed originally in 1949. After affirming that the questions were still valid, he commented:

> I would give much greater emphasis now to careful consideration of the implications for curriculum development of the active role of the student in the learning process. I would also give much greater emphasis to a comprehensive examination of the nonschool areas of student learning in developing a curriculum.[11]

Tyler concluded, "Where possible and appropriate, the students themselves should participate in the planning and evaluation of the curriculum."[12]

Greene, in an article on the artistic–esthetic and the curriculum, em-

[11]Ralph Tyler, "Desirable Content for a Curriculum Development Syllabus Today," in Alex Molnar and John A. Zahorik (eds.), *Curriculum Theory* (Washington, D.C.: Association for Supervision and Curriculum Development, 1977), p. 37.
[12]Tyler, "Desirable Content for Curriculum Today," p. 40.

phasized the importance of "moving young people to self-reflectiveness and critical awareness."[13] Greene decried ". . . the anesthetic character of so many institutions in our culture, including schools" and social structures ". . . pressing down on human beings and rendering them passive: gazers, not see-ers; hearers, not listeners."[14] From this frame of reference Greene concluded, "Curriculum, to me, ought to be a means of providing opportunities for the seizing of a range of meanings by persons open to the world, especially today."[15] Our definition of curriculum should keep open—indeed, should encourage—learners to seize or grasp a range of meanings from their world.

We define curriculum as a plan for providing sets of learning opportunities for persons to be educated. Note that the provision of sets of learning opportunities could encompass a subject-centered curriculum or a competency-based curriculum. It could also include an experience type of curriculum such as a values-clarification experience. The provision of sets of learning opportunities can also describe a learning environment where learners can grasp a range of meanings. For example, this definition encompasses the open curriculum as found in some British primary schools.

In applying this definition, the term *plan* should be viewed as an intention rather than a blueprint. An effective teacher works with a plan in the same sense that an artist starts with an image of a landscape to be painted or a head to be sculpted. As the artist works to embody this image, the image may vary. Similarly, as effective teachers embody the curriculum plan through instruction, they may vary the original plan as appropriate. Too often, ineffective teachers "plow ahead" with their plans, ignoring the learners and their interaction with the material. Curriculum plans should free teachers to be creative, not lock them into unproductive lessons.

BASIC CONSIDERATIONS IN PLANNING OPPORTUNITIES FOR LEARNING

Planning opportunities for learning requires making choices. Of the myriad of possible opportunities for learning, which ones should be selected for a given set of learners? Since curriculum choices are value-based, they cannot be determined solely through the use of empirical data. The appropriateness of a curriculum plan will be improved when curriculum decision makers (whether textbook writers, curriculum committees, or classroom teachers) have a knowledge of curriculum choices to be made and criteria to apply in making choices.

[13]Maxine Greene, "The Artistic-Aesthetic and Curriculum," *Curriculum Inquiry, 6* (1977): 283.
[14]Greene, p. 284.
[15]Greene, p. 284.

Kliebard identified four problems that arise when the central curriculum question, "What should we teach?" is confronted. "1) Why should we teach this rather than that? 2) Who should have access to what knowledge? 3) What rules should govern the teaching of what has been selected? and 4) How should the various parts of the curriculum be interrelated in order to create a coherent whole?"[16] Is there a theory that can guide in solving these problems—in making these choices?

Kliebard reviewed alternative definitions of the word *theory* as applied by Ernest Nagel. At one end of the continuum, Nagel placed hard sciences "where the term theory is usually meant to designate a system of universal statements."[17] At the opposite end of the continuum, Nagel defined theory as "any more or less systematic analysis of a set of related concepts."[18] Kliebard concluded that it may be possible to develop a curriculum theory, in the latter sense. He based his theory on the writings of Dewey:

> Through the concept of experience, Dewey hoped to tie together the two elements that constitute the heart of any curriculum theory: the child, on the one hand, with its crude, unsystematized, concrete forms of experience; and, on the other, the abstract, highly refined, and systematically organized experience of the human race.[19]

Although Dewey's ideas may provide the basis for eventual development of a curriculum theory, at this time there is no agreed-upon comprehensive theory to guide us fully in curriculum planning.

Lack of a comprehensive theory does not mean that curriculum planning must be haphazard. There are basic considerations that can guide the curriculum planner in making choices. This section examines considerations having to do with the relationship between curriculum, instruction, and teaching; historical antecedents in planning curriculum; bases for the curriculum; relation of elements of the curriculum; and the relationship between the learner and the curriculum.

Relation of Curriculum, Instruction, and Teaching

Curriculum has been defined as a plan for providing sets of learning opportunities for persons to be educated. Plans have no impact until they are set in motion; thus, learning opportunities remain only opportunities until learners become engaged with the opportunities. *Instruction is defined, then, as the actual engagements of learners with planned learning*

[16]Herbert M. Kliebard, "Curriculum Theory: Give Me a 'For Instance'," *Curriculum Inquiry,* 6 (1977): 262.

[17]Kliebard, p. 262.

[18]Kliebard, p. 263.

[19]Kliebard, p. 267.

opportunities. Thus, instruction can be thought of as the implementation of the curriculum plan.

The terms *curriculum* and *instruction* are interlocked almost as inextricably as the names Tristan and Isolde or Romeo and Juliet. Without a curriculum or plan, there can be no effective instruction; and without instruction the curriculum has little meaning.

Teaching and instruction are sometimes used interchangeably; we make a distinction between the terms. Instruction—that is, the engagement of a learner in a planned opportunity for learning—does not require a teacher. Lewis and Miel pointed out that teaching is a human function performed for another person. Thus, ". . . one might speak of self-instruction through programmed materials, a book, or film but not of self-teaching."[20] Following this logic, *we adopted a definition of teaching as a process whereby one person mediates between another person and the substance of this world to facilitate learning.* Learning is taken to be a change in the learner's behavior. Note that this definition of teaching enables us to include a variety of individuals as teachers. Parents can be teachers; so can scout leaders and peers. In fact, anyone who facilitates learning by mediating between a person and the substance of this world is a teacher. This is not to say that all teachers are good teachers nor that all teaching is effective.

An understanding of the relationships and the differences between curriculum, instruction, and teaching will improve the choices made by curriculum planners. Effective plans for opportunities for learning—curriculum—make provision for their implementation—instruction—and for the mediating function between persons and materials—teaching.

Historical Antecedents in Planning Opportunities for Learning

Curriculum planners can profit from an understanding of the history of curriculum planning. While they should not be bound in their decisions by historical precedent, to remain ignorant of such precedent can lead to repeating errors. The history of curriculum is particularly instructive because of its cyclical nature.

Although the history of education goes back to humanity's beginnings, the application of science to education is a development of the last 100 years. This history shows the influence of societal changes on education. And just as economic conditions and social ideals have ebbed and flowed during the past century, educational ideas have changed. This section provides a historical overview of three curriculum themes and their variations: procedures for planning curriculum, the learner and the nature of the curriculum, and content of the curriculum. As will become apparent,

[20]Lewis and Miel, pp. 30–31.

these three themes are interrelated as shapes and colors in an unfolding tapestry with society as a background.

Procedures for Planning Curriculum

In 1885, John Philbrick rejected the voluntary and pluralistic system of education and advocated that "one best system"[21] of education be developed and universally used. In 1918, Bobbitt applied the ideas of scientific management and developed a curriculum with objectives drawn directly from the life of adults. This approach has continued to influence curriculum, but with varying degrees of intensity. During the 1920s, several large cities (Los Angeles, Denver, St. Louis) adopted Bobbitt's approach and used procedures that were referred to as a scientific or an analytical-aims approach.

In the 1930s, according to Caswell, "three major influences turned curriculum development away from the dominant theory and procedure of the twenties."[22] The first influence was the experimentalist philosophical position that rejected a scientific approach, stressing ends before means and linear relationships between ends and means. The experimentalist position views ends and means as integrated and dialectically related. The second influence that eroded the dominant curriculum theory and practice in the 1920s was the Gestalt theory in psychology. This theory led to an organismic view of learning and development which, for many curriculum workers, replaced connectionism which had provided a good theoretical basis for the analytical-aims procedure of curriculum development. The third major influence during the 1930s was the great depression. Schools were asked to lead in social reconstruction with a curriculum related to students' identifiable and obvious needs.

Curriculum leaders associated with the Eight-Year Study[23] and the Progressive Education Association during the 1930s ". . . were centrally interested in students. They gave high priority to understanding, defining, and building on student's needs, purposes, and interests."[24] Caswell concluded that these leaders did not believe the best approach was through an analytical-aims procedure.

The development of evaluation instruments for the Eight-Year Study led in an interesting way, however, to a return to an analytical-procedures approach to curriculum. The evaluation group, headed by Tyler, demanded a more precise definition of aims. From his work, Tyler developed

[21]David Tyack, *The One Best System* (Cambridge: Harvard University Press, 1974).
[22]Hollis Caswell, "Persistent Curriculum Problems," *The Educational Forum, XLIII* (November 1978): 103.
[23]For a description of the Eight-Year Study, see Wilford M. Aiken, *The Story of the Eight-Year Study* (New York: Harper and Brothers, 1942).
[24]Caswell, p. 105.

his model referred to earlier. Tyler stated his rationale for evaluating a curriculum in terms of four questions which must be answered in developing any curriculum or plan of instruction:

1. What educational purposes should the school seek to attain?
2. What educational experiences can be provided that are likely to attain these purposes?
3. How can these educational experiences be effectively organized?
4. How can we determine whether these purposes are being attained?[25]

Tyler's curriculum model, which he continued to support but with modifications, represented a return to the earlier analytical-aims procedures.

Molnar and Zahorik believed that "the power and impact of the Tyler model cannot be overstated."[26] They pointed out that teachers and curriculum committees have viewed the asking and answering of Tyler's four questions as their primary task. They concluded, "To stand outside of Tyler is to stand outside of the dominant assumptions of American culture."[27]

Caswell viewed Tyler's approach as ". . . a step backward to the mechanistic procedures used in the twenties. It again made adult goals dominant in selecting and organizing pupil experiences."[28] Further, Caswell concluded after reviewing curriculum writings, "So far as I could detect, there was no evidence of a significant tendency during the forties and fifties to return to the mechanistic practices of the twenties."[29]

But a new set of actors entered the curriculum planning stage in the 1950s. The scientific approach to curriculum planning had virtually eliminated parents because they were not professionals. However, in the late 1940s and early 1950s, parents and other citizens found a way to participate. A wave of criticism leveled at progressive education and neglect of the three R's engulfed the schools. The 1950s also saw the Russians launching the first spacecraft, Sputnik, followed by the enactment of the National Defense Education Act (NDEA), which provided federal funds for curriculum development. The ensuing programs were, for the most part, developed by academicians who valued subject content and had little concern for the needs and interests of students. The resultant national curriculum programs, such as the "new math" instituted in the 1950s and early 1960s, reflected Tyler's model.

The Tyler model was adapted by other curriculum writers during this

[25]Tyler, *Basic Principles of Curriculum and Instruction,* p. 1.
[26]Alex Molnar and John A. Zahorik (eds.), *Curriculum Theory* (Washington, D.C.: Association for Supervision and Curriculum Development, 1977), p. 3.
[27]Molnar and Zahorik, p. 3.
[28]Caswell, p. 105.
[29]Caswell, p. 106.

period. For example, Taba's seven-step model extended Tyler's four questions.

1. Diagnosis of needs.
2. Formulation of objectives.
3. Selection of content.
4. Organization of content.
5. Selection of learning experiences.
6. Organization of learning experiences.
7. Determination of what to evaluate and of the ways and means of doing it.[30]

In the 1970s, Tyler's technological line of curriculum thinking was extended by intructional designers. For example, the four-step model used by Briggs reflects Tyler's questions.

a. Goals . . ., to be attained are identified in terms of learners' performance.
b. Evaluative measures are designed to assess attainment of goals.
c. Alternative sets of strategies are considered.
d. Design decisions (are made to) conform to the defined inputs.[31]

Popham and Baker advocated a four-step goal-referenced model:

1. Specification of objectives.
2. Preassessment.
3. Instruction.
4. Evaluation.[32]

The scientific management movement at the beginning of the century spawned Bobbitt's early work on curriculum. The resurgence in the 1960s and 1970s of efficiency drives in government, industry, and the military, with their accompanying demand for performance goals and accountability, has contributed to the popularity of, and in some cases legislative mandate for, a competency-based approach to education—an approach whose direct lineage can be traced to Bobbitt through Tyler.

Although Bobbitt's original view of curriculum is dominant today, there are other views of the curriculum development process. Macdonald, for example, would relegate talk about objectives to instruction and design educational programs to achieve three aims: socialization, development, and liberation.[33]

[30]Hilda Taba, *Curriculum Development: Theory and Practice* (New York: Harcourt, Brace and World, Inc., 1962), p. 12.
[31]Leslie J. Briggs, *Handbook of Procedures for the Design of Instruction* (Pittsburgh: American Institute for Research, 1970), p. vii.
[32]W. James Popham and Eva I. Baker, *Systematic Instruction* (Englewood Cliffs, New Jersey: Prentice-Hall, Inc., 1970).
[33]Molnar and Zahorik, p. 16.

Lewis and Miel proposed an imaging-embodiment approach to designing a curriculum. In such an approach:

> ... curriculum and instruction are each imaged as an organic whole of inter-related parts. The two wholes are in direct and constant interplay; the embodiment can be checked against the image and the next imaging can respond meaningfully to any discrepancy between intention and realization. As part of the ongoing process either image or embodiment or both can be revised to maintain the integrity and the continuities essential to an organic whole.[34]

This approach views ends and means as integrated and dialectically related, while Tyler stressed ends before means with a linear relationship between the two.

Edson identified three legacies from the emerging scientific ideology of curriculum development. "First, curriculum came to be viewed by educators as a professional, nonpolitical concern." Educators, once surprised by strong political reactions to curriculum formulations, are beginning to understand that curriculum building is a legitimate political concern. The second legacy, related to the first, is that ". . . viewing curriculum development as a rational and scientific process often obscures important power alignments among and between political coalitions, economic interest groups, and professional organizations—all of whom may benefit from curriculum change." The third legacy is that ". . . the application of scientific procedures to curriculum development suggests that curriculum is 'value free' or 'value neutral.' "[35] In fact, all of the important questions in curriculum are value questions.

What can be concluded from this brief historical review of procedures used in developing curriculum? Although there continues to be a major emphasis on an analytic-aims or scientific approach, there are diverse views as to how a curriculum should be planned or designed. Individuals responsible for developing educational programs in various settings should recognize that there is no curriculum development procedure that is universally desirable. Rather, different approaches should be employed depending upon the nature of the program planned. This book systematically considers different approaches to help the reader understand when and how they may be applied.

The Learner and Nature of Curriculum

One hundred years ago, schooling was standardized with universal expectations for students. In 1893, the prestigious Committee of Ten rejected the idea of a differentiated curriculum for high school students.

[34]Lewis and Miel, p. 159.
[35]C. H. Edson, "Curriculum Change During the Progressive Era," *Educational Leadership*, *36* (October 1978): 65.

However, forces already at work within society eventually led to a change in this position.

More than 23 million immigrants came to the United States between 1880 and 1919. Schools were expected to induct these new citizens into American society by teaching them predominant Anglo-Saxon Protestant values and English. Schools served the "melting pot" function within society. To do this required a differentiated curriculum. At the same time, developments in child psychology provided a scientific base for a differentiated curriculum. The influential psychologist G. Stanley Hall published an essay at the turn of the century on "The Ideal School as Based on Child Study."[36] Cremin pointed out that the key concept in this essay ". . . concerned the difference between the *scholiocentric* and the *pedocentric* school. The former, the dominant ideal of Western education throughout its history, fitted the child to the school; the latter, in Hall's view the only defensible ideal for a republic, fitted the school to the child."[37] Hall's position helped shift the focus of teaching from the school with its well-defined content to the children with their particular backgrounds and needs. Cremin commented that ". . . educational opportunity had become the right of all who attended school to receive something of meaning and value. The shift was truly Copernican, its effects, legion."[38] Educators accepted Hall's ideas, and by 1918 the NEA's Commission on Reorganization of Secondary Education reversed the earlier stand of the Committee of Ten. In their report on Cardinal Principles of Secondary Education,[39] individual differences among secondary school pupils were recognized and curriculum commensurate with individual ability was recommended. Dewey's writings in the 1890s and early 1900s, and especially his laboratory school at the University of Chicago, were very influential in this movement.

Various plans were developed to meet individual differences. For example, during the 1920s the Winnetka, Illinois, schools, under the leadership of Superintendent Carleton Washburne, divided the curriculum into two parts: the common essentials—the three R's, the sciences, and the social studies—and the so-called "creative activities," providing each child with opportunities for self-expression and exploration of special interests and abilities. The common essentials were individualized by allowing children to proceed at their own rate.

[36]G. Stanley Hall, "The Ideal School as Based on Child Study," *The Forum, XXXII,* (1901–1902): 24–25.
[37]Lawrence A. Cremin, *The Transformation of the School* (New York: Alfred A. Knopf, 1961), p. 103.
[38]Cremin, p. 104.
[39]National Education Association, "Cardinal Principles of Secondary Education," *U.S. Bureau of Education Bulletin, 35* (2) (1918).

The relationship between meeting individual needs and curriculum planning was recognized by Jesse H. Newlon, Superintendent of the Denver, Colorado, schools. Newlon believed that it was the responsibility of the schools to serve all comers and recognized that to do this would require some changes in curriculum. As Cremin pointed out, this idea was not new: "Rather his originality lay in his notion of how these adjustments might be accomplished. 'No program of studies will operate that has not evolved to some extent out of the thinking of teachers who are to apply it,' he wrote his board in 1923."[40] Accordingly, committees of teachers planned programs to meet the needs of Denver's children and youth.

The extent to which the curriculum should be adapted to the individual learner has been a continuing issue in American education. The right of all who attend school to receive something of meaning and value has led to court decisions on desegregation,[41] financing education,[42] and education of bilingual students.[43] The courts have established the constitutional rights of an individual to obtain a free and appropriate public education.

Children with special learning needs represent the newest group to seek this right. When Congress passed PL 94–142 (the Education of All Handicapped Children Act of 1975), they cited as one of the purposes "to assure that all handicapped children have available to them . . . a free appropriate public education."[44] The law provides that due process procedures be used in the placement of students in the least restrictive environment. Further, the law mandates that a written individual education program (IEP) shall be developed for every handicapped student and serve as a basis for monitoring and judging the educational program. Parents of all children may soon insist on IEP's.

The legacy to the curriculum planner of the shift from the scholiocentric to the pedocentric school—or the school fitted to the learner—provides important policy questions, according to Edson: "Curriculum-makers must be careful of the categories they use to differentiate children and must constantly reevaluate the organizational, ethnic, and scientific rationales for structural differentiation." Attending to learners' individual differences often results in "blaming the victims" for school failures. According to Edson, "We often obscure the ways in which schools systematically and structurally rationalize inequality." Edson also warned that "because of curriculum differentiation and the always fashionable appeal for educators to 'meet the needs of the child,' curriculum-makers often fail

[40]Cremin, p. 299.
[41]*Brown* v. *Board of Education of Topeka,* 347 U.S. 483, 493 (1954).
[42]*Serrano* v. *Priest,* 5 Cal. 3rd 584,96 Cal R ptr. 601, 487 P. 2d 1241 (1971).
[43]*Lau* v. *Nichols,* 414 U.S. 563 (1974).
[44]U.S. Congress, Public Law 94–142, Education for All Handicapped Children Act (November 29, 1975).

to address the important question of what knowledge should we as a society hold in common and why?"[45]

Edson's precautions to curriculum workers need to be heeded. The drive to assure that all who attend school will receive something of meaning and value will not diminish. In fact, this drive may be extended so that anyone who wishes to learn will be guaranteed appropriate opportunities.

The Content of the Curriculum

Changes in content of the curriculum over the past 100 years have both influenced and been influenced by procedures used in designing the curriculum. Educators' views of the relationship of the learner to the curriculum have influenced curriculum content. Changes in content were also influenced by shifts within society.

One hundred years ago, the content was organized around disciplines in order to pass the accumulated wisdom of mankind on to the young. With his introduction of the scientific or analytic-aims approach to curriculum development, Bobbitt added the skills needed by adults as legitimate curriculum content. The work of Bruner and others in the national curriculum projects reemphasized the importance of organizing curriculum around disciplines, often at the expense of equipping learners to meet adult needs.

Changes in how educators viewed learners had an even more profound impact on content. One hundred years ago, learners were expected to fit the school. As indicated in the previous section, through Hall's work at the turn of the century, the principle that schools should adapt to the learners' needs, interests, and capabilities was generally recognized. The extent to which content has reflected this principle has risen and fallen over the ensuing years. The application of the principle reached a zenith during the 1930s and 1940s with the encouragement of the now defunct Progressive Education Association.

Changes in society have had a profound influence on content of the curriculum. As our society has become more complex over the past 100 years, other educational influences such as the home, religious organizations, and the community have become less effective. As a result, schools have been asked to assume increasing responsibility. For example, at one time youth learned a vocation from their parents or from another adult in the community through an apprenticeship program. In another era, the home, church, and community were generally expected to instill moral values. As the influence of these groups has waned, schools have been expected to instill moral values. Thus, for example, state laws may require schools to teach the effects of alcohol and tobacco, and respect for law.

Over the past 100 years, the content of the curriculum has been broad-

[45]Edson, p. 68.

ened in order to meet nearly all of the educational needs of children and youth and in order to alleviate social problems. Educators were generally supportive of these changes. For example, the National Education Association report on the Cardinal Principles of Education (1918) agreed that schools should "educate for life" and adopted seven objectives: "a) health; b) command of fundamental processes; c) worthy home membership; d) vocation; e) citizenship; f) worthy use of leisure; and g) ethical character."[46] In 1944, the Educational Policies Commission reaffirmed this position in their list of "Imperative Educational Needs of Youth."[47] In 1976, Shane forecast educational needs for the next 25 years and argued "that we need to move ahead to *new* basics." He included cross-cultural understandings, empathy, human relations, and intercultural rapport as "fundamental skills" toward which schools should direct their energies.[48]

Not only have schools been asked (and agreed) to assume more of society's responsibilities, they have also provided educational programs for more people. Access to schools has been provided to handicapped children and youth who earlier were classified as uneducable. An ever-increasing percentage of students have continued through high school and entered college; more adults have returned to school.

The use of schools to solve society's problems continues. Schools have been asked to lead the way in integrating a segregated society. In the 1960s, compensatory education programs were instituted in an effort to break the cycle of poverty that had "chained" a whole class in our society.

The historical antecedents of the content of the curriculum leave a number of questions unanswered. Have the schools taken on too many responsibilities? If so, what other agencies can assist? How can all of these agencies work together in providing a total educational system? These questions are discussed in the section on relation of elements of the curriculum.

Bases for the Curriculum

Three sources have a major claim to consideration as curriculum planners make choices: society, learners, and knowledge. The values and behaviors defined as desirable by a given society help to shape the aims of education. The purposes, interests, needs, and abilities of learners should guide curriculum planners. Knowledge should be organized to assure its widest generalized meaning and most effective future use. These three bases—society, learners, and knowledge—will be discussed in detail in

[46]"Cardinal Principles," p. 5.
[47]Educational Policies Commission, *Education for All American Youth* (Washington, D.C.: National Education Association, 1944), pp. 225, 226.
[48]Harold G. Shane, "America's Next 25 Years: Some Implications for Education," *Phi Delta Kappan, 58,* (September 1976): 82–83.

Chapter 3 as processes and sources of data for curriculum planning are described. There are, however, two overarching questions of continual concern to curriculum planners: 1) What relative emphases should be assigned to society, learners, and knowledge? and 2) How are our values guiding curriculum choices that we make?

Society, Learners, and Knowledge as Bases of Curriculum

The history of education over the past 100 years, as noted in the previous section, shows how the degree of emphasis on each of the three bases shifted over time. One hundred years ago, the emphasis was almost exclusively on knowledge, an emphasis that returned in the 1950s and 1960s. Stimulated by the work of Hall and Dewey, increased attention was given to the learners at the turn of the century and reemphasized in the 1930s and 1940s. Bobbitt's analytical-aims approach emphasized the role of education in preparing individuals to live in society. This theme became more prominent in the depression years of the 1930s and again in the 1970s.

There are dangers in using one or two bases for the curriculum at the expense of others. For example, a curriculum based only on knowledge will result in a program viewed by many learners as irrelevant—unrelated to them or to society. A program catering primarily to the needs and interests of students may result in large gaps in the knowledge needed in today's world.[49] A program designed to meet society's present needs would reinforce the status quo in learners and block out their opportunities to generate new knowledge and produce new ideas.

One secret of effective curriculum planning is to assign appropriate weights to a consideration of society, learners, and knowledge. The weights assigned should shift with the type of learning opportunities being planned. However, it is difficult to imagine any effective curriculum plan that had not attended to all three bases of the curriculum.

A few illustrations will show how the assigned weights shift. A Red Cross training class will certainly have a primary focus on knowledge to be learned. However, the knowledge will be selected in relation to probable emerging needs within society, and the material will be adapted to the present level of knowledge of the students and their aptitudes. A class in painting for adults, if it is to succeed, will be geared closely to the needs, interests, and aptitudes of the learners. At the same time, a knowledge of color and techniques of mixing paints and stretching canvases should be included. The design of a college physics course will reflect organized knowledge. Its effectiveness will be reduced, however, if it completely ignores the needs and interests of learners and is not relevant to society.

[49]Some might argue that Summerhill, developed by A. S. Neill, provided such a program with an adequate knowledge base.

Values and Bases of the Curriculum

Curriculum workers will make choices regarding the relative importance assigned to society, learners, and knowledge as bases for the curriculum and the type of information considered. These choices depend upon curriculum workers' answers to such value questions as: What is the good society? What is the good life? What is the good person? Macdonald pointed out that there is no way curriculum workers "can avoid assuming choices of value and implying them in their work."[50] Also, he warned that many curriculum workers with a fundamentally technological orientation are not aware of their value base nor even aware that the values reflected in their work are not subject to their own control. "It is this value witlessness that is frightening in the technological approach, not the approach itself, since technological rationality is obviously a potential for either human good or evil."[51]

Value judgments are inherent in any statement of aims or purposes for an educational program. For example, is the purpose of education socialization of the learner? If so, what does socialization mean? To become like the teacher? To fit into the status quo? Or should schools be striving for development or liberation of learners? There are no right or wrong answers to these questions. They are value questions.

Curriculum workers need to guard against thinking of learners as objects to be manipulated and remember that they are human beings. And what does it mean to be human? Heschel, in his provocative book *Who Is Man*, identified a series of characteristics that separate man from other beings. For example, two of these characteristics, "preciousness" and "uniqueness," mean that to be human is to view oneself and be viewed by others as priceless and unprecedented. "To my own heart my existence is unique, unprecedented, priceless, exceedingly precious, and I resist the thought of gambling away its meaning."[52]

It is sobering on the one hand to realize that educational planners may unwittingly be gambling with the meaning of existence for other human beings. On the other hand, the preciousness of human life underscores the tremendous value and importance of education. To think that through designing effective opportunities for learning we may enable another human being to grasp meaning for his or her life is indeed heady. The challenge to curriculum workers is to recognize the importance of their task and the crucial role their own values play in this endeavor.

---

[50]James B. Macdonald, "Values Bases and Issues for Curriculum," in Molnar and Zahorik (eds.), p. 15.
[51]Macdonald, p. 15.
[52]Abraham J. Heschel, *Who is Man?* (Stanford, Calif.: Stanford University Press, 1965), pp. 35–38.

Relation of Elements of the Curriculum

Any set of opportunities for learning for a given learner exists in relation to other opportunities for learning. Three concepts have been used to describe these relationships: sequence, continuity, and integration. Sequence is the vertical or sequential arrangement of related learning experiences. Opportunities for learning need to be offered in a planned sequence when the learning gained from one experience is necessary as a basis for the next learning experience. Thus, sequence provides a way to recognize a hierarchical relationship between objectives and learning experiences.

The term *sequence* is also used to describe the reiteration of learning experiences, not simply as a repetition of the same material, but as a return to a similar concept or idea at a more advanced level. For example, a college composition class engages in paragraph writing but at a more advanced level than a high school class.

A type of sequencing used in national curriculum programs developed in the 1960s provides for teaching basic concepts at several points in a student's education. Set theory in mathematics, for example, is introduced in the early grades in the new math curriculum and repeated with elaboration in several subsequent grades. The term *spiral curriculum* has been applied to this sequencing.

Continuity is closely related to sequence. Continuity, however, takes place within the individual as he or she progresses over time, or in a vertical fashion, through a sequence of learning experiences. Whereas sequence is arranged by curriculum planners and teachers and is in that sense external to the learner, continuity is internal to the learner. An effective and sequential arrangement of opportunities for learning, however, can foster continuity of learning for a learner.

Integration is the horizontal relationship of learning experiences. There is integration when an individual is able to relate what he or she is learning in one class to learning in another class. Thus, concepts and skills learned in an English class may be used by a student in preparing a social studies report. The quality of educational experiences improves as learners are able to integrate their learning. Integration, similar to continuity, takes place only in the learner. Although curriculum planners can organize opportunities for learning in such a way as to facilitate integration, it is the learners who integrate what they are learning through various educational experiences.

Past efforts to facilitate integration of learning by students have focused on a school curriculum. However, integration, when appropriately viewed from the learner's perspective, applies to learning taking place in any setting, whether, for example, from television or from school. The concept of an ecological system of education is useful in viewing integration of learning.[53] Elements in this system for an individual learner are the school, the family, television, the peer group, and the community. Each of these elements exerts an educational influence on the learner. For example, community influences could include a Sunday school teacher, a sports coach, or a club leader. The learner must either integrate what he or she is learning from these various sources, or, alternatively, accept what he or she is learning from some sources and reject learnings from other sources.

The types of interactions within this ecological system of education affect the learner's ability to integrate his total learning experiences. The manner in which the various elements of the system are linked together may be studied by tracing communication channels between various parts of the system. For example, are there systematic ways to communicate between school and home? and community? and peer group? and television producers? Are there methods for providing feedback from one part of the system to another? The learner's ability to integrate knowledge from his or her total ecological system can be facilitated by good system linkage.

The degree and effectiveness of linkage within the system is a function of congruence within the system. To what extent do the various educational institutions project the same images of the culture? Do the images echo and reinforce each other—that is, do they resonate? Or are they in conflict—is there dissonance? For example, are the attitudes which the school is expected to teach regarding use of alcohol and tobacco congruent with the image of culture portrayed over television? The ease with which an individual can integrate learning from throughout his or her ecological system depends upon the congruence of the images of the culture projected.

A third type of interaction is mediation, which occurs when one institution or group directly or indirectly screens, criticizes, interprets, reinforces, or transforms the influence of another source. For example, a parent may mediate between the child and television by limiting the programs seen, by limiting the hours of viewing, or by interpreting what is seen. A parent may complement a television program by some follow-up activity, such as a trip to a zoo. Leichter states, "The essential point about mediation is that the experience in one sphere is reinterpreted through experience in another sphere."[54]

Some individuals make poor progress in school because of poor interac-

[53]Nicholas Hobbs, "Families, Schools and Communities—An Ecosystem for Children." *Teachers College Record*, 79 (May 1978): 756–766.
[54]Hope Leichter, "Families and Communities as Educators." *Teachers College Record*, 79 (May 1978): 603.

tion between elements of their ecological system. Communication is often absent, there is little congruence in the images of the culture being projected, and mediation screens and criticizes messages from other sources rather than reinforcing them. Cremin made a similar point in commenting on Coleman's report on "Equality of Educational Opportunity." After recognizing that Coleman's data suggest that the effects of schooling were less potent than had been assumed, Cremin added:

> His data did not indicate, however, that the school had no power, but rather that it was educating sequentially and synchronically along with other institutions and that its effect on different individuals was partly dependent upon what happened to them in those other institutions. It is not that schooling lacks potency; it is rather that the potency of schooling must be seen in relation to the potency of other experience (some of which is educational in character) that has occurred earlier and is occurring elsewhere.[55]

Elsewhere, Cremin made the point that "this to me is the real message of James Coleman's study of equal educational opportunity, not that the school is *powerless* but that the family is *powerful.*"[56]

Cremin concluded that we must think comprehensively about education and develop policies with respect to a wide variety of institutions that educate, not only schools and colleges. "To be concerned solely with schools in the kind of educational world we are living in today is to have a kind of fortress mentality in contending with a very fluid and dynamic situation."[57] The present authors also are of this belief, and in this book we show how a comprehensive approach toward education can be applied to curriculum planning.

The Curriculum and the Self-Directed Learner

Schools can break away from an isolated position in society by serving as clearinghouses for the many educational opportunities already available. Mitchell proposed that "the creation of networks which put people in touch with opportunities for self-development, including the school as one of those opportunities, should become the new mission of schooling."[58] As professional educators coordinate learning resources from many settings, they need to be in tune with the learners served and not reduce the linking function to a mechanical operation.

[55]Lawrence A. Cremin, *Public Education* (New York: Basic Books, Inc., 1976), p. 47.
[56]Lawrence A. Cremin, "Public Education and the Education of the Public," *Teachers College Record, 77* (September 1975): 9.
[57]Cremin, "Public Education and the Education of the Public," p. 7.
[58]Edna Mitchell, "Educational Leadership—Coming to Terms with Responsibility," in Norman Overly (ed.), *Lifelong Learning: A Human Agenda* (Alexandria, Va.: Association for Supervision and Curriculum Development, 1979), p. 169.

The central goal of schooling, and therefore of the curriculum and its planning, is the development of self-directing continuous learners. Historically, the goal of education was to liberate the learner; hence, the derivation of the term *liberal arts education.* Although statements of the goal to produce self-directed liberated learners are often found in the literature, the hard facts of practice all but deny its existence. Yet, the need to achieve the goal increases.

One certainty in an otherwise uncertain future is that mankind will continue to be faced with social, economic, and technological changes, probably of an unprecedented nature. Humanity's survival will depend upon the ability to influence these changes when possible and adapt to changes that are immutable. The ability to learn becomes crucial to survival, and education will be more and more a primordial need for each individual. Individuals need to take increasing responsibility for their own education, where the act of teaching gives way to the act of learning—where individuals become less of an object and more of a subject.

> The man submitting to education must become the man educating himself; education of others must become the education of oneself. This fundamental change in the individual's relationship to himself is the most difficult problem facing education for the future decades of scientific and technical revolution.[59]

Macdonald proposed that education should have "... the aim of freeing persons from the parochialness of their specific times and places and opening up the possibilities for persons to create themselves and their societies."[60]

In a rapidly changing world, educating people for the status quo is to educate them for obsolescence. On the other hand, we cannot give them the skills, knowledges, and attitudes they will need in a future we cannot possibly foresee. We can, however, give them the ability to be self-renewing, to create themselves and their societies in an ever-changing world, if we help them to become self-directing learners.

How can we achieve the ultimate goal of an educational system: to have the individual assume the burden of pursuing his own education? Three approaches will be described: 1) have individuals take increasing responsibility for their own learning; 2) attend to collateral learnings; and 3) broaden the base for education.

Educational experiences that provide joy and meaning will stimulate learners to take increased responsibility for their own learning. Joyce emphasized the role of curriculum workers in creating options:

[59]Edgar Faure, *Learning to Be: The World of Education Today and Tomorrow* (Paris: UNESCO, 1972), p. 161.
[60]Macdonald, p. 17.

Our efforts should be to increase on a continual basis the options that are available to the population and the flexibility with which they can be made available. As more options are developed, making more and more kinds of education commonplace, and giving students the power to educate themselves in increasingly human ways, then the curriculum worker will be making his contribution to the search for an increasingly humanistic education.[61]

The active involvement of the learner in planning his own curriculum has been advocated for a number of years. A 1957 brochure of the Association for Supervision and Curriculum Development stated:

More recently the philosophy of democratic participation and the recognition of the dynamic nature of learning have led to emphasis upon teacher-pupil planning. For the past 20 years schools have been experimenting with ways to improve the process by which children and young people help set the goals, plan the activities and evaluate the results of their work with the leadership of the teacher.[62]

Rarely, however, have learners been involved in a consistent and responsible way in planning their curriculum. Part of the reason may be a mistrust of students, according to Macdonald:

The vast majority of schools, teachers, and other concerned persons do not trust students. The basic assumption of the schools' orientation to students is that students will do the wrong thing (what you do not want them to do) unless you make them do the right thing. If this were not so, most school policies and classroom disciplinary procedures would not be justified. Surely, faith in the worth, dignity, and integrity of individuals is not in evidence.[63]

We find the conclusion inescapable that past curriculum planning has failed to involve students adequately. A strong contrast has resulted between the curriculum planned for and the curriculum experienced by students. Evidence of this dichotomy is found in the existence of a "hidden curriculum" of student strategies to pass successfully the hurdles of the formal or planned curriculum, as well as of other student-invented or student-structured systems of various "hidden" curriculums we allude to in appropriate sections of this book. Testimony as to the importance of the hidden curriculum was given by MIT psychiatrist Benson Snyder:

[61]Bruce Joyce, "Curriculum and Humanistic Education: 'Monolism' vs. Pluralism," in Carl Weinberg (ed.), *Humanistic Foundations of Education* (Englewood Cliffs, N.J.: Prentice-Hall, Inc., 1972), p. 199.
[62]Prudence Bostwick, *One Hundred Years of Curriculum Improvement, 1857–1957* (Washington, D.C.: Association for Supervision and Curriculum Development, 1957), p. 7.
[63]James B. Macdonald, "The School as a Double Agent," in Vernon F. Haubrich (ed.), *Freedom, Bureaucracy and Schooling* (Washington, D.C.: Association for Supervision and Curriculum Development and NEA, 1971), p. 237.

I have found that a hidden curriculum determines to a significant degree what becomes the basis for all participants' sense of worth and self-esteem. It is this hidden curriculum, more than the formal curriculum, that influences the adaptation of students and faculty. I know of no kindergarten, high school, or college that is without a hidden curriculum which bears on its students and faculty. Though each curriculum has characteristics that are special to the particular setting, the presence of these hidden curricula importantly affect the process of all education. The similarities in these hidden curricula are at least as important as the differences.[64]

Recognizing fully that schools differ in their methods of evaluating student progress, we can state that students by and large learn fairly early in their school careers to attach much importance to the system of marks, promotion, credits, and reports. In high school and college these paraphernalia may become such dominant student concerns as to indeed create a hidden curriculum of student communication, devices, and tactics—strategies—for succeeding in the planned curriculum. Thus, the means of meeting requirements, passing examinations, and earning teacher favor may become the ends of the student's curriculum rather than the objectives envisioned by the teachers. A fundamental change in goal setting and curriculum planning which enhances the student's role is essential in such situations.

Curriculum planning as it should be cannot result in the existence of two curriculums, the school's and the student's. The development of the life-long self-directed learner envisioned in our first assumption necessitates the end of this dualism by bringing students into the planning process early, openly, and fully.

The outcomes of a student's experience in school, or in any setting for learning, may be related then to the planned curriculum and to the student's personal or hidden curriculum. In addition, there are unanticipated outcomes that are by-products of the experience and are not outcomes sought. Dewey recognized the importance of these outcomes and referred to them collectively as collateral learning:

Perhaps the greatest of all pedagogical fallacies is the notion that a person learns only the particular thing he is studying at the time. Collateral learning in the way of formation of enduring attitudes, of likes and dislikes, may be and often is much more important than the spelling lesson or lesson in geography or history that is learned. For these attitudes are fundamentally what count in the future.[65]

One of the most important, if not the most important, collateral outcome is the desire to go on learning. Without that desire, students are unable to cope with the demands in the changing future.

---

[64]Benson Snyder, *The Hidden Curriculum* (New York: Alfred A. Knopf, 1970), pp. iii–xii.
[65]John Dewey, *Experience and Education* (New York: Collier Books, 1963), p. 48.

The impact of the social climate in an elementary school on both planned and collateral outcomes has been demonstrated by Brookover and associates.[66] They found that "more than one-half of the variance in mean achievement . . . is explained by the combination of Socio-Economic-Status, racial composition and the climate variables."[67] They were able to identify a climate variable they called "Student Sense of Academic Futility," which had the largest correlation with achievement. A high sense of academic futility was noted in schools where students felt they had no control over their success or failure in the school social systems, "the teachers do not care if they (students) succeed or not, and their fellow students punish them if they do succeed."[68] It is easy to see why a high sense of academic futility has a negative effect on academic achievement; it is important to recognize that this collateral learning will be a continuing handicap.

Not only do educational institutions influence attitudes leading to self-directed learners, but society itself plays a role. If education is a primordial need for each individual, then not only must we enrich schools and universities, but we must broaden the educational functions of society as a whole. What is needed is a social configuration that provides a "close interweaving between education and the social, political, and economic fabric, which covers the family unit and civic life."[69] Faure described such a configuration as a learning society,[70] and concluded that the movement toward a learning society "is irresistible and irreversible. It is the cultural revolution of our time."[71] The possibility of helping to create a learning society—to contribute to the cultural revolution of our time—elevates curriculum planning from a routine and mundane task to a creative life-building endeavor.

CURRICULUM PLANNING

Curriculum planning involves making a series of choices, often based on values. The preceding section presented basic considerations to guide the curriculum maker in making choices. This section describes the nature of the choices to be made and the processes to follow in making these choices.

[66]Wilbur B. Brookover, John H. Schweitzer, Jeffrey M. Schneider, Charles H. Beady, Patricia K. Flood, and Joseph M. Wisenbaker, "Elementary School Social Climate and School Achievement," *American Educational Research Journal, 15* (Spring 1978): 301–318.
[67]Brookover et al., p. 308.
[68]Brookover et al., p. 314.
[69]Faure, p. 163.
[70]The ideal of a learning society is not new. See, for example, Robert M. Hutchins, *The Learning Society* (New York: F. A. Praeger, 1968).
[71]Faure, p. 163.

Elements of a Curriculum Plan

Curriculum is defined in this book as a plan for providing sets of learning opportunities for persons to be educated. Our definition of the curriculum as a plan dictates that the curriculum anticipates the provision of learning opportunities for a particular set of objectives and a particular population. That is, the curriculum is not just any plan; it is a total plan for the program of a particular educational setting. We shall frequently refer to this plan—the curriculum—as the "curriculum plan," since this phrase is synonymous with our definition and may convey our meaning more fully to readers who have different concepts of curriculum. The curriculum plan usually incorporates many smaller plans for particular portions of the curriculum. A (partial) plan can be appropriately developed for a single set of related goals, a domain, although most curriculum plans tend to be more global (for example, general curriculum guidelines for a state or district) or more specific (for example, a course of study for one subject and level). Generally, particular plans for individual aspects of the total curriculum plan are written in such diverse forms as programs of studies, lists of activities, schedules, policy statements and handbooks, courses of study, syllabi, units of work, and learning activity packages. The total curriculum plan is rarely written as one document. In any educational setting, the most vital and influential plans may be sets of agreements reached by the faculty and by relatively small groups of teachers for achieving series of objectives formulated for particular groups of students; these agreements are rarely written down in their entirety and certainly not in a single document. A teacher's own plan for achieving particular objectives in working with a class, small group, or individual is also an aspect of the total curriculum plan.

A number of factors or elements are considered in developing a curriculum plan. The relationship of these elements to each other is portrayed in the curriculum system represented in Figure 1.1. Each element is discussed briefly in this chapter and at length in succeeding chapters. The system starts with a consideration of the functioning within society of the persons to be educated. The key question for the curriculum planner at this point is: What kinds of opportunities for learning do these persons need? want? Finding the best answer to this question will lead to describing the goals and objectives.

The nature of the educational opportunities provided depends upon the goals and objectives. As indicated in Figure 1.1, a number of considerations enter into stating goals and objectives. Ideally, the learner's personal goals and objectives will be congruent with the goals and objectives of the curriculum system. When this happens, learning is almost assured; when it does not, learning may be difficult. We suggest that goals and objectives be organized into four domains; personal development, social competence, continued learning skills, and specialization.

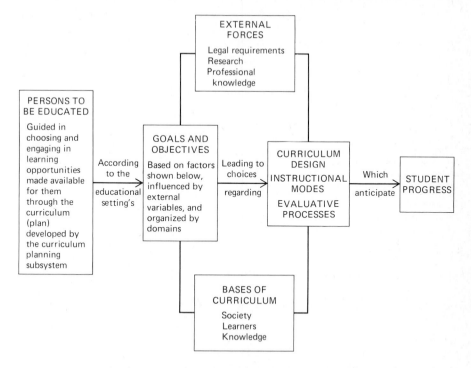

FIGURE 1.1   Elements of the curriculum system.

Agreed-upon goals and objectives provide the basis for selecting a curriculum design, choosing an instructional mode or teaching model to implement the curriculum, and evaluating the curriculum. Figure 1.2 elaborates on the portion of Figure 1.1 related to these three elements.

A curriculum design is the framework or pattern used in providing opportunities for learning. Five types of curriculum design are discussed in Chapter 5. The important decision of selecting an appropriate design is based on the goals and objectives to be achieved, the nature of the learners, and the nature of society. Political and social constraints may limit the designs to be considered.

As indicated in Figure 1.2, the curriculum planning process includes making decisions as to the instructional modes or teaching models to be used. Ideally, the curriculum plan needs to encourage flexibility and provide teachers with several suggestions for instructional modes and appropriate materials. Realistically, the selection of a particular curriculum design may limit the options available for implementation.

Curriculum evaluation of two types is suggested in Figure 1.2. Decisions need to be made and included in the curriculum plan regarding evaluation of student progress. Provisions for evaluating the curriculum plan as a plan also need to be included. The major purpose of both types of curriculum evaluation is to provide information to decision makers that

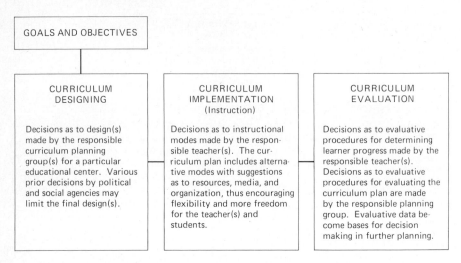

FIGURE 1.2   The curriculum planning process.

enables them to improve the quality of educational opportunities for learners.

Although a sequence of activities is implied by Figure 1.2, effective curriculum planning is not linear. It is possible to start at any point in the plan. For example, while designing the curriculum, an educator might modify one or more objectives, or, while a person is engaged with an experience, the need to modify the design may become apparent. A good curriculum plan should not be likened to a contractor's blueprint to be followed slavishly. Rather, it is similar to an artist's image to be modified as it is embodied.

Past and current practice in curriculum planning is fully described in Chapter 2, but we should note that at present it ranges from being sporadic and inadequate in far too many educational situations, to being systematic in approach and incorporating many of the processes described in this book as forward looking in others. Most models of curriculum planning followed by U.S. schools seeking continuing curriculum improvement have relied on processes of cooperative efforts at state, district, and local school levels, with input from various external agencies and from members of the school community. Unfortunately, the use of these processes has been spasmodic and ineffectual rather than continuing and influential. In *Behind the Classroom Door,* Goodlad and his associates summarized their investigations of the first four years of instruction in school, years for which cooperative and effective planning is frequently assumed to exist, as follows:

> We endeavored to secure evidence of curriculum plans being developed by the school faculty as a whole or by committees of that faculty. We encoun-

tered only one example but, admittedly, evidence here was very difficult to obtain. Nonetheless, neither observations nor interviews with teachers and principals revealed faculties at work on curriculum problems and plans. In general, each class operated as an individual unit, taking curricular direction from textbooks, courses of study, and teachers' experience.[72]

Goodlad's more recent observations resulted in a continued concern for the quality of planning and teaching in classrooms—and at all grade levels.[73] Studies similar to Goodlad's yield two observations that are pertinent here. On the negative side, one sees many schools in which the obsession with scheduling time to plan obscures the fundamental goals and processes of planning, frequently reducing the planning process to a series of rapid-fire decisions on immediate problems with little effort made to relate present crises and tasks to long-range goals. On the positive side, those cases in which comprehensive planning has been done by the individual school faculty, with adequate representation from the community and student body, give much hope that systematic planning at the school level can and does make a difference. For this difference to occur, the planning process must be based on an adequate conception of the roles of goals and objectives, and of feedback and evaluation, in relation to the curriculum plan and its implementation and to continuing efforts in planning year after year.

Goals, Objectives, and Domains

Examination of past and present practices of curriculum planning indicates a frequent lack of a continuing focus on goals and objectives, which is essential to systematic curriculum planning. Indeed, one can infer that the actual as well as the "hidden" objectives are frequently quite contrary to what is written in the curriculum guides.

One problem is the failure to relate the various components of the curriculum to long-term goals as well as to short-term specific objectives. For example, a widely cited goal of curriculum planning is to develop educational programs which help learners become increasingly self-directing. Curriculum plans that reflect this goal would need to include curriculum designs and instructional modes which extend over the entire period of schooling, and the evaluative procedures would need to appraise the growth of self-direction over an extended period as well as for short-term instructional units. But most curriculum plans are for relatively short periods, and evaluation arrangements rarely include such goals as this one, and even more rarely do they cover multiyear periods.

[72]John I. Goodlad, M. Frances Klein, and associates, *Behind the Classroom Door* (Worthington, O.: Charles A. Jones Publishing Company, 1970). p. 64.
[73]John I. Goodlad, *What Schools Are For.* (Publication of Phi Delta Kappa, 1979), p. 91.

Another problem is that a curriculum plan, in practice, tends to be a course of study or an instructional system within a subject field for achieving varied objectives (typically cognitive ones), which relate to a particular body of subject matter. One can infer from some courses of study that the objectives were determined by the subject matter rather than the reverse.

The traditional procedure of identifying curriculum components as subjects resulted in only passing attention given to the nonsubject curriculum areas of activities, services, and special programs and groupings. But many of the most important educational goals, especially those of an affective nature, are not really sought through the subjects or even the conventional nonsubject areas. To facilitate more functional groupings of learning opportunities, we use in this book the concept of a *curriculum domain* to describe *a grouping of learning opportunities planned to achieve a single major set of closely related educational goals with corollary subgoals and specific objectives.* Since planning has rarely so tied goals and curriculum, we hope that use of this approach to curriculum will help to make planning more systematic.

To illustrate our concept of a curriculum domain, we see the domain of continued learning skills as embracing the various educational goals having to do with skills and processes essential for present and future learning and including such varied learning opportunities as the following:

1. Specific instruction in reading and other initial learning skills.
2. Programmed instruction in use of library tools and sources.
3. Instruction on the use of computers.
4. Individual, student-choice reading in school and community libraries.
5. Use of group-process skills in laboratory sessions for their development and in teacher- or student-directed groups and community groups.
6. Use of television at school and at home.
7. Interviewing of peers in instructional situations and in school and community for information acquisition.
8. Teacher-guided mastery of skills unique to particular subjects and activities.

A domain can thus include a plethora of learning opportunities to be planned without needless restriction as to school subjects, learning locales, group organization, and other factors that have frequently limited goal setting and curriculum planning in general. The domain defines a broad area of the curriculum; it can be used as a set of guidelines to facilitate moving across former boundaries of subjects, activities, and services to make certain that the goals which set the domain are reflected in a plan which can be implemented and the goals achieved, regardless of whether the goals fit conventional subjects and activities.

We suggest as a broad classification of goals by domains for our reference in this and other chapters of this book four sets of goals that seem to us to be of great present and future significance: personal development, social competence, continued learning skills, and specialization. That these domains may be perennial is indicated by two similar classifications made in past decades. The analyses and deliberations regarding U.S. life and education by the Educational Policies Commission resulted in this 1938 classification of educational purposes:

1. The Objectives of Self-realization
2. The Objectives of Human Relationship
3. The Objectives of Economic Efficiency
4. The Objectives of Civic Responsibility[74]

This report describes these purposes in detail, listing many subpurposes and objectives.

Studies conducted during the 1950s at the Midwest Administration Center of the University of Chicago concerning the task of public education resulted in the following conceptual framework:

A. Intellectual Dimensions
1. *Possession of Knowledge:* A fund of information, concepts.
2. *Communication of Knowledge:* Skill to acquire and transmit.
3. *Creation of Knowledge:* Discrimination and imagination, a habit.
4. *Desire for Knowledge:* A love for learning.
B. Social Dimensions
5. *Man to Man:* Cooperation in day-to-day relations.
6. *Man to State:* Civic rights and duties.
7. *Man to Country:* Loyalty to one's own country.
8. *Man to World:* Inter-relationships of peoples.
C. Personal Dimensions
9. *Physical:* Bodily health and development.
10. *Emotional:* Mental health and stability.
11. *Ethical:* Moral integrity.
12. *Aesthetic:* Cultural and leisure pursuits.
D. Productive Dimensions
13. *Vocation-Selective:* Information and guidance.
14. *Vocation-Preparative:* Training and placement.
15. *Home and Family:* Housekeeping, do-it-yourself, family.
16. *Consumer:* Personal buying, selling, and investment.[75]

Although each of these listings includes domains similar to our own, we consider that of the Educational Policies Commission inadequate for current use because it subsumes under other purposes the skills of continued

[74]Educational Policies Commission, *The Purposes of Education in American Democracy* (Washington, D.C.: National Education Association, 1938).
[75]Lawrence W. Downey, *The Task of Public Education: The Perceptions of People* (Chicago: Midwest Administration Center, University of Chicago, 1960), p. 24.

learning. Too, both of them ignore phases of specialization other than the economic, productive ones, important as these are. For the 1980s and beyond, educational goals that relate to lifelong learning (our domain of continued learning skills) and to multifaceted interests, career and otherwise (our specialization domain), are significant and deserving of central emphasis in curriculum planning.

Personal Development

In a very general sense the entire purpose of education is to aid the development of the person. Somewhat less generally, we see much schooling that seeks in many ways at all levels to aid the individual in attaining his personal objectives, solving his personal problems, and above all establishing his concept of self. This major category of goals has been stated in many ways: "to enable the individual to achieve his potential"; "to help the individual develop a favorable self-concept"; "to guide the individual's search for self-actualization"—or "self-direction"—or "independence." Despite the controversy concerning whether the school should be interested in the "whole child," the well-recognized fact is that progress in school, academic and otherwise, is inextricably related to the total growth and development and well-being of the learner.

The personal development domain includes a vast array of learning opportunities: basic communication skills; most opportunities relating to the so-called general education objectives; value assessment and development; guidance and counseling services; health and physical education; exploratory subjects; and activities and opportunities that give each individual chances to discover areas of interest for later specialization.

Esthetic education plays an important role in personal development. Broudy lists esthetic experience as a basic ". . . because it is a primary form of experience on which all cognition, judgment, and action depend." Through the power of esthetic experience for image making, "it furnishes the raw material for concepts, and ideals, for creating a world of possibility." Broudy concluded, "Roughly, art is to feeling what science is to thought."[76]

Social Competence

American educational goals have generally given emphasis to citizenship education, social welfare, human relations, and similar phrases which we encompass under the term "social competence." Certainly, a continuous and essential goal of education in a society of human beings, and especially in one which prizes democratic values and processes, is ever-improving social competence.

[76]Harry S. Broudy, "How Basic is Aesthetic Education? Or is 'Rt the Fourth R?" *Educational Leadership, 35* (November 1977): 139.

This domain, too, includes a plethora of curriculum possibilities: the various knowledge areas included in the social sciences and humanities; languages; social interaction and organization within the schools themselves; the participation of students in the various social groups and institutions of their communities; and specific studies and skill-development activities related to particular human relations problems within the school and community, such as those involved in cultural differences and conflicts, and, again, valuing processes.

Efforts to achieve aims associated with the social competence domain can, if narrowly conceived, interfere with personal development. These aims, if restricted to socialization, can lead to ". . . the acceptance of the status-quo by definition and the replication of the present social class and role structure, ethos, and attitudinal sets by the most efficient and effective methods possible."[77] Such an approach does not result in freeing persons from the narrowness of their specific times and places and opening up the possibility for them to respond to future changes by renewing themselves and society.

Continued Learning Skills

In practice, much schooling has been preparatory for further study; the assumption seems to have been that the more knowledge a person acquires in school, the better prepared he will be for acquiring still more knowledge at higher levels. Beyond reading and some other knowledge-acquiring skills, traditionally little attention has been paid to the skills learners need to learn effectively outside of and after school. With the ever-increasing changes in today's society, it is futile to expect individuals to store up during 12 to 16 years enough information to solve future problems. Instead, there is now wide agreement that the central mission of schooling is to develop lifelong learners—individuals who are motivated to continue learning and who have the basic skills to do so. Overly referred to lifelong learning as "the latest term for the constellation of efforts designed to make education more central to the continuing search for fulfillment." He added that "the concept is too important to the quality of our future to permit it to become one more inoperative fad."[78]

To encourage lifelong learning, the continued learning skills curriculum domain includes such standard plans as instruction in reading, listening, viewing, and speaking. It encompasses as well plans generally yet to be made for teaching more advanced learning skills: interviewing, discussing, interacting; using various information-retrieval systems, including those made possible by telecommunications and computers; analyzing issues,

[77]Macdonald, "Value Bases and Issues," p. 16.
[78]Norman V. Overly (ed.), *Lifelong Learning: A Human Agenda* (Alexandria, Va.: Association for Supervision and Curriculum Development, 1979), p. 1.

selecting alternatives, trying out ideas, and other problem-solving skills; locating sources for continued study; evaluating sources and ideas; generalizing; and others.

Specialization

The specialization domain is even more difficult to categorize than the others, for what is specialized education for one individual may be exploratory or general education for another. American education clearly seeks to provide a wide and varied range of opportunities for individual students to work in depth in the areas they choose for themselves on the bases of interests and qualifications. Specialization for career purposes is generally delayed until after high school, yet many adolescents terminate, at least for some years, their education before or upon finishing high school. Even elementary school children develop strong interests in music, art, sports, and other areas that can be the basis of extended instruction and independent study. Thus, this domain includes such traditional school areas as those generally classified as prevocational or vocational and, in addition, almost any area that can be pursued in depth by an individual selecting it for specialization. In this case, specialization includes such cut-across learning opportunities chosen on the basis of individual interest as work experience, community service, or extended study in another school center, community, state, or nation.

In the 1970s, the emphasis on education for earning a living was revived as "career development" or "career education" through the leadership of the then U.S. Commissioner of Education, Sidney P. Marland, Jr. Marland noted his preference for the term *career education* since it implies a structured preparation program as an integral part of a student's academic course work throughout his school and college years. He stated: "Inherent in the concept is the principle that our schools and colleges are accountable to students not only for developing their problem-solving skills, self-awareness, and social consciousness, but for equipping them as well to earn a living in a personally satisfying career field."[79]

Critics of career education voice concern over the pervading technocratic ideology that conveys the basic message that scientific-technological knowledge leads to success. Some critics fear that values associated with careers are minimized where they are given the same objective status as work, roles, skills, and occupational choices. Bowers concluded that "career-education programs, in spite of their rhetorical commitment to such values as dignity and self-understanding, are nevertheless designed to socialize students to accept the present organization of work and technol-

[79]Sidney P. Marland, Jr., "The School's Role in Career Development," *Educational Leadership, 50* (December 1972): 203. "Education for Career Development" is the theme of this issue, which included various articles on the theory and practice of career education.

ogy as the taken-for-granted reality."[80] The authors do not condemn career education—there are good programs and poor programs. Curriculum workers and teachers need, however, to weigh potential programs—career education or any other type—by examining assumptions and values and, most of all, the total impact of programs on learners.

The four domains—personal development, social competence, continued learning skills, and specialization—represent a classification of major educational goals and related learning opportunities that seems fairly universal and therefore useful for the purposes of this book. It is not assumed that each educational setting would necessarily have curriculum plans within each of these domains, nor that additional domains cannot be developed.

The Locale of the Curriculum

The variety of possible areas of study identified within each of the four domains illustrates the growth in educational expectations. Neither schools nor any other agency or institution can singlehandedly meet these needs. Education in the future will take place in many settings and utilize a variety of resources. Tyler identified four resources we should turn to in meeting future demands for education.

1. The millions of adults, young and old, who sincerely want to make a significant contribution and welcome opportunities to help young people.
2. Community institutions that can be mobilized for education—museums, libraries, parks, playgrounds, boys' and girls' clubs, churches, and synagogues.
3. The organizations and institutions able to furnish educative employment opportunities.
4. Technological systems such as motion pictures, radio, TV, audio- and videotapes, video discs, and computers.[81]

An important step in determining goals and objectives is to decide which goals can best be achieved in one educational setting or a combination of settings. It is not satisfactory for each institution to simply set its own goals. Cooperative planning is necessary to assure that:

1. Some provision is made for achieving all major goals and objectives.
2. All potential learners have opportunities to achieve the goals and objectives.

In Chapter 4 we deal fully with the process of defining goals and domains and indicate various classifications of goals that have been made in

[80]C. A. Bowers, "Emergent Ideological Characteristics of Educational Policy," *Teachers College Record, 79* (September 1977): 44.
[81]Ralph Tyler, "Technological Horizons in Education: An Overview," *Technological Horizons, 5* (September/October 1978): 34.

American education. There we also give attention to other levels of goals and objectives, especially the development and use of objectives for particular learning opportunities.

Curriculum Designs

We see designing as the somewhat creative aspect of curriculum planning, analogous to the role of the architect in building or the fashion designer in clothing or the menu planner (not the recipe maker) in cooking. The planning group responsible, for example, for developing plans in the social competence domain for a population of middle school children, having collected and analyzed essential data and identified goals, would need to create or select a general pattern—a design—for the learning opportunities to be provided. Among their alternatives would be: 1) a subject design utilizing specific studies in the social sciences and humanities; 2) a scope and sequence plan built around a selection of persistent social competence needs; 3) an analysis of the essential skills of social competence to be taught as the basis of activity and skills groups; 4) a selection with the students of individual interests and problems related to social competence in the classroom, school, and community; and 5) others, including combinations of the foregoing. The design plan ultimately anticipates the entire range of learning opportunities within the domain for this population, or at least the points of further planning.

A curriculum design answers the following questions:

1. Who will the learners be?
2. What are the subgoals or objectives?
3. What types of learning experiences will be provided?
4. What will be the locale for the learning experiences?
5. What roles will participants play: learners, teachers, others?
6. What will be the time and space dimensions?
7. What criteria will be used for assessment?

FLEXIBILITY IN DESIGN.   Some curriculum designs anticipate considerable flexibility in teachers' choices of subject matter and activities, whereas others assume one basic route to the achievement of the objectives or coverage of the topic. Few plans anticipate adequately the wide range of individual differences within learning groups and a correspondingly wide choice of alternative learning opportunities. A flexible curriculum plan is flexible in all aspects: flexible curriculum designs, instructional modes, and evaluative procedures. Such flexibility is possible only as curriculum planners build into their designs many alternatives and as the users of the plans—teachers and students—choose freely from the alternatives.

ADOPTION OF EXTERNALLY DEVELOPED DESIGNS.   In our judgment, the most serious gap between the theory and practice of curriculum planning occurs as local planning groups and individual teachers adopt without study specific plans made external to the school center and population concerned. This practice is perhaps most obviously represented by blind adherence to a textbook as *the* curriculum design for a particular subject. The uncritical use of commercially prepared curriculum packages is little different. The curriculum design as we have presented it, developed for a particular population and for particular goals and objectives, would rarely be identical from one educational setting to another. In Chapter 5 a series of curriculum designs is presented and illustrated. Guidelines are offered for selecting appropriate designs.

Curriculum Implementation

We have defined instruction as the implementation of the curriculum plan—that is, the actual engagement of learners with the planned learning opportunities. Therefore, the curriculum planning process includes making decisions regarding instructional modes (see Figure 1.2).

Teachers and students should be given freedom in the implementation of the curriculum plan. Thus, effective curriculum plans will not prescribe instructional procedure and materials; rather, they will describe alternative instructional models and suggest a variety of instructional materials. We present in Chapter 6 our classifications of instructional models.

Curriculum Evaluation

The curriculum system also includes a plan for evaluation of the curriculum in relation to its goals. Our treatment of evaluation (Chapter 7) recognizes both formative and summative evaluation. Formative procedures are the feedback arrangements which enable the planners and implementers of the curriculum to make adjustments and improvements throughout the planning, or implementing, process. The summative evaluation comes at the end and deals directly with the evaluation of the total curriculum plan; this evaluation becomes in effect feedback for the planners to use in deciding whether to repeat, modify, or eliminate the plan with another population.

FORCES AFFECTING CURRICULUM PLANNING

The curriculum planning process just described is influenced by a number of individuals and groups. The curriculum planners' image of the ideal person living in an ideal society should guide education. Education in turn helps to shape the future of individuals and their society. To the extent that individuals and groups within our society differ in their images of ideal citizens living in an ideal society, they have varying views on the ideal curriculum plan. The extent to which different segments of society attempt to shape the curriculum provides a remarkable testimony to the potential influence of education. A brief examination of the influence of clients, critics, professionals, legislative groups, and courts is provided in this section. Subsequent chapters will provide more extensive discussions.

The Clients

The interests and needs of potential learners influence the nature of opportunities for learning engagements as clients "vote with their feet." If learners perceive the curriculum as irrelevant, adult courses fail to meet their goals, community college and university enrollments drop, community organizations lose support, youth drop out of school, and truancy rates increase. The degree of influence of the clients depends upon their control of the resources and their vocality. Note, for example, the changes in high school and college curriculums during the student activist days of the 1960s.

A powerful influence on students, and thus the curriculum, has been their desire to proceed through the educational system. The ladder system of education has brought with it a syndrome of illnesses related to the notion that the student must prepare at each rung of the ladder for the next, with the college and especially now the graduate school at the top being the determiner of educational purposes and programs below. Despite all of their services to the schools, colleges and universities have had an impact on curriculum planning that has often augured against the interests of students and that is inconsistent with the basic assumption that the central purpose of education is the development of an independent learner. Current changes in educational patterns toward more varied community college programs, intermittent study-work programs, adult education, and changing patterns of college admission may make possible lessened emphasis on presumed requirements for college preparation. In any event, more systematic processes of curriculum planning will utilize concepts of continuous experiences rather than grade norms. It is to be hoped that they will also involve systematic input and feedback from many sources, not just the level above, and will include in planning groups representatives of various levels.

Clients of compulsory school age have fewer ways to indicate their views of the curriculum plan. However, indications of student boredom and increased truancy rates may be indicative of client dissatisfaction. Parents can and do find ways to indicate dissatisfaction. Parents may enroll their child in another school, or in a few instances, undertake the teaching of their own child. Parents may also work to influence those responsible for curriculum decisions.

Since 1969, annual Gallup polls have given educational planners data as to national trends in public opinion, and many local polls on specific issues provide more relevant data for local curriculum planners. The national polls showed a continuous weakening of confidence in public schools during the 1970s. (Other institutions shared in the phenomenon.) This decline in confidence may have been related to a weakening of parental influence on the curriculum. As the influence of school boards weakened, parents found themselves increasingly isolated from decision makers in curriculum policy. If confidence in public schools is to be strengthened, citizens will need greater influence in formulating educational goals and means of achieving them. Suggestions regarding citizens' participation in curriculum planning are included in Chapter 2 and at other appropriate points in this book.

The Critics

Curriculum planners make choices based on their values and on their perceptions of the future. However, individuals and groups within society may hold different values and beliefs about the future. Critics of education express these divergent views and propose modifications in educational programs. These critics will be present in any society unless it is monolithic in its values or prohibits free speech.

Some critics focus on priorities in education and teaching methods. For example, the Council on Basic Education consistently advocates a traditional teaching approach to a subject-centered curriculum. The influence of critics increases when they reflect and support the mood of a sizable group within society. For example, the book by Flesch, *Why Johnny Can't Read,*[82] had considerable popularity during the "back to the three R's" movement of the late 1940s and 1950s. Similarly, Copperman's book, *The Literacy Hoax,*[83] caught the mood of and reinforced the "back-to-basics" drive of the late 1970s.

Revisionist critics criticize schools for the role they play in supporting a particular type of society. For example, Bowles and Gintis stated, "Education plays a major role in hiding or justifying the exploitive nature of the U.S. economy."[84] In fact, the chief problem, according to the revisionists, is not the educational system, but the social and economic system it reflects.

Another group of critics may be classified as neoromanticists. Borrowing from the work of Rousseau and Freud, they believe that the natural goodness of human nature, when not constrained by some external authority, will lead to making the right choices. The importance of personal freedom in making choices is central to the educational ideas of such reformers as Neill and Illich.[85] The neoromanticists also hold an egalitarian view of

[82]Rudolph Flesch, *Why Johnny Can't Read* (New York: Harper & Row, 1955).
[83]Paul Copperman, *The Literacy Hoax* (New York: William Morrow Books, 1978).
[84]Samuel Bowles and Herbert Gintis, *Schooling in Capitalist America* (New York: Basic Books, Inc., 1976), pp. 13, 14.
[85]A. S. Neill, *Summerhill* (New York: Hart Publishing Company, 1960); Ivan Illich, *Deschooling Society* (New York: Harper & Row, 1971).

human nature. "Not only was it essentially good, but it was equal in value and potential when expressed naturally."[86] The neoromantic approach appeals to many educators and has resulted in the formation of freedom schools and alternative schools. Some of these schools, however, run into contradictions that neutralize their educative potential and sometimes create educational anarchy in the classrooms. Bowers summarized the problem: "Since the view was widely held that all one needed to know in life could be learned from one's own direct experience, there was significant ambiguity in the role of the teacher."[87]

Curriculum planners need to take the critics seriously—other people do. Informed critics can play the important role of a "balance wheel" in an educational system beset by fads and passing innovations. To accept uncritically and act on all criticism, however, would be as harmful as ignoring it. Criticism can be useful when the curriculum planner attempts to understand the values held by the critic and the assumption he or she is making about the past, present, and future of our society. Curriculum planners should not read criticism for the purpose of refuting it nor for finding support for their own position. Criticism's value will be realized when it is read objectively to secure information for curriculum planning.

The Professionals

Teachers and administrators play central roles in shaping the curriculum for schools and other agencies. There are, however, some groups of professional educators that have special influence on curriculum planning.

Teacher Unions

New York City bargained the first significant contract with teachers in 1962. By 1979, 33 states had collective bargaining laws that affected education.[88] Lieberman commented on the impact of this bargaining, "Since 60 percent to 80 percent of school budgets are spent for personnel, virtually every aspect of education has been affected by this dramatic shift to collectively bargained terms and conditions of employment."[89] As a result, curriculum proposals may be bargained as trade-offs for economic benefits to teachers.

Collective bargaining is increasingly conducted by paid negotiators for

[86]C. A. Bowers, "Educational Critics and Technocratic Consciousness: Looking into the Future through a Rearview Mirror," *Teachers College Record, 80* (December 1978): 281.
[87]Bowers, "Educational Critics," p. 282.
[88]"State-by-State Roundup of Collective Bargaining Laws," *Phi Delta Kappan, 60* (February 1979): 472.
[89]Myron Lieberman, "Eggs That I Have Laid: Teacher Bargaining Reconsidered," *Phi Delta Kappan, 60* (February 1979): 415.

boards of education and for trade unions. Fewer people are making more and more decisions. According to Boyd, collective bargaining has resulted in a shift of ". . . large amounts of authority over the curriculum from local school districts to higher levels of government."[90] School boards and parents are the big losers in this restructuring of authority; and some parents are demanding a place at the bargaining table.

Professional Interest Groups

Teachers are not the only professionals to have formed special-interest groups. Administrators, counselors, librarians, subject field specialists, and professionals concerned with a particular level of schooling have also established groups. It has been estimated that from 250 to 300 education-related special-interest groups have offices in Washington, D.C.[91] Those interest groups that have professional development of their members as a primary goal influence curriculum planning indirectly through in-service education programs and publications. Some interest groups influence curriculum planning directly by lobbying lawmakers. Unfortunately, it appears that good will and compromise thinking among interest groups are shrinking. "Where one expects alliances, one sees battle lines; where cooperation appears natural, and more, necessary, to achieve mutual goals, there is competition and conflict."[92]

Professional Reformers

The term *professional reformer* is not used in a pejorative sense. In recent history, several groups have worked to reform curriculum. In the 1950s and 1960s, subject matter specialists, primarily in universities, worked to reform education. The launching of Sputnik by the Russians in 1957 provided a major impetus to their work. The basic rationale underlying the work of these reforming groups is presented by Bruner in *The Process of Education.*[93]

The federal government funded efforts of many professional reformers through the Elementary–Secondary Education Act (ESEA) of 1965. Not only were on-going subject-centered reform movements financed, but research and development centers (R and D centers) and regional educational laboratories (RELs) were developed throughout the United States. The purposes of these centers and laboratories were to identify good

[90]William Lowe Boyd, "The Changing Politics of Curriculum Policy-Making for American Schools," *Review of Educational Research, 48* (Fall 1978): 610.
[91]Jon Schaffarzick and Gary Sykes, "NIE's Role in Curriculum Development" (Washington, D.C.: National Institute of Education, 1977), p. 50.
[92]Schaffarzick and Sykes, p. 50.
[93]Jerome Bruner, *The Process of Education* (Cambridge, Mass.: Harvard University Press, 1960).

practice through research, develop appropriate programs and materials, and disseminate and demonstrate these materials. A national panel identified over a hundred programs deemed to be worthy of dissemination. A national diffusion network was established by the National Institute of Education (NIE) to spread these "tested" programs throughout the United States.

Philanthropic groups and foundations have also supported work of professional reformers. For example, the Ford Foundation supported early experiments with team teaching in Bay City, Michigan. The Kettering Foundation has financed vehicles for change through its support of leagues of schools. The influence of externally developed curriculums and efforts to change the curriculum will be considered in Chapter 2.

Producers of Educational Materials

Educational materials have a pervasive effect on the curriculum. A study supported by the National Science Foundation sent observers into classrooms to discover the extent to which nationally developed curriculum programs were being utilized. They found very little use of these materials and of the process and inquiry methods they advocated. What they did find was extensive use of textbooks, with teachers trying to get into the heads of pupils the information between the covers of textbooks. One of the best ways to learn about educational experiences offered in a classroom is to examine the textbooks in use. The content of some textbooks has been influenced by national curriculum projects. For example, the NSF-sponsored Biological Sciences Curriculum Study (BSCS) materials led to major revisions in the content of biology textbooks.[94]

The incidence of citizen censorship, not only of textbooks but of library books and all written materials, has reached alarming proportions. Textbook publishers feel very vulnerable to this censorship. In order to protect the large investment required for the first printing, they do not wish to risk the chance of being censored by communities or of being controversial. In some instances, content of textbooks is tailored to assume favorable consideration in the more populous states. Thus, for example, the content of textbooks used throughout the United States may be shaped by the publishers' perception of what may be acceptable in California.

Standardized tests represent another influence on the curriculum. The use of competency tests as a criterion for graduation, the publication of test results by schools, and the drive for accountability combine to exert a powerful force on the teacher. It is not surprising that when passing tests appears to be the goal of education, teachers will teach for the tests. The result is a serious constriction of opportunities for learning experiences.

The rapid increase in the use of computers in education provides the

[94]Schaffarzick and Sykes.

producers of the software with considerable influence on the curriculum. A serious lag in the production of educationally sound software may result from computer illiteracy on the part of most professional educators.

Accreditation

The intent of accreditation is to maintain some acceptable, at least minimum, level of education. Originally accreditation was largely a school–college relation that was regionally initiated at the turn of this century to facilitate college admission. The impact of regional accrediting associations on high school programs lessened with the advent of more rigorous state standards and accrediting procedures. State accreditation is a means of enforcing state regulations regarding schools, but it is also used in some states as a means of improving local educational planning processes. In any event, the local curriculum planning group must deal with the realities of accreditation requirements of whatever bodies accredit their schools; frequently, whether a major change can be made in a school's program depends on whether an exception can be made in these requirements, and fortunately most accrediting plans have procedures to encourage experimentation. In some states, local initiative is being encouraged through new patterns of accreditation and planning.

Legislative Groups

The influence of school boards on curriculum has decreased while the influence of collective bargaining has increased. Concurrently, state and national legislative bodies are exercising greater control of educational programs. This has been accomplished through the passage of legislation accompanied by the creation of regulatory agencies. Members of legislative groups are influenced by their constituents, by special-interest lobby groups, and by friends and colleagues often in the business or legal community.

Legislative groups have instituted or supported drives for accountability, competency-based education, and minimum standards for high school graduation. The role of legislative bodies in the curriculum planning process has been an expanding one. Originally, legislative bodies provided the resources for education. Next, they began to legislate goals of education. Through legislation on minimum competencies for graduation, they moved to specifying outcomes of education. Some legislation even specifies aspects of curriculum design and implementation. For example, PL 94–142 requires that an individualized education program (IEP) be developed for each handicapped child. This mandated component of an appropriate public education is used to describe, monitor, and judge programs for handicapped children.

Legislative intent regarding the curriculum is achieved through funding, or withholding funds from, programs. Regulatory agencies are established to ensure conformity. Failure to conform with specific provisions (Title IX, for example) may result in withholding all federal funds. Thus, the infusion of a relatively small percentage of funds from the federal government (8 to 10 percent) can result in broad control over educational programs.

Courts

There has been a dramatic increase in the number of state and federal court cases that have affected the organization, administration, and programs of the schools. For example, during the 108-year period between 1789 and 1896, 50 such federal court cases were heard, while during the five-year period between 1967 and 1971, 1273 cases were heard.[95]

Litigation addresses one specific question and the decision is in response to that question. This creates a ripple effect as the decision affects other parts of the system. Thus, for example, court-ordered busing to achieve desegregation weaknened already fragile bonds between schools and their communities. Courts will continue to affect curriculum plans. According to Cunningham, "There seems little likelihood that the prominence of the courts in the life of the schools will diminish."[96]

Implications for Curriculum Planning

A number of forces that influence curriculum planning, whether in schools, colleges, universities, or community groups, have been described. These forces may be viewed as external constraints which provide boundaries within which curriculum is planned. Curriculum workers may conclude that when all the constraints are considered, there remains relatively little opportunity for change. A more constructive view is to recognize the value of working with various individuals and groups in designing the best possible opportunities for learning experiences. When this is done, many of the constraints can be minimized or removed. Throughout this book we will try to show how this can be done.

WHO PLANS THE CURRICULUM?

Chapter 2 deals with specific roles of various persons in the curriculum planning process. At this point, we will refer briefly to the various actors. It could be deduced from the preceding section on forces influencing the

[95]Raphael O. Nystrand and W. Frederick Staub, "The Courts as Educational Policy Makers," in Clifford P. Hooker (ed.), *The Courts and Education,* 77th Yearbook, National Society for the Study of Education (Chicago: University of Chicago Press, 1978), p. 29.
[96]Luvern L. Cunningham in Hooker (ed.), p. xix.

curriculum that a "cast of thousands" is involved in curriculum planning. We prefer, however, to think of all the organizations and individuals associated with various external forces affecting curriculum planning as resources for the curriculum planners rather than as a part of the planning group. That is, the project directors, authors, publishers, testers, accreditors, pollsters, lobbyists, and philanthropists we identified earlier as influencing curriculum planning have much potential to affect this process, but systematic planning should elicit this potential as it is needed by the system.

The Learner in the Leading Role

We see the learners as being actively involved in planning their own curriculum. Indeed, we see them as having the lead in the drama of their engagement with the learning opportunities they select from the program planned for their educational center. Whether they spend their school day in an elementary or middle school, or in and out of their high school or college, or as a continuing learner in another setting, it is the learners themselves who must finally embrace or reject the opportunities their curriculum presents. As a member of the learner population, they also have opportunities related to their level of maturity to help in planning the total program; in this process of curriculum planning they participate but do not necessarily have the lead.

Other Roles in the Educational Center

Supporting the leading actor in the individualized curriculum drama are all the teachers, resource specialists, community educators, and others who share in teaching and guiding individual learners. For more dependent learners limited, it is hoped, to the earlier spans of the curriculum continuum, this support is quite active, providing incentives and careful guidance. For more independent learners, support is more on call of the learner. We consider especially important for more personalized curriculum planning the role of directors or counselors for personal development.

Our major concern in developing curriculum plans is to project a total program of learning opportunities keyed to the total population of the educational center and reflecting the major goals it serves. Here the leaders are those with expertise in a systematic approach to curriculum planning: persons who can move from goals to curriculum domains to curriculum designs, instructional strategies, and evaluation schemes. These leaders are variously classified as teachers, resource specialists, curriculum directors and coordinators, counselors and directors of personal development, and administrators. Whatever their titles, their roles are those needed in the systematic process of curriculum planning.

External Participants

Various persons outside the center also have significant roles to play in planning a program of learning opportunities for its students. Curriculum, instruction, and evaluation specialists from the school district offices, community educators and resource specialists, parents, and others in the community are needed in the system. A systematic process may involve the services of a curriculum designing unit outside the individual educational center staffed to provide the expertise needed by several centers or possibly all centers within the community.

The Teacher as Curriculum Planner

Past and present educational practice has enthroned teachers as the final curriculum planners for their classes. Now that educational organizations are rapidly abandoning the notion of a standard-size class as the instructional unit and substituting varied size groups with much individualized instruction, the role of the teacher in planning is also changed. We see teachers as very active participants in the planning of the total program of the educational center and of the learning opportunities within their particular domain(s) of the curriculum. In many educational centers teachers will have no "class" of their own but will instead be responsible for various groups and individuals within their domain(s). Their planning responsibility then increasingly becomes one of continuing development of the particular learning programs through which they guide their students and of planning with individual students for their continuing progress through the programs. Whether they have a set group of students for guidance over an extended period of time or a rapidly changing group as programs are completed, or both patterns, depends on the plan of instructional organization developed by the planning groups involved.

THE MARKS OF A "GOOD" CURRICULUM (PLAN)

To summarize this chapter, we present a checklist whereby a visitor to an educational center or a person employed there could investigate the quality of the curriculum (plan). No rating device is suggested, although the person using the checklist could develop some scale if this seemed appropriate. In general, affirmative answers to these questions would indicate a good curriculum:

1. Are data regarding learners, social and cultural factors, society, the nature of knowledge, and the learning process available to curriculum planning groups?
2. Are the goals of the educational center clearly stated and understood by all concerned? Are the values and assumptions underlying the goals

known? Are the goals sufficiently comprehensive, balanced, and realistic? Is there provision for modifying, dropping, and adding goals as needed?

3. Is the curriculum plan a part of a comprehensive community-wide plan for education?

4. Do the learning opportunities anticipate a progression from dependent, other-directed learning to independent, self-directed learning in accordance with the level of learners served by the educational center?

5. Do learners and teachers mutually understand the specific plans in the total curriculum plan which affect them? Do learners participate, as their maturities permit, in making the plans? Do they generally understand and agree as to what is expected of them, and why?

6. Are sets of related major goals grouped accordingly, with the learning opportunities in each set or domain selected for achieving these goals? Have sets of learning opportunities been checked as to their relation to the goals, with gaps and overlappings identified and remedied? Do the learning opportunities seem to be the best possible choices for this group of learners at this time to achieve the goals set for them?

7. Does the curriculum provide appropriate learning engagements in each of the four domains: personal development, social competence, continued learning skills, and specialization?

8. Within each domain or set of goals and related learning opportunities, is there a pattern or patterns reflecting conscious attention to curriculum designing? Are all appropriate and feasible types of learning experiences utilized?

9. Is the plan tailor-made for the particular educational center? Are any plans developed externally, adapted to the population and facilities of the educational center? Are the learning opportunities planned truly relevant to the educational needs of this population and community? Are provisions made for individual differences of learners?

10. Are demands of external forces screened through a process that keeps them in acceptable balance?

11. Is the total curriculum plan comprehensive? Does it anticipate instruction and evaluation as well as include goals and designs of learning opportunities?

12. Are the responsible planning groups representative of all persons concerned, including learners, parents, general public, and professional staff?

13. Does the plan have adequate provision of feedback from learners and other concerned groups as well as means for making modification as indicated?

14. Can the plan and each of its parts be explained sufficiently clearly to learners, parents, and other lay persons to be understood by them?

15. Is there some representative council or curriculum evaluation unit or other group or individual responsible for identifying problems and collecting problems identified by others that develop in the planning process? Is there a clear channel of communication of such problems to

those who can resolve them and a plan for reporting back to the problem identifiers the resolutions made? Similarly, is there a systematic way of securing, monitoring, and reporting action regarding suggestions for change and innovation?

16. Does the plan anticipate full use of the educational resources of the educational center, the community, and the media? Does the plan recognize that learners will have educational experiences in other settings?

17. Is flexibility built into the curriculum plan by adequate provisions for alternative learning opportunities, instructional modes, and learner and teacher options in general?

ADDITIONAL SUGGESTIONS FOR FURTHER STUDY

Austin, Gilbert R., "Exemplary Schools and the Search for Effectiveness," *Educational Leadership, 37* (October 1979): 10–14. Reviews studies of school effectiveness, and concludes that the individual school is the key: "research confirms the faith" that the people directly concerned must agree on goals and work cooperatively for them.

Beauchamp, George A., "A Hard Look at Curriculum," *Educational Leadership, 35* (February 1978): 404–409. An insightful examination of the state of the field. Its problems are labeled by this long-time curriculum student and author as: 1) definition; 2) confusion in curriculum design; 3) defects in curriculum engineering, especially in the implementation process; 4) inadequacy of curriculum evaluation; and 5) the naive state of curriculum theory development.

Cremin, Lawrence A., *Tradition of American Education.* New York: Basic Books, Inc., 1977. A most insightful and penetrating essay on the real world of education in the United States when one takes account of the many family and community activities and agencies that also contribute to the education of all of us. Pleads for a full understanding of the special role and responsibilities of the school in relation to other community institutions.

Goodlad, John I., and associates, *Curriculum Inquiry: The Study of Curriculum Practice.* New York: McGraw-Hill Book Company, 1979. The scope of the curriculum field is identified and discussed using three kinds of phenomena: substantive (goals, subject matter, materials, and the like); political-social (human processes through which some interests come to prevail); and technical-professional (processes through which curricula are improved, installed, or replaced).

Klein, M. Frances, Kenneth A. Tye, and Joyce E. Wright, "A Study of Schooling: Curriculum," *Phi Delta Kappan, 61* (December 1979): 244–248. The team that spent more than six years in a comprehensive analysis of a sample of schools in the United States present a three-dimensional model of the curriculum that constituted the basis for collecting data and drawing conclusions about the nature and status of the school's program.

Lawton, Denis, Peter Gordon, Maggie Ing, Bill Gibby, Richard Ring, and Terry Moore, *Theory and Practice of Curriculum Studies.* London: Routledge & Kegan Paul, 1978. An interesting collection of lectures originally written for the Theory and Practice of Education Course in the Diploma of Education, University of London Institute of Education. The lecture-essays are grouped into five parts: 1) Approaches Through the Disciplines; 2) Psychological Issues; 3) Philosophical and Social Issues; 4) Evaluation and Assessment; and 5) The Teacher, Accountability and Control.

Pinar, William F., "Notes on the Curriculum Field 1978," *Educational Researcher,* 7 (September 1978): 5–12. Places curriculum writers and theorists into three categories: traditionalists (people who value service to practitioners in the schools above all else); conceptual empiricists (people who tend to be trained in social science and see service to practitioners subsequent to years of research); and reconceptualists (people who tend to be trained in the humanities and believe that an intellectual and cultural distance from practitioners is necessary to develop curriculum theory). Some tenets of the reconceptualist position are set forth.

Scharffarzick, Jon, and Gary Sykes (eds.), *Value Conflicts and Curriculum Issues.* Berkeley, Calif.: McCutchan Publishing Corp., 1979. This volume of significant essays and reports is the result of the efforts of the Curriculum Development Task Force, established by the National Institute of Education in 1975, to identify major issues that arise in the planning of the curriculum and define roles and policies that should characterize future developments.

Tanner, Daniel, and Laurel N. Tanner, "Emancipation from Research: The Reconceptualist Prescription," *Educational Researcher, 8* (June 1979): 8–12. Scathing but scholarly critique of the reconceptualist position, primarily as excerpted from the writings of William Pinar, regarding curriculum and society (see Pinar, "Notes on the Curriculum Field 1978").

TWO
...
PROCESSES AND ROLES IN CURRICULUM PLANNING
■■

Curriculum is defined as a plan for providing sets of learning opportunities for persons to be educated. To develop such a plan would appear to be a simple, straightforward task. In fact, it is relatively simple to put together a poor plan based on an ill-considered mixture of assumptions, beliefs, and personal preferences. But to develop the *best* plan for a group of learners is a highly complex task utilizing facts and considerations and involving a number of decision makers. Typically, curriculum planners have overestimated the ability and training of people involved and underestimated the time required for curriculum planning.

Societal changes have made curriculum planning more complex. Boyd, after reviewing research on curriculum policy, concluded, "If there is one proposition about curriculum politics that is clear, it is that the school curriculum becomes an issue in communities and societies that are undergoing significant change."[1] This has contributed to the remarkable recent growth of the influence and authority of state and national (both governmental and nongovernmental) agencies over the curriculum.

The complexity of curriculum planning will increase as cooperative planning of educational experiences within a network of a learning system provides greater coordination between various educational agencies. However, improvement in the quality of the experiences for learners should justify the additional effort.

The greatest challenge facing curriculum planners is not new. It is the problem of implementing the curriculum plan—the problem of achieving a match between the planned and the experienced curriculum. Curriculum planners recognize that teachers hold a "pocket veto" on any curriculum plan developed. Therefore, an effective strategy for curriculum change has a double agenda: to change ideas about the curriculum and to change the human dynamics.

The complexity and challenge of planning a curriculum cannot deter the work. Rather, they underline the importance of the task and the necessity to approach it with the best possible professional knowledge. This chapter, along with the remaining chapters in this book, is designed to provide this knowledge.

[1] William Lowe Boyd, "The Changing Politics of Curriculum Policy-Making for American Schools," *Review of Educational Research, 48* (Fall 1978):582.

THE PRODUCTS OF CURRICULUM PLANNING— THE PLANS

As explained in Chapter 1 (see Figure 1.1, p. 29), the curriculum plan is regarded as an arrangement of internal variables (curriculum designs, instructional modes, and evaluation procedures) intended to achieve the particular goals and objectives of the curriculum domain(s) involved. The plan may be global, encompassing all goals and domains, or specific for an individual goal and domain or some phase thereof. Typically it is written; otherwise it is unlikely to serve as a reference for implementation and evaluation.

Broadly speaking, the products of curriculum planning include much more than written curriculum plans, or curriculum guides. Ideally, the products include changes in the behavior of learners, and, to achieve these, changes in the practices of teachers and the teaching environments which affect learners. The direct products of planning which we can analyze here are the plans to affect the people and things that constitute teaching–learning situations. We cannot lose sight of the fact, however, that changes in learner behavior are the ultimate products sought and that the goal of the curriculum planning process is to enable teachers to effect these changes. We heartily concur in Miel's classic thesis that curriculum change is "a type of social change, change in people, not mere change on paper."[2] Certainly the increased understanding of the curriculum and of the teaching and learning which generally accrues from systematic curriculum planning is an important product which almost in itself justifies the process. Teachers who are themselves becoming more knowledgeable, more skillful, and more dynamic can serve increasingly effectively as guides to learners. Hence, ultimate changes in learners and their teachers are inextricably related to the plans that are direct products of the curriculum planning process.

Curriculum Guides for School Use

Most curriculum plans developed by state and local school agencies are ultimately put in written form, thus becoming curriculum guides. One can obtain an idea of their number and variety from the hundreds of guides exhibited at each annual conference of the Association for Supervision and Curriculum Development and the annual published list of the guides exhibited. The many thousands of such guides in published form can be roughly classified as follows.

General Statements

Many school districts and even individual schools find it desirable to prepare statements of their philosophy and program of education. Such

[2]Alice Miel, *Changing the Curriculum* (New York: Appleton-Century-Crofts, 1946), p. 10.

general guides usually contain one or more of the following types of materials: philosophy and objectives; scope and sequence of learning opportunities, usually organized by subject fields; suggestions for organizing instruction; and policies relating to the curriculum. Guides for self-study, assessment programs, preparation of curriculum materials, and other purposes are also prepared.

Courses of Study

Most curriculum guides deal with the content of the curriculum areas. For the elementary and middle schools (much less frequently for high schools), these guides may indicate suggestions for organizing instruction in all curriculum areas. Many guides deal with a particular field for all levels of instruction, although separate courses of study for each high school subject are also quite common. Frequently the guides are prepared for levels: primary, intermediate, middle, junior high, and senior high school years. Their nature varies from very prescriptive outlines and minimum essentials of content to be taught to very general suggestions to teachers as to possible guidelines for selecting content and organizing instruction.

Specific Teaching Aids

Although the more useful courses of study are usually replete with specific suggestions as to materials and techniques, many publications focus on aiding teachers in particular ways. Thus, resource units may be made available for helping teachers plan their own units of work with reference to some broad curriculum topic or theme. Various types of curriculum packages, such as learning activity packages (LAPs), may be prepared externally and by teachers for student use. Detailed listings of materials, especially audiovisual ones, and guides to community resources are frequently provided. General guides to teaching, with specific suggestions on many teaching responsibilities, are also issued by some state and larger local systems.

Descriptions of Practice

Any of the above types of curriculum guides may contain descriptions of practice within the school district, but some districts also publish bulletins wholly devoted to describing curriculum opportunities and teaching practices within these districts. Although frequently directed primarily to parents and the general public, such bulletins also serve useful purposes in helping the teachers who prepare them and others who read them develop common concepts about the school program.

Curriculum Guides for Nonschool Use

Educational agencies other than schools and colleges have publications that serve as curriculum guides by providing suggestions and sometimes directions to teachers. A number of illustrations follow. Teachers in the military and in industry have instructors' manuals. Religious groups develop a sequence of lessons for Sunday school classes; lesson guides are provided for teachers based on this sequence. Youth groups, such as the Boy Scouts and Girl Scouts, have developed a series of learning experiences for their members—often organized around skills to be achieved or knowledge to be gained; leader's manuals serve as curriculum guides. Art museums provide written material to be used by their docents. Guides are prepared for teachers as they use educational television programs with students. Parent guides have been prepared to assist parents as they work with their children.

The quality of the curriculum guides prepared for nonschool use varies just as that of school curriculum guides varies. However, increasingly organizations are recognizing the importance of a scientific and rational approach to curriculum development. For example, the Girl Scouts of America employed a curriculum specialist to help them develop programs for girls in inner cities, and the main-line Protestant denominations have developed a cooperative church school curriculum with guidelines for staff development and instructional strategies.

Use and Development of Curriculum Guides

Undoubtedly, some curriculum guides are not put to good use, but we would not abandon the important process of preparing guides just because of faulty procedures or poor products in some situations. The growth that can come from cooperative work in developing guides is perhaps one of the major reasons for maintaining the production of these materials. Furthermore, good guides, well planned and well written, can be of much direct assistance to teaching personnel. We suggest the following considerations for their development:

1. Each guide should clearly indicate its intended use. Generally, there are two uses by teaching personnel: a) orientation and reference with respect to the total curriculum and the curriculum policies of the educational agency; and b) specific guidance of teachers in planning instruction.
2. Guides written to give specific help to teachers should suggest a wealth of possibilities from which the teacher may derive ideas for exploration in his or her own situation. The presentation of suggestions should be in such form as to aid the teacher in understanding and evaluating them, and also to emphasize the teacher's responsibility and opportunity to make the best plan possible for his or her situation.
3. The guides should be attractive in format, clear in presentation, and arranged to facilitate teachers' use for reference purposes. For the more specific types of guides, a looseleaf notebook arrangement is probably preferable so that the teacher can insert additional materials. Tabs, paper

of different colors, write-in sections, and other mechanical aids are helpful.

4. Most general guides are probably best used as bases of discussion. Accordingly, they should be brief, cogent, and specific as to issues and positions. References to other sources for further study and even questions for discussion may be useful in materials which are likely to be discussed in parent or teacher study groups and in faculty meetings.

The production of an effective curriculum guide is based on a number of important decisions made by various individuals and groups. Walker identified three distinct activities ordinarily called curriculum development: curriculum policy-making, generic development, and site-specific development.[3] These three activities are aspects of one overall process, curriculum development, by means of which curriculum plans are produced and educational programs are changed and improved (see Table 2.1).

Curriculum policy making establishes the ground rules, limits, criteria

TABLE 2.1 Curriculum Development Activities.

Curriculum Policy-Making	Site-Specific Curriculum Development		Generic Curriculum Development
De Jure	Phases		
Supreme Court decisions	Identify local needs or programs		Textbooks
U.S. legislative acts	Survey available generic materials		Instructional
U.S. government grants	Adapt generic materials to local needs		packages
State legislative acts	and conditions or		and systems
State board regulations	Develop site-specific materials		National
State agency standards	Implement the new curriculum as		curriculum
and policies	standard operating procedure		projects
Local agency regulations			Regional, state,
			and district
De Facto	Types of Decisions	Data Considered	guides
Community networks	Curriculum policies	Students	Leagues of
Accrediting associations	Selection of curric-	Society	schools
Testing bureaus	ulum content	Knowledge	
Advisory boards and	Technical develop-	Learning process	
panels	ment of curric-	Goals	
	ulum	External policies	
	Arrangement of	Resources	
	learning oppor-		
	tunities		
	Plan for implemen-		
	tation		

[3]Decker F. Walker, "Approaches to Curriculum Development," a paper prepared for the NIE Curriculum Development Task Force, 1976 (Washington, D.C.: National Institute of Education, 1977).

and the like which circumscribe the curricula of educational institutions within a given jurisdiction. For public schools, curriculum policy making is an official responsibility of the agencies responsible for the governance of education. In the United States, constitutionally, this responsibility rests with the individual state, where it is generally shared among the state legislature, state and local boards of education, and the state department of education. The federal government also makes curriculum policy decisions by passing legislation regulating school programs (for example, PL 94–142) and allocating funds for curriculum development. *De facto* curriculum policy may be made by quasi-official bodies to which an educational institution may choose to belong (see Table 2.1).

Generic development is the design and production of curriculum plans and materials suitable for use in schools in general or in certain types of schools or other educational agencies. Generic development requires the formation of some type of enterprise supported as a private endeavor or through public or foundation funds. Pilot versions of plans and materials are developed and tested. The pilot test results lead to the design, production, and marketing of the plans and materials (see Table 2.1).

Site-specific development refers to activities undertaken to change the curriculum of a particular educational institution. This activity holds the central place in our conception of curriculum development (Table 2.1) because, as pointed out earlier, curriculum development activities have meaning only as they result in changes in practices of teachers and teaching environments. Site-specific curriculum development demands an intimate knowledge of local conditions on the part of professionals and a willingness to recognize the existence of problems and to cooperate in efforts to solve them on the part of community leaders.

The four phases of site-specific development shown in Table 2.1 represent but one of several approaches. A major portion of this chapter entails descriptions of three different approaches to site-specific curriculum development. However, because of the impact of curriculum-policy making and generic development on site-specific development, these topics are explored first.

CURRICULUM-POLICY MAKING

Policy making is perhaps the most difficult kind of curriculum decision-making. In part, it is made difficult by the clamor of everyone to participate in it, since almost all citizens, as well as professional educators, feel they have a stake in the educational process. In the United States, curriculum-policy making involves professional organizations and more particularly legally constituted groups, namely, state and local boards of education. Nevertheless, we recognize fully that decisions concerning what to teach and what not to teach in local school districts must be shared not only by the local board of education and the professional staff but by the taxpayers and parents and the students themselves. The challenge of curriculum planning is to determine orderly processes whereby the wishes of all concerned may be considered in the final determination of curriculum policy by legally constituted authority.

De Jure Curriculum-Policy Making

A number of legally constituted bodies are concerned with curriculum policy (Table 2.1). Most of these policies are related to the operation of public schools and state-supported colleges and universities. However, other educational agencies—such as youth organizations, the Red Cross, religious groups—may also be subject to curriculum policies established externally by parent bodies.

Historically, the hallowed principle of *local control* of education guided curriculum-policy making. This was generally effective in small and relatively homogeneous districts. However, local control became less effective as school districts became larger and more heterogeneous, and it became difficult, if not impossible, to arrive at a consensus on the proper character of education for citizens in the community. But, according to Boyd, "the development that has most weakened the effectiveness of the local control principle is the remarkable recent growth of the influence and authority of state and national (both federal and nongovernmental) agencies over the curriculum."[4] This politicizing of curriculum-policy making often appears to be a contest for control among special-interest groups (often professional associations) concerned with protecting or advancing their own interests.

Federal Level

Citizens and educators generally believe that the federal government should provide resources for education—but exercise little or no control over it. However, as pointed out in Chapter 1, the federal government is influencing, and in some cases making, curriculum policy through court decisions, legislation that mandates programs, and appropriations that support categorical aid and fund curriculum development projects. Gold-hammer provided some justification for categorical aid when he recognized that "generally where the federal government has provided categorical assistance for the development of specific types of programs, these 'stimulative' grants have been in areas of significant social and community needs where little, if anything, was being accomplished by local communities and educators."[5]

There are, however, sharp differences of opinion regarding the proper

---

[4]Boyd, p. 579.
[5]Keith Goldhammer, "The Proper Federal Role in Education Today," *Educational Leadership, 35* (February 1978):350.

federal role in curriculum activities—whether it be in policy making or generic development. Proponents of a strong role claim that federal leadership is needed:

1. To address matters of clear national interest.
2. To pursue national goals.
3. To upgrade the content of instructional programs.
4. To provide coordination among the various agencies who sponsor and conduct curriculum activities.
5. To stimulate innovation and risk taking.

Other observers argue that limiting federal leadership is needed:

1. To promote local control and priority setting.
2. To return control of education to the states.
3. To reduce control over educational reform by elite groups with special influence.
4. To reduce the fickle pursuit of fads and instant panaceas.
5. To reduce inefficiency, waste, and duplication.[6]

State Level

The 50 states have varied in the ways their educational agencies influence the curriculum of their local schools and in the extent of their influence. Perhaps the most easily identifiable influences are state constitutional provisions, legislative acts, and state board or department of education regulations which prescribe subjects to be taught, graduation requirements, time allotments, and special programs and emphases. These prescriptions generally stipulate a basic program of studies for the elementary school, including the customary subjects of language arts, arithmetic, U.S. history, geography, science, health, physical education, art, and music; but they may make more specific requirements of some but not all individual subjects for the high schools. The most common requirements for the high schools have been in English and in U.S. history, with many states also prescribing mathematics, science, health, and physical education. Other more specific requirements of individual states have included state history, driver education, conservation, and drug abuse education.

A recent trend has been a rapid increase in curriculum-policy making at the state level. One stimulus has been the channeling of federal funds through the states to support programs created by the federal government. Moreover, state legislatures have become increasingly active; new

[6]See Jon Schaffarzick and Gary Sykes, "NIE's Role in Curriculum Development: Findings, Policy Options, and Recommendations" (National Institute of Education, 1977), pp. 6–8, passim.

laws and court rulings have had a major impact on the school curriculum. A majority of the states are specifying, or planning to specify, competencies necessary for graduation; many have instituted state-wide testing systems; and some are requiring parent participation in making curriculum decisions.

The extent to which states have become involved in curriculum-policy making is illustrated by the curriculum procedures included in a New Jersey law passed in 1975.

In attempting to define specific educational action, it mandates that communities shall:
1. *Develop Goals*—with involvement of teachers, staff members, administrators, board members, pupils, parents and other citizens.
2. *Establish Assessment Objectives*—goal indicators and specific levels of achievement or standards.
3. *Identify Needs*—difference between what is and what is desired (objectives).
4. *Develop and Install Educational Programs*—to provide translation from goals to reality.
5. *Evaluate Program Effectiveness*—to determine whether goals and objectives have been met and to recycle adaptive goals.[7]

This law was heralded by legislators as enhancing autonomy in the running of local schools, since the law only specifies what is to be achieved at a district level; the how is left to the locality. However, other provisions of the bill show the extent of state control over the curriculum. A school is classified as "approved," "conditionally approved," or "unapproved" based on two major factors:

1. Student performance on a minimum basic skills test administered in grades three, six, nine, and eleven.
2. School progress toward meeting its self-determined educational plan coupled with implementation of federal- and state-mandated programs.

As we see it, to ensure an adequate and indeed excellent program throughout the state, the state should set a broad framework of the school program and provide sufficient general support, with standards to be met in order to receive that support. Regulatory measures are undoubtedly needed, but if the state educational agencies stop with regulations and standards, local decision making is not aided in moving beyond requirements and minimums to ever-improving educational programs. Thus, we consider the most important function of planning at the state level to be that of working with local leadership in making plans which will aid local

[7]Kenneth D. Hall and Virginia Brinson, "What About Curriculum Reform at the State Level?" *Educational Leadership*, 35 (February 1978):344.

school districts in moving forward with their own curriculum planning. Some significant steps in this direction follow:

1. Use of state curriculum commissions, committees, and advisory groups, representing educational groups throughout the state, in determining state curriculum policies, such as those we have identified, and also in recommending ways and means whereby local systems may organize their own curriculum improvement programs. Curriculum guides may be produced through these endeavors to help local districts move into new areas of curriculum development.
2. Establishment of state curriculum evaluation commissions to carry on deliberate and informed evaluation of curriculum proposals from many sources and to serve liaison functions with such commissions in other states and with national and regional curriculum studies and projects.
3. Stimulation of professional development and school innovation through conferences, consultations, surveys, studies, and other means of focusing the attention of local educational leaders on systematic processes of change.
4. Sponsorship of curriculum research and development studies in the state, with financial and other aid to the schools serving as research centers, with adequate arrangement for field testing and dissemination.
5. Working with state-wide organizations interested in but outside the field of education in order to develop understanding and support of the educational program of the state, and also to secure suggestions for its improvement.

State activities have extended well beyond the activities outlined above. Boyd concluded, after reviewing research on curriculum-policy making, that "the curriculum-policy making system is now more complex, legalized, centralized, and bureaucratised and includes more veto points."[8] A complex hierarchy of authority involving local, state, and national levels of government has emerged and complex procedures for meshing these parts of government are necessary. The very complexity of the curriculum-policy making machinery may prove dysfunctional by preventing schools from responding to a rapidly changing society.

De Facto Curriculum-Policy Making

Educational institutions may voluntarily belong to one or more organizations and, as a condition of this membership, follow agreed-upon curriculum policy (see Table 2.1). Illustrations of possible *de facto* curriculum-policy making groups follow.

[8]Boyd, pp. 610–611.

Community Networks

In Chapter 1, it was emphasized that learning takes place in many settings—schools, homes, youth organizations, religious organizations, museums, and through radio and television. An individual learns from a number of these sources during a given period of time. To avoid redundant (or, indeed, contradictory) experiences, various educational agencies should plan cooperatively, thus creating a network of learning systems. Curriculum-policy decisions made by such a network provide a guide to each of the members.

Accrediting Associations

Schools, colleges, and universities may choose to belong to one or more accrediting associations. Admittance to such organizations and continuation of membership are dependent upon following association standards, including curriculum policies.

Testing Bureaus

Ideally, the tests used should be determined by the curriculum; in fact, the reverse may happen. Once a school or school system has adopted a testing program, the curriculum is influenced. For example, one school system appointed committees of teachers, principals, and supervisors to analyze the content of the newly adopted standardized tests "so we can change our curriculum to fit the tests." (Not surprisingly, their modified curriculum produced better results—on the tests.) The test publisher was, in fact, establishing curriculum policy for the school system.

Advisory Boards and Panels

Some educational institutions establish boards or panels to advise them on programs. For example, museums and symphony orchestras often have advisory panels of educators to help them plan educational programs, and vocational educators use advisory boards drawn from business and industry to assist in program development. Such groups participate in curriculum-policy making.

GENERIC CURRICULUM DEVELOPMENT

Generic curriculum development includes the design and production of curriculum plans and materials for use in various educational settings. As Table 2.1 indicates, these plans and materials are developed away from a specific site. The preceding section demonstrated how curriculum policy made external to the site established a "zone of tolerance" within which local educators are free to exercise professional judgment in site-specific curriculum development. The products of generic development can extend the horizons of site-specific curriculum developers by supplying ideas and materials. The same products can become a "strait jacket," although often a comfortable one, when they are adopted as the complete curriculum plan.

In the 1980s many school districts and schools model their curriculum planning on prototypes outside the districts and schools, and are even adopting, in somewhat wholesale fashion, models, plans, and systems developed elsewhere. We believe that curriculum planning should remain a local function, albeit one that is discharged more satisfactorily than has been true in many situations in the past, but we recognize and here identify the possibilities and practices of using externally developed plans and systems. Historically, and perhaps still today, the textbook is the most commonly used externally developed plan, and we consider this practice first.

Textbooks

Textbooks can be a valuable resource for site-specific curriculum developers. When developed by experts within a field, they contain useful and organized information. Observers of teaching in a developing country, where there are no funds to purchase textbooks, appreciate the value of this teaching tool.

Ideally, members of a local curriculum committee will select textbooks, and other print and nonprint material, *after* they have developed their own curriculum plans. When this process is reversed, the adopted textbook has too frequently been the only curriculum plan used. The weakness in these situations is not inherent in the textbook but rather in the absence or disregard of a curriculum plan which facilitates the proper use of the textbook in relation to the objectives of the instructional program. Curriculum planning of recent decades has tended to correct this abuse of textbooks, and greatly improved textbooks and many other instructional aids have facilitated the new plans, but no person knowledgeable about curriculum practices in U.S. schools would deny that the textbook is still the curriculum plan in many classrooms.

In such situations, the curriculum plan, if one could really call it that, follows a pattern: 1) adopt the objectives of the textbook author; 2) adopt the scope and sequence of the textbook as the design of the curriculum; 3) use whatever instructional strategies the textbook (or the accompanying manual or guide) suggests; and 4) make evaluation a series of tests (sometimes also provided by the publisher) of learners' mastery of the textbook. Ignored in general are the aspects of curriculum planning described in this book such as the studying of data about the learners involved, the relating of the curriculum goals and design to the needs of learners and the social factors operating in the community, the mapping of instructional strategies in relation to goals and learners, and the provision for continuing feedback concerning the effectiveness of the learning opportunities provided.

When other teaching–learning materials were generally lacking, when teachers had little preparation for their jobs, and when students had little competition from other media for their interests, the basic textbook was certainly a great advance as a curriculum plan over memorization of dictated and copied material. Today, greatly improved in format, content, and accompanying aids, it can still be a great resource for the instructional program, but it ought not to be used to prescribe that program for widely varying learners, classrooms, and schools. That is, we question the use of any national curriculum plan as the exact plan for any situation, and the textbook used as just described is such a national plan.

Probably most efforts toward curriculum improvement in this century have sought to diminish the use of the textbook as the curriculum plan. The curriculum movement itself, beginning in the 1920s with the aims and activity-analysis approaches of Bobbitt and Charters (described in Chapter 5), was begun and continues as a system of planning which relates instruction to educational goals and objectives rather than to textbooks alone. Each of the designs described in Chapter 5 would utilize a curriculum plan other than that of any single textbook. But the designs were reflected in textbooks, and the local plans frequently either began with the adopted textbooks or utilized them to the exclusion of all other sources of curriculum content.

As we see it, the most influential and widespread departure in local curriculum planning came in the 1950s with the national curriculum projects. A large number of districts and schools sought to incorporate or adopt the "new curricula" in their plans. Many of these projects resulted in textbooks. Although new materials are developed differently and include new curriculum content sometimes presented in whole kits of materials, these new materials could, like textbooks, also be misused by being incorporated wholesale into local curriculum plans. Hence, we doubt if curriculum planning should assume that any plan, however creatively designed, cannot at some point be reflected in a textbook or learning kit that will in some classrooms become the curriculum plan. The inferences we draw from this observation are that: 1) the curriculum plan should include alternatives as to instructional materials and strategies; 2) teachers should be helped through preservice and in-service training to make wise choices of the alternatives; and 3) whatever materials are developed and-/or purchased should be the best available, so that if alternatives are still ignored and externally developed materials are still used without adaptation, learners have as good a chance as possible under such circumstances —and the chances are poor—to have good learning experiences. In other words, if all else fails and textbooks (and kits) constitute the plans, find the best ones possible!

Instructional Packages and Systems

Current publications and publishers' advertisements use interchangeably such terms as *packages, packets, kits, instructional systems,* and others. The terms are used to cover two very different concepts: 1) a total system of learning activities and related materials for a broad area of content or a series of objectives; and 2) a particular assembly of materials for one segment of such a system, or even of a subject or other curriculum component that is not fully systematized. To eliminate the confusion here we use *instructional system* for the first, broader concept and *package* for the latter, narrower one. We consider *system* as appropriate to the former, since the more advanced instructional systems use a systems approach; we prefer *package* for the latter because of the widespread use of the term in local curriculum planning to refer to locally produced materials for specific curriculum objectives, such as the LAP (learning activity package). In this section, our reference is to the use in local curriculum planning and implementation of systems and packages developed externally, primarily the first type above.

Unruh described six characteristics of instructional systems, as we use the term, although she referred to characteristics of "well-designed teaching–learning packages . . . built as instructional systems." These characteristics have become even more important in the 1980s with the increased use of teacher aids.

1. The emphasis is on individualization in the emerging concept of teaching–learning packages.
2. Instructional systems packages are based on broad concepts organized into manageable coordinated modules.
3. Clearly stated instructional objectives convey to the student the quality of performance expected of him.
4. Multimedia learning materials of varying types are included to provide a choice of vehicles for learning for various steps in the process.
5. The package not only provides diversified materials, but also provides for diversified learning activities, particularly student–student interaction and teacher–student interaction.
6. The role of the teacher–instructor is significantly changed.[9]

Many instructional systems have been developed in recent years by commercial publishers and the large producers of educational software and hardware, frequently called learning industries, and by regional edu-

[9]Glenys G. Unruh, "Can I Be Replaced by a Package?" *Educational Leadership, 27* (May 1970):765.

cational laboratories and other organizations. Obviously, these systems vary in the extent to which they exemplify Unruh's characteristics. Even more variation is probably exhibited in the skills with which teachers use the systems, especially in relation to the alternatives emphasized by Unruh: variety of media; diversified learning activities; and teacher behavior.

Instructional systems are being developed as software for computers. Earlier efforts to develop computer assisted instruction (CAI) suffered from excessive costs and unimaginative programs. However, the cost, size, and energy requirements of computers have been reduced dramatically. By the end of the 1980s personal computers will probably cost less than $100. The linking of computers with telecommunications provides a powerful new technology for packaging and delivering instructional systems. Computers are used extensively for educational purposes in business and industry, and numerous programs are becoming available for home and school use.

Commercially or other externally developed instructional systems offer new resources to local curriculum planners. For those goals which the school or district shares with the developers of the systems, the latter may represent better plans of curriculum implementation than local groups can readily and efficiently develop. But the processes involved in the original selection of a system and its use are critical: if the right system is selected and it is used in the way any "right" system should be—that is, with careful choice for particular learners of appropriate media, activities, and teacher behavior—the system may indeed be the right plan. As to the choice of instructional systems, the following factors should be considered by individuals or groups:

1. Extent to which the system meets the six characteristics described above.
2. Congruence of local objectives and those of the system.
3. Compliance of the system with principles of human growth and development.
4. Relevance and validity of the system's contents.
5. Appropriateness of evaluation procedures used in the system.

Full consideration of these factors would in itself be a rather comprehensive type of curriculum planning, and one that seems to us of critical importance, whether the instructional system is to be purchased on these bases or ultimately to be developed locally.

National Curriculum Projects

A reform movement that produced for national use over 100 curriculums in different subjects had its roots in the years immediately following World War II. Test scores of young men recruited for the armed services revealed serious inadequacies in their preparation in science and mathematics. Part of the problem was their limited study in these fields; part of it was learning from an outmoded curriculum that did not reflect the scientific advances of the twentieth century. Scholars in a few fields, notably mathematics and science, recognized their responsibility for this condition and voluntarily launched national efforts to reform the curriculum.

The successful launching of Sputnik in 1957 provided a great impetus to the movement. Federal appropriations through the National Defense Education Act (1958) and the National Science Foundation and other educational support provisions made possible a great acceleration of curriculum development, improved facilities, and teacher education in science, mathematics, and foreign languages initially. The impetus given these subjects and widespread concern for updating curriculum content in general stimulated project development in all fields in time. Along with the interest in new content and additional trained manpower in the fields first of national defense and then of specialization in general, an accelerated effort was made to utilize more fully new technology in education. Federal expenditures for the projects through 1974 were $357 million; costs for the School Mathematics Study Group (SMSG) project were in excess of $50 million.[10]

The national curriculum project method of curriculum development is illustrated in Figure 2.1. Each project is initially aimed at the content of one subject field (for example, physics, biology or chemistry), and is frequently a year-long course, although broader projects and even interdisciplinary projects can be developed later. Scholars in the discipline define the structure of the subject field and determine the form and sequence of the presentation of the subject matter. In the second step, these same scholars work with educational practitioners and producers in preparing tentative teaching–learning materials. These materials are field-tested with classroom teachers and revised before the major implementation process begins (Step III). The curriculum materials that result are generally in the public domain and published by commercial publishers or through the project or some quasi-public educational laboratory. As the materials are used, they are subject to continuing revision.

Local curriculum planning groups have used the projects in any of these ways:

1. The general approach of the project in defining its field, usually through the selection of basic concepts, principles, and processes—the so-called

---

[10]The NIE Curriculum Development Task Force, *Current Issues, Problems, and Concerns in Curriculum Development* (Washington, D.C.: National Institute for Education, 1976), p. 11.

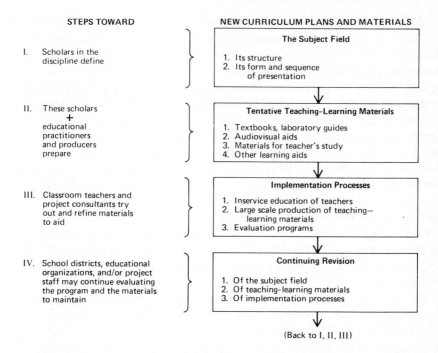

STEPS TOWARD   NEW CURRICULUM PLANS AND MATERIALS

The Subject Field

I. Scholars in the
    discipline define
    1. Its structure
    2. Its form and sequence
       of presentation

Tentative Teaching-Learning Materials

II. These scholars
     +
     educational
     practitioners
     and producers
     prepare
     1. Textbooks, laboratory guides
     2. Audiovisual aids
     3. Materials for teacher's study
     4. Other learning aids

Implementation Processes

III. Classroom teachers and
      project consultants try
      out and refine materials
      to aid
      1. Inservice education of teachers
      2. Large scale production of teaching—
         learning materials
      3. Evaluation programs

Continuing Revision

IV. School districts, educational
     organizations, and/or project
     staff may continue evaluating
     the program and the materials
     to maintain
     1. Of the subject field
     2. Of teaching-learning materials
     3. Of implementation processes

(Back to I, II, III)

FIGURE 2.1   The National Curriculum Project method of curriculum planning

structure of the subject (see Chapter 5)—may be followed or at least consulted in the development of the local curriculum plan for this field.

2. Textbooks and perhaps related learning aids which have been influenced by a project's definition of the content of a field may be selected for some use in the local curriculum plan.

3. The entire program, kit, or "package" developed by the project or its publishers may be adopted and used locally as the curriculum plan; such adoption may involve education of the staff responsible for the use of the materials.

This third approach is not much different from the practice of adopting a basic textbook as the curriculum plan. To the extent that teachers are trained in the use of the materials, and to the extent that the materials facilitate adaptation to the individual differences of learners, classrooms, and teachers, the use of the project materials can be a useful aid to local groups in developing their own instructional program. Used without adaptation to local objectives, designs, and learners, the projects can be almost as sterile and irrelevant as the worst of the textbook-alone "plans."

Research studies comparing subject matter achievement of students using the national curricula programs with that of students using traditional curricula were reviewed by Walker and Schaffarzick.[11] They looked for "signs of superiority of innovative curricula over traditional curricula." What they found was "not superiority, but parity: each curriculum did better on the distinctive parts of its own program, and each did about equally well on the parts they held in common."[12] We should not lose sight of the important finding that different curricula are associated with different patterns of achievement. Walker and Schaffarzick concluded that curriculum materials generally produce "a pattern of academic achievement consistent with the intentions of curriculum developers." This led them to advise that we "stop thinking of the curriculum as a fixed race course and begin to think of it as a tool, apparently a powerful one, for stimulating and directing the active learning capacities which are ultimately responsible for the achievement we want from schools."[13]

Conducting further studies comparing national curricula programs with traditional ones would be difficult because it would be hard to find "traditional curricula" unaffected by one or more national curriculum programs. Furthermore, as indicated previously, relatively few teachers are using all of the features of a national curriculum program. A national project that continues to have vitality and influence is the Biological Sciences Curriculum Study (BSCS). The staff publishes the *BSCS Journal.*[14] Although some other national projects have been discontinued, many of the textbooks being used reflect the national curriculum projects; thus, their influence continues.

The national curriculum reform movement was a legacy of the National Institute of Education (NIE) when it was organized in 1972. Critics of the national movement said the strategy was expensive and that "a relatively small number of projects have consumed the lion's share of the NIE budget with development activities."[15] Critics also pointed out the serious problems of adoption and adaptation of national curriculum materials. The assumption made by curriculum developers that materials could and would be picked up and used by any teacher—"teacher-proof" materials —proved faulty. Although these, and other arguments, were used to oppose funding national curriculum projects, as Schaffarzick and Sykes pointed out, "at the heart of the matter have been differences in fundamental convictions over issues of right, legitimacy, entitlement, and con-

[11]Decker F. Walker and Jon Schaffarzick, "Comparing Curricula," *Review of Educational Research,* 44 (Winter 1974):83–109.
[12]Walker and Schaffarzick, p. 108.
[13]Walker and Schaffarzick, p. 109.
[14]For a review of BSCS work, see the twentieth anniversary issue of the *BSCS Journal, 1* (September 1978); and W. V. Mayer (ed.), *Planning Curriculum Development* (Boulder, Co.: BSCS, 1975).
[15]Jon Schaffarzick and Gary Sykes, "A Changing NIE: New Leadership, A New Climate," *Educational Leadership,* 35 (February 1978):368.

trol in educational decision making, and over the goals and purposes of education."[16] After consulting with a national panel, NIE shifted its emphasis from centralized curriculum reform "to support for basic and applied research and efforts to stimulate, facilitate, and coordinate the R and D (Research and Development) work of other educational agencies."[17]

A national curriculum project, independent of federal funds and control, is operated by the Joint Council on Economic Education. This council is an independent, nonprofit organization that was founded in 1949 to encourage, improve, and serve the economic education movement. They have produced curriculum materials which are widely used in elementary schools, middle schools, high schools, and colleges. The Joint Council works through a network that covers 49 states with over 170 centers and 400 cooperating school systems. Publications of the Joint Council include *The Journal of Economic Education,* "Progress in Economic Education" (a newsletter), curriculum guides for teachers, and materials for student use.[18]

Regional, State, and Local Curriculum Materials

Federally funded regional R and D centers were established in the 1960s to contribute to the reform and continuing improvement of education. A major, though not exclusive, activity of these centers has been development of curriculum materials.[19] Although activities varied from center to center, the curriculum approaches generally used differed significantly from those used in national programs. Chase identified three characteristics of curriculum work in R and D centers:

1. There is a systematic attempt to work out cycles of need assessment, specifications of objectives, analysis of alternative strategies and treatments leading to choices among alternatives, construction of partial or tentative systems or prototypes on the basis of testing in clinical and experimental situations, installations and testing under field conditions in a variety of situations, and continuing evaluation and refinement.
2. Attention is given to all of the major elements in learning environments. The approach is one of creating systems that have as components instructional materials and media, physical settings and the development of relevant behaviors for teachers and other school personnel, family groups, and community volunteers.

[16]Schaffarzick and Sykes, p. 369.
[17]Schaffarzick and Sykes, p. 367.
[18]For information, write to Joint Council on Economic Education, 1212 Avenue of the Americas, New York, N.Y. 10036.
[19]See the periodical, *Education R & D Report,* for brief items about new projects and materials issued by the R and D labs. For copies, write to R & D Interpretation Service, CEMREL, Inc., 3120 59th St., St. Louis, Mo. 63139.

3. There is a linking of many organizations and institutions in the implementation of programs.[20]

Gagné reviewed federal accomplishments in research and development and concluded that R and D centers had "increased the awareness of the role and value of research and development among school boards, school administrators, and teachers."[21] The millennium has not arrived, but educational research has come out of the closet. Gagné also recognized that R and D centers had made significant contributions to evaluation by enlarging its scope. However, Gagné felt that little progress had been made in program development and diffusion, with much remaining to be done.

The major problem faced by R and D centers has been that their innovations are not implemented as prescribed. Pincus identified some reasons for the lack of implementation, including:

1. Researchers are interested in disciplinary prestige more than in problem solving in the schools.
2. Researchers and practitioners often don't talk the same language because their operating styles, perceptions of issues, and professional priorities are so different.
3. Research and Development agencies follow an R and D change model that views the schools as passive adopters of new products, but the schools themselves decide to adopt and implement innovations in light of a host of organizational considerations which are not incorporated in the R and D model of change.[22]

For these, and possibly other, reasons, most of the materials developed by R and D centers have had little impact on schools. The original number of R and D centers has been reduced with commensurate reduction in funding.

Federal funds (particularly authorized by Title III and Title IV of the Elementary and Secondary Education Act) support curriculum development at the state and local level. The materials developed are disseminated to other schools and school districts. The U.S. Office of Education established a National Diffusion Network (NDN) to encourage dissemination of programs of proven quality. Through a highly quantitative screening and validation program, approximately 100 programs for dissemination were identified. The network disseminates information regarding these activities to professional personnel.

[20]Francis S. Chase, "Educational Research and Development in the Sixties," *Elements of Curriculum Development* (Ontario: Ontario Institute for Studies in Education, 1971), p. 145.
[21]Robert M. Gagné, "Educational Research and Development: Past and Future," in Robert Glaser (ed.), *Research and Development and School Change* (Hillsdale, N.J.: Lawrence Erlbaum Associates, Publishers, 1978), p. 90.
[22]John Pincus, "Incentives for Innovation in the Public Schools," *Review of Educational Research, 44* (Winter 1974):132.

Various states have established banks of locally developed validated programs. For example, the Michigan State Department of Education asked local districts to nominate noteworthy programs. These projects were then visited by a panel of experts in a curricular area. The programs selected by the panels were added to the national bank and made available to key decision makers in the districts.[23]

Curriculum guides and materials developed by state departments of education are made available to school districts and schools. Many school districts provide locally developed guides to their schools. Such guides are often exchanged at national and state meetings. Drawing from national and state banks and from other districts and schools, many schools adopt programs to meet their curriculum needs. However, reliance on such programs will not be sufficient. McNeil cited a "growing uneasiness about the ability of anyone at a distance from the classroom—publishers or product developers—to design a curriculum and have it implemented as intended."[24]

Leagues of Schools

Leagues of schools may share in the development of curriculum materials as well as supply professional and moral support for mutual efforts of innovation. The terms *consortia, networks,* and *associated schools* are generally synonymous with *league.* Less formally organized than the school district with its legal status, the league cuts across district and even state lines. Planning models of this type have long been used in education, and we believe that they have more utility than ever before. For example, the Eight-Year Study involved an association of 30 schools and had ties with colleges and universities which entered into the agreement about the admission of the graduates of the schools. More recently, the federally subsidized research and development centers and the regional educational laboratories have utilized various types of networks of participating schools. The supplementary educational centers financed by Title III of the Elementary and Secondary Education Act of 1965 and its supplements have generally served a specific group of schools and in some states have melded into intermediate units. The Union Boards of New York State and similar sharing arrangements among local districts in other states have provided special tax support for cooperative educational services shared by cooperating school districts.

The League of Cooperating Schools developed in 1966 by Goodlad

[23]Olga Moir, "Locally Identified Promising Programs: Quality Control Through Professional Judgment," *Educational Leadership, 36* (October 1978):51–54.

[24]John D. McNeil, "Curriculum—A Field Shaped by Different Faces," *Educational Researcher, 7* (September 1978):22.

provides a prototype for league activity. Eighteen elementary schools in 18 separate Southern California school districts joined with the Research Division of the Institute for Development of Educational Activities, Inc. (I/D/E/A) to form the league. The beliefs that guided Goodlad in the formation of the League included:

1. The optimal unit for educational change is the single school with its pupils, teachers, principal.
2. Under certain conditions, a school can change to be more satisfactory. If change in the school is to proceed more rapidly than change in the larger system, the school will require the goodwill of that system or some compelling "different drummer," or both.
3. Because the school is in some ways an isolated, fragile culture, efforts to change will probably require a supportive reference group.
4. Changes require new knowledge, new skills, new ways of doing things.[25]

The League of Cooperating Schools is successful because it enables schools to be self-renewing as it helps them to help themselves. The League provides the needed support system in the form of people and materials. Not all leagues have as solid a conceptual base as does the League of Cooperating Schools.

Another example of a league type of activity for planning curriculum and instruction is the Individually Guided Education (IGE) network developed by the Wisconsin Research and Development Center for Individualized Schooling.[26] IGE assists elementary and middle schools to provide individualized instruction through planning by one or more instruction and research units. "The units' personnel share in deliberations and decisions about pupil needs, problems, materials, and procedures of diagnosis and instruction."[27] Smith referred to this activity as a continuous mini-workshop. The preparation of teachers for IGE has been carefully delineated, and appropriate teacher and pupil materials are available for the program.[28] Smith reported that faculty members in "IGE schools are more adaptive, flexible, and innovative with respect to instructional activities."[29]

The successful diffusion of the IGE plan has been achieved through networks in 14 states with three interlocking hierarchial levels: System-

[25]John Goodlad, "An Ecological Approach to Change in Elementary School Settings," *The Elementary School Journal,* 78 (November 1977):98.

[26]H. J. Klausmeier, R. A. Rossmiller, and M. Saily (eds.), *Individually Guided Elementary Education: Concepts and Practices* (New York: Academic Press, 1977).

[27]B. Othanel Smith, "IGE and Teacher Education," *Journal of Teacher Education,* 30 (May–June 1979):17.

[28]H. J. Klausmeier, *Individually Guided Education in Elementary and Middle Schools: A Handbook for Implementors and College Instructors* (Reading, Mass.: Addison-Wesley, 1977).

[29]Smith, p. 19.

wide Program Committees (SPCs), Regional IGE Coordinating Councils (RICCs), and a State IGE Coordinating Council (SICC). SPCs are composed of representatives from the local school system, and the regional and state councils are composed of representatives from departments of education and teacher training institutions, as well as teachers and principals. Lins reported that the agencies represented "have moved increasingly toward relying on the network structures as a means of addressing crucial issues facing education."[30] Thus, the league not only fosters IGE but serves as a mechanism for educational improvement as well. Lins said, "The IGE experience demonstrates that well-organized state networks are important in bringing about educational renewal."[31]

An illustration of a state-wide league is provided by the North Carolina League of Middle/Junior High Schools. The League of member institutions was founded in 1976 with the following major goals:

1. To serve as a clearinghouse for the exchange of ideas, materials, and personnel needed for curriculum improvement in the middle grades.
2. To facilitate continuing curriculum improvement, in-service education, school planning, and other phases of middle/junior high school education.
3. To assist in developing plans for evaluating middle/junior high schools in North Carolina.
4. To help secure and maintain support of agencies and groups in the state interested in educational improvement.
5. To represent middle/junior high school age youth in professional and public discussions of educational programs and problems.

The League is achieving its goals through an annual conference, training workshops, planned visits to schools, and the publication of a newsletter and a journal.[32]

We believe that collaboration of schools in such ventures is a great incentive and aid to curriculum planning. Actually, the plans are not developed wholly externally to the school, since through the league there is typically much opportunity for participation in planning for any common curriculum designs and much opportunity for mutual support, feedback, and modification during implementation. The league may be organized with little aim of developing common curriculum plans, as was true in the Eight-Year Study with the great freedom each school had in developing its own plan, but with the expectation of sharing, criticizing,

[30]L. Joseph Lins, "Implementing IGE: State Networks as a Strategy for Renewal," *Journal of Teacher Education*, 30 (May–June 1979):22.

[31]Lins, p. 22.

[32]"North Carolina League of Middle/Junior High Schools Newsletter," *Journal of the North Carolina League of Middle/Junior High Schools* (Boone, N. C.: Appalachian State University, n. d.).

and observing the plans of individual schools. The systematic process of site-specific curriculum planning which we will now discuss would make full provision of such sharing and collaborating among schools with common needs and interests.

SITE-SPECIFIC CURRICULUM DEVELOPMENT

Curriculum development consists of three interrelated activities: policy making, generic development, and site-specific development (see Table 2.1). Official and quasi-official bodies interact in making curriculum policy that circumscribes local decision making. External groups are sources of curriculum plans, materials, and ideas that may be used in local decision making. Given the policy constraints and the resource assistance, curriculum development proceeds at the local site. This section presents three approaches to site-specific curriculum development: structured-committee approach, inductive approach, and problem-solving approach. These are not the only approaches nor are they necessarily independent, but they are representative of different strategies.[33]

The selection of a curriculum development approach depends upon local conditions as they relate to the double agenda mentioned earlier: change in ideas about the curriculum and change in the human dynamics. Curriculum plans are useless until they are implemented in the classroom. Therefore, a brief discussion of problems and strategies of curricular innovations is presented.

Implementation of Curricular Innovations

Failure to implement new curriculum plans has both puzzled and frustrated researchers and program developers. Consequently, hundreds of studies on the implementation of curriculum innovations have been made. Fullan and Pomfret prepared an excellent review of this research, which is used extensively in this section.[34]

From their review of research, Fullan and Pomfret identified five dimensions of curriculum change: "changes in a) subject matter or materials; b) organizational structure; c) role/behavior; d) knowledge and understanding; and e) value internalization."[35] Most curriculum innovations require changes in all five dimensions. Failure to recognize the need for change in one or more dimensions may result in adopting the form but not the substance of an innovation. For example, inductive approaches to

[33]For illustrations of various strategies, see Chapters 3–7 in John I. Goodlad et al., *Curriculum Inquiry: The Story of Curriculum Practice* (New York: McGraw-Hill Book Company, 1979).
[34]Michael Fullan and Alan Pomfret, "Research on Curriculum and Instruction Implementation," *Review of Educational Research, 47* (Spring 1977):335–397.
[35]Fullan and Pomfret, p. 361.

science fail when teachers do not change their classroom behavior and continue to lecture. Fullan and Pomfret found four broad categories of factors that influence implementation: characteristics of the innovation, strategies, characteristics of the adopting unit, and characteristics of macro sociopolitical units.[36]

Characteristics of the Innovation

Innovations characterized by little explicitness (that is, described in abstract, global, or ambiguous terms) lead to user confusion, lack of clarity, and frustration. Such innovations have a low degree of implementation. Plans for continually moving toward greater explicitness during initial implementation need to be made. A second important innovation characteristic is the degree of complexity of the innovation or the difficulty in using it. Ease of implementation declines as complexity increases. Thus, new teaching strategies and role relationships with students showed lower levels of implementation than less complex changes in structure, administrative procedures, and materials.

Strategies and Tactics

Since successful implementation basically involves some resocialization of teachers and administrators, the methods employed in introducing and implementing innovations should support this process. Research suggests four important methods or strategies: in-service training, resource support, feedback mechanisms, and participation in decision making. Intensive and ongoing in-service training linked to problems of initial implementation (as distinct from preservice training) is an important factor. Such training provides "teachers with demonstration models and experiences as well as psychological reinforcement conducive to resocialization."[37]

A successful change strategy provides a feedback mechanism to identify problems encountered in implementation in order to provide support for addressing such problems. The absence of an accurate feedback network during implementation can cause critical problems. Too often high expectations for success on the part of sponsors and administrators create unrealistic pressures on teachers. This distorts feedback as teachers hide their problems and failures and make a pretense of success.

The strategy of participation in decision making was characterized by Fullan and Pomfret as "the most complex (multidimensional), controversial, and probably the most powerful determinant in a negative or positive way." The conventional wisdom, supported by psychological and sociological studies, primarily from business and industry, is that those involved in

[36]Fullan and Pomfret, pp. 367–368.
[37]Fullan and Pomfret, p. 374.

implementing a decision should participate in making the decision. Fullan and Pomfret conclude from research, "Active involvement in the development process appears to be the critical factor, rather than participation in decisions per se." They recommended that users be codeciders with authorities on initiation and adoption of innovations; be coplanners of training experience in the planning for implementation stage; and be problem solvers and evaluators during implementation.[38]

Characteristics of Adopting Units

One research study identified two contrasting types of adoption processes—opportunism and problem solving. Opportunism is responding to the availability of funds with little local commitment, while problem solving addresses itself to locally identified needs. The selection of the approaches used in the adoption and decision process "continued to play a pervasive role in the implementation," with the problem-solving mode leading to greater changes.[39]

Several studies reviewed by Fullan and Pomfret "suggest that 'organizational climate' of adopting units plays a critical role in whether and how implementation occurs."[40] The principal is a key factor in school-based change in terms of his or her support of staff through provision of materials and time, involvement of staff in decision making, and enthusiasm for the innovation. High morale of teachers is associated with effective innovation. A study cited by Fullan and Pomfret concluded "that basic teacher preparation (and development) is another critical factor in the implementation, nonimplementation, or misimplementation of the new program."[41]

Sociopolitical Factors

The previous discussion of curriculum-policy making showed the complexity of the interaction at different levels of government. Often, political decisions at the state or national level that mandate new programs are never adequately implemented. Fullan and Pomfret observed that once a political decision is made, efforts are made to obtain as many adoptions as possible in the shortest time. This approach has a negative effect on implementation because "the process of obtaining or determining acceptance by users is bypassed either because of lack of time, or because rejection or delay cannot be risked."[42] Because of the urgency of introduc-

---

[38]Fullan and Pomfret, p. 381.
[39]P. Berman and M. McLaughlin, "Implementation of Educational Innovation," *Educational Forum*, XL (1976):347–370.
[40]Fullan and Pomfret, p. 383.
[41]Fullan and Pomfret, p. 385.
[42]Fullan and Pomfret, p. 387.

ing new programs, inadequate time is spent in planning and specifying implementation strategies.

Politically determined program innovations often fail to recognize the importance of teacher incentives. The personal costs for teachers in trying new innovations are high in terms of the amount of energy, time, and sometimes trauma involved in learning new skills. Generally teachers are expected to bear these costs at their own expense. With little or no incentive and high personal costs, teachers may resist the innovation.

A Perspective on Change and Curriculum Development

This brief section has introduced some concepts related to implementation of curriculum changes. For more information, the reader is referred to:

J. Victor Baldridge and Terrence E. Deal, *Managing Change in Educational Organizations* (Berkeley, Calif.: McCutchan Publishing Co., 1975).

John Goodlad, *The Dynamics of Educational Change: Toward Responsive Schools* (New York: McGraw-Hill, 1975).

Ronald G. Havelock, *Planning for Innovation* (Ann Arbor, Mich.: Institute for Social Research, University of Michigan, 1971).

Everett M. Rogers and F. Floyd Shoemaker, *Communication of Innovations* (New York: The Free Press, 1971).

There is one inescapable conclusion: implementation of changes in the curriculum is difficult. Although the difficulty of change presents a challenge to those interested in improving education, it also is a blessing in disguise. Assume for a minute that educational change were easy. Imagine the utter chaos as schools followed one pied piper, then another, and then yet another, into educational utopias. Natural resistances to change provide a "balance wheel" effect that enables educational systems to maintain some stability.

Change, just for the sake of change, is inexcusable when the quality of educational experiences for learners is at stake. There are, however, situations when curriculum development and change are appropriate. Obviously, when an educational program must be developed where none exists, curriculum development is necessary. When there are significant changes in factors associated with education, such as the nature of learners or the nature of society, curriculum modifications are called for. Finally, inadequacies in the existing educational program may require curriculum-development activities. Check first, however, to determine if better implementation of existing programs is all that is needed.

Once a decision is made that some curriculum change is needed, a procedure for curriculum development is selected. The procedure should enable the developers to answer the question, What should be changed and what processes are necessary to implement the changes?

Procedures for curriculum development in nonschool settings vary with the organization. For some organizations, the development takes place in a national or regional office. For example, 14 major Protestant denominations cooperated in developing a curriculum for Sunday School classes.[43] Other educational agencies develop local educational programs. For example, the curriculum for a summer crafts program might be developed by a supervisor in the park department or a teacher in a class. Since there is little research or literature on developing curriculums for nonschool use, the material that follows is oriented toward curriculum development in schools. However, nonschool educational personnel can apply many of the principles in their own work.

Structured-Committee Approach

The committee approach to problems and tasks is widely used in curriculum planning. At the school level, committees of students, parents, and faculty, sometimes separately and sometimes jointly, are used for many purposes: 1) investigating specific curriculum problems; 2) developing plans for particular curriculum purposes; 3) steering faculty planning and coordination; 4) articulating instructional programs between teams, grades, subjects, and schools; 5) organizing staff-development activities; and 6) conducting curriculum research and experimentation. At the district level, curriculum councils get much of their work done by organizing committees or task forces, including persons from the council and from outside it, to perform particular tasks such as: 1) developing innovative proposals; 2) working on problems submitted through the communications channels of the council; 3) preparing curriculum plans in new areas; 4) evaluating existing programs; and 5) searching literature, practice, and research for information relative to any aspect of curriculum and instruction agreed upon as needing such review. Committees of parents and of students are organized to parallel or join in with staff committees for similar purposes, and especially for securing feedback regarding established or proposed curriculum practices.

District-Wide Curriculum Committees

School committees generally function in relation to a central or district-wide coordinating group. A popular organization for coordinating planning in school districts is the council on curriculum and/or instruction. Early examples of such councils in Battle Creek, Michigan; Glencoe, Illi-

[43]Robert E. Koenig, *Christian Education: Shared Approaches* (Philadelphia: United Church Press, 1975).

nois; Kingsport, Tennessee; Milwaukee, Wisconsin; and Minneapolis, Minnesota were described in 1950 by Caswell and his associates.[44] Some type of central council for curriculum planning continues to be used in many school systems.

The curriculum council provides a potentially effective clearinghouse for planning for a school district or other official organization of schools under a single administrative board or head. For larger districts, some plan of subdistricts, each with its curriculum council represented on an interlocking district-wide council, is desirable and frequently used. The council should represent each individual school, with some plan to ensure representation also of the central administration, community, parents, and students served. This latter representation may be secured through parallel community and student councils, with an arrangement for liaison between the school's curriculum council and the community and students' advisory councils.

The effectiveness of the role of the curriculum council in planning for the district depends to a large extent on the quality of the arrangements made for it to receive problems and proposals from the constituent units and the opportunity given these units to review recommendations made to them by the council. It is particularly important for specific aspects of planning to be assigned to task forces, each created for a particular purpose and each reporting back to the council. Such tasks of planning include: 1) review of data regarding curriculum needs; 2) selection of instructional systems or national curriculum project packages for district-wide use; 3) creation of alternative schools for particular purposes; 4) the setting of curriculum domains for district-wide curriculum designing; 5) the planning of staff-development programs relating to curriculum needs; 6) identification of problems for research; and especially 7) review of feedback from various sources on the curriculum and instructional program of the district.

Some alternatives to curriculum councils as a means of providing system-wide coordination are being developed. For example, the Upper St. Clair Township school district (Pennsylvania) has two types of district-wide committees: subject-area committees at the various levels and a K–12 panel.[45] There are curriculum leaders for each of the major subject areas in the elementary, middle, and high school levels. Each curriculum leader works with a committee composed of teachers and principals, whose role is to make recommendations involving all facets of the instructional program. The K–12 panel is composed of the assistant superinten-

---

[44]See Hollis L. Caswell et al., *Curriculum Improvement in Public School Systems* (New York: Bureau of Publications, Teachers College, Columbia University, 1950).
[45]This organization is described by Donald H. Eichhorn, "Strategies for K–12 Instructional Planning," unpublished paper, 1975.

dent in charge of curriculum and instruction, the curriculum leaders of the involved subject areas from the elementary, middle, and high school levels, and the curriculum directors. This panel does not initiate change but reviews and coordinates programs as it acts upon recommendations for change.

Curriculum change in the Upper St. Clair Township school district may be initiated by staff, students, or citizens. Their proposals are referred to the most appropriate subject-area committee for its consideration and recommendations. Recommendations from the subject-area committees are referred to the K–12 panel for their review and approval. If the recommendation involves a change in board policy, the superintendent and the board of education are provided with the opportunity to review and act upon the recommendation.

Groups of personnel especially organized for curriculum development have long been used in school districts and even in individual schools. For example, many curriculum guides have been prepared by task forces employed during the summer for this purpose. Large school districts have also arranged for the release of personnel during the school year to work with a central curriculum bureau or department to prepare curriculum guides, conduct curriculum studies, serve as executive secretaries of curriculum councils and committees, and perform similar tasks relating to the central purpose of curriculum designing (see Chapter 5). Procedures for selecting teachers to work on curriculum development is specified in some negotiated teacher contracts. For example, some contracts require that teachers serving on curriculum committees be selected from a list submitted by the teacher organization.

Some school systems have a curriculum-design component responsible for developing instructional packages that can be thought of as units of study. The designing procedures include the employment of one or more instructional design specialists, an inservice education program to prepare the staff for their involvement in the process, and the preparation of packages for individual subsystems (horizontally, subjects; vertically, grades). We emphasize, however, that many curriculum goals cannot be achieved by the usual types of curriculum packages. These are the subtle, frequently the affective, but also many times the higher cognitive objectives. For these, determined planning of learning opportunities by teachers for their particular students and groups is essential.

The school district needs input from outside the district and this may be made available through membership in leagues, through the services of supplementary educational centers and other sharing arrangements, through the organization of search parties to visit other schools and districts where needed resources have been identified, and through the services of consultants employed for particular purposes. The school district also needs specialized research and evaluation services to carry on its evaluation programs. It may very wisely identify and staff pilot curriculum centers and experimental units for the development and testing of innovative curriculum models with provision for dissemination through the council and other means. In all of these endeavors, there is need for some feedback mechanism which provides critiques of the various operations by those concerned.

School-Site Curriculum Committees

Curriculum committees at individual schools are linked to district committees. A critical requirement for effective curriculum planning at the individual school center is strong leadership. In the past, many persons who advocated centralizing curriculum planning justified their position by decrying the quality of curriculum leadership at the school and even the district level. Debates over whether the curriculum and instructional leader should be the principal or the curriculum coordinator or the assistant principal for curriculum and instruction have not resulted in providing the leadership needed. The important point is that the educational program of a school requires one qualified person to be responsible for enlisting the resources, facilitating the processes, and advising the entire staff and other participants in planning, implementing, and evaluating the program. To this end, the training of qualified persons and their assignment to individual school centers must be accelerated. Whether the school district gives this responsibility to the principal or to the curriculum coordinator, the assistant principal, or one or more unit or team leaders, the person selected must meet several qualifications. As a minimum, these qualifications should include training in group process, goal-setting, team planning and teaching, use of instructional resources, individual instruction and counseling, curriculum theory and research, evaluation, and community relations. Undoubtedly, each district would modify and expand these qualifications to conform to local needs. Our thesis is that a systematic process of curriculum planning necessitates the presence of a qualified curriculum leader, whatever his or her actual title, at every school site.

As a management center for curriculum and instruction, the individual school needs a variety of information about the students for whom it is responsible. It should also have a complete inventory of all the learning opportunities available within the community and not just those planned for implementation within the school. In addition, the management system needs some trustworthy device for accurate matching of student needs and learning opportunities. Already, computer matching of learners and opportunities is available for some levels. This does not replace the need for a good counseling system with a teacher-counselor who is knowledgeable about his or her advisees and about the learning opportunities available, serving as home base advisor or director of personal development. These advisers would need help from trained counselors and the assistance of the curriculum leader to coordinate their activities.

Many roles in curriculum planning can be and are filled by groups or teams of teachers: 1) selecting goals and subgoals for the grade, subject, section, little school or other subdivisions of a large school, or other basis of organization; 2) designing appropriate learning opportunities to achieve these goals; 3) assigning of responsibility for particular programs and students; 4) procuring needed materials; 5) scheduling instructional groups and facilities; 6) defining student evaluation procedures; and 7) planning for and conducting evaluation of particular instructional programs and, indeed, the entire curriculum plan for which the team is responsible. Whether interdisciplinary, intradisciplinary, or simply a planning group for grade or departmentalized teaching, the teaching team has fundamental decisions to make within the particular curriculum domain(s) concerned. Teams have especially significant decisions to make regarding curriculum implementation: what instructional models they will use, and when and how; individualized self-teaching; guided independent study; laboratory-type experience; group discussion, inquiry and analysis; or combinations of these.

Increasing use of team teaching in elementary and middle schools makes even more important the provision of adequate time, leadership, and facilities for team planning. As several teachers who are working together in planning, teaching, and evaluating instruction for the same groups of learners are able to share their experience and expertise, better plans should emerge. This is the goal of such planning systems as Individually Guided Education (IGE), described earlier in this chapter.

Groups of teachers might be appointed for special tasks. For example, a group might be responsible for examining the school's effectiveness in relation to one or more curriculum domains. These planning groups would require the special help of the curriculum leader in setting up their programs, and they might well benefit from the input of the curriculum council and of any league of schools or other sharing organization with which they are affiliated.

Feedback mechanisms at the school center must rely heavily on the data from students as they accept, modify, and reject the learning opportunities planned for them. Close interaction of teachers and students is imperative, but students also need the opportunity to appraise objectively their experiences and to suggest other types of learning opportunities they would like to see incorporated into their personal curriculums. Student representatives on school planning councils and special curriculum task forces are successfully used in many high schools. Middle school students are also involved in planning groups with their teachers and parents, and parents of younger elementary school children are widely used as representatives of their children. Opinion polls may be advantageously taken on many curriculum issues in the school.

Characteristics of Cooperative Group Planning

Effective curriculum planning at any level, we believe, is always cooperative, involving group decision making. Although its various stages frequently include intensive activity by individuals, at times working alone, the individual is responsible to the group of planners who review his or her proposals and tentative plans and who share his or her responsibility. Thus, even the individual teacher who ultimately plans an instructional program for a particular group of learners is responsible to colleagues in the planning group. He or she must be able to relate his or her own program to other instructional programs the learners have experienced in the past, are currently experiencing, or will experience in the future, and share responsibility with colleagues for the total instructional program. The teacher is responsible, too, for involving the learners themselves in the planning process, in ways and for purposes appropriate to their maturity. Whatever the level of planning and the group of learners, certain characteristics of cooperative planning are to be sought. These characteristics apply to the inductive and problem-solving approaches to curriculum development as well as to the committee approach.

COMMON GOALS.   Whatever the planning group and the problems for immediate focus, the common goal in curriculum planning is to provide maximally appropriate learning opportunities for the students concerned. This general goal may be broken down into many subgoals for the particular population of students for the specific phases of planning involved, but always the central focus of any planning group has to be the creation of appropriate learning opportunities. The group's effectiveness in planning learning opportunities directly relates to the clarity of its definition of subgoals, its earnestness in adhering to its goals, its consistent evaluation of the goals, and its own operation in terms of the central goal and the group's own subgoals. Thus, a teaching team planning learning opportunities for the development of skills for continued learning sets up particular skills as subgoals and devises plans whereby these skills can be acquired by the students taught by the team; other items for planning and discussion are ruled out, and intermittently the group reviews its plan in terms of relevance and feasibility for skills development by the learners concerned. That is, the group keeps asking: "Will this plan or plans accomplish our goal of appropriate learning opportunities for our students to become better equipped for self-directed learning?"

ADEQUATE REPRESENTATION AND ORGANIZATION.   Two basic principles are involved here: 1) all persons directly involved in the consequences of decisions made by a group should be represented in the decision making; and 2) the group should have whatever organization is most promising for achievement of its goals. As to the first, all curriculum decisions have direct consequences for the students, school personnel, and community involved. Whether the educators can adequately represent student and community concerns depends on such factors as the significance of the decision to students and community, the ability of the students and community to understand and deal with the issues involved, and the integrity of the educators. As we see it, many decisions are of such critical consequences to students and community that they should be directly represented, and many others are so technical and relatively insignificant that student and community representatives would not wish to be involved. For example, a decision on whether sex education is to be provided in a school program ought to be made with adequate representation of students (at early levels through their parents) and community. On the other hand, a choice of commercial instructional materials ought to be made on such technical bases as to preclude the use of student and community judgment, except as usability might be tested out with representative students or as possibly controversial content might be checked out with community representatives.

The organization should provide for the active involvement of teachers at all steps in the curriculum development process. This will often require appointing subcommittees. Our experience with curriculum committees suggests the following guidelines:

1. *Ad hoc* committees, organized for particular tasks and composed of the persons best qualified to perform the tasks, are more effective than standing committees without specific tasks to perform.
2. Committees created by a curriculum council or a school faculty or the curriculum administrator should be given as clear a definition as possible of their task, even if it is to propose their own role, with some timetable as to dates for committee reports.
3. Each committee should be given as much help as the situation permits in terms of time for meetings, resources of personnel and materials, and other specific needs the task involves.
4. Recognition for committee work is desirable and in such forms as are appealing to committee members and feasible in the situation: publication of reports, presentation to boards of education and other status groups, in-service requirement credits, reduced teaching loads, additional employment (summer), points for salary increase, direct compensation, leaves of absence, and others.

Each curriculum subcommittee or planning group should work out for itself an effective organization for achieving its goals. Items most groups need to plan for include the choice of a chairman, the system of recording, the schedule of meetings, the channeling of feedback, the use of subcommittees, the plan for reporting plans to other groups, and the process of modifying plans and making them final.

COMPETENT GROUP LEADERSHIP. Curriculum planning groups, like groups in general, need leaders competent in directing the group process. The leader recognizes that every individual in the group is a potential leader who may at any time direct group thinking by questions, observations, and suggestions. The leadership person provides every opportunity for all potential leadership within the group to exert itself. At the same time, this person gives personal leadership to the group enterprise when this seems critical. Among the specific tasks of leadership, not necessarily of a single person designated as chairman but of all who share the leadership role, are the following:

1. Maintain a comfortable environment.
2. Secure frank, full expression of ideas.
3. Summarize faithfully agreements or decisions reached and group progress from time to time.
4. Help record keepers in the maintenance of adequate notes as to the flow and results of discussion.
5. See that alternative courses of action and positions on issues are identified.
6. Determine the consensus when appropriate.
7. Recognize fully the contributions of group members.

OPEN AND CLEAR COMMUNICATION. Open and clear communication may be expected within a group when the leader operates as just described. But in curriculum planning there are continual needs for communication with other groups and individuals—the committee to the faculty, the teacher to the class, the committee or the school or district administrator to community groups and boards of education, for example. The communications network needs careful attention so that all concerned understand recommendations and actions and especially so that there is clear consideration of feedback from these persons.

Analysis of curriculum planning activities indicates that in both the planning and implementation phases a major block to action is the failure of persons concerned to understand each other. Implementation of plans made by persons other than the implementers is obviously impossible unless the plans are clearly communicated and fully understood and accepted. Even face-to-face communication breaks down because of semantic and perceptual difficulties. The use of written communications alone eliminates opportunity for discussion and constitutes an inadequate basis for curriculum planning at all levels. Systematic channels for communication clearly understood by all concerned, with information fed back to those who make suggestions, and maximum opportunity for proposals to be made and feedback about them to be gathered and considered, are essential in the planning process.

USE OF RELEVANT DATA.   Curriculum planning does not have to be a matter only of sharing opinions. Although there are points when judgment may have to be speculative, there are many others when judgments can and should be based on interpretations of facts. Facts are available and should be considered regarding the student population, community expectations, goals of the school, and all of the other items described in Chapter 3 and elsewhere in this book as basic to curriculum planning. Furthermore, research reports are available on many problems, and these are becoming increasingly easier to locate through ERIC (Educational Research Information Clearinghouse Service) and other sources. If the school uses a systematic process of curriculum planning, much input is to be considered as it is channeled from the various feedback channels that give students, faculty, and the community opportunity to make their needs, wishes, and suggestions known.

The critical characteristic of effective planning is its reliance on such data. Instead of the curriculum planning group's simply polling its members on what they think ought to be done, readiness for this question is developed through consultation of the data from the available sources. The question, "What do you think?" is more properly, "What do these data tell us needs to be done?" In the absence of data, the question may even become, "How can we find out what ought to be done?"

ADEQUATE TIME AND FACILITIES FOR PLANNING.   Entirely too much curriculum planning, especially at the school level, has had to be done within crowded time schedules and in crowded rooms. Although pleasant surroundings and adequate time do not guarantee good planning, they can certainly help. Increasingly schools are scheduling time for planning, with the groups meeting in conference rooms in the building. Spaces where planners can operate without interruption, in which boards or charts can be used to record items for all members to see, and in which audiovisual equipment can be readily used help greatly. Rapid duplication services, and perhaps dictating equipment, may expedite record keeping and the review of written materials.

Large blocks of time in which to meet are essential at many points in the group planning process, so that whole days—or, better yet, weeks, perhaps summer periods—should be set aside for this purpose. Summer workshops aided by adequate resources and needed data can be especially productive.

GROUP DECISIONS.   Groups which possess the characteristics we have described are almost certain to make decisions that reflect the best judgment of the group as a whole, or certainly of a majority of the group. The one pitfall frequently observed is a lack of awareness on the part of the group concerning the limitations of its decision-making powers. Committees that have worked out a careful plan for trying out a particular curriculum innovation in their school or district need to keep in mind that their recommendation is only a recommendation, that it must be considered by the larger faculty or community group that is responsible for the total school program. Groups are sometimes frustrated by not understanding what decisions they can make or what the force of their recommendations may be. Consequently, it is as important for the group leader to clearly identify the scope and force of the group's decision-making power as it is for him to guide the group to a decision that genuinely reflects the best judgment of group members.

The degree of autonomy granted to the local school in curriculum decision making has a direct bearing on its potential for excellence. Goodlad examined schools that had achieved marked success and found four characteristics:

1. The school as a unit has a great deal of autonomy in the system or is itself the total educational system for a given population of students in its community setting.
2. The school has a sense of mission, unity, identity, and wholeness that pervades every aspect of its functioning.
3. The principal is central to the attainment of the kind of school implied.
4. The surrounding infrastructure is supportive. The superintendent recognizes the school as the key unit for change and improvement."[46]

Based on Goodlad's observations, curriculum decisions generally should be made at the local school level, with any central council serving in a coordinating and facilitating role.

Weaknesses of Structured-Committee Approach

Although structured-committee approaches of various types have been and continue to be the prevalent modes of curriculum development, the approach has been criticized. Taba, a recognized leader in curriculum planning for many years, denounced some aspects of the committee approach as practiced in the 1950s.[47] She challenged the need for wide participation in curriculum development: . . . "it seems that almost everyone is supposed to participate: the public, the administration, students, curriculum and supervisory staff, teachers, and specialists in curriculum development, learning, child development and content." This extension in participation, she believed, had not been accompanied by a clarity of the roles each group should play; she urged that a distinction be made

[46]John Goodlad, "Can Our Schools Get Better?" *Phi Delta Kappan, 60* (January 1979):346.
[47]Hilda Taba, *Curriculum Development: Theory and Practice* (New York: Harcourt, Brace and World, Inc., 1962).

"between decisions that involve general wisdom and those that require expertise."[48]

Another criticism of the committee approach is that curriculum development often becomes a piecemeal operation. For example, too often a committee-produced curriculum guide is a "cut-and-paste job," with pieces of content shifted from one grade to another. Problems of sequence in the curriculum may develop because of a faulty division of labor. For example, developing curriculum guides by grade level may result in a failure to articulate programs between grade levels, and particularly, between different levels of schooling.

Securing appropriate representation on curriculum committees is often a problem. Too often, individuals selected are neither interested in curriculum development, nor trained in the requisite skills. Sometimes they are not even representative of their group. For example, faculty representatives to a district coordinating council may be appointed by a principal because they are effective teachers. This is not a bad criterion, but it does not assure that they will have the needed interest and skills, or that they will adequately represent their group.

One of the severest criticisms is that a structured-committee approach may result in an oversimplification of the task. Central curriculum councils may not recognize the need to experiment with pilot programs before they are implemented. The time required to develop, try out, and implement a plan may be underestimated. Too often there is no plan and thus no resources set aside for implementation.

We recognize the validity of Taba's earlier criticisms, as well as current ones cited, and know that they apply to curriculum planning as it is often practiced. However, the criticisms are not inherent to a committee approach. Through careful planning, the weaknesses can either be overcome or minimized. Accordingly, we believe this analysis of weaknesses provides a basis for strengthening a committee approach, rather than reasons for abandoning it.

Inductive Approach

The inductive approach to curriculum development as designed and used by Taba remains a viable one. She studied the problem of the gap between theory and practice in both designing and implementing curriculum plans. Taba viewed a structured-committee approach as a "top down" operation, where curriculum plans and general designs are passed down for teachers to use in developing their classroom plans. This deductive sequence starts with the mapping out of general scope and sequence and proceeds to the development of specific units to implement the se-

---

[48]Taba, p. 451.

quence. She argued that inverting this method of developing curriculum designs could help to bridge the gap between theory and practice. "Instead of starting with general designs, a start needs to be made with reconsidering and replanning learning–teaching units as the first step in curriculum development."[49] Instead of deducing classroom plans from general designs, general designs would be induced from learning–teaching units—an inductive approach.

Steps in the Inductive Approach

Taba described five strategic steps in the sequence of curriculum change.[50]

PRODUCING PILOT UNITS.   The inductive approach starts with the production of pilot units by groups of teachers. The teachers are selected according to the grade levels and subject areas to be revised. Since the entire sequence depends upon this first step, the units developed must represent the best possible curriculum planning, involving a consideration of "actual student needs, experimenting with classroom procedures, and setting objectives that are rooted in classroom reality."[51]

TESTING EXPERIMENTAL UNITS.   Since the pilot units are developed by teachers for use in particular classrooms, they need to be tried out in other classrooms. From such trials, the parts of the unit that can be used with different student populations are determined. The adaptability of the model to different teaching styles is also tested.

REVISING AND CONSOLIDATING.   Based on the tryouts, modifications are "assembled and shaped into outlines representing an appropriate general curriculum for all types of classrooms." The inductive process begins with a consideration of "the rationale for developing the units by stating the principles and theoretical considerations on which the structure of the units . . . are based." (Note this inversion of the usual sequence.) A handbook is produced, explaining the use of the unit, or units, and suggesting limits within which modifications in the classroom can take place.

DEVELOPING A FRAMEWORK.   When a significant range of units is available, they are examined for sequence and scope "by those who are competent in the theoretical aspects of curriculum development." A number of criteria to be used in making this examination are suggested by Taba. Based on this examination, shifts may be made in content or empha-

49Taba, p. 441.
50Taba, pp. 457–459, passim.
51Taba, p. 458.

sis. The product of this inductive work is "a statement of the general framework, which stakes out the scope and sequence."

INSTALLING AND DISSEMINATING NEW UNITS.   Taba recognized that the task of installation required training large groups of teachers in the use of the units. Because of the turnover of teachers, this is often a perennial task. Administrators become facilitators as they make practical arrangements, such as providing needed materials and shifting schedules.

Weaknesses of the Inductive Approach

The inductive approach is difficult to use. Teachers need considerable assistance in developing the original units. An in-depth knowledge of curriculum development is needed for the inductive steps. The principles and theoretical considerations on which the units are based are discovered in the process of revising and consolidating. Further inductive work is required in developing a framework. This work is not impossible—Taba did it with considerable success—but it requires better preparation in the theoretical aspects of curriculum development than most professionals possess.

The inductive approach requires a long period of time—depending on resources and the degree of change involved. Taba recognized, "Under the best of circumstances it is a matter of several years, rather than the year or few months usually scheduled for revision of curriculum guides."[52] Even though it may be argued that the results of an inductive approach, judged by the quality of the curriculum and its degree of implementation, justify the additional time, relatively few schools or school systems are willing to invest such long periods of time.

Taba developed the inductive approach to bridge the gap between theory and practice in both designing and implementing curriculum plans. She criticized typical curriculum development activities "because a theory of implementation is lacking." As a result, "only the form and not the substance is implemented and the essence of the idea is subverted."[53] We do not see how the inductive approach provides for any new "theory of implementation." The installation and dissemination of the curriculum developed through the inductive approach reverts to the "top down" procedure criticized by Taba. Teachers given intensive workshops and a series of in-service courses may not respond any more favorably toward inductively developed materials than toward any other material. Of course, those few teachers involved in developing the material will already be using it.

[52]Taba, p. 459.
[53]Taba, p. 441.

A better assessment of the inductive approach, including the quality of the materials produced, would be possible if it were being used. Because of the skills and excessive time required, the method as conceived by Taba is rarely used. The method has merit, in that it provides a fresh approach to closing the gap between theory and practice in designing, if not implementing, curriculum. More instances of its practice are needed for study.

Problem-Solving Approach

The problem-solving approach to site-specific curriculum development involves the faculty in identifying a local problem, seeking appropriate generic material to be adapted (if none is available, developing site-specific material) and implementing the new curriculum (see Table 2.1). A primary objective of this approach is that new curriculum material, whether adapted from generic material or produced locally, will result in changed classroom practice. Support for the approach is found in sociopsychological research on organizations. After reviewing this research, Buchanan concluded:

The effectiveness of improvement efforts is enhanced when they take place under the following conditions: The efforts are planned (a) by the members themselves, (b) in response to needs which they identify from analysis of their organization, (c) under conditions of mutual trust, and (d) where feedback concerning the effectiveness of their efforts is available.[54]

These conclusions agree with those of Fullan and Pomfret based on their review of research on implementation reported earlier.

Havelock summarized five assumptions that support a problem-solving approach:

1. The user's world is the place to begin to consider utilization of new programs.
2. A diagnostic phase, where user need is considered and translated into a problem statement, is necessary.
3. Outsiders can be useful as catalysts, collaborators, or consultants.
4. Internal knowledge retrieved and the marshalling of internal resources should be given at least equal influence with external retrieval.
5. Self-initiation creates the best motivational climate for lasting change.[55]

[54]Paul C. Buchanan, "The Concept of Organization Development, or Self-Renewal, as a Form of Planned Change," in Goodwin B. Watson (ed.), *Concepts for Social Change* (Washington, D.C.: National Training Laboratories, 1967), p. 7.
[55]Ronald G. Havelock, *Planning for Innovation Through Dissemination and Utilization of Knowledge* (Ann Arbor, Mich.: University of Michigan Press, 1971), pp. 11–13.

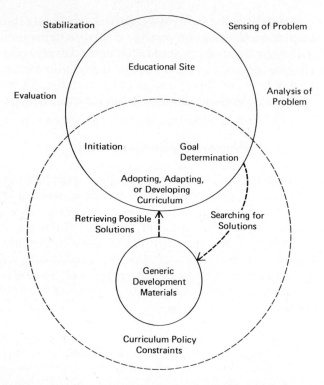

FIGURE 2.2   A problem-solving approach to site-specific curriculum development

Steps in a Problem-Solving Approach

Formulations of steps in problem solving are based on the scientific method. Lewis and Miel proposed a seven-step model[56] represented in Figure 2.2. A brief description of these steps follows. The solving of curricular problems is not as linear and sequential as the model suggests. For example, evaluation is involved at each step of the process. Steps may be revisited as appropriate; for example, at the stage of adapting an existing program or developing a new curriculum, it may be necessary to sharpen the analysis of the problem.

SENSING OF PROBLEM.   Sensing the problem is one of the most complex and difficult aspects of change. The problem may come to the faculty from an external force—for example, comments from concerned parents, a directive from the central office, a new law. There is a difference, however, between being told that you have a problem and recognizing and

---

[56]Arthur J. Lewis and Alice Miel, *Supervision for Improved Instruction* (Belmont, Calif.: Wadsworth Publishing, Inc., 1972), pp. 178–187, passim.

"owning" a problem. Problems that emerge through evaluative efforts initiated by the staff are generally more powerful motivators than those presented to them. In fact, a group will not engage in concerted problem-solving effort until there is a problem of genuine concern.

ANALYSIS OF PROBLEM. Several problems may surface, requiring that a choice be made either according to priorities or, where problems must be solved serially, to which problems must be solved first. Once the problem is identified, the staff collects data and makes a diagnosis of the problem. Faculty involvement in the collection and interpretation of data increases their acceptance of the diagnosis and the resulting plans to overcome the problem.

GOAL DETERMINATION. Assume, for purposes of illustration, that an elementary school faculty identifies as their problem a large number of poor readers in the upper grades. As part of their problem analysis, the teachers study children's standardized reading test scores from grade to grade and discover that for many children reading growth 'levels off" at grade four. The faculty sets as a goal, therefore, improvement of the reading curriculum in the fourth grade. Note from Figure 2.2 that curriculum policy (represented by the area enclosed by the dotted circle) establishes constraints as to the goals that may be selected. Thus, in our illustration, the faculty cannot solve its problem by forcing poor readers out of school. Curriculum policy also provides constraints over the type of program that can be developed and initiated.

ADOPTING, ADAPTING, OR DEVELOPING CURRICULUM. After determining their goal, the faculty looks for existing materials or programs that can either be adopted or adapted to enable them to achieve their goal. In our illustration, they seek reading programs and materials for the fourth grade. If suitable materials are found, they will be adopted, or adapted. Experience indicates that considerable staff development work is required for the successful use of externally developed curriculum material even when they are appropriate. When suitable programs and materials cannot be found, the faculty develops their own.

INITIATION. The faculty conducts pilot tests of the programs and materials to see if they solve the problem. After suitable adjustments are made, the program is initiated throughout the school.

EVALUATION. Once the program is initiated, formative evaluation begins through a systematic procedure for the feedback of data. These data are used to monitor the program and provide the basis for making appropriate modifications in the program and materials.

STABILIZATION.   After a suitable and agreed-upon period of time, data are collected for a summative evaluation. If the new program meets the test of alleviating the problem identified, its use becomes a part of the standard operating procedure. At this point the faculty, if they have the heart for it, is ready to take on another problem.

The problem-solving approach is being applied in several New York City schools. Their "High School Renewal Program" involves teachers, students, and administrators in defining their school problems and working out their own solutions.[57] The model used was developed in two high schools over a period of seven years with the assistance of 200 New York City corporations; 30 high schools were participating by 1977. The process involves an "ongoing movement through seven stages: entry, diagnosis, planning, research and development, implementation, evaluation, and institutionalization."[58] Because of its effectiveness, the model was extended into elementary and junior high schools.

Weaknesses in the Problem-Solving Approach

Critics of the problem-solving approach question the capacity of the typical teacher and faculty to innovate. Do teachers have the interest, curiosity, and ability to follow the problem-solving approach? Do they have the time? In response to the former criticism, packaged in-service education programs have been designed to strengthen a faculty's problem-solving capability.[59]

The problem-solving approach is criticized for its inadequate use and appreciation of the scope, variety, and rich potential of externally developed programs. A great many new ideas and products have been developed at considerable expense by research and development centers. Effective programs have also been developed by other users. Unfamiliarity with the vast storehouse of programs and materials must lead to "reinventing the wheel" many times over.

A major criticism of the problem-solving approach is its inability to spread new ideas rapidly. Often successful solutions to "sensed problems" entrench the status quo when what is needed is a major overhaul of programs. To borrow an example from engineering, would it make sense to invest hundreds of millions of dollars on improving the gasoline engine when the world is running out of fossil fuel? Even though school faculties work on the "right" problems, considerable time and energy will be required for significant changes to result.

[57]Marc Bassin and Tom Gross, "Renewal: A Problem-Solving Model," *NASSP Bulletin* (May 1979):43–48.
[58]Bassin and Gross, p. 45.
[59]See, for example, the "Research Utilizing Problem Solving Training Package" (RUPS) (Portland, Ore.: Northwest Regional Educational Laboratory, 1973).

Selecting an Approach to Curriculum Development

Three approaches to site-specific curriculum development have been reviewed: structured-committee approach, inductive approach, and problem-solving approach. These do not exhaust the possibilities, but are representative of the variety of approaches used. Each of the approaches has strengths and weaknesses. Actually, it is not necessary to choose just one approach. Generally, in practice, an eclectic approach, combining two or all three of these approaches, is used. For example, a district committed to school-based management may use a problem-solving approach. However, they may also have a district-wide coordinating council and provide central office support services. Teachers, as individuals or in a group, may use an inductive approach in developing a curriculum needed to solve a specific problem.

Unfortunately, there is no tested theory to guide the practitioner in selecting curriculum development approaches. The following guidelines, however, may be useful:

1. *Local-unit autonomy.* An effective curriculum is a plan to provide learning experiences for a specific group of learners, in a specific setting, and at a specific time. Those who know the learners and the setting are in the best position to develop an appropriate curriculum. We agree with Goodlad: in order to be outstanding, schools need a great deal of autonomy and a superintendent who recognizes "the school as the key unit for change and improvement."[60]
2. *High-quality curriculum.* Time and energy should not be spent in producing a poor or mediocre curriculum. The approach selected should provide some assurance that the product will be valuable. Some marks of a good curriculum plan are listed at the conclusion of Chapter 1.
3. *Implementation.* The production of the very best curriculum is of no value if it does not influence teaching. The approach(es) selected should have a reasonable chance of being implemented. Specific plans for implementation should be developed and allocations of necessary time and money should be made.
4. *Time efficiency.* The amount of time required to develop *and implement* the curriculum should be reasonable. Rapid production of material will be inefficient if implementation is protracted and possibly never completed. Other approaches may require longer production time for material, but once available and tested the material is put to immediate use.
5. *Impact on teachers.* A curriculum-development approach should have a positive impact on teachers. When the project is completed, teachers should have grown in their professional stature and feel good about themselves.

[60]Goodlad, "Can Our Schools," p. 346.

6. *Representation in planning.* We recognize the value of a broad base for curriculum development, including representation of learners, teachers, supervisors, and parents. However, we know that curriculum development is a highly complex task requiring special skills. Any approach should recognize the conflicting nature of these views. This can be done by clearly defining the roles of various groups. This point is discussed in the next section.

7. *Impact of technological developments.* A combination of shortage of energy and improved telecommunications and computer technology may influence curriculum development. The energy shortage will reduce the possibilities for face-to-face communications in school districts, between districts, and in consultative relationships. Large group meetings will become less frequent. At the same time there will be increased possibilities for conferencing via computer networks. Television and computers may become increasingly important resources not only in curriculum but also in curriculum planning.

Application of these guidelines requires professional judgment. In many cases trade-offs will have to be made. An ideal approach according to one guideline may not meet the standards suggested by another. However, if the guidelines heighten educators' awareness of the implications of their selection of curriculum development processes, they will have served their purpose.

ROLE OF VARIOUS GROUPS IN SITE-SPECIFIC CURRICULUM DEVELOPMENT

Different groups are involved in site-specific curriculum development. However, this complex task requires specific skills and understandings; therefore, careful plans are needed regarding roles to be played by various groups in order to avoid poorly prepared and implemented programs.

The curriculum approach used influences appropriate roles for various groups. For example, the roles played by teachers vary between the structured-committee, the inductive, and the problem-solving approaches. The nature of the material produced also influences the roles of the groups involved. For example, teachers will be expected to follow a rigid curriculum, but will have freedom to develop their own variation with an open-ended curriculum. The complexity of the task and the time required to perform it are considerations in assigning roles. Thus, it would be a mistake to expect parents to perform a time-consuming complex task when they have neither the time nor the skills. These general considerations need to be kept in mind as we consider the role of learners, teachers, community, and leaders.

Role of Learners

Three types of student participation in curriculum planning are envisioned. One is the involvement of students of appropriate maturity in decisions concerning the basic curriculum plan. High school students can sit in on planning groups, and their contributions are prized in a growing number of high schools that are seeking to increase student involvement. Increased involvement of younger children may be best secured through the use of parent advisors and members of planning groups, although teacher interviews of children and polling on many questions may also be useful; obviously the physical presence of young children on adult planning groups would rarely bring out student interests and needs as clearly as with more mature students.

A second way to involve students is through the collection of feedback data. This is particularly useful in the pilot-test phase of curriculum development. Results on tests provide one, but not the only, source of data. Student attitudes may be assessed through observation, discussion, and written questionnaires. The most powerful type of feedback data is available in voluntary adult or youth-group programs: Do they come?

The more universally possible type of student participation is direct consultation of the learner about his own personal curriculum. Here there is no adequate substitute for a close relation between teacher and individual student. At the elementary school level, this possibility was always present in the self-contained classroom arrangement, and now even with the use of team teaching and specialized instruction in elementary schools there generally remains some arrangement whereby each child has one teacher who is his first advisor. Although some middle schools follow the departmentalized pattern of the secondary school organization, many utilize some sort of home-base or other advisory arrangement in which each student has his own teacher-counselor. At the high school level, such arrangements are more infrequent but equally desirable.

Role of Teachers

Traditionally, teachers have been involved to a limited extent in developing, and to a greater extent in implementing, the curriculum. A new type of involvement has emerged through teacher union collective negotiations. Involvement of teachers in planning, implementing, and negotiating the curriculum is described below.

Planning the Curriculum

Teacher participation in curriculum planning has too frequently been minimal or nonexistent. When teachers had little education themselves

beyond high school and minimal if any preparation for teaching, curriculum planning was the province of textbook authors in colleges and universities and of state and district supervisory personnel. But beginning in the 1920s, as teacher preparation became more common, teachers have had increasing participation in the development of educational objectives and curriculum guides. The widespread practice of textbook adoption, and beginning in the late 1950s of adoption of materials from the national curriculum projects, frequently overlooked teacher participation and perhaps made it all too easy for teachers simply to follow plans made externally to the learning situation. By the 1970s, however, teacher organizations were frequently demanding the voice in curriculum planning most curriculum leaders would have had for them many years ago. Today there is general agreement that teachers should be involved in curriculum development. However, since curriculum development takes place at many levels and is a complex and time-consuming task, it is impossible for all teachers to be involved in all phases of curriculum development. Thus, decisions as to appropriate roles are needed. The roles assigned will depend upon the level of planning so that, for most teachers, the degree of involvement will decrease as the planning is removed further and further from the classroom.

Implementing the Curriculum

The teacher is the final decision maker concerning the actual learning opportunities provided to students, although students have the final choice regarding their response to experiences provided. The best-designed curriculum, as well as the poorest, owes its ultimate success or failure to the quality of the teacher's own planning and implementation.

Research on implementation shows that the extent to which a curriculum is implemented in the classroom is associated with teacher involvement in the process. However, it cannot be assumed that teacher involvement in curriculum development assures implementation. Benham attributed many failures at curriculum reform to the "split personality" of American education.[61] She identified two fundamentally irreconcilable rationales in American education. "The first is grounded in classical realism and idealism and finds its twentieth-century expression in essentialism and perennialism; the second combines a gestaltist world-view with elements of modern pragmatism and existentialism." Many innovations, such as "open education," failed because "the reforms themselves are grounded in the contemporary-realistic world-view, which is alien, even threatening, to most teachers."[62] Thus, most teachers may not have understood what was wanted, or if they did, they did not make a

[61]B. J. Benham, "Thoughts on the Failure of Curriculum Reform," *Educational Leadership,* 35 (December 1977):205.
[62]Benham, p. 206.

genuine commitment to ensuring its success. Benham's thesis, if correct, provides a challenge to curriculum workers. The inductive approach, in which the curriculum grows out of teacher experience, should minimize the "split personality" phenomenon.

Successful implementation of a curriculum requires in-service education of teachers. Recent developments have increased the effectiveness of these programs. Cruickshank and colleagues, from their review of a number of studies on in-service education, identified four trends:

1. A movement from a compensatory to a complementary view of inservice education. . . . Inservice education, rather than eradicating deficits, is seen as complementing and extending professional growth beyond the baccalaureate.
2. A progression from a discrete to a continuous view of inservice teacher education. . . . There is no longer a distinct line between preservice and inservice education.
3. A shifting from a relatively simple to a complex inservice teacher education operation. . . . Today's programs . . . address a wider range of topics and problems and engage a more diverse and larger clientele.
4. From a narrow control of inservice education programs by school administrators and/or university professors to collaborative governance, including the clients—teachers.[63]

The latter trend is supported by federal and state legislation, which provide that teacher centers be operated by teacher-dominated policy boards and with limitations placed on the use of funds for service contracts with colleges and universities.

Negotiating the Curriculum

The growth of collective bargaining since its beginning in 1962 was described in Chapter 1. Originally, most negotiations centered on personnel matters pertaining to salary, fringe benefits, grievance procedures, and specific working conditions. However, unions have been successful in expanding the scope of bargaining to include such activities as curriculum; class size; promotion, evaluation, and grading procedures; and the nature of new programs.[64]

A major thrust of unions is to incorporate decision-making procedures into contracts. Thus, some contracts specify the composition of textbook selection committees and procedures to be followed in changing the curriculum. Wollett foreshadowed this in 1969 when he wrote that teachers

[63]Donald R. Cruickshank, Christopher Lorish, and Linda Thompson, "What We Think We Know About Inservice Education," *Journal of Teacher Education,* 30 (January–February 1979):27.
[64]Charles W. Cheng, "Community Representation in Teacher Collective Bargaining: Problems and Prospects," *Harvard Educational Review,* 46 (May 1976):153–174.

"frequently lack a meaningful voice in determining the content of the courses they are teaching or in selecting appropriate textbooks." He concluded that "seldom, if ever, do they share a role in overall curricula planning."[65]

We have already indicated the importance of appropriate teacher participation in curriculum development, based on skills, time, and interest. Unfortunately, too often union contracts specify that building stewards, or in some instances, bargaining agents, be the participants. These individuals may or may not be qualified to contribute.

Role of Community

Community involvement in curriculum development is endorsed, in principle, by educators and laymen. There are broad disagreements, however, as to appropriate roles for lay involvement and how these roles should be played. Professionals, on the one hand, concerned with providing quality education, point out that laymen do not have the expert knowledge required to participate in all aspects of curriculum development. Laymen, on the other hand, also concerned with quality education, know that the only way they can influence education is through personnel, resource allocation and use, and curriculum. As more and more decisions are made through collective negotiations, opportunities for community involvement, even through an elected board, are reduced. Some citizens are working hard for increased community involvement as a means of improving education. For example, a national Institute for Responsive Education works to promote parent participation in curriculum, personnel, and budgetary actions.[66]

Some federal and state laws legislate a role for parents and community in curriculum policy development. For example, Title I of the Elementary and Secondary Education Act requires the establishment of a citizens advisory council; California and Florida laws require citizens advisory councils. However, few of these mandated councils have any impact. Gittell suggested "that these new structures channelled citizen energies in directions which were less productive, less likely to change institutions, and less likely to improve delivery and services than self-initiated citizen organizations."[67] The fate of mandated councils, if they are not understood and accepted by professional educators, is that the form is adopted but not the substance.

Individual parent participation is required by PL 94–142 in developing

[65]Don H. Wollett, "The Coming Revolution in Public School Management," *Michigan Law Review,* 67 (1969):1020.
[66]See their newsletter, *Citizen Action in Education,* published by the Institute for Responsive Education, 704 Commonwealth Ave. Boston, Mass. 02215.
[67]Marilyn Gittell, "Participation or Cooptation?" *Citizen Action in Education,* 57 (January 1978):5.

a curriculum plan for their child—an individualized education program (IEP). In some instances, the parent participates; in others, the parent may feel coopted.

Suggested Roles for Community Participants

We envision important roles in curriculum planning for many persons and groups in the community. The many educational agencies within a community should cooperate in assessing educational needs, establishing educational goals for different agencies, selecting appropriate curriculum designs and learning experiences, and evaluating outcomes. Chapter 8 provides a discussion of how this community planning might be accomplished. When this approach to education materializes, professional educators will assist community groups with curriculum development. The practical and immediate question remains, however: How can community participation help at each stage of curriculum development—goal setting, designing, implementing, and evaluating—under the present arrangements for education?

At the goal-setting stage of curriculum planning, various types of community advisory groups may be used. The board of education may set up a general advisory group of community representatives to advise it on many educational problems, including the goals of its system. Or it may appoint advisory groups on specific problems such as curriculum, finance, facilities, and others. Advisory groups for particular curriculum areas such as vocational education, human relations, health education, and others are also used. Even without formally organized groups of this type, the district may use some existing organization such as the PTA council for advisory functions. And individual schools may choose to use an advisory council, PTA committees, homeroom parents' organizations, Dads' clubs, and other existing organizations to seek suggestions and feedback regarding school goals.

At the curriculum designing stage, various interests in the community can be consulted for specific help in planning learning opportunities. Work-experience programs require arrangements with local businesses and industries for the work assignments to be conducted. Indeed, learning opportunities outside the school of all types need to be planned with representatives of the various agencies, organizations, businesses, and industries in which the opportunities may be made available. As the school expands into the community, new boards or councils for community education may be needed to provide closer cooperation and coordination of educational opportunities available through schools, community libraries and museums, television and radio, scout troops, youth clubs, travel tours, churches and social welfare agencies, and other community institutions.

The social competence domain of the curriculum in particular requires extensive community participation. Perhaps each school should have a community advisory council with competent specialists advising the participants on the many problems incident to opening up the community to student participation in the enterprises appropriate for student learning experiences. Such councils could sponsor community–student forums on social problems and issues in the community, as well as suggest resource persons representing all facets of community life to work with students.

Community participation in the instructional program is anticipated in the planning just described. Community resource persons assist individual students and various types of student groups with the particular expertise gained through their professions, hobbies, travels, and unique experiences. Community agencies and institutions make their resources available for the learning opportunities planned. Businesses, industries, and various community institutions provide work-experience opportunities. Especially helpful services are provided by the various types of school volunteers.[68] Parents of children in school, college and university students, and other community residents help man offices, classrooms, lunchrooms, health clinics, libraries, and other school facilities.

Curriculum evaluation cannot be adequately done without extensive community involvement. Parents' reports on their children's progress in reaching objectives, as revealed in their behavior at home, work supervisors' reports on the performance of students engaged in work experience, and other types of data from home and community are essential for evaluating many educational goals. Furthermore, a major source of data in evaluating the curriculum plan is the opinions of school patrons and community participants and observers. Comprehensive evaluation plans generally use opinion polls on both specific and broad questions relating to the school curriculum.[69]

No single formula for community participation will work for all of the thousands of U.S. communities. We would recommend as a general principle in any school community, large or small, the organization and consistent use of one or more curriculum advisory councils. Existing organizations may suffice or new ones may be needed. Answers should be sought to such questions as the following: How can the school get participation by the parents and other citizens it serves in providing the best curriculum possible for the student population? Is one general council needed or one for each curriculum domain within the plan? How can the council members be fully enough informed of school policies, goals, and programs to give school personnel reactions and suggestions useful in curriculum improvement? How can the school utilize more effectively the educational resources of the entire community? Appropriate answers will

[68]See B. DaSilva, *Practical School Volunteer and Teacher Aide Programs* (West Nyack, N.Y.: Parker Publishing Co., 1974); and Don Davies (ed.), *Schools Where Parents Make a Difference* (Boston: Institute for Responsive Education, 1976).

[69]For example, Florida law requires that an annual evaluation of the school(s) be circulated. A report of a community survey on public attitudes toward school is to be included.

result in constructive activities and ties between parents and schools; while inappropriate answers will involve parents in nonproductive ways and engender friction between parents and schools.

Participation by Exercising Options[70]

A type of parental involvement in curriculum determination has always been available to those who could afford to send their children to a private school. The number and variety of these options increased with the development of alternative schools in the late 1960s.[71] Alternative schools defy description because of their great diversity. They include, perhaps as their most numerous variety, many types of schools set up by parent and other community groups for various age levels, sometimes any age under 20. Many of these were originally established in California; a Los Angeles reporter in 1972 described these schools as follows: "Free schools, alternative schools, radical schools or new schools. Whatever you call them, they have at least one thing in common: wild flight from the precepts and practices of the cumbersome public institution they scorn as the 'big gray schoolhouse.' "[72] Initially, most alternative schools rejected authoritarian aspects of traditional schools in the belief that children's natural curiosity would express itself best in a free climate. There was faith that "students and teachers brought together would naturally deal openly and honestly with each other to create the new, effective learning environment."[73] Argyris pointed out that students and teachers discovered that with their new-found freedom they could not solve some of the school's management problems. As a result, most alternative schools gradually shifted their management style toward an authoritarian and bureaucratic approach. Disillusion occurred when teachers and pupils discovered they had re-created what they had tried to escape. Many alternative schools lasted for two years or less.

The alternative movement, however, provided a valuable impetus for change. During the early 1970s many school districts had created alternative schools within the system. Outstanding examples of these early schools were the Parkway Program in Philadelphia and Metro High School in Chicago. By 1978, Duke and Muzio wrote, "The past decade has wit-

[70]For suggestions regarding a number of options, see James S. Coleman (ed.), *Parents, Teachers, and Children: Prospects for Choice in American Education* (San Francisco: Institute for Contemporary Studies, 1977).

[71]For information on alternative schools, see Roy A. Weaver (ed.), *Changing Schools* (Los Angeles: University of Southern California, School of Education); and Mario D. Fantini (ed.), *Alternative Education: A Source Book for Parents, Teachers, Students, and Administrators* (Garden City, N.Y.: Anchor Books, 1976).

[72]Lynn Lilliston, "A Wild Flight from Public Education," *Los Angeles Times* (March 19, 1972):E1.

[73]Chris Argyris, "Alternative Schools: A Behavioral Analysis," *Teachers College Record, 75* (May 1974):434.

nessed the emergence of thousands of public schools purporting to be alternatives to conventional educational institutions."[74]

Minneapolis, Minnesota, public schools pioneered educational options by offering parents and teachers in the Southeast Minneapolis area four different kinds of elementary schools: traditional, continuous progress, British primary/integrated day, and a K–12 free program. Whereas 35 percent of the parents affected were satisfied with their schools just prior to installing the optional plan, 85 percent were satisfied four years later. "By 1978, 15,000 of Minneapolis's 23,000 elementary pupils were going to schools they and their families had chosen."[75]

Magnet schools, a variation of the alternative school, attract students from across a school district, thus integrating the schools. The Dallas, Texas, Independent School District established magnet schools at every level. The Indianapolis, Indiana, public schools developed a plan for total desegregation of their elementary school population through six distinct educational options. While the options have functioned with mixed success, their primary purpose has not yet been achieved. (The Montessori option has proven most popular.)

The term *alternative schools* has been used to describe special environments established for disruptive children or children with special needs. We prefer the original use of alternative schools as an option for parent and child, rather than a place to assign students. If more good options were available, there would be less need for special assignments.

We see two major influences on local curriculum planning of the alternative school movement: 1) the planning system must have adequate participation and feedback mechanisms to ensure the identification of student and parent interests, problems, and dissatisfactions with the school program; and 2) the alternative school within the system can be an excellent means of developing and trying out curriculum alternatives. We question the establishment of alternatives only as palliatives for the dissatisfied, although temporary conditions may necessitate such an approach. But the long-term use of alternatives should be built into the planning system.[76]

---

[74]Daniel L. Duke, and Irene Muzio, "How Effective Are Alternative Schools?—a Review of Recent Evaluations and Reports," *Teachers College Record, 79* (February 1978):461.

[75]Jane Power, "Magnet Schools—Are They the Answer?" *Today's Education, 68* (September–October 1979):69.

[76]For further information regarding alternative schools, see "A Decade of Alternative Schools and What of the Future," *NASSP Curriculum Report, 8* (October 1978); Evans Clinchy and Elisabeth Allen Cody, "If Not Public Choice, Then Private Escape," *Phi Delta Kappan, 60* (December 1978): 270–273; Daniel L. Duke and Irene Muzio, "How Effective are Alternative Schools? *Teachers College Record, 79* (February 1978): 461–483; Anne Flaxman and Kerry C. Homstead (eds.), *The 1977–78 National Directory of Public Alternative Schools* (Amherst, Mass.: National Alternative Schools Program, College of Education, University of Massachusetts); and Robert Barr, Vernon Smith, and Daniel Burke, *Alternatives in Education: Freedom to Choose* (Bloomington, Ind.: Phi Delta Kappa, 1976).

Proposals to increase parental control through a voucher system are perennial. Under this plan, schools remain public, but parents are issued educational vouchers and allowed to spend them in the school of their choice. An early and very limited experiment of this plan was tried at Alum Rock, California; variations of it have appeared on state ballots. The plan has strong advocates (for example, Coons and Sugarman).[77] The plan has equally strong critics (for example, Butts).[78]

Role of Leaders

A dictionary definition of *leader* is "a person who leads; directing, commanding, or guiding head, as of a group or activity."[79] Therefore, a leader for curriculum development is one who directs, commands, guides (or influences in other ways) the activity of developing a curriculum. This may or may not be the designated leader of the group; for example, the principal, status leader of the school, may not be the leader for curriculum development. Further, as pointed out earlier, different individuals may provide curriculum development leadership at different times. This leadership may emerge as specific needs arise.

Emergent and shared leadership is important in curriculum development. However, we believe that site-specific curriculum development requires one or more designated leaders. Ideally, these designated leaders will possess the qualities and skills that will enable them to influence the process.

Six different styles of leadership are identified and described by Lewis and Miel: autocratic, manipulative, democratic, cooperative problem-solving, laissez-faire, and permissive.[80] These styles do not exist along a continuum, nor is one given style superior in all situations. Selecting an appropriate leadership style requires a consideration of several factors. One consideration is the nature of the total organization within which the curriculum is to be developed. For example, an autocratic style might be inappropriate in a group that has volunteered to develop a new curriculum for a Boy Scout camp program.

The best style in a given situation will also depend upon the leader and the group. What assumptions do they make regarding change and the change process? Does the group or the leader hold philosophical or ethical assumptions that might dictate a particular style? What type of leadership does the group want? (Some groups may not want democratic leadership.) What styles of leadership does the leader feel comfortable with? For exam-

[77]John E. Coons and Stephen D. Sugarman, *Education by Choice: The Case for Family Control* (Berkeley Calif.: University of California Press, 1978).
[78]R. Freeman Butts, "Educational Vouchers: The Private Pursuit of the Public Purse," *Phi Delta Kappan,* 61 (September 1979):7–9.
[79]*Webster's New World Dictionary* (New York: World Publishing Company, 1962), p. 831.
[80]Lewis and Miel, p. 74.

ple, autocratic personalities find it difficult to provide democratic leadership.

The task to be accomplished influences the selection of a style. Thus, different styles of curriculum leadership might be selected for the structured-committee approach, inductive approach, and problem-solving approach. Several styles could be used with the structured-committee approach; however, the laissez-faire and permissive styles would probably be ineffective. Regardless of the style selected, the leader needs group process skills.

Similar styles could be used with the inductive approach and, again, group process skills are important. In addition, the leader needs to be an expert in developing a teaching–learning unit, since the whole process hinges on these units.[81] The leader also needs to know how to work with others in inductively building a curriculum from teaching–learning units.

The problem-solving style of leadership is most appropriate for the problem-solving approach. Such a style requires well-developed skills in group process. It also requires knowledge of specific strategies at each phase of problem solving as discussed previously. For example, at the problem-sensing stage, the leader secures feedback data that might reveal weaknesses, as well as strengths, in the program. The leader also works to create the type of school climate in which it is acceptable for a teacher to have a problem and seek help.[82]

Site-specific curriculum development cannot be viewed in isolation from the total system. The curriculum planning process will not be systematic or effective unless there is, for whatever group of schools comprise the system, a responsible and competent individual officially designated as the curriculum leader. It matters little whether his or her title is assistant superintendent for instruction, director of curriculum, director of instruction, curriculum coordinator, or any other title used to designate his or her official function.

The management of a curriculum planning system involves many tasks, but the central one is the coordination of all of the processes described in this chapter. More than almost any other educator, the curriculum leader must be able to keep straight the relation of the trees and the forest. As he or she works with individual teachers and principals, school faculties, district councils, curriculum designing units, and lay groups, he or she not only helps each individual and group to make a contribution to curriculum planning but sees to it that these contributions mesh well with each other. In the 1980s, new demands arising from public discontent with the schools and new resources through systems analysis and computer management make the role more complex but also potentially more challenging and rewarding.

[81]For assistance with this, see Taba, pp. 343–379.
[82]For other strategies, see Lewis and Miel, pp. 180–185.

Finally, the special skills and knowledge required of curriculum leaders, whether functioning at a special site or the system level, may be deduced from the dual agenda of curriculum development: first, to develop an effective curriculum plan; second, to implement the plan. To lead in the development of an effective curriculum plan requires a knowledge of the various topics covered in this text: the history and major concepts of curriculum development; processes to use in curriculum development, and data needed for this process; and ways to design, implement, and evaluate a curriculum plan. To achieve the second agenda item, the leader needs skills in working with teachers on a one-to-one basis to provide the support, encouragement, and wisdom required to take the most difficult step in all of curriculum development—for teachers to give up proven and familiar practices for the new and uncertain.

CURRICULUM DEVELOPMENT FOR BUSINESS AND INDUSTRY TRAINING PROGRAMS

Business and industry training programs are a rapidly growing sector of education. Some of the general principles of curriculum development used in schools and colleges apply to these programs. However, there are significant differences. Curriculum development in business and industry training programs is not subject to the type of external policy-making that is having an increasing influence on K–12 and postsecondary education. The plethora of generic curriculum materials (textbooks, tests, and the like) available to schools and colleges is not matched in business and industry. Further, the purposes of business and industry training programs are far more specific than the general goals of schools and colleges. In addition, clients, teachers, and policy decision makers generally agree on purposes of business and industry training programs.

Purposes of Training Programs in Business and Industry

Thousands of businesses and industries are now engaged in educational activities once reserved for schools and college. One business research group estimates that 45,000 people are employed full-time by corporations to provide education and training.[83] This does not include the thousands of supervisors and managers who instruct as a part of their job. Estimates on annual expenditures vary from $4 billion[84] up to $100 bil-

[83]Stan Luxenberg, "AT&T and Citicorp: Prototypes in Job Training among Large Corporations," *Phi Delta Kappan, 61* (January 1980):314. The January 1980 issue of *Phi Delta Kappan* includes a special section on training in business and industry that provides an excellent overview.
[84]Anthony E. Schwaller, "The Need for Education/Training Programs in Industry," *Phi Delta Kappan, 61* (January 1980):322

lion;[85] the latter figure includes the cost of apprenticeship training, on-the-job training, new-job and first-job experience, as well as the wages employees are paid while in training.

These heavy investments in training reflect corporate recognition of the value of human resource development. In a highly competitive business world, survival depends upon providing services most efficiently and profitably. Securing, maintaining and developing human resources becomes an important part of the formula for corporate success. Luxenberg points out that "it was once possible for a bright college graduate to learn skills entirely on the job. But in the computer age where whole industries change in a matter of months, new employees must be trained and then constantly retrained."[86]

The three major purposes of training in business and industry are interrelated:

1. Train new personnel employed because of turnover and growth.
2. Improve the skills and performance of present employees in their jobs.
3. Accommodate changes in knowledge and skills required by a business.

These purposes of training apply to management personnel as well as other employees. Lusterman estimated that 24 percent of the total cost of education and training in industry is for management and supervisory personnel.[87]

Recently, some businesses have incorporated "basic remedial education" into their training programs. Schwaller observed that "in many cases, depending upon the industry and its products, some new employees must be trained in basic math, reading, etc. Others must be trained in effective speaking and listening skills."[88] Lusterman estimated that corporations spend approximately $15 million per year on basic remedial courses.[89] Some corporations offer educational programs that are broader in purpose then the training and retraining of exployees. For example, college credit courses are offered by such corporations as Xerox, AT&T, Lockheed Missiles and Space, Holiday Inn, TWA, Bank of America, and IBM. McQuigg reported that "four of the largest corporations in America—IBM, Xerox, GE, and AT&T—now offer bachelor's degrees."[90] Thus,

[85]Gary J. Corrigan, "Corporate Training: A Career for Teachers?" *Phi Delta Kappan, 61* (January 1980):328.
[86]Luxenberg, p. 314.
[87]Seymour Lusterman, *Education in Industry* (New York: The Conference Board, 1977), p. 45.
[88]Schwaller, p. 323.
[89]Lusterman, p. 45.
[90]Beverly McQuigg, "The Role of Education in Industry," *Phi Delta Kappan, 61* (January 1980):325.

colleges and universities may find themselves increasingly in competition with educational programs offered by industry.

One manager of a corporate education group, Norman Smith, urged a cooperative relationship between the corporate world and universities. Smith made a distinction between corporate training with its narrowly defined objectives—eliciting in the trainee constructive on-the-job behavior and increased productivity—and liberal education. Smith recognized the importance of liberal education to provide attributes needed particularly by managers—an understanding of history, self-knowledge, motivation, and compassion. He concluded that "if we can overcome the mutual distrust between the university and the corporate world, we can tap vast reservoirs of human energy."[91]

Procedures for Curriculum Development in Business and Industry

Curriculum development strategies in business and industry training programs reflect the purpose of meeting specific training needs. This is well illustrated by the procedures followed by AT&T, the biggest private company in the world. AT&T spends about $1 billion a year in training and retraining its nearly one million employees.

AT&T has developed standardized courses "designed to teach employees only the specific information they need to do their job. To accomplish this, courses are designed around job studies and test criteria."[92] Classes are taught in local company offices or at locations near employees' homes. Courses requiring special equipment or limited to a small number of people are taught at corporate learning centers throughout the United States. The major center for technical training is the Bell System Center for Technical Education at Lisle, Illinois.

There are four departments at the Center for Technical Education corresponding to the major activities of the company: business service, engineering, forecasting, and network operations. A department board composed of management personnel heads up each department. Curriculum councils responsible for specific areas function under the departmental boards.

Line managers, as well as lower-level employees, identify areas where training is needed. The appropriate curriculum council assigns a training technologist to study the problem. According to Luxenberg, "The Lisle school employs about 80 technologists, most of them trained at the center in the young discipline of developing education and training programs." Often a change in operational procedures may eliminate the need for a

---

[91]Norman R. Smith, "Corporate Training and the Liberal Arts," *Phi Delta Kappan, 61* (January 1980):311.
[92]Luxenberg, p. 314.

training course. If a training program is required, a developmental team is assigned to design it. The first step is to write the final examination, which could "consist of a student's being required to fix an artfully broken or fouled-up piece of equipment or to solve a difficult engineering problem."[93] Courses are carefully field-tested before they are used throughout the system.

Smaller corporations do not have the large staff of AT&T. However, most of them have procedures to assure that courses are designed to meet training needs of employees. For example, a Citicorp executive requested the head of the training group to develop a course to train supervisors in making salary decisions for subordinates and presenting these decisions to the subordinate. The executive requested the course on the basis of poor supervisor performance in this area. The course designers started by interviewing supervisors and lower-level employees. They then designed a two-day workshop that included lectures, role playing, and the use of a simulated salary problem.

In most training programs, the instructors develop their own curriculum. The variety of skills this requires is reported by Corrigan, based on a survey of 2790 training specialists.[94] It was found that their roles included: 1) needs analysis and diagnosis; 2) determination of the appropriate training approach; 3) program design and development; 4) management of educational resources; 5) classroom training; 6) training research; and 7) professional self-development. Many corporations provide support systems to assist instructors. For example, IBM has a training program to help instructors become curriculum developers. As above, "it deals with such topics as project control and management, media selection and audience analysis."[95] IBM also has a developer-support organization, comprised of three departments: Publishing Support Services, Developer Support Services, and Education Computer Services.

The effectiveness of training programs operated by business and industry have caused some observers to wonder if corporations could become competitive with K–12 schools as well as universities. For example, Doll forecast a general weakening due to financial constraints. He speculated that "coincident with the growing economic crisis, a loss of confidence in public education will have taken place." As a result, Doll predicted, "Public schools at the preuniversity level will serve mainly poor children, as most parents will have enrolled their children in private and parochial schools." Corporations will be forced to pay private school tuition for children of employees—particularly children of management personnel.

[93]Luxenberg, p. 315.
[94]Corrigan, p. 329.
[95]Peter M. Dean, "Education and Training at IBM," *Phi Delta Kappan, 61* (January 1980): 318.

Doll concluded that "eventually we may see corporate private schools run by a consortium of corporations."[96]

We believe that such a resolution to the problem of financially weakened schools would be self-defeating to corporations. The survival of corporations depends upon effective education for all people, not just children of corporation employees. We believe that most corporate leaders will recognize this and seek ways to cooperate with schools in ways that will strengthen the educational and training functions of both schools and business and industry.

ADDITIONAL SUGGESTIONS FOR FURTHER STUDY

Bellack, Arno, and Herbert M. Kliebard (eds.), *Curriculum and Education.* Berkeley, Calif.: McCutchan Publishing Corporation, 1977. One of the seven-volume series, *Readings in Educational Research,* sponsored by the American Educational Research Association. This volume does not primarily report or review research but instead includes articles by various educators organized by the editors around these questions: 1) How should curriculum problems be studied? 2) What purposes should the curriculum serve? 3) How should knowledge be selected and organized for the curriculum? 4) How should the curriculum be evaluated? 5) How should the curriculum be changed?

Brandt, Ronald S. (ed.), *Partners: Parents & Schools.* Alexandria, Va.: Association for Supervision and Curriculum Development, 1979. Various authors review arguments for and examples of parent involvement in schools, and propose means of increasing the partnership. See especially the article by the late Ira J. Gordon on "The Effects of Parent Involvement on Schooling," which includes description of four models of involvement.

Daft, Richard L., and Selwyn W. Becker, *Innovation in Organizations: Innovation in School Organizations.* New York: Elsevier North-Holland, Inc., 1978. Research study using 13 suburban high schools in Cook County, Illinois, focuses on the process of innovation. Covers many aspects of innovation with some provocative findings, including positive results on innovation and change because of the employment of curriculum coordinators.

Deal, Terrence, and Robert Nolan, *Alternative Schools: Ideologies, Realities, Guidelines.* Chicago: Nelson-Hall, 1978. The ideologies the authors present range in time and concept, from John Dewey to A. S. Neill; the realities section is a description of a variety of alternative schools; and the guidelines provide excellent principles and concepts for the development of such types of schools.

Duke, Daniel Linden, *The Retransformation of the School.* Chicago: Nelson-Hall, 1978. Useful description and analysis of alternative schools based on the author's visits to a sample of 40 schools. Four chapters describe major features of these schools, with an additional section devoted to analysis of the origins of the alternative school movement.

Glaser, Robert (ed.), *Research and Development and School Change.* Hillsdale,

---

[96]Russell C. Doll, "Speculations on the Meaning of the Trend Toward Corporate Education," *Phi Delta Kappan, 61* (January 1980):336.

N.J.: Lawrence Erlbaum Associates, Publishers, 1978. Useful symposium of views on the relation of research and development to school change by eight leaders in educational research including Benjamin Bloom, Jacob Getzels, Robert Gagné, and Ralph Tyler.

Ratcliff, James L., "Meeting the Demand for Community Outreach," *The Educational Forum, 43* (March 1979):315–330. A description of procedures to be used by community colleges in developing educational programs to serve entire communities.

Schaffarzick, Jon, and Gary Sykes (eds.), *Value Conflicts and Curriculum Issues.* Berkeley, Calif.: McCutchan Publishing Corp., 1979. A series of significant essays and reports produced by the National Institute of Education task force on curriculum development. Includes discussions on legal controls over curriculum and the political setting. Recommended approaches to planning in light of the present situation in state and federal controls and financial aid are presented.

Toner, Nea Carroll, and Walter B. Toner, Jr., *Citizen Participation: Building A Constituency for Public Policy.* Washington, D.C.: U.S. Office of Education, HEW Publication No. (OE)–78–07001. Detailed suggestions for securing citizen participation in making policy regarding social issues and problems, including education.

Training and Development Journal. The official magazine of the American Society for Training and Development. It is particularly valuable for anyone involved with corporate training programs.

van Geel, Tyll, *Authority to Control the School Program.* Lexington, Mass.: D. C. Heath and Company, 1976. An authoritative book on the control of the schools through constitutional and statutory enactments and court decisions at both the federal and state levels. Cites a tremendous body of law and judicial opinions that bind the schools.

THREE

■ ■ ■

DATA FOR CURRICULUM PLANNING

■ ■

A society establishes social institutions to facilitate the education of its members; hence, curriculum planning always takes place within a social structure and is designed to contribute in major ways to the education of an identifiable group of children, youth, or adults. It follows logically that those who plan the curriculum must take into account certain basic factors within this broad structure of social function if the education provided learners is to be appropriate and valid.

DATA ESSENTIAL FOR PLANNING

An effective curriculum is based on data from three major sources: 1) the nature of the learners to be educated; 2) the society which provides and operates the educational institution; and 3) the accumulated knowledge available and feasible for educating learners. These data are used for the phases of curriculum planning described in subsequent chapters: goals and objectives, curriculum design, instructional models, and evaluative procedures (see Figure 1.1, p. 29). In addition to a general background, curriculum planners need specific information regarding the learners to be served and the nature of the local community. With this information, they are able to relate knowledge to a specific group of learners in a particular setting.

This chapter provides readers with some of the types of data and specific data necessary to build a foundation for curriculum planning. Special emphasis is given to important recent developments or, in some instances, developments just on the horizon. Sources of additional information are listed. The chapter also contains suggestions regarding types of specific data to be collected.

Three external forces especially control and influence curriculum development: legal requirements, research, and professional knowledge (see Figure 1.1, p. 29). Ways in which legislative groups, courts, and regulatory bodies control and influence the development of curriculum policy and curriculum materials were discussed in Chapters 1 and 2. These forces combine to provide a "zone of tolerance," or parameters, for curriculum development. Other forces act to extend curriculum planners' knowledge. Research and professional literature in education provide one such force. Certain concepts and theories in related disciplines (such as anthropology, sociology, political science, and psychology and its related field of neuroscience) are valuable to planners. The contributions of these disciplines are discussed in this chapter.

It should be recognized that much curriculum planning does not follow the models and the processes presented in this volume. Often, planners plunge right into the preparation of guides, instructional materials, or instructional plans without overtly and deliberately considering all of the steps listed in Chapter 1 as necessary in a systematic approach to educational planning. Whenever we observe or study outstanding educational programs, however, we are impressed with the extent to which such programs are carefully designed for the learners and appropriate to the community setting. Further, in implementing the program, teachers are applying principles derived from professional knowledge and related disciplines. In summary, the quality of a curriculum plan improves in direct proportion to the intelligent use of data discussed in this chapter.

DATA ABOUT LEARNERS

A curriculum is planned for an identified group of learners. Typically, learners have been considered as children, youth, and young adults enrolled in formal educational institutions. Life has been divided into three stages: education (as preparation for work), work, and retirement. An emerging pattern promises greater variety to life; for example, an individual will attend school for ten to twelve years, work for three or four years, return to school for another four or five years, work for eight or nine years, take a "sabbatical year," work for three or four years, return to school for a year, and so on. This pattern will result from a changing technology that requires skilled workers to be completely reeducated four or five times during their career. Retirement may well be a gradual process, with adult education programs and leisure-time activities (many also involving educational preparation and continued training) filling in the increasing time away from work. Individuals of all ages will turn to education to help them cope with changes in themselves and in society. Lifelong learning will be a reality—not just a slogan—with education available for every age group. Who, then, are the learners of today and in the future and what are they like?

Demographic Data

Elementary school enrollment, which peaked in 1969 at approximately 36,800,000, dropped steadily to approximately 31,000,000 in 1980. The maximum secondary school enrollment of 15,600,000 in 1976 is projected to drop approximately 25 percent by 1990. These remarkable shifts are caused as age cohorts of different sizes progress through their life stages.

The number of births at any time depends upon the number of women of childbearing age in the population and the fertility rate of these women. Children of the "baby boom," born in the decade following World War II, are becoming 25 to 34 years of age during the 1980s. However, this increase in the number of childbearing women is accompanied by a dramatic decline in fertility rate.[1] The fertility rate of 3.65 in 1960 declined to 1.86 in 1974.[2] The dramatic effect of this sliding birth rate is shown by these statistics: "In 1957, 35 million women of childbearing age produced 4.3 million babies; in 1976, 48 million such women bore only 3.2 million babies."[3] Thus, while the number of women of childbearing age *increased* by 37 percent, the number of children born *decreased* by 26 percent.

Several factors cause demographers to project a continuation of a low fertility rate: more women are working, divorce rates are increasing, and couples are increasingly choosing to have one child or none at all. If this low fertility rate continues, birth rates will start a sharp and protracted decline when the "small generation" which followed the "baby boom" generation dominates the childbearing age in the 1990s.

The American Association of School Administrators (AASA) prepared an excellent filmstrip on population changes, entitled "A Profound Transformation."[4] The shifts in population have had a marked effect on all of society and particularly on elementary schools. Greater changes are ahead for secondary schools as an average high school in an average community will experience approximately a 25 percent drop of enrollment from 1976 to the early 1990s. For some high schools, the drop could be as great as 40 percent. Related societal shifts will affect schools. For example, just when secondary schools will be combating dropouts to bolster dwindling enrollments, a smaller number of youths will be competing for jobs so that dropping out will be more attractive. The composition of the school group will shift if the fertility rate of women of low socioeconomic status continues to be greater than that for women of higher socioeconomic status; those who can most afford to have children are least likely to have them.

Although our discussion has focused on schools, other educational institutions will be affected. For example, various youth organizations will experience sharp declines in potential clients. Television programs geared to young adults will have fewer possible viewers.

[1]Fertility rate is defined as the average number of births that each woman in a cohort of women would have in her lifetime if she experienced the birthrate occurring in the given calendar year.
[2]Susan Abramowitz and Stuart Rosenfeld (eds.), *Declining Enrollment: The Challenge of the Coming Decade* (Washington, D.C.: National Institute of Education, 1978), p. 132.
[3]Shirley Boes Neill, "The Demographers' Message to Education," *American Education, 15* (January/February 1979): 6.
[4]American Association of School Administrators, "A Profound Transformation," filmstrip and script (Arlington, Va.: American Association of School Administrators, 1979).

Because of this "profound transformation," curriculum developers will need to:

1. Design curriculum plans that can continue to be effective with declining enrollments.
2. Develop educational programs to help students live through the changes accompanying sharp population shifts.
3. Capitalize on the opportunity to expand educational offerings to individuals of all age levels.

The book, *Declining Enrollments: The Challenge of the Coming Decade,* contains a series of papers providing demographic data on declining enrollments and their implications for schools.[5]

Curriculum planners need specific information regarding groups of learners. Table 3.1 lists some of the more important kinds of enumerative and statistical information that should be available. Some sources from which the data may be obtained are suggested, although it is recognized that these may vary among school systems or that other sources may be available. The importance of the information for curriculum planning is

TABLE 3.1 Kinds of Information Needed about Student Population

Item	Possible Sources	Suggested Uses
1. Population and enrollment data: numbers, trends, births, age distribution; race or ethnic background; projected birthrates and rates of population growth; projected enrollments.	Census data by tracts; student data records; individual school records; national and state reports on vital statistics; decennial census reports; forecast of population.	Facilities, staff, equipment, and materials needed; class size; teacher load; budgetmaking; planning desirable integration by racial and ethnic characteristics; locating buildings.
2. School progress: normal, retarded, or accelerated progress by grade, multiunit, or level.	Student records in individual schools; achievement as measured by tests.	Analyze and evaluate promotion and class assignment practices; diagnose individual needs; plan programs to meet special needs; plan for multilevel or ungraded groupings.
3. Dropouts: rate, causes, characteristics of the dropouts; school status; postschool status.	Student records, by schools and systemwide; follow-up studies; conferences; guidance records; student input before entering and after leaving school.	Critical assessment of curriculum and instruction in terms of genuine relevancy for all students; identification of potential dropouts and use of positive counseling measures; desirability of alternate types of educational programs for some students; planning part-time and informal programs for those who drop out; parent involvement; stimulating community action for better school programs.

[5]Abramowitz and Rosenfeld.

indicated in the column headed "Suggested Uses." Such a list is not exhaustive nor are the recommendations spelled out in detail.

Much of the statistical data about the student body of the school, the population characteristics of the children of the district, and follow-up studies can be compiled or be made by staff members of appropriate research or personnel bureaus; other data may be compiled by administrators or counseling personnel of the individual school. Curriculum planning committees and individual teachers should have readily available this information without spending a great deal of their time in collecting it. Interpretations of the data, however, should be made by all of those involved in the planning process, including parents.

Some data collected by a school would be useful to other educational agencies within society. Similarly, other educational agencies have information of value to curriculum planners and teachers including: membership in such groups as Boy Scouts, Girl Scouts; holders of library cards and circulation records; and participants in recreation department activities. In Chapter 8, we propose a cooperative approach to collecting data needed for social indicators of educational performance.

A precautionary note regarding the collection and sharing of information is needed. Individuals have the right to keep others from knowing private information about themselves, particularly if that information could be stigmatizing. Riskin pointed out that "information about a person's IQ and emotional condition, or his or her proclivity for dangerous behavior is potentially stigmatizing; even a very high IQ could be embarrassing to some persons." Riskin continued, "derogatory information can influence the way a person is treated for the rest of his or her life by parents and other relatives, employers, and educational institutions."[6]

The Family Educational Rights and Privacy Act of 1974, more commonly known as the Buckley Amendment,[7] requires that parents or older students have the right: 1) to review educational records; 2) to a hearing to challenge their accuracy and to ensure that they are not in violation of the student's right of privacy; and 3) to insert their own written interpretations. Riskin reports a court decision prohibiting the use of a plan to identify potential drug abusers. The court argued, "When a program talks about labelling someone as a particular type and such a label could remain with him or her for the remainder of his or her life, the margin of error must be almost nil."[8] This admonition should be heeded by all curriculum planners.

[6]Leonard L. Riskin, "Telling Tales Out of School: Some Legal Problems," *Teachers College Record, 78* (December 1976): 231.
[7]20 U.S.C., Sec. 1232g–i (Supp. IV 1974).
[8]Riskin, p. 232.

Growth and Developmental Characteristics

Another major category of data needed about learners is the nature and status of their growth and development. Much of the insight and understanding curriculum planners need in this aspect of student data relies on known generalizations about infants, children, youth, and adults. It will, of course, be necessary to check this knowledge against the population for whom a particular curriculum plan is being prepared and instruction is being provided. In fact, personalization of instruction based on the developmental status of learners is essential.

Developmental Tasks

Havighurst proposed a series of tasks that individuals must learn for health and satisfying growth, arising from three sources: 1) physical maturation (for example, learning to walk); 2) cultural pressure of the society (for instance, learning to talk); and 3) personal values and aspirations of the individual (such as choosing and preparing for a vocation).[9] Some tasks are practically universal; others, particularly those that grow out of social demands, show variation between cultures. Havighurst described developmental tasks for the following stages of growth: infancy and early childhood, middle childhood, adolescence, early adulthood, middle age, and later maturity. For example, the tasks Havighurst listed for middle age were: 1) assisting teen-age children to become responsible and happy adults; 2) achieving adult social and civic responsibility; 3) reaching and maintaining satisfactory performance in one's occupational career; 4) developing adult leisure-time activities; 5) relating oneself to one's spouse as a person; 6) accepting and adjusting to physiological changes of middle age; and 7) adjusting to aging parents.[10]

Most developmental tasks should be achieved at a certain period in life. If the task is not achieved at the proper time, it will not be achieved well and may cause partial or complete failure in the achievement of tasks to come.[11]

Stages of Personality Development

The developmental tasks described by Havighurst include all phases of growth and development. Erikson, one of the leading figures in the field of psychoanalysis and human development, identified eight stages of de-

[9]Robert J. Havighurst, *Developmental Tasks and Education* (New York: David McKay Co., Inc., 1974).
[10]Havighurst, pp. 96–104 passim.
[11]Havighurst, pp. 6–7.

velopment of a human personality.[12] In each of Erikson's stages, a central problem is posed, having both a positive and a negative outcome (for example, basic trust versus basic mistrust). While the struggle between positives and negatives must be fought through successfully if the next developmental stage is to be reached, no victory is completely or forever won. The eight developmental stages follow.

BASIC TRUST VERSUS BASIC MISTRUST (INFANCY).   The cornerstone of a healthy personality is a basic sense of trust in oneself and in one's environment. For the infant, this sense of trust requires a feeling of physical comfort and a minimum amount of fear or uncertainty. A sense of mistrust arises from unsatisfactory physical or psychological experiences.

AUTONOMY VERSUS SHAME AND DOUBT (EARLY CHILDHOOD).   As infants gain trust in their mothers, their environment, and themselves, they start to discover that their behavior is their own and to develop a sense of autonomy as they have experiences enabling them to make choices. Erikson pointed out that even as the environment encourages the child to stand on his own feet, "it must protect him against meaningless and arbitrary experiences of shame and early doubt."[13]

INITIATIVE VERSUS GUILT (PLAY AGE).   This is a period of vigorous learning leading away from the child's own limitations into future possibilities. At the same time, a sense of conscience develops as "the child is no longer guided only by outsiders; there is installed within him a voice that comments on his deeds, and warns and threatens."[14] Accordingly, the problem to be worked out at this stage is how to exercise will without too great a sense of guilt.

INDUSTRY VERSUS INFERIORITY (PRIMARY SCHOOL AGE).   If the problems of the first three stages have been well worked through, this is a period of steady and calm growth. Children need and want real achievement at this stage. Curriculum planners and teachers are challenged to help them secure it while heeding the warning of the White House report. "The chief danger of this period is the presence of conditions that may lead to the development of a sense of inadequacy and inferiority."[15]

[12] A full explanation of these stages is in Chapter 7 of Erik H. Erikson, *Childhood and Society*, 2d ed. (New York: W. W. Norton & Company, Inc., 1963).
[13] Erikson, p. 252.
[14] *A Healthy Personality for Every Child*, A Digest of the Fact Finding Report to The Midcentury White House Conference on Children and Youth (Health Publications Institute, Inc., 1951), p. 15.
[15] *A Healthy Personality for Every Child*, p. 17.

IDENTITY VERSUS ROLE CONFUSION (ADOLESCENCE). The physiological changes that accompany puberty make adolescence a period of storm and stress for many young people as they seek to clarify their own identity, what their role in society will be, whether they are children or adults. The important question is: Will I be a success or a failure? Adolescents need help as they work through the problem of identity. The White House Conference stated, "It is clear, then, that if health of personality is to be preserved much attention must be given to assuring that America makes good on its promises to youth."[16]

INTIMACY VERSUS ISOLATION (YOUNG ADULTHOOD). Once the sense of identity is achieved, it is possible for an individual to develop a sense of intimacy—intimacy with persons of the same sex or of the opposite sex or with oneself. Young people who are not fairly sure of their identity shy away from interpersonal relations and are afraid of personal communion with themselves.

GENERATIVITY VERSUS STAGNATION (ADULTHOOD). Generativity is primarily the concern in establishing and guiding the next generation. Erikson said, "The concept generativity is meant to include such more popular synonyms as *productivity* and *creativity*, which, however, cannot replace it."[17] Where individuals fail to achieve generativity, they often regress to an obsessive need for pseudointimacy with a pervading sense of stagnation and personal impoverishment.

EGO INTEGRITY VERSUS DESPAIR (SENESCENCE). Erikson's contrast between ego integrity and despair at the end of life places his whole scheme in perspective. "Only in him who in some way has taken care of things and people and has adapted himself to the triumphs and disappointments adherent to being . . . only in him may gradually ripen the fruit of these seven stages." This is what Erikson referred to as ego integrity. He described it as "the acceptance of one's one and only life cycle as something that had to be and that, by necessity, permitted of no substitutions."[18] The lack or loss of this accrued ego integration results in despair that comes from the realization that the time is now "too short for the attempt to start another life and to try out alternate roads to integrity."

This brief summary will refresh the memory of those who have read Erikson; for others, it may open new vistas worth exploring. A knowledge of the central problems humans face at each stage of development is valuable to those who plan and provide educational experiences.

[16]*A Healthy Personality for Every Child,* p. 21.
[17]Erikson, p. 267.
[18]Erikson, p. 268.

Intellectual Development

Piaget is one of today's most influential thinkers and has had a profound effect on our understanding of children's intellectual growth. A philosopher, biologist, and developmental psychologist concerned with the problem of knowledge, Piaget has evolved a theory of intellectual development from a cross-disciplinary approach and from extensive observation of his three children. His original works were published in French, and it was not until the 1950s that translations were available to American educators and psychologists. Since that time, however, he has had a major impact on curriculum development.

While some prefer to read his original works,[19] others have found it helpful to read many of the books which have been written "interpreting" Piaget to psychologists, educators, teachers, and parents.[20]

Piaget is primarily interested in understanding the qualitative development of intellectual structures, not curriculum development. However, Piaget offers several hypotheses which clearly have implications for educators. First, he suggested that there is a continual and progressive change in the structures of intelligence. The idea that behavior and thought change with age is not new. However, Piaget viewed this change occurring as the result of an individual seeking to maintain a mental balance (or equilibrium) between new events and what is already known and understood. Equilibration results from the interplay of maturation, experience with the physical environment, and experience with the social environment. This process of equilibration is continuous and progressive and leads to hierarchical structures of intelligence.

Second, these structures appear in a predictable sequence. Piaget hypothesized four successive stages of cognitive development which occur in an invariant sequence with somewhat relative time boundaries.

Stage 1. Sensory-motor. The infant's first interactions with the world are through the senses and the development of motor skills. By interacting with objects and people the infant separates "self" from "other."

Stage 2. Pre-Operational. Data gathering takes on a more organized form as the child works with things, begins to solve problems, and acquires language which allows for the labelling of actions and objects.

[19]Jean Piaget and Barbel Inhelder, *The Psychology of the Child* (New York: Basic Books, 1969); Jean Piaget, *To Understand Is To Invent* (New York: Grossman, 1973); Jean Piaget, *The Grasp of Consciousness* (Cambridge: Harvard University Press, 1976).

[20]See, for example, John H. Flavell, *The Developmental Psychology of Jean Piaget* (Princeton, N.J.: D. Van Nostrand Company, Inc., 1963); David Elkind, *Children and Adolescents: Interpretive Essays on Jean Piaget* (New York: Oxford University Press, 1974); Richard M. Gorman, *Discovering Piaget: A Guide for Teachers* (Columbus, Oh.: Charles E. Merrill Publishing Co., 1972); Mary Ann Pulaski, *Your Baby's Mind and How It Grows: Piaget's Theory for Parents* (New York: Harper & Row, 1978).

Stage 3. Concrete Operational. Inquiry becomes more like research as the individual observes the results of actions, learns from them, and begins to predict other actions.

Stage 4. Formal Thinking. Individuals manipulate ideas and propositions and test hypotheses through abstract thinking. They are no longer dependent upon direct experience.

Third, intelligent activity is an active, organized process of "assimilating" the new information to the old and of "accommodating" the old to the new. Piaget saw the processes of assimilation and accommodation as a part of "adaptation." This adaptation takes place as the learner responds to his or her new environment by relating it to the concepts (schemata) he or she already has assimilated. If the learner can do this the new experience is accommodated and can be assimilated into the structure. The art of teaching depends upon appropriately matching activity and environment with the concepts of the learner. If the discrepancy between the new activity/environment and the learner's current structure is too great the person is frustrated or simply tunes out; if there is a perfect match the result is stultifying boredom. However, when the new activity presents a challenge—meaning that is within the range of the current structure—then learning occurs.

This brief description of Piaget's theory alerts curriculum workers to the need to recognize the developmental nature of learning and the importance of the old adage that "teaching must start where the learner is." Readiness, thus, becomes an important consideration in building a curriculum. It is important to realize that Piaget's theory of cognitive development is a set of hypotheses to be tested further, although it is generally treated as established knowledge. As a set of working hypotheses, however, the theory is having a profound impact on curriculum development.

Emerging Patterns of Growth

The growth and development patterns of learners are changing. The height and weight of children is increasing and they are physically healthier. Menstruation and sex drives are developing earlier in children. Over the 60-year period between 1870 and 1930 the mean age of the onset of menstruation fell from 16.5 years to 14.5 years; between 1930 and 1970 the mean age dropped another three years, to 11.5 years.[21] These biological changes have been brought about by numerous interrelated forces including: improved nutrition and diets, more effective immunization to disease, increased use of vitamins and minerals, and diet additives given to livestock.

As a result of earlier maturation children are motivated by many drives

[21]Leslie J. Chamberlin and Ricardo Girona, "Our Children are Changing," *Educational Leadership, 33* (January 1976): 301, 302.

that only a few years ago affected youths many years their seniors. Chamberlin and Girona observed that "traits such as straining against parental authority, desire for greater freedom, and extreme loyalty to peer groups, that once characterized the late teen years now are often encountered in much younger children."[22] Earlier maturation of children accounts, in part, for the dramatic increase in the number of live births to unwed mothers. In 1975, 447,900 U.S. children were born out-of-wedlock, representing 14.2 percent of all births for that year.[23] "Of the 3.1 million live births in 1975 . . . 12,642 were to girls under 15 (years of age)."[24]

But while adolescence is beginning at an earlier age, marriage and the establishment of a career are being postponed. Thus, we have "the paradox of children who, while biologically maturing earlier, are being required to wait longer for sex, social rights, and adult obligations."[25]

Keniston observed that neither "adolescence" nor "early adulthood" quite describes today's young people and concluded, ". . . we are witnessing today the emergence on a mass scale of a previously unrecognized stage of life, a stage that intervenes between adolescence and adulthood."[26] This stage, referred to as "youth," begins at about age 18 and usually concludes at about age 24 but may continue to age 30. The educational implications of this new stage were deemed sufficiently important that the National Society for the Study of Education devoted one of their two 1975 yearbooks to youth.[27]

Keniston, writing in this yearbook, identified a series of major youth themes including:

1. Tension between self and society—the awareness of actual or potential conflict or lack of congruence between one's identity and values and the resources and demands of the existing society increases.
2. Alternating estrangement and omnipotentiality—estrangement entails feelings of isolation, unrealtiy, absurdity, and disconnectedness from the interpersonal, social world; while omnipotentiality is the feeling of absolute freedom, of living in a world of pure possibilities, of being able to change or achieve anything.
3. Change versus stasis—Youth places enormous value on change, transformation, and movement and abhors stasis. During youth we see the most

---

[22]Chamberlin and Girona, p. 303.
[23]Arthur J. Lewis, Carol Blalock, David Harrison, Paul Kajdan, Robert Soar, *Social and Economic Trends Influencing Education* (Tallahassee, Fla.: Department of Education, 1979), p. 11.
[24]Neill, p. 7.
[25]Chamberlin and Girona, p. 302.
[26]Kenneth Keniston, "Prologue: Youth as a Stage of Life," in Robert J. Havighurst and Philip H. Dreyer (eds.), *Youth*, The Seventy-fourth Yearbook of the National Society for the Study of Education (Chicago: University of Chicago Press, 1975), p. 8.
[27]Havighurst and Dreyer (eds.), *Youth*.

strenuous, self-conscious, and even frenzied efforts at self-transformation, using whatever religious, cultural, therapeutic, or chemical means are available.[28]

These "themes of youth" need to be considered by curriculum planners, especially by those who plan programs for learners between ages of 18 and 25 to 30.

The development of adults is becoming of special interest.[29] The increase in the number of adults has prompted some of this interest; but the impetus has come primarily from increased perplexities of living in a complex society. Knox indicated that developmental tasks for adults are shaped by the social setting or context, performance of life roles, physical condition, personality, and learning.[30] A major change in any of these areas has great influence on adult development. Educational and counseling resources are being developed in many communities to help adults through development periods.

Developmental Status of Children and Youth

Children and youth seem to be experiencing more than the usual difficulties in growing up. The nature and possible causes of these difficulties have implications for educational programs whether offered in or out of school.

Statistics indicating symptoms of developmental difficulties are both numerous and depressing. These include increases in suicide, homicide, illegitimate births, delinquency, and drug and alcohol abuse.[31] The public views discipline as the biggest problem schools face.[32] The incidence of violence and vandalism in schools has increased. Wynne analyzed statistics on entering freshmen at several colleges and found an increase in withdrawn attitudes among students coupled with an apparent simultaneous increase in their self-centeredness. He concluded that "successive groups of students have felt less and less relationship to the world. They have become increasingly *alienated.*"[33]

Several factors are associated with these changes in children and youth. One factor, cited earlier, is the combination of earlier maturation and later marriage. Changes within society, accentuated by a telecommunications

[28]Keniston, pp. 9–12, passim.
[29]See, for example, Gail Sheehy, *Passages* (New York: E. P. Dutton, 1976).
[30]Allen B. Knox, *Adult Development and Learning* (San Francisco: Jossey-Bass Publishers, 1977).
[31]See Edward A. Wynne, "Behind the Discipline Program: Youth Suicide as a Measure of Alienation," *Phi Delta Kappan, 59* (January 1978): 307–315.
[32]George H. Gallup, "The 11th Annual Gallup Poll of the Public's Attitudes Toward the Public Schools," *Phi Delta Kappan, 61* (September 1979): 34.
[33]Wynne, p. 310.

revolution, are also affecting youth. They are reacting to social change that is so rapid it threatens to make values, institutions, and technologies obsolete within their lifetimes.

Forces within the immediate environment, such as the family, are affecting children and youth. Increasingly, children live in families with single parents; and in two-parent families mothers are often working outside of the home. The separation of the home from the workplace ended much of children's economic usefulness at home; at the same time, the costs of raising children have risen rapidly. Coleman pointed out that "the family is increasingly, for husband and wife, a convenience institution for themselves." Because children are less central to the family, Coleman observed, "family life is less and less appropriate for the needs of children and especially young persons emerging from childhood."[34] Society has ostracized its youth, according to Smith. "Adults—parents, as well as the working community—have all but shut out the young from responsible participation in the activities by which the community improves and maintains its life."[35] The adult society denies youth the opportunity to satisfy their need to be needed.

President Pifer of Carnegie Corporation stated in his recent annual report: "We know that the abuse and neglect of children have reached shocking proportions."[36] He cited statistics regarding the number of physically, mentally, and emotionally disabled children; the number of children in foster homes; the national school dropout rate; and the number of children under 16 working in fields. "One would think," said Pifer, "that in the face of the steady decline in the numbers of young people being born today, we would be more disposed to do our best by those we have." In fact the opposite seems to be the case. "Public attitudes have turned to indifference or even downright antagonism."[37] It is ironic that Pifer's report was written in 1979—The International Year of the Child.

Pointing out the adult community's responsibility for the plight of youth does not exonerate the youth themselves. The data, however, show the decreasing adequacy of the social–psychological environment within which children and young people are growing up. The challenge to all of society, particularly to educational insitutions is to improve this environment—to heed Pifer's warning, "No nation, and especially not this one at this stage in its history can afford to neglect its children." He concluded,

---

[34]James S. Coleman, "Changing the Environment for Youth." *Phi Delta Kappan, 59* (January 1978): 319.

[35]B. Othanel Smith, "Socialization: What Can the Schools Do?" *Educational Leadership, 36* (April 1979): 454.

[36]Alan Pifer, "Perceptions of Children and Youth," *Annual Report, Carnegie Corporation of New York, 1978* (New York: Carnegie Corporation, Inc., 1979), p. 7.

[37]Pifer, p. 7.

"In the end the only thing we have is our young people, if we fail them, all else is in vain."[38]

Information Regarding Individual Learners

The general characteristics of learners, just described, need to be checked against the population to be served by a particular curriculum. The kinds of information needed about student growth and development include:

1. Physical development including health status and special physical needs.
2. Emotional and social development.
3. Psychological needs.
4. Intellectual and creative development.
5. Personal traits including motivational level and behavior.

DATA ABOUT SOCIETY

Information about society aids curriculum planners in understanding learners and in identifying social functions of educational programs. Most information will serve both functions. However, to simplify the analysis of a complex topic, information will be presented in two categories: 1) society and learners; and 2) society and functions of education.

Society and Learners

Individuals learn by observing people in their social context. In addition to the school, the social context includes the family, peer groups, community groups (such as religious organizations and youth groups), and mass communication. The educational effectiveness of any one of these agencies or groups will depend on such factors as communication between agencies and the degree of congruence of their values, goals, and methods of education. Professional educators have a special responsibility for building bridges with other elements in the students' social context. For example, communication between school and home can be fostered as parents become directly involved in all phases of their child's education. Thus parents can play a role in determining purposes and objectives for schooling and in evaluating the consequences of schooling. Parents can also work hand-in-hand with teachers as volunteers in the classroom. Parents can assist their own children in learning. Such activities will not only improve communication, but may lead to greater congruence between the school and the home regarding values, goals, and methods of education. Also,

[38]Pifer, p. 11.

school environments need to be related to work environments. Programs described in Chapter 5 as illustrative of social problem/activities curriculum design show how this may be done.

Family

The American family, as indicated in the previous section, is undergoing sweeping changes. The greatest change has been the increase in the number of mothers of children under 18 working outside the home—from 9 percent in 1940 to almost 50 percent by 1976.[39] An increase in divorce rate has resulted in one child out of six living in a single-parent family, almost double the percentage in 1950. As a consequence, children have less meaningful contact with adults. Working is competing with the raising of children.

Featherstone pointed out, however, that "the family in some form continues to be the paramount institution for child rearing. Despite the rising divorce rate, 98 percent of American children are in some form of family setting."[40] For the benefit of society, other educational institutions should work with the family to strengthen it. Effective ties between schools and the home are particularly important.[41] These ties can be strengthened as teachers and curriculum planners become familiar with family and home conditions of students, and become aware of such things as: socioeconomic status of the family; occupations, composition, and status of the family; educational level of parents; cultural and intellectual climate; community activities; and emotional climate.

We urge thoughtful and professional utilization of these data. For teachers to categorize (or stigmatize) learners on the basis of information about their homes is to limit both the learners' and the teachers' own horizons unnecessarily. Families in our society need neither pity nor condemnation; they need help that comes from professionals who care and are willing to share in the task of developing healthy personalities in healthy families.

Peers

Peer groups become more influential as children and youth have fewer meaningful experiences with adults. During all but the earliest years of life

[39]Lewis, et al., p. 11.
[40]Joseph Featherstone, "Family Matters," *Harvard Educational Review, 48* (February 1979): 23.
[41]The following books regarding the family are recommended: Mary Jo Bane, *Here to Stay* (New York: Basic Books, 1979); Advisory Committee on Child Development of the National Research Council, *Toward a National Policy for Children and Families* (Washington, D.C.: National Academy of Sciences, 1976); Kenneth Keniston, *All Our Children* (New York: Harcourt, Brace, Jovanovich, 1977).

the peer group is an important source of influence and support. Next to parents, peer groups exert the most influence for most children, with schools following. The peer group contributes to school attitudes, achievement, and self-concept in childhood and to social development in adolescence. Peer groups exert pressure on their members toward conformity that can either support or block change.

Dunphy suggested that the family offers only a limited set of roles for the child to experience.[42] Peer groups, however, provide an opportunity for the child to participate in a broader range of roles. Childhood groups carry over into small and cohesive unisex cliques in adolescence. Numbers of cliques may organize into heterosexual crowds.

Educators recognize that peer groups can either encourage or discourage educational achievement among their members. When the shared values of the peer group are consistent with those of society and of the school, they can be a powerful socializing force. Often, however, their shared values do not support institutional and societal goals. In either event, peer groups will have a powerful effect on learners and educators need to be aware of the nature of peer groups among learners.

Community

The community played an important educational role in nineteenth-century America. Values taught in the home and in religious organizations were supported by the community. Children and youth learned occupations from parents or other adults in the community. However, communities lost much of their educational influence as they became larger, more heterogenous, and less cohesive.

Communities are regaining some of their educational programs; however, curriculum planners must be aware of the changing nature of communities and the new definitions of communities arising from new patterns of social interaction. For example, busing is creating extended, nongeographical communities; ethnic identity and religious affiliations establish additional community patterns. Government-related agencies such as museums, libraries, and arts-and-crafts centers conduct educational programs. Private industry spends over four billion dollars a year on education for their employees and families. In 1978 the military spent 5.8 billion dollars on training. National voluntary agencies offer educational programs—for example, Boy Scouts, Girl Scouts, Campfire Girls, 4-H Clubs, and Red Cross. Religious organizations offer educational programs. Any number of skills can be learned through private lessons—from swimming and horseback riding to ballet and piano.

There are varied opportunities for learning within most communities.

---

[42]D. Dunphy, "The Social Structure of Urban Adolescent Peer Groups," *Sociometry, 26* (1963): 230–246.

Curriculum planners need to have information regarding these programs. With such a knowledge, curriculum planners can improve educational programs in any one of three ways:

1. Recognize total educational experiences of learners in planning their curriculum.
2. Utilize other educational agencies in planning a community-based educational program for a group of learners.[43]
3. Cooperate with other educational agencies in developing a coordinated community-wide plan for education.

Mass Communication

The time-honored concept of the school as the center of a learner's educational experience may be changing. Today children and youth are immersed in an alternative and a highly competitive "educational system" including films, television, radio, pop music, and comic books. As meaningful contacts with adults in the home decreased, mass media, particularly radio and television, filled some of the empty hours.

Television is found in 97 percent of the homes in the United States. "Children from ages 2 to 11 average almost 26 hours of television per week and adolescents from ages 12 to 27 average 22 hours."[44] Estimates of the total hours of television watched by children in the United States by the time they complete high school vary from 15,000 to 20,000, compared to 11,000 to 12,000 hours spent in the classroom.

There are several reasons for television's popularity. Television asks nothing of the viewer except visual and auditory attention. The programming requires no thought or skills from the viewer. Television provides interesting visual images accompanied by music, dialogue, story lines, and attractive people. Furthermore, it allows the viewer to participate vicariously in numerous activities.[45] No wonder classroom teachers find television a stiff competitor for children's attention.

Television is influential—witness an expenditure of over 6.5 billion dollars in 1976 for television commercials. Because television is persuasive and since it is value laden, "it is under constant scrutiny by those who see values challenged, moral and ethical systems degraded, and children subjected to excessive crime, violence, sex and tasteless as well as sometimes false advertising."[46] Research evidence gives credence to some of these

[43]See, for example, Barbara M. Shoup, *Living and Learning for Credit* (Bloomington, Indiana: Phi Delta Kappa, 1979).
[44]Lewis, et al. p. 14.
[45]Neal J. Gordon, "Television and Learning," in Herbert J. Walberg (ed.), *Educational Environment and Effects* (Berkeley, Calif.: McCutchan Publishing Corporation, 1979), pp. 57–59 passim.
[46]Lewis, et al., pp. 14, 15.

concerns. Gordon discovered, after viewing a number of studies, "that television aggression leads either to an increased proclivity toward violence, a greater tolerance of violence, or a slower reaction toward violence.[47]

Regardless of its possible weaknesses, television provides an educational environment. Curriculum planners need to be aware of the types of programs viewed by learners. This may enable them to devise learning experiences to improve learners viewing skills. Curriculum planners may wish to incorporate some of the better television programs into their plans. Improved videotaping equipment makes television more accessible for classroom use.

Computers may join books, magazines, films, and television as means of mass communication. Advances in electronic technology may make personal, notebook-sized computers available for less than one hundred dollars by the end of the 1980s. Microcomputer hardware and educational programs already have a large home market. Will computers in the home join television in competing for children's attention? The educational uses of computers are discussed in Chapter 8.

This section has shown how the children and youth we teach are molded and shaped by their environment. Today's environment is radically different from the one encountered by learners just 30 years ago. A knowledge of this emerging society helps curriculum planners understand the influence of the environment on learners.

Society and Functions of Education

Dewey considered education to depend on two interacting factors—the learner and the social and cultural milieu in which the education is being provided. The two factors are equally significant and are always present in any learning situation. In fact, it is impossible to plan and carry out an educational program without giving the fullest consideration to both the characteristics of the students to be educated and the nature of the society which establishes the schools.

Schools have been established historically by a social group to serve these functions:

1. Transmit the culture.
2. Contribute to the socialization of the young.
3. Aid in the preservation of the society as a nation.
4. Contribute to the preparation of the young for adulthood.
5. Assist in the personal development of the young members of the society.

Obviously these functions are not clear-cut, discrete categories of purposes served by the schools; they intertwine and are complementary,

[47]Gordon, p. 61.

perhaps even reciprocal, aspects of the total process of growing up in a society. But they do constitute major points of emphasis, controlling approaches to curriculum development and program planning and constituting varying patterns of design in the fabric of education. Moreover, educators must recognize that a school must serve adequately and appropriately those functions deemed essential and highly desirable by the citizens who exercise political control over the local school systems by the vote and other means or these persons will force changes in the school's staff, policies, curriculum, and program of instruction.

The general functions of education are discussed in more detail in Chapter 4 and ways in which all educational agencies can work for their achievement are explored.

The nature of a given society influences the functions assigned to educational institutions and how they are achieved. For example, the choice of culture to be transmitted and the method of transmission are greatly influenced by the family, peer group, community, and mass-communication media. Data regarding these aspects of society—work and leisure, environment and energy, technology, and values—follow.

Work and Leisure

Work is a basic source of meaning for citizens. Even the hard-core unemployed seem to associate self-esteem with work. In one survey of unemployed, 84 percent answered they would work even if they could live comfortably without it.[48]

The world of work is changing:

1. Participation of women in the work force has increased steadily since 1950.
2. Percentage of jobs in the service industries has increased while those in manufacturing has decreased.
3. Major growth is anticipated in jobs related to the processing and storage of information.
4. Many children in elementary schools today will hold midcareer jobs that have not been thought of as yet.
5. Leisure time will be increased.

Curriculum planning at all levels of education provides for some type of vocational preparation—this may be general preparation or specific occupational training. Hence data are needed regarding the nature and character of career opportunities, potentialities for particular types of occupations, and interests and needs of individual students. Table 3.2 suggests the kinds of information needed.

[48]H. R. Kaplan and C. Tausky, "Work and the Welfare Cadillac: The Functions of and Commitment to Work Among the Hard-Core Unemployed," *Social Problems 19* (Spring 1972): 475.

TABLE 3.2 Kinds of Information Needed about Career Potentialities

Item	Possible Sources	Suggested Uses
Career plans: extent of continuation in college and other postsecondary institutions; current career choices and plans; career patterns of graduates; mobility among young persons; occupational patterns in the community; occupational trends, locally and nationally; opportunities for career education in the community or area; situation among minority groups in postsecondary schooling and occupational opportunities.	Follow-up studies of graduates; guidance records; conferences; census data by tracts; Department of Labor studies for U.S. and local and/or state on occupations, manpower needs, employment trends, occupational outlook.	Courses to be offered; cooperative work-study programs; guidance programs; providing postsecondary opportunities for occupational preparation; establishing close working relations with collegiate institutions; programs to provide scholarships and special opportunities for members of minority groups.

Preparation enabling a person to find immediate employment fulfills only a portion of education's responsibility. It is no longer possible for one educational program to give a person all the skills he or she will need throughout a career. A fundamental part of work preparation, therefore, is to give individuals the skills and attitudes that will enable them to continue their learning as they undertake retraining.

Educational institutions need to help individuals select and participate in activities that will give meaning to their increased leisure time. Such activities would include discovering and enjoying music, art, literature, photography, and sports as well as enjoying and preserving the natural environs. The pursuit of further education is a worthwhile use of leisure time for many citizens.

Environment and Energy

The related problems of securing enough energy and protecting our environment are major societal concerns. Education will play a major role in finding and applying solutions to these problems. The solutions found will have, in turn, an impact on education.

Energy, environment, and life style are closely interrelated. An optimum relationship can be maintained when a three-cornered dynamic equilibrium exists among energy conservation, transmission, and use at one point, a rational program for protecting and conserving the environment at a second point, with the triangle completed through the maintenance of a stable and economic system.[49] Failure to maintain equilibrium among these three points can result in a collapse of the triangle—and of society.

Facts on energy and environment are easy to find; agreement on the

[49]Lewis, et al., p. 50.

facts is hard to come by. It is generally recognized, however, that the supply of gas and oil is finite—whether it will last for 20 or 200 years is subject to debate. It is agreed that as energy becomes scarcer, the energy required to secure any additional energy increases; thus the net energy gained decreases. Most authorities agree that the solutions to our energy problems will require finding new sources of energy and reducing our energy needs by changing our life styles.

Major educational programs are needed to make citizens aware and knowledgable about energy and environmental problems. Transmitting information alone may not produce the needed attitude changes; educational programs are needed to change attitudes. Programs will use a variety of materials and experiences and be interdisciplinary in nature. These programs should be conducted by various community educational agencies—not just the schools.

Technology

Rapid advances in technology, particularly computer and telecommunication technology, have changed the United States from an industrial to a postindustrial society. Bell described a postindustrial society as having two major characteristics: "the centrality of theoretical knowledge and the expansion of the service sector as against a manufacturing economy."[50] In this postindustrial society, collecting, storing, processing, and exchanging information plays a key role. There is an increasing dependence on science as the means of innovating and organizing technological change.

Masuda proposed that we are in the midst of an information revolution, based on computers and telecommunications, that "will have a far more decisive impact on human society than the 'power' revolution resulting from the invention of steam engines."[51] Computers hold great potential for automation and knowledge creation. However, they also pose the threat of a computer-managed society in which "ruling elites would guide the 'managed' (persons and things) using information networks as control mechanisms."[52] Masuda described such a society as inhuman or alienated from humanity. "A completely automated state would be an intellectual ice age."[53] There are a number of alarming indications that we are moving in this direction. For example, the development of integrated computer systems makes possible the assembling of quantities of data on an individ-

[50]Daniel Bell, *The Coming of Post-Industrial Society*, 2nd ed. (New York: Basic Books, Inc., 1976), p. xix.
[51]Yoneji Musuda,"Automated State vs. Computopia: Unavoidable Alternatives for the Information Era," in Andrew A. Spekke (ed.), *The Next 25 Years: Crisis and Opportunity* (Washington, D.C.: World Future Society, 1975), p. 360.
[52]Masuda, p. 364.
[53]Masuda, p. 364.

ual including: income tax return, credit card transactions, trips by airlines, medical examiniations for life insurance policies, and miscellaneous information gathered by private investigators.

Values

One function of educational institutions is to transmit the culture. The values held within a society influence decisions regarding aspects of the cultural heritage to be transmitted. Political, economic, moral-ethical, and social values all influence what is in the curriculum and how it is taught.[54]

Rapid technological and social changes, some of which have been described above, have produced a lack of consensus in values—even within a local community. Thus a major and difficult task for curriculum planners is to identify varying values held by the community. Unfortunately, the verbal and nonverbal signals are not always consistent. For example, a state law may require educators to teach "the evil effects of alcohol" to students who see alcohol advertised in the popular magazines and portrayed on television as a way to improve personal relationships and solve problems.

Curriculum planners need to attend to the fundamental values held within the total society and to values and mores within the local community. Table 3.3 describes the nature of the information needed, possible sources, and suggested uses.

Armed with data collected from sources, such as those suggested in Table 3.3, the curriculum planner decides how national and local values should affect the curriculum. Note that this decision is based on values. Wise curriculum planners work with citizens' groups in considering values and the curriculum.

Educational institutions transmit values through planned instruction as well as through what is rewarded and punished.[55] The messages do not always agree. For example, schools teach students to value knowledge and test them on the recall of facts.

Many educational institutions have greater freedom to teach values than do schools. For example, since religious groups have a relatively homogeneous clientele, they can teach moral and ethical values. Schools, however, find it difficult to transmit values directly on account of cultural heterogeneity and lack of consensus.

Many of the dilemmas facing society can be resolved only through the application of values. Educational institutions, especially schools, would be abandoning their responsibility if they attempted to be value free. This

[54]For an analysis of these values as they pertain to education see Lewis, et al., pp. 64, 65.
[55]For information on the teaching of values see R. Freeman Butts, Donald H. Peckenpaugh, Howard Kirschenbaum, *The School's Role as Moral Authority* (Washington, D.C.: Association for Supervision and Curriculum Development, 1977).

TABLE 3.3 Kinds of Information Needed about the Values
of the Culture and the Social Group

Item	Possible Sources	Suggested Uses
1. Values: the fundamental values of the people as a nation; basic tenets of democracy; the essence of our cultural ethos.	Great documents of the American people; writings of scholars, statesmen, interpreters of the American scene; U.S. Supreme Court decisions; literature, drama, essays; writings of journalists and columnists; TV programs that interpret American thought and actions.	Constitute basic elements in program planning, including organizational and administrative arrangements, curriculum, school policies and regulations; nature and character of discipline; plans for desegregation; implementation of concept of equality; selection of staff members; defining goals and objectives.
2. Values of a less basic nature: the mores and traditions of the citizens of the local school district and of subgroups within the community; evidence on pluralism in values; diverse points of view on morality; evidence of anomie, despair, lack of commitment or faith in American beliefs; factors in alienation of youth.	Opinion polls; community surveys; editorials in local news media; selection of news and "slanting" in local press; city ordinances on liquor, pornography, amusements; views of political leaders and office holders; activities and views of local civic, patriotic, educational, and political action groups; "ear-to-the-ground" listening; shrewd observations.	Same as above; in addition: providing opportunities for students to express and state views on values, mores, traditions.

does not mean they should practice indoctrination, however. "Education will be most effective if it can help learners develop and clarify their own beliefs and values . . . less effective when it attempts to inculcate a predetermined set of beliefs and values."[56]

DATA ABOUT KNOWLEDGE

Information about the learner, society, and knowledge may be likened to the legs of a three-cornered stool supporting curriculum planning. If one of these legs is too long—or too short—curriculum planning loses its balance. Chapter 1 provides a description of the relative emphasis given to each of these bases over the past 100 years.

The "back-to-basics" move beginning in the middle 1970s placed a greater emphasis on meeting societal needs at the expense of providing knowledge. "Functional literacy," the goal of the "back-to-basics" move, stressed the ability to use reading and computation in life situations. For

[56]Lewis, et al., p. 65.

example, competency examinations required for high school graduation tested students' ability to read and complete a job application and balance a checkbook. The ability to recognize and analyze great literature or to write acceptable prose was not tested. It may be noted that the "back-to-basics" drive was coincident with an antiintellectual, populist move in American society.

The technological changes described earlier require a new and probably different emphasis on knowledge in the curriculum. Throughout this book there is an emphasis on a community-wide approach to education. However, we view formal educational institutions with highly qualified teachers as central to the provision of knowledge. Children can learn to read and compute in any one of several settings, for example, from reasonably intelligent parents and/or from computer programs. However, a teacher with a thorough grasp of the subject is required to help a learner understand the concepts that underlie a discipline such as physics. This is not a plea to return to business as usual in a traditional subject-centered approach to education. The material that follows shows that new developments in knowledge may require new approaches to curriculum planning and teaching.

New Developments in the Nature of Knowledge

The amount of knowledge[57] available has grown exponentially rather than linearly. Thus, the more knowledge available the faster it grows, and there is no end in sight. For example, the number of scientific journals has been doubling approximately once every 15 years. The nineteenth-century concept of science was one of a bounded or exhaustible field of knowledge whose dimensions would eventually be filled in. Now, however, "we assume an openness to knowledge which is marked by variegated forms of differentiation."[58] This differentiation is well illustrated by the publication *Encyclopedia Britannica*. From its inception in 1745 until the 1785 edition it was assembled by one or two men who encompassed the knowledge of the world. In 1785, consultants were used for the first time; for the 1965 edition over 10,000 consultants worked on the Encyclopedia.

Knowledge and a Technological Age

Knowledge plays a central role within the new dimensions of the postindustrial society as described by Bell.[59]

---

[57]We use Bell's definition of knowledge as "a set of organized statements of facts or ideas, presenting a reasoned judgment or an experimental result, which is transmitted to others through some communication medium in some systematic form." Bell, p. 175.
[58]Bell, p. 186.
[59]Bell, pp. xvi–xviii passim.

1. Centrality of theoretical knowledge. Every society has existed on the basis of knowledge, but only now is codification of theoretical knowledge the basis of innovations in technology.
2. Spread of a knowledge class. The fastest growing group in society is the technical and professional class.
3. Change from goods to services. The new services will be primarily human services and professional and technical services.
4. Change in the basis for merit. Awards will be based more on education and skill and less on inheritance or property.
5. Economics of information. For the optimal social investment in knowledge, we have to follow a "cooperative" strategy in order to increase the spread and use of knowledge in society.

Will educational programs, as they are now organized, enable society to support the "centrality of theoretical knowledge"? How can educational institutions foster a cooperative strategy in the spread and use of knowledge?

Storing and Processing Information

The procedures used in storing and processing information depend upon the technology available. Before writing was developed, humans stored information in their memory and transmitted it orally from generation to generation. Writing, and later print, opened up far more effective means for recording information and transmitting it to others. Electronic technology triggered a quantum leap in the storage and transmitting of information. For example, it is possible to store all of the content of 300 books of 250 pages each on one video disc. The developer of the PLATO computer system estimates that by 1985 he can place all of the information in the entire University of Illinois library in a computer-accessible one-inch cube.

Fortunately, the remarkable capacity to store massive information is accompanied by an equally remarkable capability to retrieve it. Computers can be programmed to search through vast amounts of information in milliseconds. Further, the linking of telecommunications and computers makes it possible in search through data banks in different geographic locations.

Information in a book is available to those who have the book provided they can read it. Computer-stored information is available to those with the computer hardware and software, if they know how to access information from a computer—that is, if they have computer literacy.

Knowledge and Curriculum Planning

Does computer capability for storing and processing information make the acquisition of knowledge obsolete? Definitely not; but there are implications for what should be studied and how it is to be studied. The question, What shall be taught? is not new; but the answer may be.

One clue to the answer may be deduced from Whitehead's definition of education as "the acquisition of the art of the utilization of knowledge."[60] In addition to having knowledge that could be utilized, Whitehead emphasized that learners need to develop an "appreciation of the structure of ideas" and the need to see "the bearing of one set of ideas on another."[61] Whitehead reversed the old proverb about the difficulty of seeing the wood (forest) because of the trees and said, "The problem of education is to make the pupil see the wood by means of the trees."[62]

A Map of Knowledge

Curriculum planning that enables learners to see the forest, and not just the trees, is based on some map of knowledge. A familiar way to map knowledge is through the use of scholarly disciplines defined as organized fields of inquiry, pursued by particular groups of specialists. Foshay viewed a discipline as "a way of making knowledge." He said that a discipline may be characterized "by the phenomena it purports to deal with, its domain; by the rules it uses for asserting generalizations as truth; and by its history."[63] A discipline has substance, method(s) of inquiry, and a history.

Phenix developed an alternative map of knowledge by categorizing disciplines into six "realms of meaning": *Symbolics* (ordinary language, mathematics, nondiscursive symbolic forms); *Empirics* (physical science, biology, psychology, social science); *Esthetics* (music, the visual arts, the arts of movement, literature); *Synnoetics* (personal knowledge); *Ethics* (moral knowledge); and *Synoptics* (history, religion, philosophy).[64] Descriptions of these realms of meaning provide a useful guide for curriculum planners.[65] One type of map of the cognitive field widely used by curriculum planners is Bloom's taxonomy.[66] This taxonomy is discussed in Chapter 4.

Selection of Content

The information explosion makes it difficult to select the most important content. Clearly there is no time to waste on useless content or on the

[60]Alfred North Whitehead, *The Aims of Education* (New York: Mentor Books, 1929), p. 16.
[61]Whitehead, p. 23.
[62]Whitehead, p. 18.
[63]Arthur W. Foshay, "A Modest Proposal," *Educational Leadership, 18* (May 1961): 511.
[64]Philip H. Phenix, *Realms of Meaning* (New York: McGraw-Hill Book Company, 1964).
[65]For an alternative map of knowledge see Paul H. Hirst, *Knowledge and the Curriculum* (London: Routledge and Kegan Paul, Ltd., 1974).
[66]Benjamin S. Bloom, *Taxonomy of Educational Objectives: Cognitive Domain* (New York: David McKay Co., 1965).

memorization of subject matter that can easily be retrieved. The following guidelines may assist curriculum planners as they choose from the various disciplines the content for general education.

1. Content should illustrate and clarify the representative ideas of a discipline—in Whitehead's terms, it should help the pupil see the wood by means of the trees.
2. Content should give students an understanding of the fundamental structure of the discipline.
3. Content should exemplify the methods of inquiry used in the discipline.
4. Concepts and principles selected should provide the broadest and most comprehensive view of the world.
5. Balance should be maintained between content that is rigorous and deep and content that is practical and immediate.
6. Content should appeal to the imagination of students—hard enough to be challenging yet within the students' grasp.

Content selected according to these guidelines provides a general education base. Students with particular interests will specialize in one discipline, or eventually, in a subspeciality within the discipline. Their purpose extends beyond understanding the structure and methods of inquiry of the discipline; they aim, ultimately, to produce new knowledge.

Curriculum planners should remember that these guidelines relate only to the selection of content in relation to knowledge. The other data bases discussed earlier in this chapter also need to be considered in planning the curriculum: the nature of learners and the nature of society.

Selection of Methods

Communications technology vastly simplifies acquiring, storing, and retrieving information vital to scientific inquiry. This frees people to do more of what they, and only they can do—think. As a consequence the ability to synthesize and apply knowledge takes on greater worth. An understanding of structure and the ability to generate new knowledge in a discipline will be increasingly valuable. Teaching methods should be selected to reflect this shift.

Typically methods of teaching subject matter have focused on helping learners to acquire and retain information. Teachers have developed the curriculum by listing the facts and the interpretations they wanted students to learn. The material is presented through lectures, films, books, filmstrips, and so on. The students are then tested on their ability to recall the facts and interpretations. A different approach is needed if we are to teach students to think.

Teaching requires the ability to use reason in analyzing and synthesizing information in order to make generalizations. When intuition is added to this process, new ideas may be born. Computers cannot process information in these ways; but humans can if they are helped to learn how. To achieve this goal, Bruner advocated a discovery method of teaching. He described one arithmetic project team that devised methods "which permit a student to discover for himself the generalization that lies behind a particular mathematical operation." He contrasted this with "the method of 'assertion and proof' in which the generalization is first stated by the teacher and the class asked to proceed to the proof."[67] This "discovery method" influenced a number of national science curriculum projects, particularly in mathematics and science.

Foshay described the use of a discovery approach in teaching history.[68] Since history is a disciplined way of confronting the past, learners would be asked to consider the kind of data they would need to reconstruct a period in history; given these data they would be asked to draw conclusions and make generalizations. Foshay's method would convert learners into "producers of knowledge, not mere passive consumers." France has produced this type of material required for this method of teaching history. An album "Documents of the History of France" has been assembled. This album "is put into the hands of the student in the lycée who is directed to do no less than to rediscover French history from the primary sources on which it is based."[69]

Although this method was advocated twenty years ago, it is used in few classrooms. One reason is because it is more demanding on teachers. If learners are to "discover a discipline," their teacher needs to know how the discipline is structured and what method of inquiry can be used. It is difficult to arrange materials and learning experiences that will enable learners to discover generalizations. Another reason for avoidance of the discovery method is that most curriculum planners believe that far more subject matter needs to be "covered" than can be learned through the discovery approach. ("Imagine," they might say, "how long it would take a student to write the history of France"!) This argument needs careful consideration. Clearly, more subject matter can be covered with a traditional approach than by a discovery method. However, the quality of learning in the discovery approach may more than compensate for less content. The test will be in the learner's ability to process, organize, and utilize information. Nevertheless, some balance needs to be worked out between presenting generalizations to learners and having them discover the generalizations.

Applications to curriculum development and teaching from the emerging field of cognitive science may improve the effectiveness of teaching subject matter.[70] The field of cognitive science brings together people

[67]Jerome Bruner, *The Process of Education* (Cambridge, Mass.: Harvard University Press, 1960), p. 21.
[68]Foshay, pp. 511, 512 passim.
[69]Foshay, p. 515.
[70]George J. Posner, "Tools for Curriculum Research and Development: Potential Contributions from Cognitive Science," *Curriculum Inquiry, 8* (1978): 311–340.

working in cognitive psychology, artificial intelligence, and linguistics. "The aim of these researchers is to understand what is involved in intelligent behavior. In particular, this extends to an understanding of how knowledge is organized to permit storage, retrieval, and utilization of knowledge."[71] From the curriculum planners' perspective, one of the most significant aspects of human information processing is long-term memory where people store everything they know. Cognitive science is posited on the assumption that long-term memory consists of schemata, that is "data structures for representing the generic concepts in memory."

This idea of a patterning of elements in the mind is not new; it goes back to the work of such psychologists as Piaget, Bruner, and Ausubel. "Most cognitive psychologists believe that what we know and how our knowledge is organized (that is, schemata) are primarily determinants of what we perceive, what we can do, and how we think."[72] What is new is that recent developments in cognitive science have increased the "precision with which we are now able to specify the cognitive structures and processes required to perform tasks."[73]

A representational system for information stored in the long-term memory is made up of semantic networks. This system is of particular interest to curriculum planners since these networks show the interrelated structure of concepts. Posner described possible uses of semantic networks in analyzing a discipline, specifying learning outcomes, analyzing content of instructional materials, and evaluating student learning.[74] Much work remains in developing applications of cognitive science to curriculum. However, the possibility of analyzing knowledge, by means of semantic networks holds promise.

EXTERNAL FORCES

In addition to the various legal and extralegal factors described in Chapters 1 and 2, two other types of external forces influence curriculum decisions—research and professional knowledge.

Research

Information that can help in curriculum planning may be found in research publications; scholarly reports of commissions, agencies, and institutes; and the views and recommendations of recognized authorities on education and related areas.

[71]Posner, p. 312.
[72]Posner, p. 315.
[73]Posner, p. 315.
[74]Posner, pp. 323, 333. passim.

In recent years the federal government has allocated considerable sums of money to support research projects, task-force studies, investigations and studies by commissions, and innovations and experiments in education, as well as to disseminate the findings and recommendations of such undertakings. Nonprofit foundations, state governments, universities, and individuals have also contributed to the large volume of literature now available to planners.

The role of the federal government in curriculum development was described in Chapter 2. The federal government's major sponsorship of educational research activities began with the establishment of the first Research and Development centers in 1963 under the Cooperative Research Act. These centers carry on specialized research of a generally sophisticated nature on designated aspects of education. Usually a center works with cooperating schools in implementing new programs or new approaches to education that embody its research findings. Each center issues reports, newsletters, and similar literature on its activities.

In 1964 the Gardner Task Force recommended the expansion of regional R and D centers and educational labs. The passage of the Elementary and Secondary Education Act in 1965 resulted in the establishment of an additional 20 R and D centers and educational labs. By the end of 1966 there were 11 R and D centers and 19 educational labs. By 1968 this number began to decline until by the end of the decade of the 1970s there remained nine R and D centers and eight educational labs.

Since its founding in 1972, the National Institute of Education (NIE) has absorbed under its authority many of the research, development, and dissemination activities previously carried on by the U.S. Office of Education. For example, R and D centers and labs are financed through NIE. In establishing NIE, Congress declared that "the federal government has a clear responsibility to provide leadership in the conduct and support of scientific inquiry into the educational process."[75] The act assigned these responsibilities to the NIE:

1. Helping to solve or alleviate the problems of and achieve the objectives of American education.
2. Advancing the practice of education as an art, science, and profession.
3. Strengthening the scientific and technological foundations of education.
4. Building an effective educational research and development system.

In the late 1970s, NIE deemphasized improving instruction through materials development. In 1977 NIE gave top priority to sponsoring the conduct, syntheses, and dissemination of applied research on issues of

[75]"Educational Amendments of 1972," Public Law 92–318, 92nd Congress, S. 659 (June 23, 1972), Title III.

curriculum and instruction. The development of new instructional programs received lowest priority.

A major source of information on student performance is the National Assessment of Educational Progress (NAEP). Since 1969 NAEP has tested individuals selected from four age groups—9, 13, 17, and 26.[76] By using scientifically selected samples, NAEP has gathered census-like information about levels of achievement in science, citizenship, writing, reading, literature, music, social studies, and consumer skills. The assessment is based on ability to perform tasks. For example, in the music assessment, exercises were used to determine what proportion of the population could follow the score while listening to a piece of music. Repetition of the tests in cycles makes it possible to compare progress over a period of years. It is also possible to examine results in relation to such factors as sex, color, type of community, region of the United States, and level of education of parents.[77] NAEP operates with federal funds, through NIE, and is conducted by the Education Commission of the States.

A research dissemination activity of particular interest to curriculum planners is NIE's sponsorship of the Educational Research Information Center (ERIC) which is concerned with the dissemination aspect of the federal research program in education. The national center publishes monthly, with an annual compilation, an index to educational research and scholarly publications. Entitled *Resources in Education,* it is available on a subscription basis from the Government Printing Office. This publication is the best listing in this country of educational research and scholarly kinds of information; it is well indexed by title, subject, and author, and each item is briefly annotated. The U.S. Office of Education makes available for purchase film copies or printouts of each of these reports. Recent issues have included curriculum guides put out by school systems, state education departments, and other agencies, with brief annotations on each.

Moreover, ERIC has established a number of research clearinghouses, each one responsible for a specific area of education. The clearinghouse collects research reports and other useful publications, sees that they are listed in *Resources in Education,* and often publishes bulletins that report on developments in its areas. Educators may write directly to each clearinghouse for information about its services and publications.[78] ERIC publishes *Current Index to Journals in Education* (CIJE), a monthly guide to periodical literature, with coverage of more than 700 educational and

[76]For information on NAEP and results of assessment see Simon S. Johnson, *Update on Education* (Denver, Colo.: The Education Commission of the States, 1975).

[77]For assessment results write to National Assessment of Educational Progress, Suite 700, 1860 Lincoln Street, Denver, Colorado, 80203.

[78]For a listing of clearinghouses, together with complete directions on the use of ERIC, see the pamphlet "How to Use ERIC" (Washington, D.C.: The National Institute of Education, no date).

education-related publications. ERIC materials are on computers with on-line access through six different software systems.

ERIC provides a vast amount of information and the system is used extensively (in one year almost 10 million persons used ERIC products and services). As might be anticipated in any operation as vast and diverse as the ERIC system, the material stored is uneven in quality. However, when used with discretion it is a valuable source of information on research.

Professional journals are a major source of research information for curriculum planners. Three publications of the American Educational Research Association (AERA) are cited here because of their general usefulness in reporting research. The *Review of Educational Research* contains authoritative reviews of scholarly research related to a particular topic. For example, the review of "Research on Curriculum and Instruction Implementation" is cited frequently in Chapter 2.[79] The reviewers synthesized the research findings and developed some hypotheses worthy of testing. The AERA publication, *Educational Researcher* contains frequent articles related to curriculum planning by leading researchers.[80] A third AERA publication, *American Educational Research Journal,* contains reports of individual research studies.[81] Many other scholarly journals, often associated with particular subject fields, publish research studies.[82]

Professional Knowledge

Research studies provide one source of professional knowledge for curriculum planners; knowledge can also be gained by reading accounts of good practice, visiting other educational centers, and consulting with experts in education. Behavioral sciences provide another source of knowledge. This section describes the types of knowledge that may be obtained from four behavioral sciences: political science, anthropology, sociology, and psychology; and suggests possible sources of information.

Political Science

Many educational institutions, especially public schools, colleges, and universities, are subject to political control and direction; they are instruments of social groups, and the groups collectively exercise their control

---

[79]Michael Fullan and Alan Pomfret, "Research on Curriculum and Instruction Implementation," *Review of Educational Research, 47* (Spring 1977): 335–397.

[80]See, for example, Roger D. Gehlbach, "Individual Differences: Implications for Instructional Theory, Research and Innovation," *Educational Researcher, 8* (April 1979): 8–14.

[81]See, for example, Don Beeken and Henry L. Janzen, "Behavioral Mapping of Student Acitivity in Open-Area and Traditional Schools," *American Educational Research Journal, 15* (Fall, 1978): 507–517.

[82]For a ranking of leading journals see Terrence S. Luce and Dale M. Johnson, "Rating of Educational and Psychological Journals," *Educational Researcher, 7* (November 1978): 8–10.

through political action. Public schools are especially susceptible since decisions made by boards of education and the staffs must fall within legal structures that have been politically determined. Those who administer and staff the schools are inevitably engaged in the science or art of political government. It is especially important that curriculum planners recognize fully the political control of schools, for it must be a major consideration in decision-making. It is because they are political institutions that the schools today are being subjected to pressure from all sides. Lasswell defined politics as "who gets what, when, and how."[83] Since schools and universities use such a large share of public tax funds, they are affected by politics.

Political control of the schools imposes three important obligations on educators:

1. Know the constitution and laws to which schools are subject and the court decisions that interpret these instruments.
2. Understand the nature of the power structure and views, expectations, and demands of those who exercise power at all levels of government and the judiciary.
3. Determine a proper role for themselves in political action.

In the past the public strongly believed that teachers and administrators should not engage in overt political activity, especially of a partisan nature or that related directly to the operation of the schools. But this is obviously an undesirable, if not impossible, restraint. Who is in better position to seek quality in U.S. education than those who devote full time to the field? Educators must be advocates for schools; they must endeavor to influence political action, promoting desirable plans and programs and opposing undesirable ones. The situation in recent years with respect to accountability drives, desegregation, busing to alleviate segregation, providing equality in financial support for all children, and many other issues illustrates the necessity for educators, especially those with major responsibilities for planning, to engage in political action.

The National Society for the Study of Education yearbook, *The Politics of Education* provides a useful overview of the applications of political science to education.[84] The book, *A Systems Analysis of Political Life*, provides a model that can readily be applied to schools.[85] Books by Kim-

---

[83]Harold D. Lasswell, *Politics: Who Gets What, When, and How* (Cleveland, Oh.: Meridian Books, 1958), p. 187.
[84]Jay D. Scribner (ed.), *The Politics of Education*, The Seventy-sixth Yearbook of the National Society for the Study of Education (Chicago: University of Chicago Press, 1977).
[85]David Easton, *A Systems Analysis of Political Life* (New York: John Wiley and Sons, 1965).

brough and by Nunnery and Kimbrough provide guides to the study of community power structures and their influence on education.[86]

Anthropology

Educators recognize the usefulness of political science; however, uses of anthropology in designing educational programs are not generally understood. Anthropologists have studied change in a variety of settings. From their case studies[87] they "can state in quite precise behavioral language why apparent changes that arise from coercive pressure are in truth illusory; why involvement is a necessary condition of learning; why a custodial environment inhibits or destroys initiatory capacities; or why highly structured supervisory systems produce individual pathologies and low productivity."[88] Anthropologists have found that changes in education require changes in society, a principle that is often overlooked in practice.

Anthropologists recognize that "you cannot separate the consequence of experience as learning from the social setting in which it occurs."[89] A person becomes human within a social context and is a part of the whole. As a result of their systemic approach anthropologists provide valuable insights on such topics as:

Cultural conditions of learning
Cultural differentiation
Development of morals
Education as transmission of culture

Whereas psychology focuses on the behavior of individuals, anthropology is concerned with the behavior of individuals in groups and thus provides a useful perspective on education that takes place in groups. Anthropologists, from their study of human organizations, have shown that schools are "a deculturing influence that fosters alienation from the community."[90] Had findings from anthropological research influenced the formulation of schools, they would be quite different institutions and many of today's problems would have been avoided.

[86]Ralph B. Kimbrough, *Political Power and Educational Decision Making* (Chicago: Rand McNally and Co., 1964); Micael Y. Nunnery and Ralph B. Kimbrough, *Politics, Power, Polls, and School Elections* (Berkeley, Calif.: McCutchan Publishing Corp., 1971).
[87]For an illustration of such a case study see Elizabeth M. Eddy, "Educational Innovations and Desegregation: A Case Study of Symbolic Realignment," *Human Organization, 34* (Summer 1975): 163–172.
[88]Solon T. Kimball, *Culture and the Educative Process: An Anthropological Perspective* (New York: Teachers College Press, 1974), p. 275.
[89]Kimball, p. 276.
[90]Kimball, p. 277.

Kimball's book, *Culture and the Educative Process,* provides an overview of anthropology and specific applications to education. A book edited by Wax and colleagues, *Anthropological Perspectives on Education* also shows applications to education. Niehoff's book, *A Casebook of Social Change,* contains valuable insights on the change process. For an interesting anthropological case study on the induction of new teachers see Eddy's, *Becoming a Teacher.*[91]

Sociology

The aim of sociology is to provide relatively precise descriptive and explanatory categories for understanding the complicated phenomena of social behavior. The usefulness of data from this field of education has been recognized in recent years.[92] Many of the data presented in this chapter's section on "Data about Society" were drawn from sociological materials. Studies of the change process conducted by sociologists have influenced the research and literature on educational innovation.[93]

Sociological studies have examined social class influence on schools. Coleman and colleagues conducted the best known such study.[94] They concluded that the socioeconomic level of a student's school had more effect on his or her achievement than any other measureable factor except the socioeconomic level of the home. Coleman's data have been reworked and his conclusions challenged by other sociologists.[95]

Sociological research that has provided insights on the governance of schools includes studies of: federal influence in education, the school in its power environment, authority system of the school, and bureaucracy in education.[96] Sociologists have studied problems of interpersonal relationships by examining roles of personnel within a school and possible conflicts between and within these roles.

The National Society of Education (NSSE) Seventy-third Yearbook, *Uses*

[91]Murray L. Wax, Stanley Diamond, Fred O. Gearing (eds.), *Anthropological Perspectives on Education* (New York: Basis Books, Inc., 1971); Arthur Niehoff (ed.), *A Casebook of Social Change* (Chicago: Aldine Publishing Company, 1969); Elizabeth Eddy, *Becoming a Teacher* (New York: Teachers College Press, 1969).

[92]There is a Sociology of Education section in the American Sociological Association and AERA has established a Social Context of Education Division.

[93]Rogers and Shoemaker prepared a particularly useful summary of this research. Everett M. Rogers with F. Floyd Shoemaker, *Communication of Innovations: A Cross-Cultural Approach,* 2d ed. (New York: The Free Press, 1971).

[94]James S. Coleman, et al., *Equality of Educational Opportunity* (Washington, D.C.: U.S. Government Printing Office, 1966).

[95]See, for example, Christopher Jencks, et al., *Inequality: A Reassessment of the Effect of Family and Schooling in America* (New York: Harper & Row, 1972).

[96]For summaries of these and other sociological studies see C. Wayne Gordon (ed.), *Uses of the Sociology of Education,* The Seventy-third Yearbook of the National Society for the Study of Education (Chicago: University of Chicago Press, 1974).

of the Sociology of Education, presents a series of articles around four major topics: youth culture; equality of educational attainment; race/ethnic desegregation, integration, and decentralization; and the role of federal government in education.[97] The journal, *The Sociology of Education,* published by the Sociology of Education section of the American Sociological Association, contains useful papers and descriptions of research studies.

Psychology and Neurosciences

The field of psychology has made many contributions to curriculum planning and teaching. In fact, psychology played a leading role in shaping schools and profoundly influenced what happens within classrooms. Data regarding human development have come in large part from psychological studies. In addition, psychology has contributed ideas to a vast array of educational topics as diverse as motivation and self-concept. Of major interest to curriculum planners is the contribution of psychology to learning theory.

Learning Theory

The familiar stimulus-response (S-R) reinforcement model has been used by generations of teachers. In this model behavior is viewed as the association between stimuli and responses. Learning is represented in terms of the systematic changes in S-R associations that occur because of appropriate reinforcement, that is an event that strengthens responses.[98]

An outgrowth of S-R reinforcement learning theory, behavior modification,[99] is based on four ways in which behavior change may be brought about: 1) reorganizing the person's environment; 2) deliberately training new responses; 3) altering the person's repertoire of verbal controlling responses; 4) changing motivational conditions. One type of behavior modification, operant conditioning, emphasizes the role of specific consequences, or reinforcements, in altering the strength of a preceding response. Behavior modification is used by many teachers and serves as a basis for some commonly used curriculum designs. Behavior modificaion has its critics, some of whom challenge its philosophical assumptions.[100]

Cognitive field learning theory is concerned with meaningfully learned

[97]Gordon (ed.), *Uses of the Sociology of Education.*
[98]For a brief discussion of the S-R reinforcement model see Robert E. Silverman, "Using the S-R Reinforcement Model in the Classroom," in Elliott W. Eisner and Elizabeth Vallance (eds.), *Conflicting Conceptions of Curriculum* (Berkeley, Calif.: McCutchan Publishing Corp., 1974), pp. 64–69.
[99]For a comprehensive discussion of behavior modification see Carl E. Thoresen, (ed.), *Behavior Modification in Education,* The Seventy-second Yearbook of the National Society for the Study of Education (Chicago: University of Chicago Press, 1973).
[100]See, for example, Michael Scriven, "The Philosophy of Behavior Modification," in Thoresen (ed.), *Behavior Modification in Education,* pp. 422–445.

material.[101] Meaningful learning, according to cognitive psychologists, requires that new material be related to relevant aspects of existing cognitive structure, the resulting new meaning be reconciled with established knowledge, and be recorded in more familiar language. Note the relationship between this definition of meaningful learning and Piaget's explanation of the accommodation and assimilation of information. Concepts from the emerging field of cognitive science are consistent with cognitive-field learning theory.

Curriculum planners recognize that there is no right or wrong learning theory; each has strengths and weaknesses. Some curriculum planners make their selection of learning theory based on the nature of material to be learned. For example, an S-R reinforcement or behavior modification approach can be effective with rote learning and simple skill development, while cognitive learning theory will be effective with concept development.

Neurosciences and Education

The opening sentence in the book, *Education and the Brain,* is "The human brain is probably the most complexly organized matter in the universe."[102] Chapters in the book, written by researchers in biology, biopsychology, neurobiology, neurology, neuropsychology, psychology, educational psychology, and psychobiology convince the reader of the truth of this sentence. Furthermore, they provide information that can have a profound impact on curriculum planning and teaching.

Earlier conceptions of learning and learning theory were based on the behavior and performance of learners. Newer conceptions are emerging from studies of the brain and the processes involved in learning. "Learners are not passive recipients of (environmental) information given to them. They actively construct their own meanings from the information they are taught."[103] The human brain actively selects, transforms, organizes, and remembers information and through this process constructs models of the world. The pattern-detecting apparatus developed by the brain is the result of stimulation and experience.

A recent finding of particular interest to educators is that the cortical hemispheres of the brain characteristically organize and encode information in different ways. The left cortical hemisphere (in most people) "spe-

[101]See David P. Ausubel, Joseph D. Novak, Helen Hanesian, *Educational Psychology: A Cognitive View* (New York: Holt, Rinehart, and Winston, 1978).

[102]Timothy J. Teyler, "The Brain Sciences: An Introduction," in Jeanne S. Chall and Allan F. Mirsky (eds.), *Education and the Brain,* The Seventy-seventh Yearbook of the National Society for the Study of Education (Chicago: University of Chicago Press, 1978), p. 1.

[103]M. C. Wittrock, "Education and the Cognitive Processes of the Brain," in Chall and Mirsky (eds.), *Education and the Brain,* p. 64.

cializes somewhat in a propositional, analytic-sequential, time-oriented serial organization well adapted to learning and remembering verbal information." Reading, writing, and computation would be performed primarily by the left hemisphere. The right hemisphere specializes in an "appositional, synthetic-gestalt organization well adapted to processing information in which the parts acquire meaning through their relations with the other parts."[104] Perception and interpretation of paintings would be illustrative of activities performed by the right hemisphere.

Samples argued that education and culture have been biased against right-hemispheric thought.[105] He developed materials that would not only enhance the left-hemisphere functions, "but would invite into concert those magical qualities of the right hemisphere as well." He concluded, after years of testing and evaluating, that when "one invites *both* mind functions into equal partnership, three things characterize the learning ecology: 1) higher feelings of self-confidence, self-esteem, and compassion; 2) wider exploration of traditional content subjects and skills; 3) higher levels of creative invention in content and skills."[106] A realization that the "brain constructs meaning in at least two different ways, by imposing analytic and holistic organizations upon information,"[107] could lead to new and better organizational strategies in designing curriculum and sequencing instruction.

Individuals develop different ways of perceiving, conceptualizing, and organizing information. These cognitive styles may be associated with the relative importance of the hemispheres in learning—analytic-cognitive style associated with the left hemisphere and a global-cognitive style with the right. The curriculum and its implementation will be improved when it is based upon an understanding of the individual student's previous learning and cognitive strategies.

Further research will provide additional insights on how the brain processes and organizes information. Chall and Mirsky projected a future in which a series of tests administered by a team of specialists would enable educational neuroscientists to "perform an accurate assessment of the child's developmental stage, his particular strengths and weaknesses, the instructional materials he would best be able to handle, and the problem areas that would most likely be encountered during his educational career."[108] After painting this utopian picture, they added "it must be realized that it cannot be applied in the absence of that most effective and essential of all educational forces—able, patient, and caring teachers."[109]

[104]Wittrock, p. 65.
[105]Bob Samples, "Mind Cycles and Learning," *Phi Delta Kappan, 58* (May 1977): 688–692.
[106]Samples, pp. 689, 690.
[107]Wittrock, p. 100.
[108]Chall and Mirsky (eds.), *Education and the Brain*, p. 378.
[109]Chall and Mirsky (eds.), p. 378.

SUMMARY

An effective curriculum will be based on data about learners, society, and knowledge. This chapter presents summaries of recent developments in each of these areas. Sources of further information are also included. Curriculum planners will also be assisted by knowledge from various disciplines. This chapter provides summaries of the types of information to be obtained from political science, anthropology, sociology, and psychology and neuroscience. Even though legal restrictions provide constraints for curriculum planners, given the vast amount of data already available—and much more is to come—well-informed curriculum planners can design exciting and effective educational programs within the constraints.

A global (right-hemisphere) consideration of data presented in this chapter suggests an emerging frontier in curriculum development. The cyclical nature of the relative emphasis placed on learners, society, and knowledge as bases of the curriculum has been described. The emphasis on "functional" literacy has given societal needs the foremost position. The next swing in the cycle may be a return to a greater emphasis on knowledge. A chief motivation for this swing could be the increased importance of knowledge, reported in the description of a postindustrial society. However, there is not likely to be a return to the traditional teaching of subjects. New developments in cognitive science and in the study of the brain could lead to a new and much more profound transmittal of knowledge. This could be an exciting, revitalizing time for education and curriculum planners could play a key role in developing the new frontier.

The possibility of a shift in emphasis toward knowledge as a determinant illustrates the tendency to view each source of data—learners, society, bodies of knowledge—as a separate entity. Effective curriculum planning requires that data from all these sources be synthesized and used for curriculum decision-making. However, the kinds of information taken into account, the relative weight assigned to the information, and the conceptual scheme used in its synthesis depends upon the value orientation of the planners. Again, we see how curriculum planning starts and finishes with the value commitments of the planners.

ADDITIONAL SUGGESTIONS FOR FURTHER STUDY

Bachman, Jerold G., Patrick M. O'Malley, and Jerome Johnston, *Adolescence to Adulthood: Change and Stability in the Lives of Young Men.* Ann Arbor, Mich.: Institute for Social Research, 1978. Reports a longitudinal study of 2200 boys entering tenth grade in 1966. Data collected every two years (through 1974) are used to identify factors which precede and often influence educational and occupational attainment. A variety of dimensions of development are dealt with; for example, self-esteem, motives, affective states, values, views on social issues, job attitudes, delinquency, and drug use.

deLene, Richard H., *Small Futures: Children, Inequality, and the Limits of Liberal Reform.* New York: Harcourt Brace Jovanovich, 1979. This study, made under the aegis of the Carnegie Council on Children, is a profound as well as startling document on the nature and effects of inequality on children, and the shameful efforts, often misguided, this nation has made, in contrast to other highly developed countries, to eliminate such inequalities.

Lawrence, Gordon, *People Types & Tiger Stripes.* Gainesville, Fla.: Center for Applications of Psychological Type, Inc., 1979. A practical guide to using the Myers-Briggs Type Indicator in assessing a student's psychological type and using this information in planning curriculum and instruction.

Jencks, Christopher, and others, *Who Gets Ahead? The Determinants of Economic Success in America.* New York: Basic Books, Inc., 1979. In this new report Jencks and his associates have used a large body of new data and extensive analysis to "assess the impact of family background, cognitive skills, personality traits, years of schooling, and race on men's occupational status, earnings, and family income." The group concludes that "the best readily observable predictor of a young man's eventual status or earnings is the amount of schooling he has had."

Keniston, Kenneth and the Carnegie Council on Children, *All Our Children: The American Family under Pressure.* New York: Harcourt Brace Jovanovich, 1977. A report of a study of the relationship between the nature of contemporary American society and child development. Some of the anxieties, worries and obstacles that a changing society is creating for American parents and youth are described.

Longstreet, Wilma S., *Aspects of Ethnicity: Understanding Differences in Pluralistic Classrooms.* New York: Teachers College Press, 1978. Provides fresh, practical suggestions in the area of multicultural instruction by helping teachers and curriculum workers understand five interrelated aspects of ethnicity: verbal communication, nonverbal communication, orientation modes, intellectual modes, and social value patterns.

National Association of Secondary School Principals, *Student Learning Styles: Diagnosing and Prescribing Programs.* Reston, Va.: The Association, 1979. Several authors report research and practice in the identification of student learning styles and in the application of knowledge about learning styles to the individualization of education.

Postman, Neil, "The First Curriculum: Comparing School and Television," *Phi Delta Kappan, 61* (November 1979): 163–168. Compares the characteristics of the TV curriculum and the school curriculum, concluding that "the real pragmatic issue is not TV but its relationship to other systematic teachings in the information environment."

Report of the National Commission on Youth. *The Transition of Youth to Adulthood: A Bridge Too Long.* Boulder, Colo.: The Westview Press, 1979. The National Commission on Youth argues that a transition to adulthood made exclusively through the school is an environment rich in information but poor in maturing experiences. Service-learning activities—a social apprenticeship in a community-based setting—are described.

Swick, Kevin J., and R. Eleanor Duff, *Parenting.* What Research Says to the Teacher Series. Washington, D.C.: National Education Association of the United States, 1979. An all-too-brief but succinct and relevant summary of theory, practice, and research on the role of parents in the development of children. Includes descriptions of specific programs of parent education.

FOUR

■ ■ ■
DEFINING GOALS AND OBJECTIVES
■ ■

Armed with the types of data described in the previous chapter, the curriculum planner is ready to define goals and objectives (see Figure 1.1, p. 29). The importance of this step cannot be overemphasized since there are two ultimate tests of any educational program: 1) Does it achieve the broad purposes and general goals of education for which it was designed? and 2) Are the purposes and goals valid for those to be educated? Defining goals and objectives is an important creative task requiring the careful exercise of value judgments. The assistance of various individuals and groups is needed in clarifying philosophical positions and agreeing on values that will guide education.

This chapter describes how educational institutions are established to serve purposes within a society. Ways in which educational institutions can be structured and programs organized are discussed. Procedures for formulating purposes and general goals and for defining subgoals and instructional objectives are also considered.

EDUCATIONAL INSTITUTIONS AND THEIR PURPOSES

Human societies have, throughout time, possessed a common need to transmit their cultural heritage to oncoming generations. In our society this responsibility is shared, with schools and colleges being assigned a major share. Beyond schools and colleges, however, numerous individuals and institutions educate—parents, siblings, peer groups, adults, as well as such institutions as churches, synagogues, libraries, museums, and radio and television stations. Failure to recognize the multiplicity of educative individuals and institutions has led to placing inordinate responsibilities on schools and colleges—responsibilities they cannot always fulfill.

A basic assumption of this chapter, and of this book, is that individuals and institutions providing an educative influence should share in society's responsibility for education. Cremin said, "To be concerned solely with schools, given the educational world we are living in today, is to have a kind of fortress mentality in contending with a very fluid and dynamic situation." He added, "Education must be looked at whole, across the entire life span, and in all situations and institutions in which it occurs."[1]

This chapter presents a broadened planning base appropriate to an

[1]Lawrence A. Cremin, *Public Education* (New York: Basic Books, Inc. Publishers, 1976), p. 59.

holistic approach to education. Ideally, as a first step a community determines the purposes to be served by all of its educational institutions. Then, through comprehensive planning, responsibilities of each institution are agreed upon.

A society establishes and supports educational institutions for certain purposes; that is, it seeks to achieve certain ends or attain desired outcomes. Efforts to direct the experiences of learners, whether children or adults, constitute preferences for certain human ends and values. Education is a moral venture, one that necessitates choosing values among innumerable possibilities. Educators identifying purposes for an educational institution need to comprehend the nature of human growth and development, and understand the essential characteristics of society as it exists today and as it may become in the foreseeable future. Not only do institutions have purposes, teachers and students also have purposes.

Teachers Have Purposes

In curriculum planning we should recognize the role of the teacher in setting goals and objectives for the interactive processes that constitute the educational experiences of students. The teacher is actually the interpreter, the arbitrator, and the guide in the implementation of the purposes of the institution. Any formal statements of purpose must be translated into learning opportunities for students, and the guidance and development of such experiences is primarily a teacher's responsibility. Much attention is devoted to this matter throughout the book.

The teachers' own value systems, their views of the goals to be served by the school program, and their concepts of the nature and meaning of a stated goal, constitute the filter of meaning through which educational purposes are applied in planning. The teachers' own values, too, are the starting point for their own planning and for their whole approach to presenting learning opportunities in the classroom.

Students Have Purposes

Students have purposes when they engage in learning opportunities. The degree of congruence that exists among the purposes of the three parties in the educational process—the educational institution, the teachers, and the students—is a crucial matter. The overwhelming assumption in schools, historically and currently, is that a high degree of uniformity of purpose exists. In fact, most modes of teaching, including those used recently in specific skill development, operate overtly on this assumption. But such a presumption is not justified. Students establish their own purposes, goals, and objectives.

In recent years a number of sociologists and psychologists have pointed out that students, though they may pay obeisance to the goals of the teacher and of the school, also are participants in a "hidden curriculum" and a mode of socialization that may be largely or even totally ignored in the official educational program. The students often formulate their own desired outcomes from various elements of school life without the help or cooperation of teachers or school administrators.

Achieving a high measure of congruence among the goals and purposes of the school (or any other social institution for educating young people), of the teachers who guide the learning experiences of students, and of the students themselves is a desirable basis for building an effective curriculum. This chapter considers the process of choosing goals and the means by which those who are involved in curriculum planning may approach this important task.

ACHIEVING PURPOSES OF EDUCATION

Talk about purposes or aims of education is as old as education itself. Education is generally recognized to have dual purposes: to prepare individuals to be productive members of society and to enable individuals to develop their own potential. For example, Cremin summarized Dewey's view on the purpose of education: "The aim of education is not merely to make citizens, or workers, or fathers, or mothers but ultimately to make human beings who will live life to the fullest."[2] The two purposes—development of society and of the individual—are closely interrelated; a democracy cannot have one without the other, and their formation should go hand in hand.

Purposes of education are achieved as individuals learn to perform specific behaviors and develop certain personal traits. Thus a first step in planning an educational program is to find answers to two general questions: 1) For a person to achieve this purpose or major goal, what does he or she need to be able to do? 2) For a person to achieve this purpose or major goal what kind of a person does he or she need to be? Answers to these two questions may be summarized by statements of 1) behaviors to be learned, and 2) human traits to be developed.

The contrast of behaviors to be learned and human traits to be developed is used to emphasize that there is more to education than learning a set of behaviors. Education includes the development of such human characteristics as morals, attitudes, appreciations, and values. If educators fail to recognize the need to help individuals develop these traits, the result of their labor may be individuals who have the necessary skills but lack the human characteristics to use those skills effectively. The term *human traits* has been selected rather than human values or human

[2]Lawrence A. Cremlin, *The Transformation of the School* (New York: Alfred A. Knopf, 1961), pp. 122–123.

attitudes because it encompasses both of these concepts as well as related terms such as appreciations and self-understanding.

A specific illustration will help to show the contrast between behaviors to be learned and human traits to be developed. Assume that one purpose of education is "to enable human beings to live life to the fullest." A general goal to be achieved, in order to realize this purpose, is "to assist individuals to become self-directed learners." (Obviously a series of assumptions have been made—and value judgments exercised—in stating the purpose and general goal; but that is the nature of curriculum planning.) Table 4.1 lists the major categories of behaviors to be learned and human traits to be developed.

Individuals become self-directed in their learning only when they are able to perform the necessary behaviors and possess the appropriate human traits; in other words, both lists in Table 4.1 must be attended to. Thus, individuals who have developed all of the behaviors listed but do not believe they can learn, or do not enjoy learning, or do not have the self-discipline to follow through will not be self-directed learners. Similarly, individuals who have an interest in learning and believe they can learn will not be self-directed learners until they develop the necessary skills.

The behaviors to be learned and the human traits to be developed are not learned independently. While the two categories are useful for planners, unified experiences are essential for learners. For example, the enjoyment of reading may start as a parent reads stories to a child, as the child "reads" the pictures in a book or "reads" the funnies with mother or father. That trait may continue to be developed as the child enters school and discovers the magic of learning about other people and being transported to mysterious places through symbols in a book. Or the joy of reading may be snuffed out as the child fills in the "umpteenth" work sheet on the letter "a."

TABLE 4.1 Illustration of General Goal Analysis

General Goal: To assist individuals to become self-directed learners	
Behaviors to be Learned	Human Traits to be Developed

To be self-directed learners, individuals need to be able to:
 Read
 Write
 Use a computer
 Analyze information
 Synthesize information
 Utilize problem-solving methods
 Organize their own learning
  experiences
	To be self-directed learners, individuals need to be persons who:
	 Believe they can learn
	 Enjoy learning
	 Enjoy reading
	 Recognize the value of learning and of
	  education
	 Have a sense of control over their own
	  lives
	 Have the self-discipline to organize and
	  follow through on learning experiences

Behavior-oriented learning activities are time and task specific. For example, children learn to write through a sequential series of tasks to be mastered including: printing letters, printing words, learning to spell, learning cursive writing, learning to write sentences, and so on. The behaviors to be learned are determined by making a series of choices concerning general goals, domains, subgoals, and instructional objectives. In the following section we discuss the nature of these choices and who should make them.

Human traits to be developed are not time-specific nor can they be atomized into tasks to be learned. For example, the development of an individual's belief in his or her ability to learn probably starts with early interactions with persons and things in the environment and receives a major boost from experiences in childhood. However, beliefs in one's capability to learn continue to be reinforced, or undermined, by experiences throughout a lifetime. Erikson's eight stages of man, described in Chapter 3, suggest that different types of development occur at different stages as positives and negatives are fought through (for example, industry versus inferiority in childhood); but that no victory is completely or forever won. We shall further discuss the development of human traits after considering behaviors to be learned.

Hierarchy for Organizing Performance-Oriented Learning Experiences

Specific behaviors to be learned are determined through a series of hierarchical steps that move from the general to the more specific.

Definition of Terms

The terms *purposes, aims, goals,* and *objectives* all designate intent, or outcomes desired. In general usage they may be used interchangeably, but in curriculum planning some differentiation in meaning is desirable.

Purposes is used here in a broad sense to refer to a desired result; it is the most inclusive of the terms defined here and is used generically to mean the reason for which something exists or is done. The term *aims* is generally used interchangeably with purposes.

General goals mean the end, the result, or the achievement toward which effort is directed. The term is used extensively in this chapter to designate the broad significant outcomes desired from an educational program.

Domains designate a large group of learning opportunities, broad in scope, that are planned to achieve a single set of closely related educational goals. Domains are categories for classifying major goals and related learning opportunities; they do not state the purposes of the school but rather the aspects of human development for which goals have been formulated.

Subgoals further define the major goals that constitute domains of the curriculum. They state in more specific terms the nature of the ends sought in the learning opportunities provided within a domain. They are the basic elements in the detailed job of curriculum planning.

Objectives state the specific, overt changes in student behavior that are expected to result from participation in a unit of learning activities. Obviously, they develop more explicitly the general goals and their respective subgoals for the purpose of planning instruction.

Relationships in Hierarchy

A hierarchy of goal definition is envisioned. Overarching the entire process is the determination of a system of values derived from the culture of the social group, since all educational planning must be based on a value system. From these values, purposes or aims of education are stated and then identified. The achievement of purposes requires that general goals, organized by domains, be stated. These general goals constitute the broad categories of the overall curriculum plan. Subgoals for each general goal are then formulated which further define the nature of a domain. The subgoals are the basis for detailed curriculum planning. Finally, objectives that will contribute significantly to the attainment of the subgoals are selected. Instruction is planned and carried forward on the basis of these objectives. Some of these objectives, of course, may not be in written form but may be clearly envisioned in the mind of the teacher, perhaps with some actually being formulated as instruction is underway.

The hierarchy of purposes, goals, subgoals, and objectives is illustrated in Table 4.2. This figure provides only one illustration from among several statements that could be included under each heading. Thus, for example, another specific objective could be stated: Be able to state the requirements for filing as a presidential candidate in the United States.

Participants in Organizing Learning Experiences

Everyone who is directly concerned with the process of education should participate in some way at some level in determining the goals and

TABLE 4.2 Hierarchy of Purposes, Goals, Subgoals and Objectives (Illustrative Statements)

Purpose:	Be effective citizens in a democratic society.
General Goal:	Participate intelligently in the democratic process (Domain of Social Competence).
Subgoal:	Be informed on constitutional provisions of government.
Objectives:	Demonstrate ability to answer correctly questions regarding procedures concerning the methods of electing a United States President.
Specific Objective:	Be able to indicate basis on which electoral votes are assigned to states.

objectives of education. This means learners themselves; teachers in various educational institutions; members of boards of education; citizens of the community, particularly the parents of school children; and representatives of appropriate governmental bodies should share in formulating purposes.

The roles of individuals and groups vary with levels on the hierarchy (see Table 4.2). The nature of the groups involved and their proposed function at various stages is portrayed in Figure 4.1. We recommend broad participation in agreeing upon purposes of education and the general goals of education. Following consensus on the general goals, an agreement needs to be reached among various educational institutions regarding the role that each will play. The general public should assist with this assignment of educational roles and approve the plan. Each educational institution then proceeds with defining subgoals and instructional objectives.

What we propose as a community-wide approach to education is not present practice. Therefore, we elaborate on procedures to achieve a community-wide approach in Chapter 8. In this chapter we report on present practice as it pertains to schools. Most of the ideas discussed, however, can be used equally well in other educational institutions.

Identification of Fundamental Values and Interpretation of Student Data

All of the groups just listed should participate in the identification of fundamental values and their relation to the students to be served. It is, after all, the people as a social group who espouse a set of values and beliefs that characterizes democracy in the United States.

Direct involvement, however, may be limited. Some school systems prepare a statement of beliefs as a basis for further planning, but whether written or not, the values, ideals, and beliefs of the people are inevitably the basis for the formulation of general goals, subgoals, and objectives. If a formal statement of beliefs is prepared, representatives of students, parents, and other citizens should participate with teachers in the development of the statement; it should be presented and discussed at open meetings in the community, and it should finally be adopted by the board of education. Some programs for goal definition refer to this initial step as "evolving an educational philosophy." In preparing such a statement the kinds of information and data described in Chapter 3 should constitute basic sources.

Formulation of General Goals and Subgoals by Domains

The definition of goals for the school is a professional responsibility, although citizens, scholars, educational leaders, students, statesmen, and

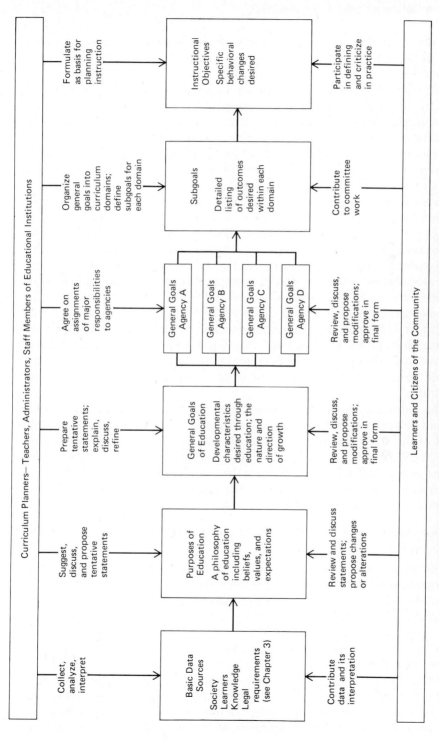

Curriculum Planners— Teachers, Administrators, Staff Members of Educational Institutions

Collect, analyze, interpret

Suggest, discuss, and propose tentative statements

Prepare tentative statements; explain, discuss, refine

Agree on assignments of major responsibilities to agencies

Organize general goals into curriculum domains; define subgoals for each domain

Formulate as basis for planning instruction

Basic Data Sources
Society
Learners
Knowledge
Legal requirements (see Chapter 3)

Purposes of Education
A philosophy of education including beliefs, values, and expectations

General Goals of Education
Developmental characteristics desired through education; the nature and direction of growth

General Goals Agency A
General Goals Agency B
General Goals Agency C
General Goals Agency D

Subgoals
Detailed listing of outcomes desired within each domain

Instructional Objectives
Specific behavioral changes desired

Contribute data and its interpretation

Review and discuss statements; propose changes or alterations

Review, discuss, and propose modifications; approve in final form

Review, discuss, and propose modifications; approve in final form

Contribute to committee work

Participate in defining and criticize in practice

Learners and Citizens of the Community

FIGURE 4.1   The process of defining the goals and objectives of educational institutions.

competent analysts of the social scene should share in the process. Goals should be of two types, behaviors to be learned and human traits to be developed.

The whole apparatus for curriculum planning and development, which was treated in detail in Chapter 2, is involved in the definition of goals. As suggested there, system-wide committees may be established, each building may have a curriculum-planning committee, committees may be established for each domain and subject field or area of study, or other procedures may be followed. In any instance, the formulation of goals is a major responsibility of such committees.

In the process of planning it is desirable for every committee to include at least two types of nonprofessional persons—lay citizens and students. Other persons may be appointed as full-fledged members of the committee or used in a consultative capacity. These should include scholars in the appropriate subject fields, anthropologists, psychologists, psychiatrists, and specialists in mental health, instructors in teacher-preparation institutions, and, in many instances, observers of life in the United States. In the prevocational, vocational, and applied fields of study, leaders in the occupation or field may be committee members. Such committees will, of course, draw on the kinds of basic data listed in Chapter 3 and mentioned above. Goal setting without a deep and penetrating analysis of these data would be in complete contradiction to the principles of sound curriculum planning.

The culminating aspect of these efforts to define goals for the school should be a critical examination of the selected goals by appropriate members of the staff. The adoption of goals should involve all members of a building staff for any sets of goals unique to that building and all members of the system staff for those affecting the entire school system. Often such discussions may be held in smaller subgroups, with only representatives of these groups coming together for final approval at the system level.

Determination of Objectives for the Instructional Program

The final stage in the formulation of purposes for the school is the preparation of lists of objectives for the instructional program. Obviously, these should be consistent with and contributory to the attainment of the general goals and subgoals previously defined. Inasmuch as these objectives specify the kinds of learning experiences the teacher chooses to develop with a group or with individual students in striving to achieve these goals, the responsibility for their formulation devolves primarily on the teacher or team of teachers who guide the learning activity. In curriculum planning, however, it is common practice for committees of teachers and staff personnel to prepare instructional guides for courses, a cluster of courses, a unified segment of learning opportunities, and, in terms of our recommendation, the domains of the curriculum. In addition to lists of goals for the subject, field, segment, or domain, such guides may contain lists of objectives for each unit of instruction or activity or a comprehensive list in the introductory section.

Committees of professional organizations, textbook writers, and similar groups or individuals often publish lists of recommended goals and objectives. The Center for the Study of Evaluation, a federally funded agency at the University of California at Los Angeles, established an Instructional Objectives Exchange which uses computerized methods of recording and retrieving behavioral objectives for teachers' use.

Regardless of who prepares them, it should be recognized that lists of packaged objectives are helpful to teachers and curriculum committees *provided* planners critically consider the validity of the objectives for their particular instructional program. It is essential that a teacher choose objectives that are appropriate for a unit of instruction for a student or group, giving full consideration to all factors that must be taken into account in any specific piece of curriculum planning. Scissors-and-paste methods of planning a curriculum are to be vigorously condemned when items are uncritically used, but utilizing existing materials of all sorts to glean ideas, suggestions, and items that will enhance planning is simply sharing professional knowledge.

Illustrations

A model program for community and professional involvement in the establishment and implementation of educational goals and objectives was developed by the Program Development Center of Northern California.[3] This model has been used by a number of schools and school systems. The Workshop Packet has been updated[4] and contains all of the materials needed for community groups to follow the model.

The first step in the model program is to send community participants a list of eighteen general goals of education. These goals vary from "develop skills in reading, writing, speaking, and listening" to "develop good character and self-respect." Participants are given the opportunity to add other general goals. In a general meeting of community participants each individual ranks the 18 goals as well as any others added by the community through a forced choice technique. Small groups of participants (four members) develop a consensus ranking of the goals. A mathematical consensus is then calculated from results of these small group meetings.

A list of the general goals and their ranking is distributed at a second community meeting. Each participant is asked to respond for each of the

[3]B. Keith Rose, *Workshop Packet for Educational Goals and Objectives* (Bloomington, Ind.: Phi Delta Kappa, Inc., no date).
[4]*Educational Planning Model* (Bloomington, Ind.: Phi Delta Kappa, Inc., 1978).

eighteen or more goals to the question: "How well are the current school programs meeting this goal?" They respond by checking a Likert type scale with the following designations: "extremely poor," "poor," "fair but more needs to be done," "leave as is," "too much is being done." Concurrently teachers and students are marking a similar scale in response to the question, "How well are my school's current programs meeting this goal?"

As a result of this work, the community is aware that: the district has goals, these goals are ranked in priority order, and some of these goals are not being met as well as they should be. "The next step is to express each goal in terms clearly conveying to the community the desired level of performance each child should attain."[5]

The National Assessment of Educational Progress (discussed in Chapter 3) developed a list of educational objectives as a basis for their assessment in each of several learning areas. The term *objectives* was used by the National Assessment as "goals for the education of young Americans."[6] National panels were used in selecting possible objectives. These objectives were subjected to three tests. "First, the objectives had to be considered important by scholars within a given learning area." Second, the objectives had to be "acceptable to most educators and be considered desirable teaching goals in most schools." Finally, "the objectives had to be considered desirable by thoughtful lay citizens."[7]

One other illustration of securing community participation will be considered. The Ministry of Education in British Columbia distributed a brochure which included a "proposed statement of the goals of general education in the province."[8] The brochure states that the aim of general education "is to provide all students with the opportunity to develop their full potential as individuals and as members of society."[9] A series of goals follow, such as "To Develop the Skills of Reading." Subgoals are also listed, for example, "During the primary years students should learn a basic sight vocabulary."[10] A tear-out questionnaire asks respondents to suggest modifications in the goals. Respondents are asked to place themselves in one of five categories: parent, student, teacher, trustee, other.

These illustrations represent three different approaches designed for different populations. The approaches have the common characteristic of

[5]Rose, p. 17. A programmed course for the writing of performance objectives is included in the packet.
[6]Simon E. Johnson, *Update on Education* (Denver, Colo.: The Education Commission of the States, 1975), p. 28.
[7]Johnson, p. 28.
[8]Ministry of Education, "What Should Our Children Be Learning?" (Victoria, British Columbia: Ministry of Education, 1976).
[9]Ministry of Education, p. 4.
[10]Ministry of Education, p. 8.

seeking broad citizen participation in the formulation of goals and objectives.

Organizing Learning Experiences for Development of Human Traits

Purposes of education are achieved as individuals learn behaviors and as they develop human traits. Procedures for determining behaviors to be learned have been discussed; this section describes strategies for identifying human traits to be developed. We hope the reader raised a skeptical eyebrow when he or she read the goals, subgoals, objectives, and specific objectives related to becoming effective citizens in a democratic society (Figure 4.2). The reader may have asked, "Will a knowledge of constitutional government, including provisions for electing the U.S. President through a vote of the electoral college, cause an individual to participate intelligently in the democratic process? Are not citizens' attitudes, beliefs, and values as important, or even more important, in assuring their intelligent participation in the democratic process?" The answer to the last question is an unqualified yes. Intelligent participation in the democratic process requires that acquiring new knowledge, behaviorally defined, be accompanied by the development of such human traits as: faith in the democratic process (but coupled with a realistic understanding of its weaknesses as well as its strengths); belief that one's views make a difference; and confidence in duly elected officials (but with enough skepticism to monitor their activities in order to use constitutional procedures for the removal of corrupt individuals).

Are educational institutions equally effective in achieving both halves of a complete education—learning new behaviors and developing human traits? Goodlad, a respected educational leader, provided his answer, "In recent years, we have become almost exclusively preoccupied with, at best, only half of each goal for schooling—the behavioral half."[11] According to Goodlad, educational aims refer "to conditions and traits to be cultivated in human beings . . . they say little about goals in the behavioral sense and nothing about objectives."[12] And yet, he added, "We have bemused ourselves with the notion that breaking important human traits into dozens of hundreds of pieces leaves us with a proper definition of man, and that demonstrated competence in each little piece, defined behaviorally, gives us the human we sought to describe in the first place."[13]

[11]John I. Goodlad, "On the Cultivation and Corruption of Education," *The Educational Forum, 22* (March 1978): 276.
[12]Goodlad, p. 276.
[13]Goodlad, p. 276.

Illustrations cited earlier support Goodlad's contention that there is a preponderance of concern with the behavioral half. The workshop model for community participation in developing goals and objectives specifies the expression of each goal as "the desired level of performance each child should attain."[14] No reference is made to human traits to be developed. The British Columbia statement of goals includes the aim "to provide all students with the opportunity to develop their full potential . . ."[15] and yet all of the goals and objectives are behaviors to be learned. These illustrations were not singled out to mark poor practice; rather they represent the best of usual practice.

One consequence of emphasizing the behavioral half is to fragment human traits into hundreds of pieces. Goodlad observed that when this happens, "The specific piece becomes an end in itself, whether or not the student cheated in acquiring it or was turned off in the process."[16] Success in school as measured by grades and proficiency tests, "correlates not at all with most of the human traits set forth in our educational aims—not compassion, not honesty, not good workmanship, not faith in others, not the pursuit of happiness—not anything our aims address."[17] To overcome these problems requires an understanding of why the imbalance between behavioral learning and human trait development occurred and what can be done to redress the balance.

Reasons For Underemphasis on Development of Human Traits

The idea of two types of goals is not a new one. In the 1950s Bloom and his colleagues focused attention on two distinct domains of objectives: cognitive and affective.[18] Their cognitive domain is similar to our behaviors to be learned. Some goals we characterize as human traits to be developed, such as initiative, extend beyond the usual interpretation of Bloom's affective taxonomy (discussed later in this chapter). Why have educational institutions focused so completely on the cognitive or behaviors-to-be-learned aspect of education at the expense of a total education?

The adoption of a factory model for education set the stage for a drift toward a predominant, almost exclusive, behavioral emphasis in education. A factory receives raw material, processes it, and turns out a product.

---

[14]Rose, p. 17.
[15]Ministry of Education, p. 4.
[16]Goodlad, p. 276.
[17]Goodlad, p. 276.
[18]Benjamin S. Bloom (ed.), *Taxonomy of Educational Objectives: The Classification of Educational Goals, Handbook I Cognitive Domain* (New York: Longmans, Green and Company, 1956); David R. Krathwohl, Benjamin S. Bloom, and Bertram B. Masia, *Taxonomy of Educational Objectives: The Classification of Educational Goals, Handbook II: Affective Domain* (New York: David McKay Company, Inc., 1964).

The effectiveness of a factory depends on its productivity and its efficiency. There is a specific product that can be measured and workers in the factory can be held accountable. Some educators have found counterparts to these characteristics in schools.[19]

Recent developments in business and industry continue to have an impact on schools. Systems analysis, first used in business and industry, was subsequently applied to education. The systems approach is linear and requires a clear statement of the goals or objectives to be achieved stated, preferably in behavioral terms. For example, Schutz, Baker, and Gerlach specified, "The verb in a well-formed objective describes a behavior or a product of behavior. A *behavior* is any learner performance, action, or operation which is observable."[20] The management by objectives approach, and the accompanying accountability movement, reinforced the emphasis on behaviors to be learned. Applicants for most federal grants in education are required to specify objectives or goals in behavioral terms and make provision for their evaluation.

Statements of goals and objectives in behavioral terms have proven very useful in designing instructional programs. Since we tend to do what we can do well, the demonstrated value of behaviorally stated objectives has reinforced their use.

Balancing the Learning of Behaviors and the Development of Human Traits

There is no intent to eliminate the learning of behaviors—a vital part of education. What is needed is to give sufficient attention to the development of human traits to assure a balance between learning of behaviors and development of traits.

Studies conducted by Raven in the United Kingdom showed:

teachers, parents, pupils, and ex-pupils all think that education should be primarily concerned with the development of such characteristics as initiative, the ability to work effectively with others, the ability to communicate effectively, self-confidence, and the ability to make one's own observations and learn on one's own.[21]

In a follow-up study in Ireland, Raven found that "teachers think that insufficient time is devoted to fostering these qualities and that, as a result,

[19]The extent to which schools have been influenced by the factory model was well documented by Callahan. See Raymond E. Callahan, *Education and the Cult of Efficiency* (Chicago: University of Chicago Press, 1962).
[20]Richard E. Schutz, Robert L. Baker, Vernon S. Gerlach, "Stating Educational Outcomes," in Robert L. Baker, Richard E. Schutz (eds.), *Instructional Product Development* (New York: Van Nostrand Reinhold Company, 1971), p. 6.
[21]John Raven, "On the Components of Competence and Their Development in Education," *Teachers College Record, 78* (May 1977): 457.

they remain poorly developed among pupils." Apparently the United Kingdom shares our problem of an imbalance between behaviors to be learned and human traits to be developed. Teachers in Ireland said they devote insufficient time to human goals "partly because the examination does not recognize and reward activity, either on their part or on the part of their pupils, directed toward achieving these goals, and partly because they are themselves none too clear about how to achieve them." Both of these reasons could be echoed on this side of the Atlantic.

Curriculum planners need to be as deliberate and thoughtful in identifying human traits to be developed as they are in listing behaviors to be learned. See, for example, the illustration in Figure 4.1.[22] Similar human traits will appear in relationship to several goals and could, for purposes of clarity, be synthesized within four domains: personal development, social competence, continued learning skills, and specialization.

The development of human traits depends upon the quality of a learner's experience. Educators need to plan experiences that will enhance the development of human potential. For example, Kohlberg's approach to moral development recognizes the importance of the environment in providing quality experience.[23] Kohlberg identified six stages of moral development from stage 1, "the punishment-and-obedience orientation," through stage 6, "the universal-ethical-principle orientation."[24] To help students progress through these stages, Kohlberg and his colleagues, designed "a just community school" in four public high schools.[25] Students have experience in "discussing real-life moral situations and actions as issues of fairness and as matters for democratic decision." Kohlberg was clear on the human traits he wanted to develop and designed appropriate experiences for their development. He believed that "a participatory democracy provides more extensive opportunities for role taking and a higher level of perceived institutional justice than does any other social arrangement."[26]

The linear or step-by-step approach that works well in achieving performance objectives may not be effective in the development of human traits. Soltis provided a useful analogy in this regard.[27] A farmer utilizes

---

[22]Excellent suggestions for human traits to be developed are to be found in Raven, pp. 457–474.

[23]For a valuable discussion of various approaches to moral education see R. Freeman Butts, Donald H. Peckenpaugh, and Howard Kirschenbaum, *The School's Role as Moral Authority* (Washington, D.C.: Association for Supervision and Curriculum Development, 1977).

[24]Lawrence Kohlberg, "The Cognitive-Developmental Approach to Moral Education," *Phi Delta Kappan, 61* (June 1975): 670–677.

[25]For a firsthand account of a visit to one of the four "just community" schools and an appraisal of its effectiveness see Howard Muson, "Moral Thinking, Can It Be Taught?" *Psychology Today, 12* (February 1979): 48–68, 92.

[26]Kohlberg, p. 676.

[27]Jonas F. Soltis, Review of Paul H. Hirst, *Knowledge and the Curriculum* (London: Routledge and Kegan Paul, Ltd., 1974) in *Teachers College Record, 80* (May 1979): 781–782.

a linear approach: the soil is prepared, fertilizer is added, seeds are planted, crops are irrigated and cultivated, and finally the crop is harvested. According to Soltis, another general form of rational-intentional activity is clearly reflected in the activities of teaching. "Even though it lacks the ideas of order and sequence leading toward a goal, it is still goal-directed and calls for intelligent, rational activity on the part of the actor."[28] He illustrates this activity by means of a soccer player who has two important goals: kick the ball through his opponent's goal and prevent the opponent from kicking the ball through his team's goal. A soccer player's strategies cannot be linearly determined in advance. For example, to always kick the ball at the opponent's goal would be ineffective. Often it is better strategy to kick the ball laterally or back to a teammate. The skillful soccer player is constantly assessing the situation and responding in terms of that context. Similarly, for example, a skillful teacher, with a goal of helping a child develop compassion, watches for opportunities to provide experiences that will increase the child's compassion.

Responsibility for behaviors to be learned can be allocated among community groups and individuals. Responsibility for the development of human traits, however, is shared by all educative institutions. For example, the development of honesty depends upon experiences provided in the home, school, Sunday school, scout organization, and through reading books in a library. When agencies work at cross-purposes through experiences they provide, development may be stunted or even thwarted.

A final suggestion for redressing the balance is to use contextual criteria in evaluating the quality of educational experiences, not simply summative evaluation of objectives. Goodlad proposed that this process begin at the local school level as students, teachers, parents, and community members seek answers to three questions:

1. What is our school doing for humans who live and work there that we wish to maintain and strengthen?
2. What do we not like that could be improved or eliminated in a few weeks or months?
3. With what qualities do we wish to imbue everything that transpires in our school?[29]

More specific suggestions for evaluating the quality of experiences are included in Chapter 7.

We emphasize again the interrelated nature of behaviors to be learned and human traits to be developed at the instructional level. The two categories for classifying goals are useful approaches for the curriculum planner to use in planning, selecting, and directing learning experiences with students. It does not mean, however, that there are two distinct and

[28]Soltis, p. 782.
[29]Goodlad, p. 277.

separate types of learning experiences. The teacher must be aware of both types of goals in carrying on learning activities. Some activities will give much greater emphasis to behaviors to be learned; others will emphasize the development of human traits. Too often, however, we fail to make the human trait development aspects of a school activity an overt, identifiable, and eagerly sought aspect of the experience.

FORMULATING PURPOSES AND GENERAL GOALS

We move from a discussion of the general nature of purposes, goals, sub-goals, and objectives and their interrelationships to a consideration of the development of specific statements of purposes and general goals.

The nature of society influences the purposes and goals for education; at the same time, achievement of educational purposes and goals influences the future of society. Therefore, to adopt a purpose or an aim for education is to make a commitment to some long-range goal for society. The purpose of education also represents an answer to the question, "What would we have the twenty-first-century human be?" The selection of purposes and related general goals is a highly subjective activity growing out of philosophical assumptions and value positions rather than from objective data.

Preparing Statements of Purposes

Most statements of purpose emphasize the development of a good person who will, in turn, develop and support a good society. Dewey's statement of aim, quoted earlier, showed this dual nature—to make citizens and to make human beings who will live life to the fullest. Whitehead, in his essay "The Aims of Education," placed major emphasis on the development of the individual. He was very clear on what it takes to develop individuals. "Culture is activity of thought, and receptiveness to beauty and humane feeling. Scraps of information have nothing to do with it. A merely well-informed man is the most useless bore on God's earth. What we should aim at producing is men who possess both culture and expert knowledge in some special direction." Whitehead recognized that humanity's culture "will lead them as deep as philosophy and as high as art."[30]

Macdonald, a contemporary curriculum leader, identified three aims of education frequently mentioned in the literature: 1) socialization, 2) development, and 3) liberation. Socialization, as an aim, relates to the training potential of the school and, according to Macdonald, rests on "the

[30]Alfred North Whitehead, *The Aims of Education* (New York: Mentor Books, 1929), p. 13.

acceptance of the status quo by definition and the replication of the present social class and role structure, ethos, and attitudinal sets."[31] Development, according to Macdonald, involves "the concept of an elite group that knows what 'direction' development must take and how to guide this process." Macdonald's use of development differs from ours in that he implies a molding of the individual. Our use of development builds on the work of Erikson and others, and is closer to Macdonald's concept of liberation. Macdonald viewed liberation as "freeing persons from the parochialness of their specific times and places and opening up the possibilities for persons to create themselves and their societies."[32] Argyris struck a similar note for liberation when he wrote, "Man is free to the extent that he makes choices, that he consciously strives to design his life, that he accepts personal responsibilities for his behavior."[33] The purpose of a liberal education is to liberate humans in this way.

One other statement rounds out the illustrations of purposes of education. Butts, an educational historian, said, "Achieving a sense of community is the essential purpose of public education."[34] Butts called for a mobilization of the public schools "on the task of building a sense of civic cohesion among all of the people of the country."[35]

A variety of statements of purposes of education has been presented to enable curriculum planners to see the range of possible aims. Rather than to adopt one of these statements, or any other, curriculum planners should, after thoughtful consideration, develop their own statement of aims or purposes of education to guide them through the process of curriculum development. In the preparation of such a document the total planning group must seek to answer two basic questions: What essentially are the ideals of United States society? and What are the responsibilities and functions of educational institutions in educating people to live in this society now and for the rest of their lives?

The statement of purposes written by the Commission on the Reorganization of Secondary Schools (see next section) illustrates answers to these questions. The Commission stated that "education in a democracy, both within and without the school, should develop in each individual the knowledge, interests, ideals, habits, and powers whereby he will find his place and use that place to shape both himself and society toward ever

[31]James B. Macdonald, "Values Bases and Issues for Curriculum," in Alex Molnar and John A. Zahorik (eds.), *Curriculum Theory* (Washington, D. C.: Association for Supervision and Curriculum Development, 1977), p. 16.

[32]Macdonald, p. 17.

[33]Chris Argyris, "Essay Review" of B. F. Skinner, *Beyond Freedom and Dignity* (New York: Alfred A. Knopf, 1971) in *Harvard Education Review 41*, (November 1971): 561.

[34]R. Freeman Butts, "The Public Schools: Assaults on a Great Idea," *The Nation, 16* (April 30, 1973): 554.

[35]Butts, p. 559.

nobler ends."[36] In this statement, the Commission reaffirmed the values of a democratic society and the responsibilities of educational institutions, "both within and without the school" toward learners.

Preparing Statements of General Goals

Curriculum planners use their statement of purposes of education to formulate broad general goals. These goals provide the structure for building the curriculum. The scope of the entire educational program of the school, the broad design of the curriculum, and the nature of the learning opportunities provided, including courses and various other parts of the program, are embodied in the defined goals of the educational institution.

Ideally, general goals should be developed and agreed on by a representative group of citizens. Following this agreement, responsibilities should be shared among cooperating educational institutions. In present practice, however, schools are defining goals after securing advice and assistance from students, parents, and citizen groups. Although the following material relates to schools, it will prove valuable for planning by any educational institution.

Some examples of broad general goals that have been widely used and cited over the years may be informative in determining the nature of the undertaking. Undoubtedly the most famous of all statements on the purposes and nature of schooling is the aforementioned *Cardinal Principles of Secondary Education* prepared by the Commission on the Reorganization of Secondary Education and published in 1918. Although the work of the Commission was directed particularly at goal definition for secondary schools, the statement is applicable to all levels of education and constitutes a point of view worthy of the fullest consideration by all planning groups. Based on the statement of purpose adopted by the Commission included in the previous section, the Commission listed seven areas of daily living which should be covered in the school program and stated the broad goals to be sought in each area:

CARDINAL PRINCIPLES OF SECONDARY EDUCATION

1. *Health*
The secondary school should therefore provide health instruction, inculcate health habits, organize an effective program of physical activities, regard health needs in planning work and play, and cooperate with home and community in safeguarding and promoting health interests.

[36]Commission on the Reorganization of Secondary Education, U.S. Office of Education, *Cardinal Principles of Secondary Education* (Washington, D. C.: Government Printing Office, 1918), Bulletin No. 35, p. 9.

2. *Command of fundamental processes*
The facility that a child of 12 or 14 may acquire in the use of these tools is not sufficient for the needs of modern life.

3. *Worthy home membership*
Worthy home membership as an objective calls for the development of those qualities that make the individual a worthy member of a family, both contributing to and deriving benefit from that membership.

4. *Vocation*
Vocational education should equip the individual to secure a livelihood for himself and those dependent on him, to serve society well through his vocation, to maintain the right relationships toward his fellow workers and society, and, as far as possible, to find in that vocation his own best development.

5. *Civic education*
Civic education should develop in the individual those qualities whereby he will act well his part as a member of neighborhood, town or city, State, and Nation, and give him a basis for understanding international problems.

6. *Worthy use of leisure*
Education should equip the individual to secure from his leisure the recreation of body, mind, and spirit, and the enrichment and enlargement of his personality.

7. *Ethical character*
In a democratic society ethical character becomes paramount among the objectives of the secondary school.[37]

Two decades later, the Educational Policies Commission, established by the National Education Association to recommend school policies, published an important statement on the functions of education in U.S. society. The Commission declared that formal education has these basic functions:

In any realistic definition of education for the United States, therefore, must appear the whole philosophy and practice of democracy. Education cherishes and inculcates its moral values, disseminates knowledge necessary to its functioning, spreads information relevant to its institutions and economy, keeps alive the creative and sustaining spirit without which the letter is dead.[38]

The Educational Policies Commission followed this statement of purpose with two additional reports worthy of citation here as examples of general goals for the schools.

The Purposes of Education in American Democracy, published in 1938, proposed that educational goals be defined in terms of four aspects of human responsibility. The categories and two examples for each one follow:

[37]Commission on the Reorganization of Secondary Education, pp. 11–15.
[38]Educational Policies Commission, National Education Association, *The Unique Function of Education in American Democracy* (Washington, D. C.: The Association, 1937), p. 89.

THE OJECTIVES OF SELF-REALIZATION

The Inquiring Mind. The educated person has an appetite for learning.
Character. The educated person gives responsible direction to his own
life.

THE OBJECTIVES OF HUMAN RELATIONSHIPS

Respect for Humanity. The educated person puts human relationships
first.
Democracy in the Home. The educated person maintains democratic
family relationships.

THE OBJECTIVES OF ECONOMIC EFFICIENCY

Occupational Efficiency. The educated producer succeeds in his chosen
vocation.
Consumer Judgment. The educated consumer develops standards for
guiding his expenditures.

THE OBJECTIVES OF CIVIC RESPONSIBILITY

Social Justice. The educated citizen is sensitive to the disparities of human circumstance.
Conservation. The educated citizen has a regard for the nation's resources.[39]

Continuing its efforts to assist educators in planning, in 1944 the Commission proposed a set of what we designate as general goals for secondary
schools. The list is entitled "Imperative Educational Needs of Youth." This
statement has been used extensively by curriculum planning groups at the
secondary school level. In light of its significance and continued use it is
quoted here in full:

1. All youth need to develop salable skills and those understandings and
   attitudes that make the worker an intelligent and productive participant
   in economic life. To this end, most youth need supervised work experience as well as education in the skills and knowledge of their occupations.
2. All youth need to develop and maintain good health and physical fitness.
3. All youth need to understand the rights and duties of the citizens of a
   democratic society, and to be diligent and competent in the performance of their obligations as members of the community and citizens of
   the state and nation.
4. All youth need to understand the significance of the family for the individual and society and the conditions conducive to successful family life.
5. All youth need to know how to purchase and use goods and services
   intelligently, understanding both the values received by the consumer
   and the economic consequences of their acts.
6. All youth need to understand the methods of science, the influence of

[39]Educational Policies Commission, National Education Association, *The Purposes of Education in American Democracy* (Washington, D. C.: The Association, 1938), pp. 50, 72, 90, 108.

science on human life, and the main scientific facts concerning the nature of the world and of man.

7. All youth need opportunities to develop their capacities to appreciate beauty in literature, art, music, and nature.
8. All youth need to be able to use their leisure time well and to budget it wisely, balancing activities that yield satisfactions to the individual with those that are socially useful.
9. All youth need to develop respect for other persons, to grow in their insight into ethical values and principles, and to be able to live and work cooperatively with others.
10. All youth need to grow in their ability to think rationally, to express their thoughts clearly, and to read and listen with understanding.[40]

To what extent can these earlier significant statements of goals provide a guide to curriculum workers today? Shane sought an answer to that question by interviewing forty-six national and international leaders in politics, science, the arts, and education and ninety-five secondary-school age youth.[41] He asked interviewees to update the Seven Cardinal Principles of Education in anticipation of the twenty-first century. Shane found that "all save a few members of the NEA International Panel feel that the seven goals have retained their usefulness even after the passage of nearly 60 years." He also found that some of the "meanings originally associated with the cardinal principles were no longer adequate for learning and living in an interdependent human community."[42] For example, while interviewees vigorously reaffirmed the importance of basic skills as a part of "Command of Fundamental Processes," they added three categories of fundamental skills:

1. Humanistic process skills—including human relations and group processes.
2. Neoacademic skills—including a knowledge of sources and the understanding and use of computer languages.
3. Anticipatory skills—including the ability to see relationships and to make correlations.[43]

Shane summarized an additional observation made by many panel members, "The original cardinal principles did not distinguish between the general responsibilities for education and those that were best assumed by or shared with agencies such as the church, the community, and the family." They suggested that, "now we must look at the total learning system. Except for literary, and possibly vocational efficiency, the cardinal principles are tasks for other educational agencies beyond the school walls.

[40]Educational Policies Commission, National Education Association, *Education for All American Youth* (Washington, D.C.: The Association, 1944), pp. 225–226.
[41]Harold G. Shane, *Curriculum Change Toward the 21st Century* (Washington, D.C.: National Education Association, 1977).
[42]Shane, p. 41.
[43]Shane, p. 45.

These include the home, church, and peer groups as well as media."[44] We agree with the panel's observation and in this book show how a curriculum may be designed for a total learning system.

The examples of general goals presented here are meant to be provocative; each community will need to develop its own statement of goals. Shane's approach to goal setting suggests a procedure that could be followed by a community-wide curriculum committee: Ask a number of leading citizens and educators how they would change the Seven Cardinal Principles of Education to prepare people for the twenty-first century. A summary of their responses, compared with those from Shane's panel, should provide valuable information.[45]

Curriculum planning groups are often impatient in stating general goals because they feel that general goals bear little or no relationship to educational programs. There are at least two reasons for this. First, general goals promise far more than any one institution can deliver. This problem can be alleviated through adoption of realistic goals and an appropriate allocation of responsibility to different institutions within the total learning system.

A second reason that general goal statements have had little impact on classroom practice stems from the failure of curriculum planners to complete the task of goal definition as it is presented in this chapter. Obviously, further steps must be taken to translate these general goals into specific curriculum goals and instructional objectives. All too often efforts in the past, until the behavioral approaches became widely accepted in the 1960s, ended with lists that read well when suitably printed and framed or distributed in booklet form to teachers and citizens. It was the failure to complete the process of definition that should be criticized, not the products themselves.

Identifying Curriculum Domains

Part of the process of goal definition is the identification of broad domains of the curriculum as the basis for designing the educational program, further defining subgoals, stating instructional objectives, selecting curriculum content, and planning appropriate instructional modes.

In Chapter 1 the conception of curriculum domains is presented, and in Chapter 5 the use of domains as a basis for designing the curriculum is considered in detail. Here we relate the determination of appropriate domains to the formulation of general goals and subgoals.

In preparing the general goals of the school, work committees can readily begin to organize groups of closely related sets of desired outcomes. Such groupings may center around the activities of human beings, for example, as they grow and develop personally, live together in a social

[44]Shane, p. 42.
[45]Shane, pp. 40–55.

group, work together in sustaining and improving the life of each individual and the group collectively, govern themselves, or rear their children. Other bases for grouping major goals of schooling may also be used.

We propose for the consideration of planning groups four major domains within which general goals and correlative subgoals may be grouped for planning and instructional purposes: personal development, social competence, continued learning skills, and specialization. The rationale for such a classification is given in Chapter 1.

To assist curriculum planners, we review here some other schemes that have been used to designate the broad areas of the curriculum.

The *Cardinal Principles of Secondary Education,* already cited, listed seven categories of "activities of the individual"; these areas could very well be used as domains for curriculum and instructional planning, although we do not believe that adequate attention is given to the fullest development of the individual learner in terms of his capabilities and to the continuous, lifetime nature of learning itself.

The four categories of purposes delineated by the Educational Policies Commission may be used as the domains for organizing and planning the curriculum and carrying on the instructional program: Self-Realization, Human Relationships, Economic Efficiency, and Civic Responsibility.

Broudy, Smith, and Burnett envisioned a high school program for general education organized around five basic strands: symbolic studies, basic sciences, developmental studies, esthetic studies, and molar problems.[46] A complete program of education would need to include, in addition, a domain devoted to specialization.

The domains developed by Bloom and his colleagues, frequently used by curriculum workers, classified educational goals into three domains: cognitive, affective, and psychomotor.[47] Cognitive objectives "emphasize remembering or reproducing something which has presumably been learned, as well as objectives which involve the solving of some intellective task."[48] Six types of cognitive objectives are described, building from the simpler to the more complex intellectual tasks: knowledge, comprehension, application, analysis, synthesis, and evaluation. By far the largest proportion of educational objectives fall into the cognitive domain. Unfortunately, most of the cognitive objectives used in schools are at the lower levels of "knowledge" and "comprehension."

Affective objectives "emphasize a feeling tone, an emotion, or a degree

[46]Harry S. Broudy, B. Othanel Smith, and Joe R. Burnett, *Democracy and Excellence in American Secondary Education* (Chicago: Rand McNally and Company, 1964), p. 83.

[47]Bloom, *Taxonomy: Cognitive Domain;* Krathwohl, et al., *Affective Domain;* and Anita J. Harrow, *A Taxonomy of the Psychomotor Domain: A Guide for Developing Behavioral Objectives* (New York: David McKay Company, Inc., 1972).

[48]Krathwohl, et al., p. 6.

of acceptance or rejection."[49] These objectives are often expressed as interests, attitudes, appreciations, and values. This domain is organized into five categories from the lowest to the highest level: receiving (attending), responding, valuing, organization (conceptualization of a value), and characterization by a value or value complex.[50] The psychomotor objectives "emphasize some muscular or motor skill, some manipulation of material and objects, or some act which requires a neuromuscular coordination."[51] Examples would be related to physical education, vocational education, handwriting, and speech.

Joyce's proposal for curriculum domains most closely parallels the conception we present in this book:

> The primary task in selecting an educational mission is to identify the domains through which the program will enter the life of the learner in order to change his responses to living in the world. . . . Although these domains are not mutually exclusive (personal creativity, for example, may be an avenue to improve interpersonal and academic performance), we can use these three categories, the personal, the social, and the academic, to sort out some of the possible functions of education.[52]

We do not intend to be arbitrary or dogmatic about the designation of the domains, although we believe that the inclusion of the domain of specialization is highly desirable in all of these proposals. We recognize, as Joyce does, that there may be some overlapping in the scope and nature of the domains and that programs developed for one domain may—and should—contribute to development in one or more of the others.

We have emphasized that the curriculum domains are not themselves educational goals. They constitute the broad organizing elements of the curriculum plan, comprising a set of closely related major goals and subgoals that provide the basis for developing learning opportunities of all sorts, including subjects and courses, activities, community experiences, independent learning activities, informal types of school programs, and the like.

Validation of Goals and Objectives

Before discussing subgoals and instructional objectives, the important question of validation is addressed. How does the curriculum planner, the

[49]Krathwohl, et al., p. 7.
[50]Krathwohl, et al., p. 35.
[51]Krathwohl, et al., p. 7.
[52]Bruce R. Joyce, "The Curriculum Worker of the Future," in Robert M. McClure (ed.), *The Curriculum: Retrospect and Prospect,* 70th Yearbook, Part I, National Society for the Study of Education (Chicago: University of Chicago Press, 1971), p. 332.

teacher, or the administrator know whether the goals and objectives defined for curriculum and instruction are valid, that the best possible choices of goals and ends have been made, and that the best educational route has been selected for the students for whom the curriculum is planned and instruction is carried on?

We emphasize again that educators must obtain as much pertinent data as possible about the young people to be educated, for a curriculum is always planned for students, and about the society that establishes and controls the schools. Then lists of goals and objectives may be formulated that constitute the very best and most astute judgment the planning group can make on the basis of these data. Obviously, there is no one-to-one relation between a specific item of data and a particular goal or objective. Goals or objectives cannot be deduced directly from bits of data. Nor can any computer generate valid goals, regardless of the sophistication of the programming. Rather, the intelligence, insight, values, attitudes, and beliefs of human beings are the crucial factors in choice making. Wise choices cannot be made without the most complete data obtainable, but judgment must still prevail.

Thus, curriculum workers engaged in the definition of goals continuously check the validity of these goals against the basic data obtained from their two sources. They also use all the results of such a broad, continuous program of evaluation of the entire educational program as discussed later in this book, in examination and validation of purposes. Curriculum planning must be an ever-continuing cycle of obtaining data, defining objectives, providing learning experiences, evaluating instructional outcomes, re-examining data, and appraising goals in light of all factors.

One further point should be made. A curriculum worker, including a teacher carrying out instruction, may have to discard or to include certain goals or objectives because of legal requirements, court decisions, or state or local regulations. Such a situation does not invalidate otherwise sound purposes; it simply means that the school must operate within a legal structure which in itself is an expression of the values and social expectations of those who control it. If educators believe that the goals that must be rejected are valid, they should seek to have these goals accepted by those who oppose them. If the goals are not valid in terms of the basic data sources, they should not be included in the school program.

DEFINING SUBGOALS AND INSTRUCTIONAL OBJECTIVES

Translating general goals into a curriculum plan, and, ultimately into experiences for learners, requires that goals be defined in terms of subgoals and that instructional objectives be generated from subgoals. The quality of education hinges, in part, on how well this is done and on the procedures followed in defining subgoals and generating instructional objectives. Alternative processes are examined in this section.

Subgoals

Subgoals are basic elements in curriculum planning, the statements of the outcomes desired that postulate the kinds of learning opportunities that should be provided students. Subgoals are consistent with the general goals of the school, but they are much more detailed and specific, spelling out the parameters and nature of a domain of the curriculum.

Goals should be analyzed into two types of subgoals: human traits to be developed and behaviors to be learned. The specifying and achievement of human trait development is discussed earlier in this chapter. This section deals primarily with behaviors to be learned, although, as indicated previously, the two are interrelated.

Defining the behaviors to be learned in relation to a general goal is a job requiring professional skill and a great deal of effort. The task primarily falls on the educator, but a number of other specialists should be involved rather extensively in the preparation of these subgoals and in planning the content and kinds of learning activities to be provided. Particularly, specialists in the substantive content of the broad areas of study, for example, and psychologists, sociologists, philosophers, political scientists, and anthropologists, should participate in these aspects of curriculum planning.

Should subgoals be stated behaviorally? Considerable controversy raged in the early 1970s about the extent to which subgoals should be stated in behavioral terms. The movement to state goals in behavioral terms is often credited to Tyler, who, directing the evaluation program for the Eight Year Study of the Progressive Education Association in the 1930s, wrote that "each objective must be defined in terms which clarify the kinds of behavior which the course should help to develop among students; that is to say a statement is needed which explains the meaning of the objective by describing the reactions we can expect of persons who have reached the objective."[53] The demand for stating all objectives in a behavioral form, which developed in the 1960s and continued into the 1970s, accompanied the application of systems analysis to education and the press for accountability.

The advocates of behaviorally stated goals and objectives revolted against broad statements of goals that are so vague that they are meaningless as a basis for planning specific parts of the curriculum or carrying on

[53]Ralph W. Tyler, *Constructing Achievement Tests* (Columbus, Oh.: Ohio State University, 1934), p. 18.

instruction.[54] Such general listings provide no help to the teacher in determining what content to select, what learning experiences to develop with students, or how to evaluate the outcomes of instruction. A few advocates proposed that all objectives be stated in behavioral terms.

There is a strong antibehavioral objectives group including such leaders as Eisner, Kliebard, and Macdonald.[55] Arguments against using behavioral objectives include:

1. They focus teaching principally on facts at the expense of more complex and higher-level behavior.
2. The concept is inflexible and dehumanizing.
3. Creativity and spontaneity in the classroom is discouraged.
4. Human behavior is broader in scope than the sum of specific bits of behavior learned in isolation.

Opponents of behavioral objectives advocate instead a much broader, more flexible, and open-ended type of definition. They argue that human behavior is broader in scope and purpose than the sum of specific bits of behavior learned in isolation. Behavioral objectives of the performance type fail to take account of the higher and more complex levels of functioning.

Although the debate over behavioral objectives has subsided somewhat, the basic disagreements that caused the debate have not disappeared. These disagreements surface in discussions regarding which instructional designs to use, teaching models to follow, and evaluation procedure to employ. The sharp lines of distinction between proponents and opponents of behavioral objectives have disappeared, however, so that the most ardent supporter for behavioral objectives admits that some valid educational objectives cannot be stated behaviorally. Similarly, the most vociferous of the opponents of behavioral objectives can see their utility for some purposes.

We view behavioral objectives as tools whose effectiveness depends upon the skill with which they are used and the appropriateness of their use. Their appropriateness will depend upon the nature of the objectives to be achieved, the curriculum design selected, the teaching method to

[54]See, for example, R. F. Mager, *Preparing Instructional Objectives* (Palo Alto, Calif.: Fearon Publishers, 1962): W. J. Popam, et al., *Instructional Objectives: An Analysis of Emerging Issues* (Chicago: Rand McNally and Co., 1969).
[55]See, for example: Elliot W. Eisner, "Instructional and Expressive Educational Objectives: Their Formulation and Use in Curriculum," in Robert E. Stake (ed.), *Instructional Objectives* (Chicago: Rand McNally and Company), 1969, pp. 1–31; Arthur W. Combs, *Educational Accountability: Beyond Behavioral Objectives* (Washington, D. C.: Association for Supervision and Curriculum Development, 1972); Herbert M. Kliebard, "Reappraisal: The Tyler Rationale," *School Review, 78* (February 1970): 269–270; James B. Macdonald, "Myths about Instruction," *Educational Leadership, 22* (May 1965): 613–614.

be employed, and the procedures to be followed in evaluating the objectives.

Instructional Objectives

A next step in determining the purposes for which schooling should be provided is to state the outcomes desired from participation in a specific learning opportunity or group of related opportunities provided by the school. Usually, curriculum literature designates these as intructional objectives. Obviously, instructional objectives stem from the subgoals and constitute statements of outcomes that would contribute fully to the realization of general goals.

Educators have raised two issues with respect to the definition of instructional objectives. First, they are concerned with the form in which the objectives should be stated. Second, they question whether objectives for instruction should be overtly formulated at all.

We have already considered in the previous section arguments for and against stating educational purposes in behavioral terms. The points of view summarized there apply equally well to the formulation of goals or objectives. Hence no further discussion of that matter will be given here, but several additional points are appropriate.

The second point raised about instructional objectives by curriculum theorists has to do with the undesirability of defining objectives prior to engagement in the learning activity. Kliebard issued the challenge:

One wonders whether the long-standing insistence by curriculum theorists that the first step in making a curriculum be the specification of objectives has any merit whatsoever. It is even questionable whether stating objectives at all, when they represent external goals allegedly reached through the manipulation of learning experiences, is a fruitful way to conceive of the process of curriculum planning.[56]

Macdonald, in identifying six myths of instruction, stated that

it is difficult to see how meaningful, integrated behavior could result from a formal series of sequential rational decisions. . . . Another view . . . would state that our objectives are only known to us in any complete sense after the completion of our act of instruction. No matter what we thought we were attempting to do, we can only know what we wanted to accomplish after the fact.[57]

Our reaction to these points of view is that every teacher engaged in instructional activities is seeking some learned behaviors whether these

[56]Kliebard, pp.269–270.
[57]Macdonald, pp. 613–614.

are stated in written form or exist in the mind of the teacher. If a teacher, for example, is directing an activity in which students are adding columns of three-digit numbers, he or she has at least one important behavioral outcome in mind—each student should be able to add the column after suitable instruction. That objective is obvious to anyone—teacher, students, curriculum director, principal, evaluator, parents.

Good instructional practices and meaningful, purposeful learning experiences for students call for a full recognition by the teacher and the students of the significant outcomes that ought to be attained through participation in the planned instructional activity. The students should know what is *expected* of them in the way of learning outcomes—in terms of knowledge, attitudes, concepts, and skills, for example—so that they may engage purposefully and meaningfully in the learning activities that teachers, in light of their recognition of these desired outcomes, are developing with them.

Teachers need to recognize, however, that different types of objectives require different types and degrees of specificity. Determining the type of objectives and their degree of specificity a priori, as advocated by supporters of behavioral objectives, rules out the possibility of having the nature of the objective dictate its style and specificity.

It may not be necessary or even desirable for skillful teachers to set down in a guide or instructional plan all of their objectives in detail, but we suggest that the most important ones be acknowledged by teacher and student and thus become the basis for planning and carrying on learning activities.

This is not to say that some unplanned or unexpected outcomes will not result; it is hoped that they will occur, especially from heuristically designed sets of learning opportunities. We reject a narrow conception of instruction in which students move mechanically from one class exercise to the next in pursuit of prescribed sets of objectives. The skillful teacher is always flexible and adaptable, quick to take advantage at any time of a learning situation which offers worthwhile experiences for the participants, but always assessing the value of the activity in light of a clearly identified set of desired outcomes.

In other words, the teacher's activities should include contextual goal-oriented responses, comparable to those of soccer players, and not be limited to the linear approach, appropriate for farming.

Divergent views on the statement of objectives stem, in part, from a failure to distinguish between behaviors to be learned and human traits to be developed. If no distinction is made, and this is common practice, and *all of education* is to be encompassed in behavioral objectives there is good reason for the alarm expressed by Kliebard, Macdonald, and others. Bear in mind, however, that our discussion of instructional objectives pertains to only a portion of education—the learning of behaviors.

Sources of Assistance

An excellent source of subgoals and objectives is the French report.[58] For each of the twelve designated goal areas, the book lists a great number of subgoals, with illustrative behaviors which constitute in fact instructional objectives (the extent of the list is shown by the fact that it extends for 123 pages).

A somewhat comparable report for the elementary school, although we emphasize that French's goals are appropriate for that level also, was prepared by Nolan Kearney. It is entitled *Elementary School Objectives* (New York: Russell Sage Foundation, 1953). It presents instructional objectives classified in nine categories that constitute aspects of living.

Most available sets of subgoals and objectives are prepared for subject fields. Such lists may be useful to committees that work on those types of curriculum plans. Unfortunately, few lists are available for other kinds of learning opportunities, such as community experiences, noninstructional activities, interactive relations of teachers and students, and the like, except as these activities stem from and relate directly to a course offering. Hence, curriculum committees will largely need to start from scratch in preparing subgoals and objectives for programs of this kind.

Many handbooks and other publications are issued by a number of professional organizations concerned with curriculum and teaching in a subject field. Most teachers are aware of such publications for their area of specialization.

A very useful guide and source of help in writing subgoals and objectives for subject fields is the *Handbook on Formative and Summative Evaluation of Student Learning* by Bloom, Hastings, and Madaus.[59] It contains a chapter on each of 11 subject fields and includes suggestions for use of a two-dimensional chart in defining objectives.

Another useful kind of source is that of curriculum guides prepared by other school systems, state departments of education, national curriculum planning groups, and other agencies concerned with curriculum development. A guide to these curriculum bulletins and materials is the annual booklet issued by the Association for Supervision and Curriculum Development, *Curriculum Materials.*

THE NEEDS ASSESSMENT APPROACH

A procedure for defining the purposes of a school program came into use in the early 1970s—in fact, it was forced on the schools by the federal

[58]Will French and associates, *Behavioral Goals of General Education in High School* (New York: Russell Sage Foundation, 1957).
[59]Benjamin S. Bloom, J. Thomas Hastings, and George F. Madaus, *Handbook on Formative and Summative Evaluation of Student Learning* (New York: McGraw-Hill Book Company, Inc., 1971).

government if they sought certain kinds of support. Title I of the Elementary and Secondary Education Act of 1965, and subsequent amendments, provided federal support for approved school programs for educationally deprived children. In regulations for administration of the Act, local educational agencies had to meet a requirement which stated: "The project for which an application for a grant is made by a local educational agency should be designed to meet the special educational needs of those educationally deprived children who have the greatest need for assistance."[60]

Similarly, the regulations for the administration of Title III of the Act prescribed the following:

> *Assessment of educational needs.* The State plan shall identify the critical educational needs of the State as a whole and the critical educational needs of the various geographic areas and population groups within the State, and shall describe the process by which such needs were identified. This process shall be based upon the use of objective criteria and measurements and shall include procedures for collecting, analyzing, and validating relevant data and translating such data into determinations of critical educational needs.[61]

Inasmuch as states have sought federal funds available under the Elementary and Secondary Education Act, they set about to implement the needs-assessment project, periodically updating the data. Local school systems and other educational agencies eligible for funds, likewise, have had to make such assessments to meet state requirements.

According to the needs-assessment approach, a need exists when there is a discrepancy between a desired or acceptable state of affairs and an observed state of affairs. A needs assessment, therefore, consists of the following steps:

1. Identify the goal areas important to the educational program.
2. Develop or identify indicators or measures for these goal areas.
3. Set acceptable levels on these measures.
4. Apply the measures.
5. Compare the acceptable level with the actual level. If the actual level is below the acceptable level a discrepancy exists and a need has been demonstrated.

Anderson, Ball, and Murphy defined the above steps as the "objective" approach and suggested that when appropriate measures could not be found or developed a "subjective" approach be used.[62] In such an ap-

[60]U.S. Office of Education, *Financial Assistance to Meet the Educational Needs of Educationally Deprived Children: Regulations* (Washington, D.C.: Government Printing Office, 1969), p. 11.
[61]"Title 45—Public Welfare, Chapter I—Office of Education, Department of Health, Education and Welfare," *Federal Register, 37* (November 11, 1972): 24076.
[62]Scarvia B. Anderson, Samuel Ball, Richard T. Murphy and Associates, *Encyclopedia of Educational Evaluation* (San Francisco: Jossey-Bass Publishers, 1977), pp. 245, 255.

proach a rating scale is developed for judging the degree to which present performance in the goal area is acceptable. This technique, as was used in the model program for community and professional development, was described earlier.[63] It is possible and in some instances desirable to combine objective and subjective measures in judging the present level of performance.

Needs assessment has become a common phrase in the lexicon of educators. For example, in-service education for teachers is often based on a "needs assessment." Its uncritical use, however, may have unfortunate consequences. Sergiovanni observed that needs assessment may be unnecessarily rigid in its effects on teachers and pupils "and narrow in its concept of education. One is reminded of a funnel as one sees such plans in operation."[64] In needs assessment there is a progression from broad agreements with respect to purposes and goals—the top of the funnel— to specific measurable objectives—the narrow opening at the bottom. Sergiovanni proposed a process that might be likened to an hourglass configuration. The broadening, below the narrow opening, taking place when the "development of educational goals and objectives is related to a broader context which includes the school's organizational and management system as well as its educational design."[65]

Needs assessment can lock an educational system into maintaining the status quo unless some provision is made for anticipating future needs. One wonders, for example, if a 1905 needs assessment of the training needs of buggy-whip makers would have produced anything other than better buggy whips. Blanchard described a needs-assessment procedure that could overcome this limitation by incorporating future needs.[66] A school faculty gathered the usual data regarding present needs including: student and staff attitudes toward the school program, test results, post-graduation studies, and dropout studies. They also identified future needs through "an intensive session including simulations and media presentations on possible and probable futures in a number of fields including education." Staff members used a Delphi technique to select probable and preferable futures. Blanchard found that "information from futurists stretched thinking beyond the present."[67] Thus the goal areas used as a basis for discrepancy analysis had a future orientation. A consideration of the future is increasingly important in designing educational programs for children and youth in light of rapid and often incomprehensible change.

[63]Rose, *Workshop Packet for Educational Goals and Objectives.*
[64]Thomas J. Sergiovanni, "Synergistic Evaluation," *Teachers College Record, 75* (May 1974): 547.
[65]Sergiovanni, p. 548.
[66]Lois Jerry Blanchard, "Creating a Climate of Rapid Response to Needs for Change," *Educational Leadership, 36* (October 1978): 37–40.
[67]Blanchard, p. 39.

MINIMUM COMPETENCY TESTING

By 1980 minimum competency testing had become a popular procedure for establishing educational objectives and evaluating their achievement. For purposes of this discussion we accept the definition of minimum competencies as "the basic proficiencies in skills and knowledge needed to perform successfully in real-life activities."[68] Establishing objectives through minimum competency tests may short-circuit some of the steps characteristic of effective curriculum planning. The competency-testing movement is based on a narrow view of the purposes and general goals of education. But generally assumptions regarding purposes and goals are neither stated nor examined.

Background

The Denver public schools pioneered the movement when, in the early 1960s, they required successful completion of competency tests in language arts, reading, spelling, and arithmetic for graduation. In 1973 the Oregon State Board of Education established six goals for their schools and, based on these goals, identified 20 areas of personal, social, and career development as necessary to survival in modern life. That same year the Oregon legislature passed a law requiring graduates of the class of 1978 to show proficiencies in these 20 areas. Interest in the Oregon legislation spread rapidly; by the end of the decade most of the states had adopted some type of minimum competency testing.[69]

There were several reasons why minimum competency testing spread so rapidly. It was a natural extension of the movement, already described, toward a systems-based rationalized approach to education and promised to "provide a handle" to accountability. It was a response to the public's concern for declining test scores, high numbers of illiterates within our society (one study placed the figure at 23 million), and the dismay expressed by college officials, business firms, and public agencies over the inability of some high school graduates to write. State legislators, often goaded by constituents, viewed minimum competency testing as a way to raise standards in the schools and get "back-to-basics."

Impact of Minimum-Competency Movement on Education

Enthusiasm for minimum-competency testing "stems from a belief that the testing of essential skills and competencies will help raise academic

[68]Barbara Soloth Miller (ed.), *Minimum Competency Testing* (St. Louis, Mo.: CEMREL, Inc., 1978), p. 13.
[69]*The NAEP Newsletter,* 12 (August 1979): 1 reported, "While 37 states have mandated minimum competency testing in schools over the past two years, a few of the remaining 13 have sought some form of alternative to the state-mandated programs."

standards and increase educational achievement."[70] The extent to which the movement has succeeded depends upon the answers to a series of questions: What is meant by academic standards? How is educational achievement to be measured? and What groups will be considered in assessing achievement—college-bound, dropouts, and "bottom half of the class"?

Academic Standards

Haney and Madaus distinguished knowledge and skills and suggested that "the language of minimum-competency testing suggests concern, not with the broader goals of education, but more narrowly with the issue of skill acquisition."[71] Good competency tests are viewed as congruent with the tasks of life. The movement has focused attention on the social-preparation function of education at the expense of personal development and knowledge acquisition.

Leight, a critic of competency-based education, cited Pennsylvania's "Project 81" to illustrate the erosion of the subject curriculum.[72] In project 81 competencies are used to describe "two senses of achievement: 1) a level of knowledge of skill development, and 2) a demonstration of skills or knowledge in an area of application in life."[73] The goals of Project 81 are to redefine the purposes of public education in terms of competencies and to shift curriculum and graduation requirements away from courses and credits to the newly defined competencies.

Will competency based testing raise academic standards? It is probable that minimum standards will be raised in regard to skills development and the application of these skills to life situations. However, enhancing these standards could weaken standards in the subject matter curriculum and thus fail to produce the desired improvement in Scholastic Aptitude Test (SAT) scores. Weakening standards in the subject matter curriculum will be of concern to subject specialists in higher education responsible for the development of new knowledge.

Educational Achievement

Minimum-competency testing should improve minimum levels of achievement on the minimum-competency tests. Students and teachers have a clear idea as to what is expected of them. Teachers report that

[70]Walt Haney and George Madaus, "Making Sense of the Competency Testing Movement," *Harvard Educational Review, 48* (November 1978): 463.
[71]Haney and Madaus, p. 465.
[72]Robert L. Leight, "Political Goals as Educational Goals," *The Educational Forum, 63* (March 1979): 331–343.
[73]Leight, p. 338.

students are motivated to study for the test. Further, mutual motivation for passing the test encourages students and teachers to shift from their traditional adversarial roles and become allies in passing the examination. While it is true that some poorer students will become discouraged and drop out of school, this in itself will raise minimum competency scores. Levels of achievement on measures other than the minimum competencies need to be investigated as suggested in the next section.

Implications for Curriculum Planners

Curriculum planners should recognize the validity of citizens' concerns that led to minimum-competency testing. Citizens generally view the move as an important way to improve the quality of education. Educators who simply oppose the movement may have little influence on public opinion or on the course of public education. An alternative approach is to help citizens and legislative groups work through the questions that need to be answered in order to have an effective competency-based program. Brickell raised seven questions critical to establishing effective competency policy:

1. What competencies will you require?
2. How will you measure them?
3. When will you measure them?
4. How many minimums will you set?
5. How high will you set the minimums?
6. Will they be for schools or for students?
7. What will you do about the incompetent?[74]

As curriculum planners work with citizens in answering these policy questions they should relate the questions to the total curriculum. They should also help citizens examine the real values, and not just the rhetoric, that lead to competency testing. To what extent was prescriptive legislation motivated by political considerations? Are the weak (victims) being punished for political reasons? Is there a "fiddling" with passing scores to keep political balance? Are politicians using back-to-basics and minimum-competency testing to divert the public's attention from the need for adequate financing for quality education?

Curriculum planners should help citizens understand the legal and ethical issues related to using a competency test as a requirement for a diploma. According to McClung, director of the Law and Education Center at the Education Commission of the States, "Denial of a diploma means, in effect, state certification of incompetence and, therefore, second-class

[74]Henry M. Brickell, "Seven Key Notes on Minimum Competency Testing," in Barbara Soloth Miller (ed.), p. 47.

citizenship."[75] McClung identified four problems often associated with using competency testing as a basis for awarding diplomas.

1. Failure to provide students with adequate notice that a competence test will be used as a requirement for a diploma.
2. Failure to match assessment with what is taught.
3. Inadequate recognition of racial and linguistic differences.
4. Omission of plans for the assessment of handicapped students.

Failure to recognize and find resolutions for the latter two problems, warned McClung, "may simply carry forward the effects of past racial and linguistic discrimination in violation of federal law."[76]

Another responsibility of curriculum planners is to encourage and assist in the design of a program to evaluate all of the consequences of a minimum-competency program. Scores on the minimum-competency tests should be one consideration. However, the evaluation should also monitor achievement levels of all students, but particularly average and above-average students in all areas. Dropout rates should be included in such an evaluation, as well as studies of the success of graduates in postsecondary work. The results of such evaluation will make it possible to improve the minimum-competency program and, at the same time, improve other aspects of the program.

SUMMARY

This chapter describes four steps in the important process of determining educational goals and objectives: stating purposes of education, identifying goals and domains, listing subgoals, and stating objectives. The community needs to agree on broad general purposes to be achieved by all of its educational institutions. This statement should reflect community-wide values and be based on the nature of the immediate and the larger society, on the nature of potential learners of all ages, and on the nature of knowledge. These bases are discussed in Chapter 3.

Given a statement of the purposes of education, the community agrees on the general goals to be achieved by all of its educational institutions. Several illustrations of such goals are included in this chapter. Decisions are then made regarding each institution's responsibilities for the general goals. Major responsibilities for each goal could be assigned to a particular institution with other institutions assisting. For example, the major educa-

---

[75]Merle McClung, statement made in Assessment Conference reported in "Lawyers Look at Competency Testing," *NAEP Newsletter, XII* (August 1979): 1.
[76]McClung, p. 2.

tional responsibility for health might be assigned to the family, with assistance from health agencies and schools.

Subgoals are of two types. One type specifies the behaviors to be learned; the other specifies the human traits to be developed (see Table 4.1, p. 161). These subgoals may also be categorized into domains. The behaviors to be learned are then organized into instructional objectives which become the basis for organizing instruction. There are advantages and disadvantages in stating instructional objectives in behavioral form. The choice of whether or not to use a behavioral objective depends upon the characteristics of the subgoal and the nature of the learners and teachers.

The second type of subgoal—human traits to be developed—might be illustrated by one component of the general goal: to make individuals self-directed learners. To achieve this goal individuals need to be persons who "believe they can learn." This trait cannot be developed by breaking it down into specific tasks to be learned. Rather its achievement will result from the quality of experiences provided. Further, such human traits cannot be developed and then forgotten. For example, a person who believes he can learn in middle school may have that belief severely shaken, or even destroyed, by subsequent experiences in high school or college.

We emphasize that all of these steps are closely interrelated and not necessarily linear. Thus, for example, in selecting instructional objectives it is important to keep in mind the purposes of education and the general goals to which the objective is related. Failure to do this results in losing sight of the forest because of the trees; needless thrashing around in the underbrush results.

The formulation of the aims, goals, and objectives for any educational institution or agency is a very demanding, time-consuming, and sometimes frustrating job; yet it is an essential aspect of curriculum planning, a major factor in determining the quality of the program. These definitions may range from an overt, specific act of behavior to a broad, fundamental statement of a concept of humanism. The quality of living for children, youth, and adults is at stake in these efforts.

ADDITIONAL SUGGESTIONS FOR FURTHER STUDY

"Competency in Education," *The High School Journal, 62* (entire issue, January 1979): 157–206. Lead articles by Admiral Hyman G. Rickover ("Competency Based Education") and Mary F. Berry, then Assistant Secretary for Education, HEW ("Student Competency Testing") present arguments for and against national competency testing. In addition, there are several other articles on minimum-competency testing, including a discussion of legal aspects, and a report on a study of opinions on competency-based teacher education.

Farquhar, Elizabeth C., and Karen S. Dawson, *Citizen Education Today: Developing Civic Competencies.* Washington, D. C.: U.S. Office of Education, OE Publication No. 79–07007. This final report of the USOE Citizen Education Project reports the status of citizen education, cites the need for leadership in its improvement, and sets nine goals for leadership activities that should concern educational planners.

Gardner, John, *Morale.* New York: W. W. Norton and Company, 1978. Gardner writes that "when the regeneration of societies has been achieved, as it often has been over the course of history, the agents of that achievement have been people with the capacity to hope." (p. 150) The recommendations Gardner makes for helping poeple develop the capacity to hope have profound implications for determining the purposes of education.

Goodlad, John I., *What Schools Are For.* Bloomington, Ind.: Phi Delta Kappa Educational Foundation, 1979. An insightful and profound treatise on the goals, functions, and aims of education. In Chapter 3 twelve categories of goals are listed.

Jaeger, Richard M., and Carol Kehr Tittle (eds.), *Minimum Competency Achievement Testing: Motives, Models, Measures, and Consequences.* Washington, D.C.: American Educational Research Association, 1980. Examines policy issues in minimum-competency testing and considers the consequences of such testing for students, teachers, schools, courts, and society. Case studies of minimum-competency testing are included.

Kerr, Clark (chr.), *Giving Youth a Better Chance: Options for Education, Work, and Service.* A report of the Carnegie Council on Policy Studies in Higher Education. San Francisco: Jossey-Bass Publishers, 1979. This very important study concludes that one-third of American youth are "ill-educated, ill-employed, and ill-equipped to make their way in American society." It proposes a radical restructuring of American high schools with much greater opportunities for noncollege-bound students to participate in apprenticeships and acquire job skills.

National School Public Relations Association, *The Competency Challenge: What Schools Are Doing.* Arlington, Va.: The Association, 1978. Provides a concise update of state programs on competency testing as well as providing several "case studies" of local districts' competency efforts.

National Task Force on Citizenship Education, *Education for Responsible Citizenship.* New York: McGraw-Hill, 1977. A distinguished panel places the civic education of children and youth squarely within the mainstream of American schooling. Twenty-one recommendations for strengthening civic education are offered—ten are addressed specifically to the school curriculum.

Perkinson, Henry J., *The Imperfect Panacea: American Faith in Education 1865–1976,* 2d ed. New York: Random House, 1977. An epilogue for 1976–1979 added to the first edition continues the historical examination of American education as the panacea for the nation's social problems. Useful reminder of the continuing social dilemmas which education seeks to resolve, still without complete success.

Postman, Neil, *Teaching as a Conserving Activity.* New York: Delacorte Press, 1979. Postman readily acknowledges that he repudiates his earlier writings that called for radical reforms in the program of schooling and now insists that "the last thing that teaching needs to be in our present situation is revolutionary, groundbreaking, and highly charged with new values." He believes that "the most important contribution schools can make to the education of our youth is to provide them with a sense of coherence in their studies that is a sense of purpose, meaning, and interconnectedness in what they learn."

"Reconsidering the Goals of High School," *Educational Leadership, 37* (January 1980). A number of noted authors describe appropriate goals for high schools in the 1980s.

Tyler, Ralph W. (ed.), *From Youth to Constructive Adult Life: The Role of the Public School.* Berkeley, Calif.: McCutchan Publishing Corporation, 1978. Diverse authors, including Harry S. Broudy, James S. Coleman, Stephen K. Bailey, and Robert J. Havighurst, address the problem of transition. One section gives particular attention to the transition from school to work.

FIVE

···

SELECTING APPROPRIATE CURRICULUM DESIGNS

■■

$\quad$**C**urriculum planners make choices regarding the use of one or more curriculum designs following the identification of goals and objectives (see Figure 1.1, p. 29). By design is meant a particular shape, framework, or pattern of learning opportunities; thus, for any particular population, the scope and types of learning opportunities identify a curriculum design. Since the opportunities are not all provided at once, and since they lack the permanent structure of a building or the texture and color of a dress, the design is not so rapidly visualized. Yet when one observes a group of students closely following a textbook or syllabus in a subject field, it is apparent that the curriculum design is at least for this time and place a subject-focused one; if the same group is observed vigorously pursuing a discussion of happenings in their school community, it is apparent that more than one theory of design is operative in their total curriculum plan. That is, alternative designs may be used even in the same overall curriculum plan.

$\quad$Educators have a variety of designs to choose from that differ not only in form, but, more basically, differ in their underlying assumptions and value positions. According to Eisner and Vallance, the resulting richness of issues and values in the curriculum field "provides an arena that can be either a dynamic and stimulating resource or a conceptual jungle difficult to define and almost impossible to manage."[1] This chapter helps readers find their way through this conceptual jungle by describing five different curriculum designs focused on: subject matter/disciplines, specific competencies/technology, human traits/processes, social functions/activities, and individual needs and interests/activities.

$\quad$The first part of the chapter describes steps involved in curriculum designing followed by a description of alternative designs. Guidelines for selecting appropriate designs are summarized to conclude the chapter.

STEPS IN CURRICULUM DESIGNING

As presented in this book the curriculum planning process involves four principal phases:

[1] Elliot W. Eisner and Elizabeth Vallance (eds.), *Conflicting Conceptions of Curriculum* (Berkeley, Calif.: McCutchan Publishing Corporation, 1974), p. 2.

1. Setting major goals, domains, and objectives through basic data analysis.
2. Designing a curriculum plan or plans consistent with major goals, domains, and objectives.
3. Anticipating curriculum implementation (instruction).
4. Planning curriculum evaluation.

Our concern here is with the second phase, designing, and we now consider the process in detail. Our treatment assumes the prior selection of major goals, domains, and objectives as described in Chapter 4.

Step One—Considering Basic Factors Relating to the Major Goal and Domain

Curriculum planners use data about social aims and needs; learners and the learning process; and knowledge requirements when they identify goals, domains, and objectives. These same data need to be considered in designing curriculum (see Figure 1.2, p. 30) and in addition, curriculum planners need to focus on specific data relevant to a domain and population when these are known. For example, assume that the faculty of a middle school has identified as one of its major goals assisting each of its students to explore and identify special interests that can become bases for continued and successful learning and living. Immediately such questions as the following are raised: What special interests do our students already have? What other interests are appropriate and feasible for such a population? Of present and possible interests, are any unacceptable in this community? Of present and possible interests, which have carry-over effect into future academic-, career-, or leisure-oriented activities? Of present and possible interests, which are possible for development within our school and community? Consideration of these types of questions is essential to further planning within this particular domain.

Step Two—Identifying Subgoals of the Domain

The hierarchy of goals and objectives was fully explained in Chapter 4. Designing requires goal setting on a second level. It involves moving from the broad goal of a domain to subgoals that are hypothesized as achievable for a particular population and within the potentials of the domain. Subgoals need not be narrowly stated; they may be open-ended statements of desired outcomes broadly defined.

For example, we can easily assume that any elementary school faculty would set as one broad goal helping its students to attain skills of continued learning. Within the learning skills domain subgoals would be set relating to skills of reading, listening, questioning, organizing information, and others. The more specific the data the faculty has consulted regarding the current status of student learning skills, the more specific subgoals become.

Or, for another example, a high school faculty might place high priority on the major goal of developing skills of independent, self-directed learning. Its study of the nature of such learning activity and its analysis of the needs of the students in this area would lead to subgoals relating to independent study practices, motivation for independent learning, selection of curriculum options, self-evaluation patterns, and others.

Step Three—Identifying Possible Types of Learning Opportunities

The third step in curriculum designing is a blend of visionary brainstorming and realistic appraisal of actual possibilities. For example, the middle school faculty seeking to develop a special interests domain has to reconcile all of its dreaming, perhaps augmented by the hopes of the students themselves, with activities that are actually possible given the personnel and facilities of the school and community. The limitations may be far less than those usually operating if the faculty includes the possibilities of community facilities, public media, and community resource people.

At this stage some tentative classification is helpful both to extend the listing of opportunities and to lead toward the selection of designs. Thus one type of learning opportunity would be that of short-term exploratory courses in such areas as arts and crafts, industrial arts, music, art, and foreign languages. Another might be mini-courses related to fields of social studies and language arts: short-term arrangements supplementing basic instruction in these fields that would focus on political parties, local history, individual historical events or movements, dramatic productions, literary types or pieces, and other interests. Another type of learning opportunity would be independent study projects for students with special interests in any subject field, that is, individual projects growing out of but not required in regular group instruction. Still another type of learning opportunity, perhaps the most common, would be special activities organized for and largely by students and related to any of a very wide range of possibilities, from acrobatics to xylophones.

Similarly, in any domain this step involves identification of a few organizing centers or learning opportunities, a trial classification of these, usually according to the way in which they are provided, an extension of types that seem to persist in discussion and planning, and the ultimate development of agreed-upon, possible opportunities classified tentatively as a basis for relating them to design principles.

Step Four—Settling on Appropriate Curriculum Designs

With the domain determined, subgoals tentatively set, and possible types of learning opportunities explored, the planning group is ready for the step that is given major attention here: considering and selecting design alternatives.

A high school curriculum council seeking to develop an area or domain of specialization would undoubtedly list many subgoals relating to a wide spectrum of specialized interests to be served and advanced by the high school curriculum. If the group is or becomes knowledgeable about alternative curriculum designs, it is unlikely to settle on any one design focus for the very wide range of specialization opportunities. Instead, it might categorize opportunities into several designs.

An expected area of specialization for many students would be preparation for further study after high school in one or more subject areas. Advanced offerings in English, foreign languages, mathematics. science, and social studies would be made available for these students, and the subject matter/disciplines design would define the scope and sequence of these opportunities.

As their area of specialization many students might choose the expressive arts. Here there is no specific design principle more applicable than the one we later describe as individual needs and interests/activities.

Although music, for example, includes systematic and sequential instruction for specific musical performance, individual interests and needs would determine the grouping and to some extent the scope and sequence of other learning opportunities. Similarly, effective programs in other specialties within the arts field also seem much more appropriately planned by a needs and interests principle than by other designs.

Some high shool students would specialize in skills training for occupations they can enter after high school, and for them specific vocational training would be made available. This specific training is appropriately designed in accordance with the specific competencies/technology design.

Still other specialization programs may be developed by other design principles. Thus, the specialization domain, embracing many types of specialized interests and related learning opportunities, also requires several curriculum designs. Other domains—for example, social competence —may also involve more than one design. The domain of continued learning skills seems clearly to match in purpose and scope the design principle we describe as human traits/processes.

It should be emphasized that a planning group may well set domains other than the four we have illustrated, but the matching of domains and designs is a process requiring the steps described above as well as a knowledge of alternative designs. Without such steps and such knowledge, designing is lacking or inadequate, as is generally the case when all learning opportunities are reduced to so-called subjects and designed according to the traditional subject design with its attendant textbooks, homework, examinations, and credit units.

Step Five—Preparing Tentative Design Specifications

Step five is a refinement of step four. At the latter point the designing group makes a trial listing of types of learning opportunities—study units, skills sequences, activity groupings, subjects or courses, mini-courses, community experiences, independent studies, and so forth—as a basis for selecting design principles. Once the designs have been selected, learning opportunities are more deliberately planned. Thus a plan for the domain of social competence might include at least two major designs, subject matter/disciplines and social functions/activities. In the first category would be placed specific subject matter related to the goal—history of the movements in the world and in the United States to advance human rights and the conditions of human life; concepts in sociology, political science, economics, and other social sciences; and other subject matter. The design specifications would indicate organizing centers for this content and possible instructional organizations such as interdisciplinary units, mini-courses, and semester-or year-long courses.

In the second category—social functions/activities—the designing group might place many learning opportunities frequently classified as "activities": student government, homeroom, community services, student forums, civic participation, human relations councils, and others.

A tentative design specification should provide answers to these questions posed in Chapter 1:

1. Who will the learners be?
2. What are the subgoals or objectives?
3. What types of learning experiences will be provided?
4. What will be the locale for the learning experiences?
5. What roles will participants play: learners, teachers, others?
6. What will be the time and space dimensions?
7. What criteria will be used in assessment?

Step Six—Identifying Implementation Requirements

Implementation of a curriculum plan, instruction, is discussed in Chapter 6. However, in anticipation of the implementation and with tentative decisions made regarding the questions just listed, the designers can identify requirements for implementation. Imagine that a middle school planning group has designed a series of teaching units around the subject matter of human relations movements and events and has planned for these units to be developed for two teams of 120 students each. Implementation requirements would include arranging for the appropriate team teachers or leaders, especially in social studies and language arts, to prepare the detailed unit plans, deciding on a physical setting for large-group instruction, and ordering any special materials.

Implementation requirements for some designs can be more demanding. For example, a design in the personal development domain might include systematic instruction in sex education, drug abuse, or other sensitive areas. For this, implementation may well require advance communication with parents, approval of appropriate community groups and agencies, and enlistment of special professional assistance in instruction. Or the social functions/activities design for learning opportunities through civic participation would likely require considerable advance spadework in the community to identify and screen possible opportunities in government agencies, civic associations, and other organizations.

CURRICULUM DESIGNS AND CONCEPTIONS OF THE CURRICULUM

Selecting a curriculum design is not as simple as saying, "I'll take this one." Each design grows out of a series of assumptions regarding: 1) purposes and goals of education; 2) sources of objectives; 3) characteristics of learners; 4) nature of the learning process; 5) type of society to be served; and 6) nature of knowledge. Furthermore, the design selected influences, and in some cases dictates, instructional strategies, roles of teachers and learners, instructional materials, and evaluation strategies. Selecting the appropriate design, therefore, is a highly professional task requiring a knowledge of various possible designs and an understanding of the value commitments embedded in each design.

The importance of value commitments in the selection of a curriculum design cannot be overemphasized. Curriculum planners might well engage community, staff, and students in a dialogue about the philosophical bases of the assumptions and values that undergird this choice making. And just as selecting curriculum designs is an on-going process, so should there be a continuing dialogue about educational values and assumptions and their philosophical underpinnings.

Unwarranted Limitations

Curriculum planners should not limit their thinking to the five designs presented in this book. An examination of their values may lead them to creative planning that dares to move beyond the existing. The designs described in this chapter should stimulate a consideration of several options, not stifle thinking.

Curriculum workers are unduly restricted when they decide a priori to use only one design throughout the curriculum; indeed, the preoccupation of some curriculum theorists with a single principle or focus may be partially responsible for the confusion in curriculum work. We believe that a curriculum design does involve the selection of a single designing principle. The fallacy lies in the assumption that the single principle—the discipline or some other—can and should be applied to the entire curriculum. Adherence to a single design eliminates learning opportunities which cannot be so designed. Curriculum planners should design whatever learning opportunities are most appropriate for the domains and objectives: in other words, design should follow function rather than vice versa, and consequently a comprehensive curriculum plan may utilize more than one design. Any curriculum theory which posits a single design as appropriate to the total array of learning opportunities a school can provide is faulty. We believe that any one of the five designs we describe would be the most effective design for some aspects of some educational programs; we also believe that not one of the five designs would be best for every educational program.

A gap often exists between broad goals of the curriculum and classroom practice. This may be a consequence of trying to accomplish all goals with only one or two curriculum designs. For example, the goal of producing functionally literate citizens will be achieved with difficulty in a subject matter/disciplines curriculum design; while the specific competencies/technology design is well adapted to this goal. The conclusion is simple: curriculum workers should be fully cognizant of possible designs and make deliberate choices among them.

Optional Designs

Various categories of curriculum designs are found in curriculum publications. For example, McNeil described a humanistic, social reconstructionist, technological, and academic subject curriculum.[2] In another instance, Eisner and Vallance identified five orientations to curriculum: the development of cognitive processes; curriculum as technology; self-actualization, or curriculum as consummatory experiences; social reconstruction-relevance; and academic rationalism.[3] There are similarities, as well as differences, between our designs and those of other writers.

Distinctions among our five curriculum designs are based on the predominant source of data for the goals and objectives. Thus, for example, the primary source of data for the subject matter/disciplines design is organized subject matter. Since the method of presentation is through

[2]John D. McNeil, *Curriculum: A Comprehensive Introduction* (Boston: Little, Brown and Company, 1977).
[3]Eisner and Vallance, pp. 5–14 passim.

organized disciplines we refer to the design as subject matter/disciplines. Table 5.1 summarizes the designs, the primary source of data for goals and objectives, and usual ways to organize instruction.

Humanism is not listed as a distinct curriculum design since we believe that a "humanistic curriculum" is not restricted to any particular design. Because of its importance, however, it is discussed following the five curriculum designs.

DESIGNS FOCUSED ON SUBJECT MATTER/DISCIPLINES

We now consider particular curriculum designs. The dominant concept of the curriculum, historically and currently, is that of school subjects taught by teachers and learned by students. Correspondingly, the dominant curriculum design is that of a curriculum framework of subjects, usually but not necessarily derived from the major disciplines of knowledge, with the framework reflecting design decisions as to specific subjects and their scope and sequence. In describing this design and the other designs included in subsequent sections of this chapter, we will deal with its characteristic features, the arguments or case for it, and its applications, both actual and potential, and limitations.

Characteristic Features

The most characteristic and comprehensive feature of the subject matter/disciplines design is the relative orderliness of this pattern. The cur-

TABLE 5.1 Curriculum designs

Curriculum Designs	Primary Source* of Data for Goals and Objectives	Usual Ways to Organize Instruction
1. Subject matter/disciplines	1. Subject matter to be learned	1. By disciplines (for example, chemistry)
2. Specific competencies/ technology	2. Competencies to be acquired	2. Through instructional designs (for example, learning modules)
3. Human traits/processes	3. Human traits of learners to be developed	3. Through planned processes (for example, values clarification exercises)
4. Social functions/activities	4. Needs of society	4. Through community activities or 1, 2, or 3 above (for example, "get out the vote" campaign)
5. Individual needs and interests/activities	5. Needs and interests of the learners	5. Through independent learning activities or 1, 2, or 3 above (for example, learning to paint)

*All data sources listed in Chapter 3 must guide the selection and organization of a design, but each design as noted below gives emphasis to one type of data more than the other types.

riculum plan appears neatly divided into subjects, which themselves frequently are subdivided according to school grades and even marking and reporting periods. The Carnegie unit system entrenched this design and a related schedule in the high school with the original definition (1909) of a unit of credit as the study of a subject in high school for one period a day throughout the school year. Even before such a curriculum accounting system was developed, the subject design was regularized to facilitate the expansion of schooling for America's expanding population. The educational historian Lawrence A. Cremin credits the efforts during the 1870s of a St. Louis school superintendent, William Torrey Harris, to define the term *curriculum* as the beginning of the modern curriculum movement. Cremin interprets Harris' theory of education and the curriculum as holding the curriculum responsible for making the accumulated wisdom of the race "economically and systematically available" and describes Harris' "analytical paradigm" as embracing the following components:

> There is the learner, self-active and self-willed by virtue of his humanity and thus self-propelled into the educative process; there is the course of study, organized by responsible adults with appropriate concern for priority, sequence, and scope; there are materials of instruction which particularize the course of study; there is the teacher who encourages and mediates the process of instruction; there are the examinations which appraise it; and there is the organizational structure within which it proceeds and within which large numbers of individuals are enabled simultaneously to enjoy its benefits.[4]

This, Cremin writes, set forth "all the pieces ... for the game of curriculum-making that would be played over the next half-century"; indeed, Cremin further shows, as we will review later, the marked similarity between Harris' efforts at curriculum reform in the 1870s and those of other reformers in the 1950s and 1960s.

A more significant type of orderliness characterizes the subject matter/disciplines design, however, than these somewhat mechanical aspects. This is the inherent principle or structure of a discipline. The structure of a discipline is the set of fundamental generalizations that bind a field of knowledge into a unity, organize this body of knowledge into a cohesive whole, fix the limits of investigation and inclusion of knowledge for the discipline itself, and provide the basis for discovering what else exists within the field. Thus, each of the traditional school subjects such as mathematics, chemistry, and physics, which are well-ordered disciplines, has its own distinct design, and the school curriculum planner has only to determine what of this design to use, and when and how. But the structure of

[4]Lawrence A. Cremin, "Curriculum-Making in the United States," *Teachers College Record,* *73* (December 1971): 210.

other subjects created for practical and important purposes is very unclear, if not completely lacking.

Hence with the subject matter/disciplines design there is a confusion as to what is a subject and what internal logic there is in the design. At least three usages of the term "subject" confuse the subject matter/disciplines design principle of internal order. First, in the selection of a particular phase of a discipline for school study such distortion can occur as to make invalid the usual structure of the discipline. For example, various efforts to select and simplify aspects of mathematics and physical science, respectively, into so-called practical or general mathematics and consumer or practical chemistry necessitate the creation of special scope and sequence plans for these courses. Second, the widespread practice, especially in the elementary school curriculum, of encompassing materials from more than one basic discipline, for example, incorporating history and anthropology into social studies, has also necessitated special designing of some order of the content. Third, in many cases the established disciplines do not offer students opportunities to learn to deal with problems of living, and new organizations of content that are basically extradisciplinary or perhaps interdisciplinary have been created and classified as subjects. Business education, consumer education, driver education, drug education, environmental education, family life education, homemaking education, health education, industrial arts education, physical education, and sex education are just a few of the many such subjects.

Thus, while the established disciplines and the subjects clearly derived from them have an order or structure which marks their designs, many so-called subjects have no inherent design, and their planning may well use any of the other design principles we are considering. In practice, these latter subjects may be so diverse and their design of such varied quality as to make the total design appear confused and shapeless when the same schedule and instructional organization are used for all curriculum elements from algebra to office machines or from athletics to zoology. This is not so much a criticism of the subject matter/disciplines design as it is a comment on its bastardization.

The Case for the Subject Matter/Disciplines Design

Curriculum publications have long been replete with arguments for and against a curriculum organization based on subjects. One of the most persistent and perhaps the most influential arguments has been that of educational convenience; that is, since knowledge is organized into disciplines which can be used or adapted as school subjects, the easiest way to set a school curriculum, the argument says, is to use these subjects, providing a matching instructional organization and student progress system. Selecting and teaching subject matter and testing student knowledge

thereof is the process, and it is argued that this can be readily implemented by knowledgeable teachers, organization into classes, and written
tests. This argument of convenience assumes that schools, colleges, teachers, parents, and citizens in general are geared to the subject-centered
curriculum and support wholeheartedly this organizational plan. In effect,
the argument is for maintaining the status quo because it is simpler to do
so; we cannot accept this view. The case has to rest on the relative values
of the subject design.

The values of the design are derived from the important role of knowledge in the curriculum. Here there can be no real quarrel, for there would
indeed be no curriculum if there were no content, no knowledge to use
as the substance of experience. The kinds and amounts of knowledge and
its availability for school use are major determinants of the curriculum.
Since knowledge is organized into disciplines, it follows logically that the
disciplines are primary sources of curriculum content.

Curriculum theorists who argue for subject matter/disciplines designs
generally assume a continuing process of changing knowledge and changing subject matter in the curriculum. Their case emphasizes the fact that
the disciplines and correspondingly the school subjects have an internal
structure to which new knowledge can be added and from which obsoles-
cent knowledge can be dropped. The bodies of subject matter, they believe, best help the learner to test out information, to answer questions,
to inquire, to reconstruct his or her own knowledge and use it—in short,
to develop his or her intellectual powers.

The subject matter/disciplines designers generally assume that there is
a body of knowledge that constitutes the curriculum and that the task of
designing involves decisions as to what phases and organizations of knowledge are to be taught to whom, and when and how. Thus Henry Clinton
Morrison, whose Morrisonian unit curriculum and instructional system
greatly influenced high school curriculum planning from the 1920s into
the 1950s and even later, described the curriculum as "constant and universal." Thus "the content of Education is at bottom the same the world
over, and the framework upon which that content is hung, namely, the
Curriculum, is the same in essentials. The *pedagogical problems* arise in
the fields of programming and of teaching."[5] In *The Curriculum of the
Common School* he identified major phases of twelve "universal institutions" (language, mathematics, graphics, science, religion, morality and
moral institutions, art, civics, politics, commerce, industry, and health)
that he considered to be "the curriculum of the common school," or as he
further defined it, "the content of the general education of the common
man."

[5]Henry Clinton Morrison, *The Curriculum of the Common School* (Chicago: University of
Chicago Press, 1940), p. 5.

In *A Functional Curriculum for Youth,* published a decade after Morrison's book, William B. Featherstone also upheld the role of the subjects and emphasized the necessity of selecting and programming appropriate content, noting that "the practical problem of how to program a curriculum so that the essential contents—essential for general education—of all necessary subjects can be taught effectively has become increasingly difficult to solve satisfactorily."[6] He argued for a selection of content to be based on the "functions" of the curriculum and proposed a curriculum plan not unlike our own concept of "domains." The four functions Featherstone outlined were integration, supplementation, exploration, and specialization; this view involved a different conception of the functions of the subjects and their solution, but not their abandonment:

> Efforts to devise a suitable curriculum by vitalizing the conventional subjects, reshuffling them into new patterns, or amalgamating them into broad fields do not seem promising. It is probably not necessary to scrap the entire conventional curriculum, but it is apparent that an improved conception of the structure and functions of the curriculum is needed before one can decide what parts of the old curriculum can be salvaged and for what purpose.[7]

In fact, Featherstone's theory justified existing subjects and called for new ones to serve the specialization function.[8]

A major improvement in the subjects/disciplines approach occurred in the 1950s and 1960s through the national curriculum projects (see Chapter 2). Foshay appraised this development and concluded that there was "more progress in curriculum making for intellectual development in the fifties and sixties than at any other time in this century."[9] These national curriculum projects viewed intellectual behavior as an active process of inquiry and problem solving.

The basic intents of the national curriculum projects were described by Bruner in his widely cited report of the 1959 Woods Hole Conference of project directors, in which he advanced the case for teaching the structure of the subjects: "The curriculum of a subject should be determined by the most fundamental understanding that can be achieved of the underlying principles that give structure to that subject."[10] When students learn the structure of a discipline they understand how things are related. Bruner saw several advantages to learning the structure of a discipline. First, it

[6]William B. Featherstone, *A Functional Curriculum for Youth* (New York: American Book Company, 1950), p. 112.
[7]Featherstone, p. 133.
[8]Featherstone, p. 143.
[9]Arthur W. Foshay, "Toward a Humane Curriculum," in James John Jelinek (ed.), *Education in Flux—Implications for Curriculum Development* (Tempe, Ariz.: Professors of Curriculum, 1979), p. 101.
[10]Jerome S. Bruner, *The Process of Education* (Cambridge, Mass.: Harvard University Press, 1960), pp. 31–32.

makes a subject more comprehensible. Second, it improves memory since it allows learners to place detail into a structured pattern. Third, an understanding of fundamental principles and ideas facilitates a "transfer of training" to similar principles. Eisner and Vallance commented on this new development. "The structure of knowledge orientation is a dynamic new development within a very old field."[11]

Thus, proponents of the subject matter/disciplines design have going for them the undeniably strong argument that knowledge is of necessity at the base of the curriculum. Knowledge is organized into disciplines, and school subjects organized out of these disciplines can be the skeleton of the curriculum. Further, the structure-of-knowledge approach provides a powerful tool for selection of content and organization of instruction.

Applications and Limitations

Knowledge from the disciplines as reflected in the organization of school subjects has been and remains the dominant design of curriculum planning. It will continue to be an important curriculum design even though it has limitations. Understanding these limitations enables curriculum planners to make the best use of the subject matter/disciplines design.

As pointed out previously, many subjects have been added to the curriculum to meet specific needs; illustrations include business education, driver education, drug education, and industrial arts education. Although such subjects have no real basis in original disciplines, such factors as accrediting standards, graduation and college entrance requirements, elementary school time allotments, and secondary school schedules have recognized subjects as the curriculum, so that whatever has been added, however unrelated it might be to the traditional disciplines, has been classified as a subject. Once so classified, the subject has tended to become fixed and the curriculum that much more inflexible.

A first step for curriculum planners, therefore, is to determine if an area designated as a subject has its roots in a discipline. This is not to disparage in any way subjects without a discipline base; rather it is to recommend that alternative curriculum designs be considered for such subjects. For example, of the subjects listed above, business education, driver education, and industrial arts education could probably be effectively taught using a specific competencies/technology design. And drug education might use either a human traits/processes or a social functions/activities design.[12]

Does the tremendous increase of available information, described in

[11]Eisner and Vallance, p. 13.
[12]For information regarding the comprehensiveness and extent of high school courses see Susan Abramowitz, et al., *High School '77. A Survey of Public Secondary School Principals* (Washington, D. C.: National Institute of Education, 1978), pp. 72–77.

Chapter 3, present a limitation of the subject matter/disciplines approach? It is no longer possible for an individual to encompass even a small portion of the knowledge available; furthermore, computers provide virtually instantaneous access to vast stores of information. These developments have made obsolete the value of memorizing large amounts of information. They have also increased the value of understanding the structure of the disciplines. Without such knowledge individuals will be unable to determine what computer-stored information to access—nor what to do with it once they have it. Whitehead's admonition, cited earlier, becomes particularly pertinent in an information/computer age: "The problem of education is to make the pupil see the wood by means of the trees."[13] Content needs to be selected carefully to illustrate and clarify the structure of a discipline.

Developers of the national curriculum programs beginning in the 1950s and 1960s found that a careful selection of content and materials did not assure effective instruction. The attempt to produce "teacher-proof" materials failed. A curriculum exemplifying a subject matter/disciplines design is easy to teach poorly and difficult to teach well. It is easy to assign material to be read, have students recite, and test for recall of information. It is difficult to provide experiences that demonstrate basic principles and concepts, help students understand and verbalize them, and assess students' growth in understanding the structure of a discipline. Teachers need a firm grasp of the structure of the disciplines they are teaching as well as assistance in implementing a subject matter/disciplines curriculum.

Probably the chief limitation of the subject matter/disciplines design, however well planned and implemented, is the lack of direct relation of the organized subject matter to the problems and interests of the learner. Caswell stated in 1946 that "the conventional curriculum framework is the greatest single obstacle to the development of a program in the high school which provides the necessary assistance to youth in achieving in actual living the various developmental tasks which our society demands."[14] Two decades later the schools were still being criticized for the same reason, but it was not until the student uprisings in colleges and universities in the late 1960s and their counterparts in high schools that curriculum planners once again were compelled to focus on the matter of relevancy. Bruner, whose work led to a renewed emphasis on the subjects, in 1971 expressed "doubts as to whether the conventional models, the forms of our knowledge, are appropriate to our purposes in our times,"

[13]Alfred North Whitehead, *The Aims of Education* (New York: Mentor Books, 1929), p. 18.
[14]Hollis L. Caswell, "Curriculum Proposals for the Future," in Hollis L. Caswell (ed.), *The American High School,* Eighth Yearbook of the John Dewey Society (New York: Harper & Brothers, 1946), p. 140.

reflecting that "perhaps new requirements of action were proving the inadequacy of our models as they have emerged historically."[15] In fact he called for a moratorium or de-emphasis on structure of subjects in favor of attention to more urgent problems:

> If I had my choice now, in terms of a curriculum project for the seventies, it would be to find the means whereby we could bring society back to its sense of values and priorities in life. I believe I would be quite satisfied to declare, if not a moratorium, then something of a de-emphasis on matters that have to do with the structure of history, the structure of physics, the nature of mathematical consistency, and deal with curriculum rather in the context of the problems that face us.[16]

Bruner's somewhat belated recognition that there is more to education than studying the disciplines underscores the importance of maintaining a balanced emphasis on all of the goals of education. His message also reminds us of the value of relating subjects to the interests of students and showing the relevance of subjects to today's world.

Some of the national projects that are continuing under the auspices of R and D centers and regional labs are broader in conception and incorporate some of the principal points of other designs although remaining within the subject matter/ disciplines design.[17] For example, the Biological Sciences Curriculum Study (BSCS) material relates the study of biological sciences to present day ecological concerns.[18]

A final limitation of the subject matter/disciplines design, as it is often applied, was seen by Whitehead as "the fatal disconnection of subjects which kills the vitality of our modern curriculum." He set the matter straight in a particularly expressive statement:

> There is only one subject-matter for education, and that is Life in all its manifestations. Instead of this single unity, we offer children—Algebra, from which nothing follows; Geometry, from which nothing follows; Science, from which nothing follows; History, from which nothing follows; a Couple of Languages, never mastered; and lastly, most dreary of all, Literature, represented by plays of Shakespeare, with philological notes and short analyses of plot and character to be in substance committed to memory. Can such a list be said to represent Life, as it is known in the midst of the living of it? The best that can

[15]Jerome S. Bruner, *The Relevance of Education,* Anita Gil (ed.) (New York: W. W. Norton and Company, Inc., 1971), p. xii.

[16]Jerome S. Bruner, "The Process of Education Reconsidered," in Robert R. Leeper (ed.), *Dare to Care/ Dare to Act* (Washington D. C.:Association for Supervision and Curriculum Development, National Education Association, 1971), pp. 29–30.

[17]For descriptions see the newsletter, *Educational R & D Report,* issued by the R & D Interpretation Service, CEMREL, Inc. 3120 59th St., St. Louis, Mo.

[18]W. V. Mayer (ed.), *Planning Curriculum Development* (Boulder, Colo. Biological Sciences Curriculum Study, 1975).

be said of it is, that it is a rapid table of contents which a deity might run over in his mind while he was thinking of creating a world, and had not yet determined how to put it together.[19]

Since Whitehead wrote that statement, over 50 years ago, various interdisciplinary approaches have been tried. The fusion or broad fields approach combined different disciplines, for example, language arts and social studies. Such approaches have limitations; for example, Taba pointed out "it is possible that this treatment of knowledge fails to produce disciplined knowledge because insignificant details have been replaced by unintelligible generalizations."[20]

The core curriculum, developed in the 1930s and 1940s, disregarded subject boundaries as it drew upon diverse forms of knowledge. An effort was made to relate the core curriculum to life interests and student problems. For example, "living in the community" might serve as the core for tenth grade science, art, and social studies. The core curriculum came under increasing criticism in the 1940s and 1950s, and was virtually forgotten as the national curriculum projects forged ahead in the 1950s and 1960s.

What of the status of interdisciplinary approaches today? Cohen concluded from her doctoral study that, "interdisciplinary education is very much alive." One reason she cited is that "in contrast to the 1940s and 1950s, interdisciplinarity today is seen by nations and organizations throughout the political spectrum as a weapon for survival."[21] For example, "it took interdisciplinary ecology to discover that D.D.T., a chemical triumph, was a biological and social disaster."[22]

An illustration of an interdisciplinary approach is a correlated science program developed at the University of Florida laboratory school, P. K. Yonge. The correlated science program grew out of faculty concern with "the inability of students to see the interrelationships that exist in the environment and among disciplines, the excessive overlap from one course to another . . . and the total neglect of the interaction of science and society."[23] The faculty identified six major concepts as focal points for breaking down the barriers between disciplines: orderliness, change, equilibrium, models, quantification, and technology. To illustrate, "The theme of Change considers the dynamic character of our total environment, the

[19]Whitehead, p. 18.

[20]Hilda Taba, *Curriculum Development: Theory and Practice* (New York: Harcourt, Brace and World, Inc., 1962), p. 395.

[21]Mary Cohen, "Whatever Happened to Interdisciplinary Education?", *Educational Leadership, 36* (November 1978): 124.

[22]Cohen, p. 125.

[23]Thomas Gadsden, Jr., Virginia F. Allen, and William L. Dixon, "Cutting Boundaries With Correlated Science," *School Science and Mathematics, LXXV* (January 1975): 80.

inevitability and desirability of change in the total universe, on and within the earth, in ecosystems, in societies, and in individuals."[24] Enrollment in the elective course increased threefold, and graduates report their "success in science in college and perhaps more important, their increasing ability to see interrelationships."[25]

We have described new developments in the tradition-bound subject matter/disciplines design. What of the future? Eisner and Vallance observed, "Academic rationalism is alive and well. The problem is to understand why we are so defensive about it."[26] The design has come under attack because it provided an inadequate design for all of education. However, it would be difficult to defend a total educational program that did not include some systematic study of the disciplines.

DESIGNS FOCUSED ON SPECIFIC COMPETENCIES/TECHNOLOGY

The most narrow or limited design possibilities are those that focus on specific competencies. It matters little whether the competencies are stated in terms of the activity analysis procedures of the 1920s, the related job analysis used in vocational education for many years, or the competency- or performance-based curriculum and instructional plans widely promoted in the 1970s.

Characteristic Features

The performance-based objectives and curriculum plans advocated in part as a phase of the accountability movement beginning in the 1960s seem distinctly related to many earlier curriculum theories and practices that also emphasized performance. Obviously, all curriculum plans anticipate some type of eventual performance on the part of the learner, but the design we are describing assumes a direct relation among objective, learning activity, and performance. Other designs assume a much less direct relation among these components, and to some extent they anticipate that the learners' ultimate behavior will be the outgrowth of many learning experiences through which they fashion their own performance objectives and standards.

The specific competencies/technology design is based on a sequential analytic approach to curriculum development:

[24]Gadsden, et al., p. 83.
[25]Gadsden, et al., p. 86.
[26]Eisner and Vallance, p. 13.

1. Identify all tasks or jobs for which preparation should be provided.
2. Determine what one would need to know and do in order to perform these tasks or do these jobs.
3. Arrange tasks and jobs in appropriate courses.
4. Organize the knowledge and skill for each task or job into a hierarchy.
5. Determine what one needs to know for mastery of each knowledge or skill item.[27]

The result of this task analysis, generally stated as one or more behavioral or performance objectives, provides input to an instructional design system. These systems are concerned with the how and not the what of education; they seek to provide the most efficient means of communicating knowledge and facilitating learning. It is in this sense that technology is a part of the specific competencies/technology design.[28]

In a specific competencies/technology design, the desired performances are stipulated as behavioral or performance objectives or competencies, learning activities are planned to achieve each objective, and the learner's performance is checked as a basis for moving from one objective to another. Thus, in typing instruction learners must demonstrate their knowledge of the keyboard before they move to mastery of particular typing forms. In golf they learn and show how to grip the club before they learn and show how to make particular strokes with it. In social studies they learn how to read a map and demonstrate this competency before they learn about and demonstrate their knowledge of particular geographic locations and relations. Thus, a design based on specific competencies is characterized by specific, sequential, and demonstrable learnings of the tasks, activities, or skills which constitute the acts to be learned and performed by students.

The Case for Designs Focused on Specific Competencies/Technology

The earliest published justification of a competency-based curriculum design appeared in 1918 in Bobbitt's *The Curriculum*. In this and a related volume (1924) describing the Los Angeles curriculum program, Bobbitt argued for an activity analysis approach to curriculum planning. His theory, he said, was "simple":

[27]See Donald E. Orlosky and B. Othanel Smith, *Curriculum Development, Issues and Insights* (Chicago: Rand McNally College Publishing Company, 1978), pp. 105–121.
[28]For a complete description of instructional design systems see Robert M. Gagné and Leslie J. Briggs, *Principles of Instructional Design*, 2d Edition (New York: Holt, Rinehart and Winston, Inc., 1979). For illustrations of instructional design systems see the periodicals: *Educational Techonology* and *Journal of Instructional Development*.

The word *curriculum* is Latin for a *race-course,* or the *race* itself—a place of deeds, or a series of deeds. As applied to education, it is that *series of things which children and youth must do and experience* by way of developing abilities to do the things well that make up the affairs of adult life; and to be in all respects what adults should be.[29]

In further developing this theory Bobbitt distinguished between "directed" and "undirected" training experience. He proposed that the curriculum aim at objectives not attained by undirected training and that "the curriculum of the directed training is to be discovered in the shortcomings of individuals after they have had all that can be done in the undirected training."[30] Bobbitt recognized that his activity analysis procedures would be more easily applied in "spelling, grammar, and other subjects that result in objective performance, such as pronunciation, drawing, music, computation, etc.," but argued that it was equally valid in its application to all other fields, including "civic, moral, vocational, sanitational, recreational, and parental education":

Only as we agree upon *what ought to be* in each of these difficult fields, can we know at what the training should aim. Only as we list the errors and shortcomings of human performance in each of the fields can we know what to include and to emphasize in the directed curriculum of the schools.[31]

To Bobbitt the case for a curriculum based on activity analysis and leading to performance was basically that of the lack of relevance, in more recent terminology, of past curriculum practice to present human needs and the resultant deficiencies in human affairs. By focusing education on the "shortcomings of children and men" the schools can discharge new and needed functions, he argued.[32] Bobbitt's report of curriculum development in Los Angeles presented a classification of hundreds of objectives by subject fields; however, he cautioned against starting with the subjects in this description of the process of defining abilities.[33] Thus to Bobbitt the essential step in designing was the development of objectives by analysis of human needs and deficiencies of undirected training; this step, he felt, would give the schools proper focus:

The comprehensive working list of abilities should be put into printed form. This makes them definite. It prevents their becoming confused and changed through processes of discussion. It enables all concerned to have the same things before them and the same things in mind at once. It enables one to see the entire range of abilities as he considers any one of them or any group of

[29]Franklin Bobbitt, *The Curriculum* (Boston: Houghton Mifflin Company, 1918), p. 42.
[30]Bobbitt, p. 45.
[31]Bobbitt, pp. 51–52.
[32]Bobbitt, p. iv.
[33]Franklin Bobbitt, *How To Make a Curriculum* (Boston: Houghton Mifflin Company, 1924), pp. 39–40.

them. It assists in seeing each in relation to all. It prevents losing sight of any one of them. It assists in providing a broad common ground of understanding for all concerned.[34]

More detail on activity analysis was presented by W. W. Charters in his 1923 publication, *Curriculum Construction,* which Bobbitt cited frequently in his book of the following year as the source to follow in the analysis process. Charters proposed that the curriculum should be derived from both "ideals" and "activities": "Activities are not carried on without ideals to govern, and ideals will not operate except through activities." Activity analysis was regarded by Charters as an extension of job analysis, which, he suggested, could be done through at least four methods: 1) introspection, 2) interviewing, 3) working on the job, and 4) questionnaires. He also described the "difficulty analysis" Bobbitt had cited and summarized the importance of the whole process in these words:

> In determining the activities upon which instruction is to be given, analysis is necessary. This may be done by the use of job analysis in certain types of situation, or by setting up control elements in informational analysis. Difficulty analysis indicates the duties and information upon which special emphasis must be laid in the curriculum. Without such analysis we are entirely at a loss to know how to proceed in building the curriculum.[35]

Charters' "rules for curriculum construction" gave major emphasis to the definition of objectives, ideals, and activities.[36] Thus, Charters and Bobbitt some 60 years ago were arguing for a designing process that would give priority in curriculum planning to analytical procedures focused on teaching students to perform the activities and demonstrate the ideals determined by analysis of human needs and activities as significant for direct training. In this way, they reasoned, the curriculum would be more relevant, more attainable, and more efficient.

Undoubtedly, these early curriculum theorists substantially influenced processes of curriculum development by their emphasis on specific objectives and on analytical procedures for designing them. They placed objectives before subject matter and called for a curriculum plan which would be built around specific life activities of adults. Their theories did not include a detailed plan for relating instruction to each activity or objective, although they clearly anticipated a close relation.[37] It was over four decades later that a movement toward the use of behavioral objectives

[34]Bobbitt, *How To Make a Curriculum*, p. 37.
[35]W. W. Charters, *Curriculum Construction* (New York: The Macmillan Company, 1923), p. 40.
[36]Charters, p. 102.
[37]See Bobbitt, *How To Make a Curriculum,* pp. 44–45.

linked objectives, instruction, and performance in a narrower sense than Bobbitt and Charters had advocated. The behavioral objectives movement is discussed in Chapter 4, and here we merely note the use of this approach in a competency-based curriculum design.

Instructional systems design, also called educational technology, links objectives, instruction, and performance through a series of steps: 1) ordering the objectives and subobjectives and placing them in a time frame; 2) selecting instructional activities to promote the attainment of the objectives within the time period; 3) conducting a preassessment to determine entry level behaviors of learners; 4) providing instruction; 5) evaluating achievement on a criterion-referenced test.

Obviously, there are major differences between the specific-competencies design of Bobbitt and Charters in the 1920s and those of its proponents 60 years later, of whom Popham is probably the most articulate and prolific writer.[38] In both sets of theories, however, much emphasis is placed on the definition of objectives as the first step in curriculum development; indeed, this emphasis characterizes most curriculum design theories proposed in the 60 years between Bobbitt's and Popham's writings. A characteristic more unique to these two theorists is their insistence that the objectives should be focused on what the learner is to learn to do, not on what he is to study or to experience or even to know. But Bobbitt and Charters envisioned performance in far more general terms than do competency-based curriculum protagonists of today. Furthermore, the former seemingly viewed their objectives, though pointed to performance, as more general guidelines for instruction; educational technology relates the classroom transaction and the criterion-referenced test to specific objectives, so that the quality of teaching and learning can be assessed in terms of the objectives sought. Thus, the case for the specific competencies/technology design, with its performance standards and tests, includes the argument that both student and teacher performance can be effectively determined by this model.

Applications and Limitations

The use of a specific competencies/technology design has grown constantly since the early work of Bobbitt and Charters. Vocational educators were early adopters using task analysis to specify the skills or competencies to be learned. Their interest has long continued. For example, the National Center for Research in Vocational Education at Ohio State University publishes modules and guides to using competency-based materi-

[38]See, for example, W. James Popham and Eva L. Baker, *Classroom Instruction Tactics* (Englewood Cliffs, N.J.: Prentice-Hall, Inc., 1973).

als. In another instance, recently thirteen states formed The Vocational-Technical Education Consortium (V–TECS).[39] Each member state is charged with developing catalogs for specific occupational areas and making them available to other states. A catalog is a complete, job-sequenced list of tasks performed by workers in a specific occupational area. A 15-step model, beginning with a needs assessment and ending with publication of a revised catalog, is followed.[40]

The specific-competency approach received a major boost with the refinement of instructional systems design in the 1960s. The value of this new educational technology, developed to achieve specified behaviors in the most efficient manner, was demonstrated conclusively in military education programs. Competency-based education expanded from vocational education to encompass educational programs from preschool through graduate schools.[41]

There is widespread application of the specific competencies/technology design to teaching the basics of reading, math, and other skills in elementary, middle, and even high schools. It is a particularly common design for remedial programs at all levels. The design's popularity has led to its misapplication as efforts have been made to apply the design to all goals of education.

The specific competencies/technology design is being used in various professional schools. For example, the dentistry program at the University of Florida is competency based. Modules have been produced based on carefully developed task analyses and employing sophisticated computer programs. Criterion-referenced examinations are used throughout the program. Also, a number of teacher-training programs have been competency based. Gage and Winne observed in 1975, "The dominant new movement in teacher education during the last decade has unquestionably been performance-based teacher education (PBTE)."[42] Several states have mandated competency-based teacher education.[43] Special education teachers make extensive use of a competency-based approach. The minimum competency testing movement, described in Chapter 4, provided a further impetus for using a specific competencies/technology design.

[39]Vocational-Technical Education Consortium of States, 795 Peachtree Street, N.E., Atlanta, Ga. 30308.
[40]For a description of these steps see *Bank Teller* (Tallahassee, Fla.: Department of Education, Career Education Center, 1976), pp. xi, xii.
[41]For descriptions of a number of such programs see Eva L. Baker, "The Technology of Instructional Development," in Robert M. W. Travers, *Second Handbook of Research on Teaching* (Chicago: Rand McNally and Company, 1973), pp. 267–275.
[42]N. L. Gage and Philip H. Winne, "Performance-Based Teacher Education," in Kevin Ryan (ed.), *Teacher Education,* Seventy-fourth Yearbook, National Society for the Study of Education (Chicago: University of Chicago Press, 1975), p. 146.
[43]For example, to be certified in Florida a teacher must demonstrate 23 generic competencies.

The specific competencies/technology design can be applied whenever one or more behaviors to be learned can be specified through a task analysis. Orlosky and Smith identified three types of task analysis fulfilling entirely different needs: topic analysis, job analysis, and skills analysis. A topic analysis is a detailed analysis of intellectual tasks such as solving quadratic equations or deriving a formula. Job analysis relates to tasks involving physical or psychomotor skills concentrating on what is done when the task is complete, for example, renewing the contact points in a car. Skills analysis "involves the further analysis of psychomotor tasks, but this time concentrating on how the job is accomplished."[44] For example, analyze the skills needed in using a feeler gauge to renew the contact points in a car. Orlosky and Smith describe specific procedures to be followed in making each type of task analysis. In other words, they present a task analysis of making a task analysis.[45]

After a task analysis has been completed, an instructional system needs to be designed and criterion-referenced tests constructed. Instructional systems design is discussed in Chapter 6 and criterion-referenced measurement is described in Chapter 7.

Some limitations of a specific competencies design were included in Chapter 4. Critics of the design charge that its implementation is boring for students and teachers alike. However, such a criticism can be, and has been made of any curriculum design. But students with some learning styles are easily bored by the routine that accompanies many competency programs.

The major limitation of the specific competencies/technology design is that it cannot deal with all of education. Education has a dual nature: to help individuals learn behaviors and to help individuals develop human traits (see Chapter 4 for an extended discussion). The specific competencies/technology design is well-suited to helping individuals learn behaviors; it is seriously limited in helping them develop human traits. For example, it is well suited to helping prospective teachers learn to operate audio-visual equipment but is inadequate in helping them develop the human trait of "caring." This limitation is not a problem when it is recognized that a specific competencies/technology design is a valuable tool that will enable learners to achieve some types of educational goals. The limitation is a problem, however, when instructional systems designers try to use their tool for all educational goals. When that happens, for example, the human trait of "caring" is broken down into tasks to be performed; if that proves impossible, it leads to a decision that producing caring teachers is not important after all. Neither option produces caring teachers.

[44]Orlosky and Smith, p. 109.
[45]Orlosky and Smith, pp. 109–121.

Fortunately, many leaders in instructional design recognize it is not a universal tool and realize that its value depends upon its effective use for appropriate goals.[46]

DESIGNS FOCUSED ON HUMAN TRAITS/PROCESSES

The two designs just described, subject matter/disciplines and specific competencies/technology, are used frequently and are relatively easy to identify and describe. The human traits/processes design is utilized less widely than it is advocated, has not been clearly defined, and is difficult to spot in action. Nevertheless, we view this as an important emerging curriculum design.

Characteristic Features

The application of all curriculum designs influences the development of human traits. Furthermore, some type of process is involved in implementing all curriculum plans. What then distinguishes the human traits/processes design from other designs? The human traits/processes curriculum design has two features: 1) the development of predetermined and specific human traits is the central goal; and 2) the implementation processes are deliberately selected to achieve the central goal.

The dual nature of educational objectives—behaviors to be learned and human traits to be developed—is discussed in Chapter 4. While the specific competencies/technology curriculum design focuses on behaviors to be learned, the human traits/processes design focuses on traits to be developed. A listing of some of these human traits illustrates their nature. Raven identified a series of traits related to human resource development, including the ability to:

Work effectively with others
Communicate effectively
Lead effectively
Follow effectively
Make one's own observations
Learn on one's own
Make decisions
Make good judgments
Invent
Forecast
Plan

[46]See, for example, Walter Dick, Lou Carey, *The Systematic Design of Instruction* (Glenview, Ill.: Scott, Foresman and Company, 1978), pp. 2–4.

Monitor the effects of one's own action
Take corrective action when necessary
Tolerate ambiguity.

Raven gave special emphasis to these traits:

Creativity
Initiative
Self-confidence
Sensitivity to one's feelings and emotions.[47]

The list is impressive in the relevance of each item to human trait development. Furthermore, once developed these traits can be maintained with minimum use. Items on this list differ from lists of competencies to be learned in two important ways. First, learning these human traits involves "a much greater integration of the thinking, feeling, and behavioral components of action than do traditional learning activities."[48] Second, the educational goal of developing these human traits involves values, judgments; in comparison, developing competencies is often relatively value-free. For example, some citizens objected to the use of *Man, a Course of Study* (MACOS), a process approach to teaching social studies, because it encouraged students to think for themselves and, as a result, to question some of their parents' dogma.

Raven concluded that self-confidence and sensitivity to one's feelings and emotions were central to the development of other human resource traits. In order to illustrate the use of the human traits/processes curriculum design, Raven's analysis of self-confidence will be used. Self-confidence, according to Raven, would seem to mean:

1. Knowledge, based on experience, that one can work with others, that one can take a leadership role, that one can enlist others' help and support.
2. Knowledge, based on experience, that one can take effective corrective action if activities one has initiated do not turn out as expected.
3. Knowledge, based on experience, that one's judgment and ability to make decisions are good.
4. Knowledge, based on experience, that one can cope with new situations and new people.
5. Knowledge, based on experience, that one can do at least some things better than other people.
6. Knowledge, based on experience, that, should the need arise, one can change the pattern of one's competencies, learn to do new things.

[47]John Raven, "On the Components of Competence and Their Development in Education," *Teachers College Record*, 78 (May 1977): 457–475.
[48]Raven, p. 459.

7. Knowledge, based on experience, that one can master tasks that at first appeared to be too difficult.[49]

This brings us to the heart of the human traits/processes design. Note in the preceding list that in every instance the knowledge is *based on experience*. To develop desired traits students need appropriate experiences. Therefore, educational processes are organized to provide these experiences. The efficacy of these experiences is increased as learners have opportunities to analyze and think about the experiences in relationship to the traits. Human trait development is also enhanced as learners observe role models who have and are using the desired traits.

We turn to some early proposals and illustrations of curriculum designs comparable to our human traits/processes design. The national curriculum projects beginning in the 1950s, were based on two important goals: to help learners understand the structure of a given discipline; and to enable learners to discover the method of inquiry appropriate to a given discipline. The second goal is realized as students have experiences enabling them to develop appropriate problem-solving traits. For example, *Science—A Process Approach* organized science in the elementary school around such processes as observing, classifying, interpreting, and experimenting with materials drawn from the various sciences to develop these processes.

Some uses of the human traits/processes design focus on valuing processes. In 1963 Wiles proposed four curriculum domains—analysis of experiences and values, acquisition of fundamental skills, exploration of the cultural heritage, and specialization and creativity—and suggested the following design for the first of these, values analysis:

> In the school, each pupil will spend six hours a week in an Analysis Group. With ten other pupils of his or her own age and a skilled teacher-counselor he or she will discuss any problem of ethics, social concern, out-of-school experience, or implication of knowledge encountered in other classes. No curriculum content will be established in advance for the Analysis Groups. The exploration of questions, ideas, or values advanced by group members will constitute the primary type of experience.
>
> The purpose of the Analysis Group will be to help each pupil discover meaning, to develop increased commitment to a set of values, and to offer opportunity to examine the conflicts among the many sets of values and viewpoints held by members of the society.[50]

Elements of Wiles' ideas are incorporated in present value clarification programs.

An early statement on a type of processes design is Parker and Rubin's

[49]Raven, pp. 465–466.
[50]Kimball Wiles, *The Changing Curriculum of the American High School* (Englewood Cliffs, N.J.: Prentice-Hall, Inc., 1963), p. 301.

Process as Content; what they were "after," they wrote, was "an expanded preoccupation with the processes embodied in the phenomenon of human living."[51] They contrasted content and process:

> The crux of the assumed contradiction between content and process lies in the difference between passive and active approaches to learning. . . .
>
> Where the stress is upon process, the assimilation of knowledge is not derogated, but greater importance is attached to the methods of its acquisition and to its subsequent utilization. Therefore, a discrimination must be made between knowing something and knowing what it is good for. Knowledge becomes the vehicle rather than the destination.[52]

Parker and Rubin did not outline a single model of a curriculum design; indeed, they called for research and development to produce designs. They did, however, describe three models as beginning points, two of which could be fitted into existing designs and the third of which made learning processes the bases of curriculum organization. They built into the latter model "intake," "manipulative," and "applicative" operations: "The learning situation, at least as we conceive of it, consists of three interacting operations; the learner must take in data; he must manipulate it; and he must apply it."[53] They recommend using these guidelines in the selection of curriculum opportunities:

> First, some forms of knowledge have general applicability whereas others do not; to the extent that it is possible, the curriculum should be restricted to that which does.
>
> Second, processes which have a broad usefulness to be the primary, rather than the subsidiary benefit of content, should be used. They are not only to be regarded as a means to an end, but both as means and ends. In what may by now be an overly trite observation, the work of moment and the distinguished achievements of our society are performed by men conspicuous by the intellectual processes they muster to their cause.
>
> Third, exposing the learner to a variety of processes will not serve our purpose. He must suffer more than mere exposure. He must grasp the nature of the process and grasp how it got that way; he must know where it has been used in the past and where it might be used in the future; and he must know how to use it in diverse contexts, to modify it as circumstances demand, to fit it to his purpose, and to assess its results.[54]

Schaefer proposed that the school become a center of inquiry to help learners develop traits that would prepare them for a lifelong pursuit of knowledge. "By a school organized as a center of inquiry, then, I imply

---

[51]J. Cecil Parker and Louis J. Rubin, *Process as Content: Curriculum Design and the Application of Knowledge* (Chicago: Rand McNally & Company, 1966), p. 11.

[52]Parker and Rubin, p. 2.

[53]Parker and Rubin, p. 62.

[54]Parker and Rubin, p. 13.

an institution characterized by a pervasive search for meaning and rationality in its work." He would encourage students and teachers to make systematic inquiry into the substance and meaning of studies. "How else," he asked, "can students learn to learn?"[55]

The most comprehensive process-centered curriculum design is that of Berman, who sees as the aim of education the development of "process-oriented" persons, or "persons who are able to handle themselves and the situations of which they are a part with adequacy and ease. Such persons are the contributors to as well as the recipients of society's resources."[56] She described in detail eight process skills: perceiving, communicating, loving, decision-making, knowing, organizing, creating, and valuing. Berman described six curriculum designs, not espousing a particular one, and the process skills involved in each. Three of these designs maintained a subject organization and the other three an organization based on her proposed processes.

Our reason for labeling the human traits/processes design as emerging is apparent. One example gives problem-solving in a discipline a separate and significant role. Others focus on valuing processes as a major component of the curriculum design. The common element in these illustrations is their emphasis on the development of human traits and on processes as dynamic curriculum elements as compared with more fixed structures of knowledge; their diversity is in their definitions of processes and in the extent to which the processes constitute organizing centers in the curriculum plan.

The Case for Designs Focused on Human Traits/Processes

Curriculum designs that focus on process skills are based on one or more of the following arguments:

1. Since one of the most significant goals of schooling is the development of human traits such as lifelong learning skills and interests, curriculum plans should make these skills and interests central.
2. The curriculum should be planned and organized so as to have maximum carryover into life processes and skills; greater carryover is likely when the curriculum design directly reflects these processes and skills.
3. The process of valuing and other processes having a high affective element can be taught as well as essentially cognitive skills; the former should be as well represented in the curriculum as the latter.

[55]Robert J. Schaefer, *The School as a Center of Inquiry* (New York: Harper & Row, Publishers, 1967), p. 3.
[56]Louise M. Berman, *New Priorities in the Curriculum* (Columbus, Oh.: Charles E. Merrill Publishing Company, 1968), p. 10.

One of the most eloquent and prolific spokesmen for the lifelong-learning focus is John W. Gardner, who served education as head of the Carnegie Corporation foundation and as U.S. Commissioner of Health, Education and Welfare. He emphasized the notion of education for self-renewal as follows:

> We are moving away from teaching things that readily become outmoded, and toward things that will have the greatest long-term effect on the young person's capacity to understand and perform. Increasing emphasis is being given to instruction in methods of analysis and modes of attack on problems. In many subjects, this means more attention to basic principles, less to applications of immediate "practical" use. In all subjects it means teaching habits of mind that will be useful in new situations—curiosity, open-mindedness, objectivity, respect for evidence and the capacity to think critically.[57]

Whitehead warned against "inert ideas," that is to say, "ideas that are merely received into the mind without being utilized, or tested, or thrown into fresh combinations. . . . Education with inert ideas," he warned, "is not only useless: it is, above all things, harmful."[58] The human traits/processes design attempts to overcome "inert ideas," as learners are directly involved in the process.

The human traits/processes design is particularly useful in teaching valuing and goals in the affective domain. Clute emphasized the importance of schools that "give careful attention to the needs and purposes of the learner and utilize programs and practices designed to help each individual develop skills, attitudes, and understandings necessary for individual self-fulfillment."[59] It is to be hoped that any curriculum design would promote the goal of humanistic education; it is recognized, however, that a human traits/processes design is essentially appropriate for this purpose.

Applications and Limitations

A variety of applications of the process design are presented to show the range of possibilities. Berman indicated that "children and youth need help in learning behavior associated with the decision-making process," and urged that schools "provide settings in which processes of decisions

[57]John W. Gardner, *Self-Renewal: The Individual and the Innovative Society* (New York: Harper & Row, Publishers, 1963), pp. 22–23.
[58]Whitehead, p. 13.
[59]Morrel J. Clute, "Humanistic Education: Goals and Objectives," in *Humanistic Education: Objectives and Assessment,* a report of the ASCD Working Group on Humanistic Education, Arthur W. Combs, Chairperson (Washington, D.C.: Association for Supervision and Curriculum Development, 1978), p. 9.

are analyzed, taught, and evaluated."[60] She proposed starting by letting children, within a structure provided by the teacher, plan some of their own time. Gradually teachers can provide opportunities for children to move:

1. From nondecision to decision.
2. From impulsive decisions to reflective decisions.
3. From mundane decisions to creative decisions.
4. From decisions requiring little searching for new ideas to decisions requiring much searching.
5. From decisions focusing basically on self to decisions incorporating self and others.[61]

Berman's suggestions show a teacher how to gradually increase children's opportunities and responsibilities in directing an aspect of the process of education.

Process skills are also emphasized in most plans of group guidance. For example, our conception of the middle school home base group, comparable to Wiles' analysis groups cited earlier, is somewhat descriptive of various home base advisory groupings in operation in many middle schools:

[issues] arising almost daily in the lives of middle school children are treated in various ways in the home-base group. Total group discussions may at times be desirable, usually preceded by an analysis of the issue through pupil or teacher presentation, a film or other aid, or the services of resource persons. Small groups within the home-base group may be formed to analyze each issue, with resultant total group consideration of alternative positions. Committees functioning on a continuing basis may bring periodic reports to the total group. The essential points are that issues which are real to the students be identified and considered, that alternative positions be fully explored, and that the consequences of preferred positions be clearly understood.[62]

Wright and Casteel showed how the characteristic of courage can be developed while teaching critical reading skills. After the presentation of printed material, students respond on an individual value sheet. For example, after reading five vignettes of courageous acts, students select the most courageous act and defend their choice in a small group discussion.[63]

A full explanation of an inquiry training model is provided by Weil and

[60]Louise M. Berman, "More Than Choice," *Educational Leadership, 35* (March 1978): 425.
[61]Berman, "More Than Choice," p. 429.
[62]William M. Alexander and others, *The Emergent Middle School,* 2d ed. (New York: Holt, Rinehart and Winston, Inc., 1969), p. 67.
[63]Robert G. Wright, J. Doyle Casteel, "Teaching Critical Reading Skills: Value Sheets as a Means to This End." *Research Bulletin, 10* (Summer 1976).

Joyce.[64] They believe that "students can become more and more conscious of the process of inquiry, and that this process can be taught to them directly."[65] The model proposed has five phases:

Encounter with the problem
Data gathering: verification
Data gathering: experimentation
Formulating an explanation
Analysis of the inquiry process.

The human traits/processes design is used with a number of approaches to values education. Kirschenbaum pointed out that *moralizing* is a common approach to values education. The problem with this approach is that children "are being bombarded from all sides with different messages about what values to pursue and what goals to strive for to be successful, to belong, to be popular, and to succeed with the other sex."[66] A values clarification approach, however, extends beyond moralizing and teaches people a process which they can apply to values choices throughout their life. Kirschenbaum described seven subprocesses necessary for values clarification: "a) choosing from alternatives, b) choosing after considering consequences, c) choosing freely, d) prizing and cherishing one's choices, e) publicly affirming one's choices, f) acting on one's choices, and g) acting with a repetition and pattern in one's choices."[67] Values clarification as a process approach is not limited to schools. Kirschenbaum reported that "the YMCA, for example, has recently launched a major values education program of national scope, based largely on the values clarification approach. . . ."[68]

There are several limitations in the use of human traits/processes designs. Planning processes to develop human traits is a difficult task, and to date, well-formulated procedures for doing this have not been developed. Since human trait development is influenced by a learner's total experiences, it is difficult to assess the impact of any particular educational experience on the development of a trait. In other words, just because a process design is being used does not mean the desired human traits will develop. For example, Lockwood reviewed the research related to values clarification programs and concluded, "there is no evidence that values

[64]Marsha Weil and Bruce Joyce, *Information Processing Models of Teaching* (Englewood Cliffs, New Jersey: Prentice-Hall, Inc., 1978), pp. 123–196.
[65]Weil and Joyce, p. 128.
[66]Howard Kirschenbaum, "Values Education: 1976 and Beyond," in R. Freeman Butts, Donald H. Peckenpaugh, and Howard Kirchenbaum (eds.), *The School's Role as Moral Authority* (Washington, D. C.: Association for Supervision and Curriculum Development, 1977), p. 56.
[67]Kirschenbaum, p. 57.
[68]Kirschenbaum, p. 53.

clarification has a systematic, demonstrated impact on students' values."[69] However, he did find evidence suggesting that value clarification may possibly affect students' classroom behavior.

Another limitation to using a human traits/processes design may be lack of public support. Although parents may agree that development of human traits is important, they will not assign it a higher priority than learning behaviors, particularly the basics. Further, there is no consensus on which traits should be developed and how.

In spite of its limitations, the human traits/processes design appears to present the best opportunity for developing some critical human traits, including processes of living and learning. It is true that these traits can either be fostered or inhibited by other curriculum designs, but none of the others have the development of human traits as their central purpose. We believe, therefore, that the human traits/processes design needs to be refined through information based on research growing out of its careful application.

DESIGNS FOCUSED ON SOCIAL FUNCTIONS/ACTIVITIES

Each curriculum design reflects a position regarding the relative emphasis given to the major determinants of the curriculum. Thus, the three designs discussed previously emphasize, respectively, the role of organized knowledge, behaviors to be learned, and human traits to be developed. We turn now to the designs which emphasize society as an influence on curriculum development.

Characteristic Features

The socially focused designs are not as sharply delineated as those described previously. One important feature of these designs is that they are rooted in society and social problems. However, other designs may also use society as a base. For example, a social-needs analysis can provide competencies used in a specific competencies/technology design. Thus some state minimum competencies programs, such as the one in Pennsylvania, test the basic skills required to function in a society. Another example: some traits used in the human traits/processes approach, such as the ability to lead effectively, stem from societal needs. Goals in a social functions/activities design are usually achieved through engagements in social activities. However, as indicated in Table 5.1., these goals may also be

[69]Alan L. Lockwood, "The Effects of Values Clarification and Moral Development Curricula on School-Age Subjects: A Critical Review of Recent Research," *Review of Educational Research, 48* (Summer 1978): 344.

achieved through the study of disciplines or through a linear competency type of approach.

Three organizational themes are included within the social functions/activities design: 1) the social living or persistent life situation approaches based on the belief that the curriculum design should follow the persistent functions, areas, or life situations in humanity's existence; 2) approaches that organize the curriculum around aspects of problems of community life; and 3) the social action or reconstruction theories that hold the improvement of society through direct involvement of the schools and their students to be a major goal or even the primary goal of the curriculum.

A curriculum design based on the social living or persistent life situations approach exhibits an organizational pattern derived from studies of group life. Caswell, who in the 1930s directed numerous state curriculum programs that utilized this design, and Campbell, his colleague, explained the concept in the 1935 publication, *Curriculum Development:*

> Studies of group life show that there are certain major centers about which the activities of individuals and the plans and problems of the group tend to cluster. These centers, which may be referred to as social functions, tend to persist and to be common for all organized groups. . . . Since these centers or social functions represent points about which real life activities tend to gather and organize, it is considered reasonable that a curriculum which is concerned with guiding children into effective participation in the activities of real life may appropriately use these social functions as points for emphasis and orientation in outlining the curriculum.[70]

The Virginia state course of study developed through this procedure used the following list of major functions of social living:

Protection and conservation of life, property, and natural resources
Production of goods and services and distribution of the returns of production
Consumption of goods and services
Communication and transportation of goods and people
Recreation
Expression of aesthetic impulses
Expression of religious impulses
Education
Extension of freedom
Integration of the individual
Exploration.

The recent movement to add courses and programs in parenting and consumership in the high schools illustrate current trends in the use of this type of curriculum design.

[70]Hollis L. Caswell and Doak S. Campbell, *Curriculum Development* (New York: American Book Company, 1935), p. 173.

A design based on community problems might focus on functions and aspects thereof that are significant in the community concerned. Seay, for example, classified the "problems of people" basic to the program of the community school as those of food, clothing, shelter, recreation, health, citizenship, morality and religion, and work.[71] A quarter of a century later, Olsen and Clark developed a list of life concerns to be considered in the community education programs. New community concerns are shown in the items they added such as: communicating ideas and feelings, satisfying sexual desires, enriching family living, adjusting to change, and controlling the environment.[72]

There is no shortage of community problems to be addressed. High on the list are energy, conservation, land use, consumerism, health, abortion, and equality among all races. In addition to these and other current problems, it is important to anticipate emerging critical problems. (Applications of future forecasting to education are described in Chapter 8.) Teige and colleagues, with the support of the National Science Foundation, identified critical future national and international problems.[73] Many of the problems they forecast will influence local communities, for example: police alienation from the populace, potential for new urban violence, cumulative effects of pollution, loss of political and social cohesion, chronic unemployment, and teen-age alcoholism.[74] Some high school and community college classes are studying these and other future problems.[75]

A notable illustration of a community problems approach came from a rural consolidated high school in Holtville, Alabama, during the Great Depression. The students and faculty studied their community and found such problems as spoilage of canned meat. The school, with the cooperation of the farmers, built a slaughterhouse and a meat freezing plant. They processed meat and rented storage space. They developed a hatchery to serve farmers. In these, and other ways the school improved the living conditions in the community.[76]

---

[71]Maurice F. Seay, "The Community School: New Meaning for an Old Term," in Nelson B. Henry (ed.), *The Community School,* Fifty-second Yearbook, Part II, National Society for the Study of Education (Chicago: University of Chicago Press, 1953), pp. 3–4.

[72]Edward G. Olsen and Phillip A. Clark, *Life-Centering Education* (Midland, Mich.: Pendell Publishing Company, 1977), p. 109.

[73]Peter Teige, Willis Harman, and Peter Schwartz, "The Problem of Critical Problem Selection," in Harold A. Linstone, W. H. Clive Simmonds, *Futures Research: New Directions* (Reading, Mass.: Addison-Wesley Publishing, 1977), pp. 230–249.

[74]Teige, et al., pp. 242–248 passim.

[75]For descriptions of representative programs see Alvin Toffler (ed.), *Learning for Tomorrow, The Role of the Future in Education* (New York: Random House, Inc., 1974), Appendix, pp. 345–399.

[76]*The Story of Holtville:* A Southern Association Study School (Nashville, Tenn.: Cullum and Ghertner, 1944).

The social reconstruction concept has been less fully developed as a curriculum design than as an educational philosophy. Whereas advocates of a community school would have schools improve the existing society, social reconstructionists would use schools to build a new society. It is not surprising that there are few illustrations of such schools; society is not likely to support institutions advocating its reconstruction. A wave of proposals for radical school reform, many leading to societal changes, were made during the late 1960s.[77] A few political freedom schools were established, primarily in large city ghettos, but most of them lasted only a year or two.

A less radical approach to change is to provide opportunities for political socialization of students. Fantini proposed a program to develop these objectives:

> In order to develop skills in social action, the learners must be given opportunities in real life situations. Roles are learned from participation in reality contexts. This means that students would be working with poverty agencies, early childhood units, governmental institutions, hospitals, old age homes, etc. By relating to these clinical environments, students would acquire both the language and the behaviors necessary to deal with current social problems. The school would help the student conceptualize social realities and assist him in the process of developing alternative approaches to improving the environment of all people.[78]

Fantini's proposals, considered avant-garde by some, pale in comparison to the realities of Holtville.

In summary, the socially centered curriculum designs have as their central element a focus on social activities and/or functions, and these define the scope of the curriculum or a major portion of it. These activities and functions may be the centers around which instruction is organized or they may serve primarily as criteria for the selection of content within the subject or other organizational unit. In the broader design of social functions these elements are somewhat universal and timeless; in the social action program the criteria are the problem areas or "realities" in which students can participate effectively.

The Case for Designs Focused on Social Functions/Activities

There are two primary arguments for socially centered curriculum designs: 1) they are relevant to student needs and concerns and are therefore of significance and interest to students, and 2) they can directly contribute to the continual improvement of society by meeting its needs.

[77]For a good summary of these proposals see Ronald Gross and Beatrice Gross (eds.), *Radical School Reform* (New York: Simon and Schuster, 1969).

[78]Mario D. Fantini, *The Reform of Urban Schools for the 70's,* Preliminary Series (Washington, D. C.: National Education Association, 1970), p. 45.

Relevance to Students

Caswell and Campbell justified the social functions procedure on the assumption that "the activities of children in school should be organized in such a way as to carry over with the greatest ease to life situations."[79] Stratemeyer and her associates employed the concept of "persistent life situations" in a curriculum where: "The content and organization of learning experiences are determined by the experiences of learners as they deal with everyday concerns and the persistent life situations which are a part of them (these situations of everyday living take the place of 'subjects' and the varied other ways of focusing the curriculum)."[80] Stratemeyer and her collaborators claimed that the persistent life situations approach would aid balanced development, continuity, depth of learning, economy of time, wise selection of content, and varied experience.[81]

A forceful argument for student involvement in social activities comes from ideas expressed by Greene. Speaking from the perspective of existentialist philosophy she contrasted the "new freedom" with the "moral life." "I associate an unreflective, sometimes benign and drifting life with what I am arbitrarily calling the 'new freedom'; I associate a reflective and committed way of acting with what I am calling the 'moral life.' "[82] Greene believed that the moral life can result from "an effort to carry out a plan in a space where there are others ... gearing into a shared world that places tasks before each one who plays a deliberate part." Greene pointed out that "to have experiences of carrying projects into effect has to do with being adult. It has to do with dignity and the quest for ways of expressing a vision, defining a commitment—achieving a sense of freedom and responsibility."[83] There has been a rapid development of programs that provide opportunities for students to be involved in the wider community. The success of these programs is probably related to students' quest for the 'moral life'—for achieving goals identified by Greene: being adult, finding dignity, expressing a vision, defining a commitment, and achieving a sense of freedom and responsibility.

Fortunately, awarding credit to high school students for community service meets with widespread approval: "Eighty-seven percent of all respondents (to a Gallup Poll) would like to have juniors and seniors earn course credit for giving service to the community."[84]

---

[79]Caswell and Campbell, p. 173.
[80]Florence B. Stratemeyer, Hamden L. Forkner, Margaret G. McKim, and A. Harry Passow, *Developing a Curriculum for Modern Living*, 2d ed. (New York: Teachers College Press, 1957), pp. 116–117.
[81]See Stratemeyer, et al., pp. 121–140.
[82]Maxine Greene, *Landscapes of Learning* (New York: Teachers College Press, 1978), p. 148.
[83]Greene, pp. 152–153.
[84]George H. Gallup, "The 10th Annual Gallup Poll," *Phi Delta Kappan, 60* (September 1978): 41.

Needs of Society

The community school movement originated as a means of improving the immediate community. When describing aims of the community school earlier in this century, Seay wrote of "the power of education when put to work to improve community living" and stated that the community school would result in "an improvement in the living conditions and standards of the community" and "the development of the appropriate skills, values and concepts to the end that individuals will function more effectively in all their independent and cooperative undertakings."[85] The Holtville community school, described in the previous section, demonstrates the power of community education.

Olsen and Clark expanded the concept of community education to a life-centered education. They believed that "the central focus of our formal educational institutions should be on *improving the quality of human living.*"[86] Their proposal for a life-centering education extends concerns for the quality of life from the immediate community to all of humanity and from present concerns to future concerns as well. In this they reflect the emerging concern for futurism in education.

Toffler, a well known futurist, pointed out that "all education springs from some image of the future. If the image of the future held by a society is grossly inaccurate, its education system will betray its youth."[87] Benjamin (alias J. Abner Peddiwell) in his classic satire on the curriculum, illustrated problems associated with faulty images of the future. He put in the mouth of the old man of the tribe the traditional argument for the established fundamentals (here "the saber-tooth curriculum"):

> With all the intricate details of fish-grabbing, horse-clubbing, and tiger-scaring —the standard cultural subjects—the school curriculum is too crowded now. We can't add these fads and frills of net-making, antelope-snaring, and—of all things—bear-killing. . . . You must know that there are some eternal verities, and the saber-tooth curriculum is one of them.[88]

Failure to recognize the new image of a world that required, for example, netting of fish rather than simply grabbing them led to a betrayal of the youth.

Educating individuals for the present works when the future is like the present. But the future will be very different from the present. Although we cannot know the exact shape of the future, it is possible to anticipate in general terms probable future developments—both new problems and new opportunities. Shane advocated a new approach to planning the

[85]Seay, p. 11.
[86]Olsen and Clark, p. 15.
[87]Toffler, p. 3.
[88]J. Abner Peddiwell, *The Saber-Tooth Curriculum* (New York: McGraw-Hill Book Company, 1939), pp. 41–44.

curriculum: "Education should be designed for persons of all ages in anticipation of what these humans will need to know and be able to do to survive in the future."[89] Application of a future orientation to curriculum planning is described in Chapter 8.

There are two futures: the one we are drifting into and the one we want. The nature of education our society provides now will have an important bearing on the quality of our future. Accordingly, some futurists believe that in addition to preparing individuals to live in the future, education should help to shape that future. Toffler said, "Just as all education springs from some image of the future, all education produces some image of the future."[90] Bowman and his colleagues are strong proponents of an activist role for education in producing that image. "Education must be an institution for planning desired change in a crises-era." They proposed, "Learning must also be participatory—social change priorities and parameters of choice must be part of the curriculum of the future."[91]

This type of school action through the social curriculum seems to us directly related to the educational philosophy of reconstructionism, as far removed as that philosophy is from the other socially focused designs we have considered. That is, while the social activities and community-centered approaches aim toward social improvement, they do not call on the schools to lead in social action and reform movements as does reconstructionism. According to Pratte's interpretation of the works of the leading spokesman for this philosophy, Theodore Brameld, it has not resulted in a curriculum design but only in a point of view.[92] But designs are suggested in recent interpretations of a social action curriculum. Fantini and Weinstein argued, for example, that "the present social context makes the reconstructionist point of view more relevant than ever" and that "skills development in the social action process is mandatory for keeping a democratic society healthy, vital, and growing." Accordingly, they proposed "a spiral of social action projects."[93] They described an eighth-grade project which involved the students in a local election and another project resulting in improvement of the school cafeteria and concluded: "We recommend not only decision-making and power-experience, but also the focus of learning on constructive utilization of power through a social action

[89]Harold G. Shane, *Curriculum Change: Toward the 21st Century* (Washington, D. C.: National Education Association, 1977), p. 79. See Toffler, *Learning for Tomorrow,* for illustrations of a future-oriented curriculum.

[90]Toffler, p. 19.

[91]Jim Bowman, Fred Kierstead, Chris Dede, and John Pulliam, *The Far Side of the Future: Social Problems and Educational Reconstruction* (Washington, D. C.: World Future Society, 1978), p. 136.

[92]Richard Pratte, *Contemporary Theories of Education* (Scranton, Pa.: Intext Educational Publishers, 1971), p. 236.

[93]Mario D. Fantini and Gerald Weinstein, *Toward a Contact Curriculum* (New York: Anti-Defamation League of B'Nai B'rith, n.d.), pp. 30–31.

curriculum—that is, of course, if we really want an active citizen rather than merely a talkative one."[94]

Apple and King questioned the ability of schools to provide a role in reconstruction of society because schools "seem to act latently to enhance an already unequal and stratified social order."[95] They hypothesized that "schools do work. In an odd way, they may succeed in reproducing a population that is roughly equivalent to the economic and social stratification in society."[96]

Freire, a leading protagonist of a reconstructionist approach to education, opposed schools in Brazil as oppressive organizations. He shared in the life of poor Brazilians and witnessed what he called the culture of silence of the dispossessed. He viewed their ignorance and lethargy as a product of the whole economic, social, and political situation and concluded that the educational system was a major instrument for maintaining this culture of silence. He viewed the "educated" man as the adapted man "because he is better 'fit' for the world. Translated into practice, this concept is well suited to the purposes of the oppressors, whose tranquility rests on how well men fit the world the oppressors have created, and how little they question it."[97] Freire decided that educational institutions in Brazil could not be reformed; therefore he worked with the poor and developed an independent adult education program designed to lead to a liberation of the oppressed. The effectiveness of his work resulted in his being exiled from Brazil by a military government.

Others have taken up Freire's theme. Illich in *Deschooling Society* and Reimer in *School is Dead* proposed a complete educational revolution. It is doubtful whether such notions could be acceptable to either school personnel or even parents, since Reimer wrote that "perhaps the most important single thing that individuals can do" to revolutionize the social system is "to take back their responsibility for the education of their children."[98] These views may not affect the public school curriculum at all, but they do grow out of the problems of people the world over. Conceivably, social action curriculums could lead to study and action which would eliminate schools as we have them. Illich's proposed alternatives of "networks" may be suggestive of other curriculum designs.[99]

[94]Fantini and Weinstein, p. 33.

[95]Michael W. Apple and Nancy R. King, "What Do Schools Teach?" in Alex Molnar and John A. Zahorik (eds.), *Curriculum Theory* (Washington D. C.: Association for Supervision and Curriculum Development, 1977), p. 125.

[96]Apple and King, p. 124.

[97]Paulo Freire, *Pedagogy of the Oppressed* (New York: Heider and Heider, 1970), p. 63.

[98]Everett Reimer, *School Is Dead: Alternatives to Education* (New York: Doubleday and Company, Inc., 1971), p. 194.

[99]See Ivan Illich, "Education Without School: How It Can Be Done," Daniel U. Levine and Robert J. Havighurst (eds.), *Farewell to Schools???* Contemporary Educational Issues, National Society for the Study of Education (Worthington, O.: Charles A. Jones Publishing Company, 1971), and criticisms of this proposal by other authors. Also see Ivan Illich, *Deschooling Society* (New York: Harper & Row, 1971) for Illich's full analysis and proposals.

Applications and Limitations

The social functions/activities design has had wide application, although we know of no schools in which it is the sole focus of the curriculum. Instead, social-centered designs affect the selection of subject matter in subject-organized programs or the choice of activities in less structured programs.

Some applications have been in use over a period of years. For example, interdisciplinary units of work in elementary and middle schools are frequently chosen because of their relation to social functions, activities, or persistent life situations. The core programs of middle, junior high, and high schools are frequently based on analysis of social problems. Vars described structured core programs as "categories of human experience that embrace both the personal problems, interests, and needs of students and the problems confronting contemporary society."[100] A quarter of a century earlier the influential *Education for All American Youth* recommended a "common learnings" core for high schools and junior colleges that would include six areas, four of which emphasized social functions:

1. Civic responsibility and competence.
2. Understanding of the operation of the economic system and of the human relations involved therein.
3. Family relationships.
4. Intelligent action as consumers.
5. Appreciation of beauty.
6. Proficiency in the use of language.[101]

Similarly, the social functions/activities design is widely used in interdisciplinary courses in colleges.

The social functions/activities design is also followed within the social studies field as a basis for organizing units of work at all levels. Indeed, entire courses in secondary and higher education are built around major social functions, particularly in the areas of economics, political science, and sociology.

Recent applications of the social functions/activities design include the "community as a classroom." The Parkway Program in Philadelphia is generally credited with sparking the movement in urban centers toward school programs that use community facilities on a massive scale with minimal central school facilities (therefore, the term "school without

[100]Gordon F. Vars, "A Contemporary View of the Core Curriculum," in Gordon F. Vars (ed.), *Common Learnings: Core and Interdisciplinary Team Approaches* (Scranton, Pa.: International Textbook Company, 1969), p. 8.
[101]Educational Policies Commission, *Education for All American Youth* (Washington, D.C.: National Education Association, 1944), pp. 249–250.

walls"); Parkway's first director, Bremer, emphasized "the city" as a major aspect of the curriculum:

> Every student must come to know the city, the complex of places, processes, and people with which he lives. He must know it for what it is, understand it in terms of what it can do, and respect it for what it could be. He must know it, respect it, and revere it simply because he is about to change it—not do it violence, not destroy it, but change it—that is, transform it in terms of the principles of its being into what, potentially, it already is. Since the Parkway Program has the city as its curriculum, it must have the city as its campus. This is the educational reason for the school without walls. To learn about the city, to let it become familiar, to see it as the earthly counterpart of the City of God, can be accomplished only in the city; only academics suppose that this is learned in a course called Urban Dwelling 1 followed by Urban Dwelling 2.[102]

Deutschlander referred to "the curriculum beyond the school" as action learning, that is "planned activities organized through a school that provides a chance to learn by doing." He pointed out that "very often the experience will take place out in the 'real world' where other adults are producing goods or producing services needed or wanted by the community or individuals in the community."[103] Hedin and Conrad identified five types of student-community learning models distinguished by the manner and degree to which they were integrated to the school's regular academic program: volunteering for service through a volunteer bureau, engaging in community action for credit, using the community as a laboratory for existing courses, participating in a community involvement class, and developing skills through direct experience. Their descriptions of these various types of programs show the variety of opportunities for learning that a community may provide.[104]

The social functions/activities design may be applied to educational experiences sponsored by nonschool agencies. For example, the National Commission on Youth proposed a year of service-learning for young people. They argued that "a transition to adulthood made exclusively through the school is an environment rich in information but poor in maturing experiences."[105] The goal of service-learning is not to discuss public problems but to do something about them. Manning held that "service-learning is not a concept in which one learns, then practices until proficiency is developed; in learning one is performing; in performing, one is caring;

[102]John Bremer and Michael von Moschzisker, *The School Without Walls: Philadelphia's Parkway Program* (New York, Holt, Rinehart and Winston, Inc., 1971), pp. 46–47.

[103]Gary H. Deutschlander, "Action-Learning—The Curriculum Beyond the School," *NASSP Bulletin,* 58 (November 1974): 33.

[104]Diane Hedin, Dan Conrad, "Some Action Learning Models," *NASSP Bulletin,* 58 (November 1974): 22–28.

[105]David L. Manning, "Service-Learning and the Transition of Youth to Adulthood," *NASSP Bulletin, 63* (December 1979): 86.

in caring, one is contributing."[106] Thus service-learning blends all four facets of service: learning, performing, caring, and contributing.

The limitations of the social functions/activities design are evident, since it is used generally for only a portion of the curriculum. Even at Parkway, with its emphasis on the social problems of urban life, tutorials in basic skills, experiences in the arts, and learning opportunities other than those unique to the city were used. And even the social action educational revolutionists recognize the importance of specific learning opportunities for individuals to develop competence in learning skills and specialized interests and occupations.

But this design theory is highly applicable to some curriculum domains, especially to the one we designate as social competence. Study and experience in persistent social activities and problems, organized when possible to ensure consideration and involvement of students, seem to be mandatory educational components if young people are to have happy, successful, and constructive relations with their fellows in a complex society.

DESIGNS FOCUSED ON INDIVIDUAL NEEDS AND INTERESTS/ACTIVITIES

The movement away from the traditional curriculum of school subjects has usually been toward a program that emphasizes the interests and needs of students. This approach was used in the eighteenth century by Rousseau in the education of Emile, by Pestalozzi early in the next century in Switzerland, and to an extent by Dewey in his laboratory school in 1896–1904. During the present century, each of the designs we have considered other than the subjects design has moved toward the child. Now we turn to designs that more directly use learner needs and interests as a base. Variously called child-centered, experience-centered, and progressive education and, more recently, open, alternative, and humanistic education, all of these twentieth-century efforts reflect, we believe, the influence of Dewey. In *Experience and Education* Dewey included such key statements as these: "a coherent *theory* of experience, affording positive direction to selection and organization of appropriate educational methods and materials, is required by the attempt to give new direction to the work of the schools"; and "it is a cardinal principle of education that the beginning of instruction shall be made with the experience learners already have; that this experience and the capacities that have been developed during its course provide the starting point for all further learning."[107] Some of the child-centered activity programs developed by

[106]Manning, p. 87.
[107]John Dewey, *Experience and Education* (New York: The Macmillan Company, 1938), pp. 21, 88.

Dewey's followers lacked the attention to substantive material and continuity of child growth and development advocated by Dewey, and current emphasis on student-centered programs does not always acknowledge the Dewey philosophy or such similar models as those described in John and Evelyn Dewey's *Schools of Tomorrow* (1915). But Dewey's influence on the movement to incorporate more student-serving learning opportunities into the curriculum has been very great, and it may be argued that more recent models have advanced but little, if any, from Dewey's at the turn of the century.

The Association for the Advancement of Progressive Education formed in 1919, had as its aim "the freest and fullest development of the individual, based upon the scientific study of his mental, physical, spiritual, and social characteristics and needs." The views of this association, later called the Progressive Education Association (PEA), were consonant with those of Dewey as indicated by their statement of principles:

1. Freedom to develop naturally.
2. Interest the motive of all work.
3. The teacher a guide, not a task-master.
4. Scientific study of pupil development.
5. Greater attention to all that affects the child's physical development.
6. Co-operation between school and home to meet the needs of child-life.
7. The progressive school a leader in educational movements.[108]

To some extent, the principles were prophetic as a commission of the PEA formulated and carried out the celebrated Eight-Year Study during the 1930s. The subsequent history of the association, with a change of name in 1944 and its final demise in 1955, is well documented by Cremin.[109] To some extent the fortunes of curriculum designs attending to the needs and interests of students paralleled those of the PEA.

Perhaps the lag in using the learner-centered focus has resulted from a tendency on the part of curriculum planners to interpret the needs and interests design as one based on *common* needs and interests of learners rather than on those of the particular population to be served. Reflected in curriculum plans, this interpretation could, and sometimes did, become the rationale for teaching what had been taught before or for implementing some other design that did not involve the study of children's needs and interests. Research in this area in recent years, however, has made it possible for curriculum planners to develop a better base for student-centered designs. Modern learning theory and widespread dissatisfaction of students and their parents with traditional practice are moving curriculum and instruction toward designs that focus on genuine student

[108]Lawrence A. Cremin, *The Transformation of the School* (New York: Alfred A. Knopf, 1961), pp. 240–245 passim.
[109]Cremin, *Transformation of the School,* pp. 250–270.

needs and interests. We will examine these applications in a subsequent section.

Characteristic Features

A curriculum design focused on individual needs and interests/activities has these characteristic features, we believe:

1. The curriculum plan is based on a knowledge of learners' needs and interests in general and involves diagnosis of the specific needs and interests of the population served by the plan.
2. The curriculum plan is highly flexible, with built-in provisions for development and modification to conform to the needs and interests of particular learners and with many options available to the learners. In fact, the learner may develop his or her own curriculum plan in some designs, but with guidance in selecting options and in planning.
3. The learner is consulted and instructed individually at appropriate points in the curriculum and instructional process.

Curriculum designs focused on individual needs and interests/activities make frequent though not exclusive use of a student activity instructional approach. However, other approaches are used; for example, a student interested in pursuing the study of a particular subject might use a discipline approach. Or, a student interested in learning a skill could use a module developed through an instructional system design.

The Dewey School at the University of Chicago, which was in operation from 1896 to 1904, as described by Mayhew and Edwards in *The Dewey School* and by other authors,[110] seems to have illustrated our three features. In theory and practice this school aimed at the progressive growth of children toward responsible participation in present and future social life. Hines wrote that "the school was not primarily child-centered or subject-centered, it was community-centered."[111] However, he presented it as a first and exemplary illustration of the children's "interests and needs emphasis in progressive education" and extolled its accomplishments.[112]

The "project method" was advocated by Kilpatrick, a leading interpreter of Dewey, and was the subject of a much cited study by Collings

[110]Katherine Camp Mayhew and Anna Camp Edwards, *The Dewey School* (New York: D. Appleton-Century Company, 1936; reprinted by Atherton Press, 1966); Harold Rugg, *Foundations of Modern Education* (Yonkers, N.Y.: World Book Company, 1947); Cremin, *Transformation of the School;* and Vynce A. Hines, "Progressivism in Practice," in James R. Squire (ed.), *A New Look at Progressive Education* (Washington, D. C.: Association for Supervision and Curriculum Development, 1972).
[111]Hines, p. 122.
[112]Hines, pp. 137–138.

in McDonald County, Missouri. Kilpatrick's introduction to Colling's report of his study explained the needs and interests rationale.[113] Collings described the curriculum design of the experimental school as follows:

> The above program of studies represents four types of child projects—Play, Excursion, Story, and Hand—experimentally determined on the basis of affording boys and girls opportunity to realize their own purposes during the operation of the Experimental School. Play Projects represent those experiences in which the purpose is to engage in such group activities as games, folk dancing, dramatization, or social parties. Excursion Projects involve purposeful study of problems connected with environments and activities of people. Story Projects include purposes to enjoy the story in its various forms —oral, song, picture, phonograph, or piano. Hand Projects represents purposes to express ideas in concrete form—to make a rabbit trap, to prepare cocoa for the school luncheon, or to grow cantaloupes.[114]

Collings' description of the experimental school curriculum included some details of several projects and long lists of others under each type.

Most applications of a needs and interests/activities approach were in elementary schools. The subject matter/disciplines approach, organized by Carnegie units and reinforced by college entrance requirements, discouraged its use in high schools. However, a commission of the PEA worked to bring progressive education to high schools by formulating the Eight-Year Study wherein over 300 colleges agreed to waive their admission requirements for recommended graduates of the 30 secondary schools participating in the study. A number of curriculum reforms emerged in the experimental schools as teachers worked to meet needs and interests of students. Subject barriers were lowered or removed as teachers combined subjects to study social problems identified by students. At Denver's South High School students had extensive work experience in the community—a practice some 35 years ahead of its time.[115]

A follow-up study of graduates from the Eight-Year Study was conducted by comparing matched pairs of experimental and control students. On a number of measures, students in the experimental schools were more successful in college. In spite of its apparent success the Eight-Year Study has had little lasting effect on secondary education. Cremin commented on the value of the study and its five-volume report: "It is a pity they appeared in the middle of a war, for they never received the atten-

---

[113]William Heard Kilpatrick, "Introduction," in Ellsworth Collings, *An Experiment with a Project Curriculum* (New York: The Macmillan Company, 1923), pp. xvii–xviii.
[114]Collings, p. 48.
[115]A series of publications on the study were issued, with a summary report by the chairman: Wilford M. Aiken, *The Story of the Eight-Year Study* (New York: McGraw-Hill Book Company, Inc., 1942).

tion they deserve; even after two decades the challenge and excitement of the venture are apparent to the most casual reader."[116]

A 1953 publication, *A Public School for Tomorrow,* described the Matthew F. Maury School in Richmond, Virginia. This description, also introduced by Kilpatrick, reported on 18 years of experience in trying "to provide for every child, whatever his ability, the kind of environment that will bring growth upward and outward toward self-enhancement."[117] The chapter headings indicate the scope of the curriculum:

We Plan our Living
We Play, We Eat, We Rest
We Listen, We Talk, We Read, We Write
We Need Music Every Day
We Use Art in Our Search for Beauty
We Deal with Quantity and Space
We Explore Our Universe
We Seek To Live Well with Others
We Work To Be at One with Our Community

But no specific units, grade placements, and time allotments were given, since the Maury design was one for planning rather than a fixed plan.[118]

Another child-centered school has been the subject of several books. Summerhill, in England, has received much attention in educational literature. This school is perhaps a prototype of some more recently established "free" and other alternative schools in the United States. Its director, Neill, stated that it was started "*to make the school fit the child*—instead of making the child fit the school" and was based on faith in "the goodness of the child."[119] A decade after Neill's book was published 15 authors contributed to *Summerhill: For and Against* some widely varying opinions about the school's philosophy and program. We consider Hechinger's opening comment a fair appraisal of the Summerhill idea:

Summerhill is not a school but a religion. That is why one can be intrigued by it—can even admire it—without being converted to it. To derive benefits from it for one's children requires religious faith in the efficacy of its myths. As with every religion, faith distilled into fanaticisms can be dangerous. But there is so much essential goodness of intent and spirit in Summerhill that its doctrine may—in modified form—be most beneficial to ordinary parents who send their children to a variety of ordinary schools.[120]

[116]Cremin, *Transformation of the School,* pp. 253–254.
[117]Marion Nesbitt, *A Public School for Tomorrow* (New York: Harper & Brothers, 1953), p. 101.
[118]Nesbitt, pp. 21–22.
[119]A. S. Neill, *Summerhill: A Radical Approach to Child Rearing* (New York: Hart Publishing Company, Inc., 1960), p. 4.
[120]Fred M. Hechinger in *Summerhill: For and Against* (New York: Hart Publishing Company, Inc., 1970), p. 35.

Certainly Summerhill is an extreme application of the needs and interests design, lacking as it does the balance of freedom and guided options available in most child-centered schools of the past. However, the continuation of the school after the death of its founder speaks to its vitality.

Thus, these child-centered schools, primarily elementary schools, have typically exhibited the features listed at the beginning of this section, although some descriptions are somewhat vague as to how learners' needs and interests are identified and how learners are guided in their choice making. Current efforts toward curriculum individualization, especially in middle and high schools and in post-high school education, may be more completely designed in terms of these features. Before turning to these efforts we should review (see Chapter 2) the movement toward various types of "free" and "alternative" schools.

The common denominator of these various schools, many of them unidentifiable and many of them temporary, has been that they are "free" of, or "alternative" to, public schools and are typically organized by parents, teachers, or even students because of dissatisfaction with public schools. However, in the 1970s some public school systems created their own alternative schools or subsystems, so that this common denominator is not wholly inclusive. Kozol's book, *Free Schools,* deals primarily with only one type of school.[121] Kozol's free schools are concerned with the needs and interests of their students, but many of these needs are those of the entire ghetto community, and the educational program is decidedly realistic.[122] The chief generalization we can make about the curriculum design of the several varieties of free and other alternative schools is that one could find some such schools with as traditional designs as the most traditional public school and others as free and unstructured as Summerhill. Their relation to the needs and interests design stems primarily from the origin of these schools: they are generally created to meet some needs and interests of particular students which the founders see as being unmet in conventional public schools.

The Case for the Needs and Interests/Activities Design

Our study of the theory and practice of the needs and interests/activities design suggests three major arguments for it: 1) learning opportunities based on needs and interests are more relevant to the learners; 2) the needs and interests design involves a high degree of motivation and therefore success of the learner; and 3) achievement of the individual's potential is facilitated by this design.

The validity of the first argument is obvious; that is, if the learning opportunity is truly chosen because of the individual's needs and interests,

[121]See Jonathan Kozol, *Free Schools* (Boston: Houghton Mifflin Company, 1972).
[122]See, for example, the description of one unidentified school in Kozol, p. 74.

it surely must relate to them. As to the second argument, the reasoning is similar, but it must be noted that motivation is a highly internalized matter and that learners are not necessarily motivated for a learning opportunity planned externally.[123] Dewey had emphasized the importance of building on the "natural learning" of the child, explaining the curriculum of his laboratory school as based on this motivation principle.[124] Many years later the same principle was developed by Crary; describing the "natural learner" as "tireless," he wrote:

> Too often the school slanders its pupils. It judges them lazy, weary or inattentive; it acts as though these were natural characteristics of learners. On the contrary, these are protective poses of people who are unwilling to invest themselves in adventures not their own. When the school helps students to discover the mountains they want to climb it also discovers their energies and capacities.[125]

As to the third argument, facilitating the achievement of the individual's potential, this is the argument for all plans and strategies of individualization, including some categorical arrangements such as multiple tracks that we consider fallacious. Which curriculum designs focused on individual needs and interests represent the best approach has not been demonstrated, but certainly there is much evidence from research and observation that diagnosis of individual student needs and interests and provision for them are essential in good education. We accept Benjamin's argument which is charmingly presented as that of Old Man Coyote: "Old Man Coyote insists that the boy whose mathematical, linguistic, geographical, or other peaks of ability are built to great heights will have his valleys of ability in other areas pulled up toward his peaks until the sum of his achievements will be far above the minimum essentials ever set by plodding plainsmen."[126]

Applications and Limitations

We have already cited many applications of the needs and interests/activities design. Here we point only to a few that seem of particular significance for the future. In doing so, we should also note that the chief limitation of this design is its possible neglect of social goals. If the needs

[123]See L. Thomas Hopkins, *Interaction: The Democratic Process* (Boston: D. C. Heath and Company, 1941), for the insistence of one strong advocate of the experience curriculum that the learner's "real felt needs" be basic.
[124]Quoted in Mayhew and Edwards, p. 33.
[125]Ryland W. Crary, *Humanizing the School: Curriculum Development and Theory* (New York: Alfred A. Knopf, 1969), p. 114.
[126]Harold Benjamin, *The Cultivation of Idiosyncrasy,* Inglis Lecture, 1949 (Cambridge, Mass.: Harvard University Press, 1949), p. 19.

and interests principle is fully utilized, especially as excluding learning opportunities not based on learners' "felt" needs, there is no assurance of learners becoming equipped to participate effectively in social activities, particularly those of adulthood involved in work and citizenship. Hence we see the needs and interests design as especially appropriate for the personal development domain and for some aspects of the continued learning skills and specialization ones, but not for the social competence domain.

The most common approach to meeting the needs and interests of learners is the categorical grouping of students for special programs believed by the planners to match the needs and interests of the students concerned. Ability and other forms of homogeneous grouping at all levels, curriculum tracks in the high school, multiple curricula in colleges and universities, and the electives system itself in secondary and higher education have been widely provided as approaches to individualizing curriculum. Efforts of this kind are also represented by a multiplicity of programs for such special groups as the academically talented, the disadvantaged, dropouts (actual and potential), the gifted, the mentally handicapped, minority, cultural, and ethnic groups, the physically handicapped, the socially and emotionally maladjusted, underachievers, and others. These various programs have generally included curriculum plans that focus on the needs and interests of learners within the categories, our first characteristic feature of the needs and interests design. But these approaches have not necessarily had the flexibility and student involvement in planning that we also consider characteristic.

The predominant use of the needs and interests design in curriculum planning is in the provision of *options* for individual students. For example, the middle schools provide many special-interest activities, exploratory courses, and other experiences aimed at giving each student opportunities to explore and deepen his or her own interests. The system of elective courses in high schools and colleges, as well as the wide range of activities open to students, is currently being expanded by the offering of mini-courses planned with students to fit special needs and interests.

Currently the movement in higher education toward "open university" arrangements and continuing education in general illustrates the options feature of the needs and interests design. Drucker argues for continuing education which assumes "that the more experience in life and work people have, the more eager they will be to learn and the more capable they will be of learning."[127] Mondale advocated a concept of "lifelong learning as inclusive of many separate programs and concepts that have developed in recent years." He included: "adult basic education, occupa-

---

[127]Peter F. Drucker, *The Age of Discontinuity* (London: William Heinemann, Ltd., 1969), p. 302.

tional training, independent study, parent education, education for personal development, remedial education, continuing education, and education for groups with special needs." To arrange programs to meet these various needs and interests, according to Mondale, "demands the very best thinking of our most creative educators and social philosophers."[128]

Curriculum plans emphasizing the options concept can and generally do have the three features of a needs and interests/activities design: 1) the options are based on knowledge of learner characteristics; 2) scheduling and other arrangements facilitate ready selection and choice of options, with counseling services available to help students; and 3) students are actively involved in planning and evaluating the options in general and for themselves in particular.

As to future applications, we suspect that the establishment of so-called free and other alternative forms of schooling will continue, although it seems probable that these may increasingly be developed within rather than without public school systems. It is even conceivable that Illich's "networks" concept may be developed under public auspices, with computerized management. "Open" universities and schools may also be expected to utilize the needs and interests design in offering a great variety of student-requested programs.

The open classroom is an application of the needs and interests design that appeared to hold promise in the 1960s and early 1970s. The open classroom combines ideas from the earlier progressive education, experimental English primary schools, and modern technology. In the open classroom there are a variety of learning centers and students have opportunities for guided exploration and participation in these centers. As open classrooms spread, teaching practices within the classroom varied considerably. Research has been thwarted because of the great variation of practices labeled open education. Attempts at definition have caused researchers to box themselves into a corner "for the more tightly they have defined the open classroom, the fewer classrooms can be found to fit the description. Finally, the model has become so exacting and exclusive that *no* classrooms conform to it."[129] Open classrooms may share in the epitaph of other innovations—"killed by 'friends' who adopted the form but never understood the notion."

Independent study, which is both a curriculum option and an instructional strategy—indeed both a means and an end (independent learning) —seems to us to be an especially useful application of the needs and interests activities design. It is largely an individually motivated and a guided learning activity:

[128]Walter F. Mondale, "The Next Step: Lifelong Learning," *Change, 8* (October 1976): 43.
[129]Roland S. Barth, "Beyond Open Education," *Phi Delta Kappan, 58* (February 1977): 491.

Independent study is considered by us to be learning activity largely motivated by the learner's own aims to learn and largely rewarded in terms of its intrinsic values. Such activity as carried on under the auspices of secondary schools is somewhat independent of the class or other group organization dominant in past and present secondary school organizational practices, and it utilizes the services of teachers and other professional personnel primarily as resources for the learner.[130]

Although many usages of the term are misapplications,[131] many schools, colleges, and universities do have planned guidance of a wide variety of independent study opportunities conforming to the needs and interests principle.

It is the needs and interests principle rather than a particular design which has most influence and applicability. Within each of the other designs—including subject matter/disciplines—points arrive in planning curriculum and instruction at which decisions must be made regarding each student's program and progress. To the extent that consideration is given to the individual student's needs and interests in these decisions, the principle is utilized. We believe that such utilization is an essential phase of the curriculum planning needed now and hereafter.

HUMANISTIC EDUCATION

Five curriculum designs have been considered in some detail. Each of these, we believe, has been sufficiently described in theoretical works and applied in practice to be classified as a curriculum design, despite the considerable varieties in practices within each category. Humanistic education has also been identified as a curriculum design by some authors.[132] We believe humanistic education should not be restricted to one curriculum design, but rather should permeate all curriculum designs.

The history of humanistic education has been reviewed by Foshay.[133] In the 1920s and 1930s there was considerable support for humanistic education around the theme of the "whole child." According to Foshay, "The movement of the twenties and thirties suffered a sad fate. It lost its edge and generated into moralizing and sentimentalism. Events overwhelmed it: the Second World War, the political reactionism of the fifties, the educational conservatism of the fifties and sixties."[134] Interest in hu-

---

[130]William M. Alexander, Vynce A. Hines, and associates, *Independent Study in Secondary Schools* (New York: Holt, Rinehart and Winston, Inc., 1967) p. 12.
[131]See William M. Alexander and William I. Burke, "Independent Study in Secondary Schools," *Interchange, 3* (Numbers 2–3, 1972): 102–113.
[132]For example, John D. McNeil, *Curriculum: A Comprehensive Approach* (Boston: Little, Brown and Company, 1977).
[133]Foshay, pp. 97–113.
[134]Foshay, p. 98.

manistic education increased in the 1970s. Foshay speculated that this renewed interest could have been caused by a combination of such factors as: increased threat to individual identity; impact on the social consciousness of assassinations, the Vietnam War, the disaffection of the young; a reaction against the conservative thrust to make of teaching a set of impersonal techniques.

Increased interests in humanistic education led to the publication by the Association for Supervision and Curriculum Development (ASCD) of their 1977 Yearbook, *Feeling, Valuing, and the Art of Growing: Insights into the Affective.*[135] A later publication, *Humanistic Education: Objectives and Assessment,* was a report of the ASCD Working Group on Humanistic Education.[136] That group defined humanistic education as "a commitment to education and practice in which all facets of the teaching-learning process give major emphasis to the freedom, value, dignity, and integrity of persons."[137] Note the emphasis on "all facets of the teaching–learning process."

The ASCD Working Group identified seven goals for humanistic education:

1. Accept the learner's needs and purposes and develop experiences and programs around the unique potentials of the learner.
2. Facilitate self-actualization and strive to develop in all persons a sense of personal adequacy.
3. Foster acquisition of basic skills necessary for living in a multicultural society including academic, personal, interpersonal, and economic survival proficiencies.
4. Personalize educational decisions and practices—include students in the processes of their own education via democratic involvement in all levels of implementation.
5. Recognize the primacy of human feelings and utilize personal values and perceptions as integral factors in educational processes.
6. Strive to develop learning environments which are perceived by all involved as challenging, understanding, supportive, exciting, and free from threat.
7. Develop in learners genuine concern for the worth of others and skill in conflict resolution.[138]

[135]Louise M. Berman and Jessie A. Roderick (eds.), *Feeling, Valuing, and the Art of Growing: Insights into the Affective* (Washington, D.C.: Association for Supervision and Curriculum Development, 1977).

[136]Arthur W. Combs (Chairperson), David N. Aspy, Doris M. Brown, Morrel J. Clute, Laurabeth H. Hicks, *Humanistic Education: Objectives and Assessment* (Washington, D.C.: Association for Supervision and Curriculum Development, 1978).

[137]Morrel J. Clute, "Humanistic Education: Goals and Objectives," in Combs, et al., p. 9.

[138]Clute, pp. 10–14 passim.

Some of these goals can be achieved with any of the five curriculum designs described in this chapter. Some of the goals can be achieved more readily by certain designs. For example, the human traits/processes and interests and needs/activities designs lend themselves more readily to achieving these goals than do the subject matter/disciplines and specific competencies/technology designs.

It will be unfortunate if the present drive for humanistic education loses its edge, as did the drive in the 1920s and 1930s, through sentimentality, moralizing, and rhetoric. We believe the goals stated by the ASCD Working Group can lead to needed action. To be achieved these goals should influence the development of a curriculum design, guide in the implementation of that design (instruction), and provide some of the questions to be answered in the evaluation of educational programs.[139]

GUIDELINES FOR APPROPRIATE CURRICULUM DESIGNS

Curriculum is a plan for providing sets of learning opportunities for persons to be educated. The development of that plan (see Figure 1.1, p. 29) involves considering the major purposes and aims of education; identifying goals, subgoals, and objectives; selecting a curriculum design and writing a plan. All of these activities are guided by data about the learners, the society served, and the nature of learners. Knowledge from different disciplines is used in developing the plan.

The curriculum design selected has a direct bearing on the instruction provided. To paraphrase Toffler's comment on education and the future: just as all education springs from some image of a curriculum design, all curriculum designs produce characteristic types of education. For example, the widespread use of the subject matter/disciplines design to cover all goals and domains has been primarily responsible for the gap between educational goals and instructional practices; a curriculum "locked in" to that single design cannot achieve all of the goals.

No one curriculum design can be adequate for the total curriculum plan of an educational institution serving a varied population with multiple goals. Instead, we see the curriculum planners as properly selecting appropriate designs for particular curriculum goals, domains, and objectives. Inevitably, designing is an area of decision making to be shared by those immediately responsible for the curriculum plan of a particular educational setting.

Table 5.2 has been developed to aid curriculum planners in selecting appropriate curriculum designs. To use this guide for planning, the curriculum worker begins by considering the nature of the goals and objec-

[139]See Foshay for a concrete proposal for implementation of a humanistic education.

TABLE 5.2 Selecting Curriculum Designs

If Curriculum Planners Intend to:	Consider Using This Design:	Consider Organizing Instruction:
Provide organized knowledge, for example, knowledge in the biological sciences	Subject matter/ disciplines	Around disciplines of knowledge
Develop specific competencies or skills, for example, ability to add, ability to type	Specific competencies/ technology	Through an instructional system design based on a task analysis
Develop human traits, for example, knowing how to learn, ability to solve problems, ability to lead effectively, ability to be analytical about one's values	Human traits/ processes	Through planned processes involving extensive experiences related to the traits sought
Relate education to society, for example, assist learners to deal with persistent life situations, improve the local community, reconstruct society	Social functions/ activities	Through engaging learners in social activities and extensive study of social and community problems and programs
Meet the needs and interests of learners, for example, learn to paint, establish good relationships with peers	Needs and interests/ activities	Through engaging learners as individuals or in groups in activities related to their needs and interests

tives to be achieved. These goals and objectives are then related to one of five statements listed in Column 1. For example, assume that a goal is to help students develop the ability to solve problems dealing with human relations. This goal is most closely associated with "Develop human traits." Accordingly, the curriculum worker might consider using the human traits/processes design and plan experiences that enable students actually to solve human relations problems. Note, however, that the goal may also be associated with "Relate education to society" or "Meet the needs and interests of learners." Hence social functions/activities and needs and interests/activities could also be considered as alternative curriculum designs.

In order to select appropriate curriculum designs it is essential that curriculum planners be knowledgeable about curriculum designs and the designing process. Without some understanding of past and current efforts to develop designs more appropriate to the goals and domains of the school curriculum, planners continue to repeat the mistakes they have made in the past. They need to recognize many so-called innovations as renovations and be able to at least turn to the sources which have described and evaluated these. They need to identify the background of a new theory formulation and find the elements of it that have not been previously tested as well as those that have been. Thus a major justification for the study of curriculum designs as presented in this chapter is to aid curriculum planners in adding to their own store of knowledge to help them understand, classify, and evaluate curriculum design theories and proposals.

But curriculum planners cannot confine their designing efforts to reflection about past and present. The planners must also fit appropriate designs to their particular goals and domains. Design gives a curriculum plan a framework for its organization, implementation, and evaluation. It constitutes an order, however flexible and changing, for the organization of sets of learning opportunities. Thus, with goals established and domains tentatively organized around sets of goals, planners must identify the learning opportunities appropriate to their goals, domains, and populations and anticipate them in detail by fitting opportunities and design principles together in a promising framework.

In this chapter we have given detailed consideration to the characteristic features, cases for, and applications and limitations of five general designs. Each design is really a classification of design theories that focus on the same organizing principle or at least on very closely related organizing principles. We believe that curriculum planners need to be cognizant of these five design possibilities, and of the multiple patterns each entails, in order to make intelligent decisions about their own plans.

Once a design is selected an actual plan is produced, generally in a written form. The nature of the plan will vary considerably depending upon the curriculum design being used. For example, a plan utilizing a specific competencies/technology design will include instructional objectives, usually stated as behaviors to be learned; plans for preassessment of learners; descriptions of materials to be used and the sequence of their use; and test items to use in evaluating the achievement of objectives. The plan may be "packaged" in the form of a module. By way of contrast, another plan following the human traits/processes design might include: a statement of the human trait(s) to be developed; ways to assess present level of development of learners in relation to traits, often through observational techniques; suggested types of experiences to be offered; and ways to evaluate the quality of the experiences provided.

Regardless of the design followed, the curriculum plan should generally include a description of the learners; purposes and general goals, possibly organized by domains or objectives; types of learning experiences to be provided; locale; general time and space allocations; assessment procedures; and roles of various participants.

It is wise to move as carefully and rapidly as possible to test chosen designs. Selection or development of an appropriate design for a series of learning opportunities related to some curriculum domain and a set of its subgoals is an important step toward an effective curriculum plan, but this step is primarily that of giving order to the plan. It is in the translation of that order into practice through wise planning and execution of the implementation phase—instruction, in its broadest sense—that the plan is really tested.

ADDITIONAL SUGGESTIONS FOR FURTHER STUDY

Bock, Daniel R., "Summerhill: It's Alive and Well," *Educational Leadership, 35* (February 1978): 380–383. Useful addendum to the work of Neill and his critics. Bock was able to visit the school despite the ban on visitors at the time, and found the over 50-year-old institution still flourishing and inspirational.

Della-Dora, Delmos, and Lois Jerry Blanchard (eds.), *Moving Toward Self-Directed Learning.* Washington, D. C.: Association for Supervision and Curriculum Development, 1979. Gives a needed emphasis to the processes involved in self-directed learning and its development in schools. Reviews theory, research, and practice with some concluding suggestions for developing self-directed learning programs.

Goodlad, John I. and associates, *Curriculum Inquiry: The Study of Curriculum Practice.* New York: McGraw-Hill Book Company, 1979. Chapter 9 is a case study of the designing of curricula within a large school system. The description includes an account of data sources used and the transactional processes involved in relating the work of decision-making agents in the societal area, the institutional area, and the instructional area.

Gower, Robert R., and Marvin B. Scott, *Five Essential Dimensions of Curriculum Design: A Handbook for Teachers.* Dubuque, Ia.: Kendall/Hunt Publishing Co., 1977. The purpose of this book is to provide teachers with a mode of inquiry that will allow them to explore curriculum designs and consider how these influences might be used to achieve educational purposes. A Lens Theory describes how a teacher may select appropriate designs.

Posner, George J., and Alan N. Rudinsky, *Course Design: A Guide to Curriculum Development for Teachers.* New York: Longman, 1978. A limited, specific manual to be followed in the development of a course ("as much as a whole year's work or as little as a four-week 'minicourse'") in secondary and postsecondary institutions. The formula presented assumes the course design should include: 1) rationale; 2) learning outcomes; 3) conceptual map; 4) instructional plan; and 5) evaluation plan.

Schaffarzick, Jon, and David H. Hampson (eds.), *Strategies for Curriculum Development.* Berkeley, Calif: McCutchan Publishing Corp., 1975. Essays by nine curriculum developers describing their approaches to the task. Although some of the procedures are more fully reported elsewhere by such developers as Ralph Tyler, James Popham, and Elliot Eisner, the collection here facilitates a comparison such as is presented in the final chapter.

Schiro, Michael, *Curriculum for Better Schools.* Englewood Cliffs, N.J.: Educational Technology Publications, 1978. The author identifies four curricular ideologies—Social Efficiency, Scholar Academic, Child Study, and Social Reconstruction—and then analyzes many recent curriculum projects and proposals in terms of these four types of curriculum plans. Various charts and models are used in the treatment.

Synergist is published three times each year by ACTION'S National Student
Volunteer Program, 806 Connecticut Avenue, N.W., Washington, D.C. 20502.
Articles in the journal contain descriptions of principles of service-learning and
its philosophical bases. Case studies of effective service-learning programs described in the journal provide excellent illustrations of social functions/activities
curriculum designs.

Weller, Richard H. (ed.), *Humanistic Education: Visions and Realities.* Bloomington, Ind.: Phi Delta Kappa, 1977. Contains chapters analyzing humanistic education in relation to such areas as social action, human development, and
educational administration. Chapters are written by many of the leaders in the
field of humanistic education such as Michael Apple, David Aspy, and James
Macdonald.

SIX

...

PLANNING CURRICULUM IMPLEMENTATION: INSTRUCTION

▪ ▪

The purpose of all curriculum planning is to provide opportunities for an individual student or a group of students to benefit maximally from participation in selected learning activities. As the students partake of learning opportunities, whether these are planned by the teacher, or improvised on the spot by the teacher or student(s), or both, such participation becomes a learning experience which may result in personal growth. This is the process of instruction.

Instruction is thus the implementation of the curriculum plan, usually, but not necessarily, involving teaching in the sense of student-teacher interaction in an educational setting. There would be no reason for developing curriculum plans if there were no instruction. Curriculum plans, by their very nature, are simply efforts to guide and direct in one way or another the nature and character of the learning opportunities in which students participate. All curriculum planning is for naught unless it influences and shapes the things which students do. Obviously, the planner must see instruction and teaching as the summation of his efforts.

This chapter considers the link between the learning activities suggested in the curriculum, the preinstructional plan developed by the teacher, and the actual instruction. A variety of teaching models is described and their relationship to the five curriculum designs is explored. In addition, three of the persistent and emerging areas that need to be considered in planning instruction are discussed in this chapter: individualization of instruction, mainstreaming of handicapped students, and the "unstudied curriculum."

INSTRUCTIONAL PLANNING AND THE CURRICULUM

Instruction is the actual engagements of learners with planned learning opportunities. We have portrayed instuction as the implementation of a curriculum plan. However, as we shall see, this is an oversimplification; there may be little relationship between the official or stated curriculum and the actual engagements of learners.

Designing the Curriculum and Planning Instruction

A curriculum plan may suggest, or specify, student activities as well as materials to be used. The teacher's individual preinstructional plan also includes student activities and teaching materials. How do these two sets of plans mesh? Where does the curriculum plan stop and the teacher's plan begin? We can examine these questions through metaphors explaining the relationship between the educational plan, or curriculum, and the implementation of that plan, or instruction.

One metaphor likens the curriculum to a blueprint for a building and instruction to its construction. The teacher then is a craftsman whose skill is measured by the correspondence between the blueprint and the building. Another metaphor likens the curriculum to the game plan a coach presents to his or her players before the big game; instruction is the playing of the game. While the players are expected to follow the game plan, they are also expected to make intelligent improvisations. The curriculum could be thought of as a commission to an artist while the creation of the work of art is the instruction. The teacher in this metaphor becomes a creative artist. Finally, and with tongue-in-cheek, the curriculum plan might be likened to a political platform of a successful candidate and instruction the subsequent legislative session where laws are passed.

Metaphors may conceal more than they reveal as reality is warped to fit an analogy. They can be used, however, to stimulate new thinking on an old topic. The metaphors in the preceding paragraph suggest a variety of relationships between the instructional plans included in the curriculum and those developed by the individual teacher. If the curriculum is a blueprint, very specific plans for the building are included: specific space allocations, elements to go into the building, and detailed directions for their assembly. Two assumptions are made—the blueprint will be appropriate in a variety of educational settings and the teacher has the necessary materials, tools, and skills to follow the blueprint. Curriculum plans that result in a series of modules or in a reading series with a carefully spelled-out manual for teachers fit the blueprint metaphor. The legal requirement in some states that students must "Pass" a set of prescribed examinations conforms to this type of a curriculum plan.

The game plan metaphor assumes a clear goal to be achieved through a strategy of reaching several subgoals. The details of achieving these subgoals are left to the ingenuity of the players. Two assumptions guide this metaphor. First, a clearly identified major goal and subsequent subgoals are understood and accepted by the players. Second, players have the ability to achieve the goals and the ingenuity to improvise within, or even outside of, the game plan in order to achieve the major goal. Glasser's "reality therapy" through classroom meetings would fit the game plan metaphor.[1]

In the third metaphor, artists may be commissioned to compose a piece

---

[1] William Glasser, *Schools Without Failure* (New York: Harper & Row, 1969). William Glasser, "Ten Steps to Good Discipline," *Today's Education,* 66 (November–December 1977): 61–63.

of music for a particular occasion, or to paint a mural for the lobby of a large building, or to make a sculpture for some area. A few great works of art have resulted from such commissions, for example, the painting on the ceiling of the Sistine Chapel; a great many mediocre works have also resulted. Great artistic works may emerge when those granting a commission pick a talented artist and then get out of the artist's way. In other words, frame the commission in broad terms and allow the artist to be creative. Is this a metaphor for curriculum? If so, it would suggest that an effective curriculum provides only the broadest outline of goals—a canvas for the artist to paint on—and that teachers are artists. Is Summerhill an illustration? Would progressive educators in the 1930s and 1940s have claimed this metaphor?

We hesitate to comment on the political metaphor, and yet there is a lesson to be learned. A curriculum and a political platform may be viewed as handy documents to display at appropriate times, but ignored in the "real world" of the classroom or conveniently forgotten in the heat of a legislative session.

These metaphors illustrate that some types of curriculum plans include more detailed directions for implementation (instruction) than do others. In fact, the basic preplanned curriculum may be the textbook itself, with perhaps an accompanying teacher's manual, and a teacher may follow this plan quite rigidly. Generally plans that follow the subject matter disciplines or specific competencies/technology design provide more complete information for implementation than do those using human traits/processes, social functions/activities, or interests and needs/activities. There is a complementary relationship between the degree of specificity in the curriculum plan and preinstructional planning required of the teacher. Figure 6.1 shows that when plans for implementation are more complete, less preinstructional planning is required of the teacher. As the

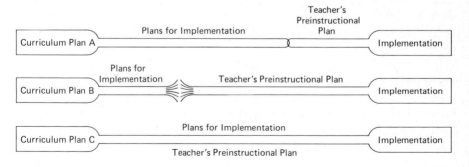

FIGURE 6.1   Relationship between teacher's preinstructional planning and the curriculum

figure suggests, the linkage may be direct when the curriculum plans are more specific; while the linkage may be tenuous when implementation plans are in the form of suggestions.

Curriculum Plan A is less demanding on the teacher's time and energy and less dependent upon the teacher's ability to design instruction; this increases the possibility that it will be implemented. However, the rigidity that provides the advantage becomes a disadvantage when the curriculum plan does not "fit" the learners. Curriculum Plan B offers the possibility of overcoming this problem by providing plenty of freedom for teachers to adapt the curriculum to the learners but at the price of requiring additional teacher time and energy in preinstructional planning.

Curriculum plans represented by A and B in Figure 6.1 are typically developed externally and given to the teacher. However, when the teacher participates in the development of the original curriculum plan (represented by Plan C in Figure 6.1) there may be little or no distinction between the original curriculum plan and the teacher's preinstructional plan.

The perceptive reader may have added a curriculum Plan D to Figure 6.1—a plan that does not connect in any way with the teacher's preinstructional planning. In this case the teacher is marching to a different drummer and the preinstructional planning may simply be a decision to use a textbook or notes used last year. A major purpose of this chapter is to help curriculum planners counteract this all-too-frequent practice.

A teacher's preinstructional plan and a curriculum plan may not connect if a teacher neither understands nor accepts the basic assumptions of the plan. Bussis and colleagues demonstrated this situation through an interview study of teachers in "open education" schools.[2] Open education, they believed, emphasizes "the central role of both teacher and child in decisions that determine the nature and course of learning."[3] They contrasted this participation with conceptions of instruction where teachers' decisions are based on criteria external to the learners. They considered both a deep-level curriculum, "referring to the purposes and priorities a teacher holds for children's learning," and a surface curriculum, "referring to the manifest activities and materials in a classroom."[4] The researchers found that for 12 percent of the teachers, " 'grade-level facts and skills' is clearly the dominant priority, and there is little evidence of experimentation or change in the surface curriculum from what the teachers have been practicing previously." They found that another 22 percent shared the grade-level facts and skills priority, "but there is much evidence of

---

[2]Anne M. Bussis, Edward A. Chittenden, Marianne Amarel, *Beyond Surface Curriculum* (Boulder, Color.: Westview Press, 1976).
[3]Bussis, et al., p. 2.
[4]Bussis, et al., p. 4.

change and experimentation with the surface curriculum." The remaining teachers placed priority on initiative/independence of children and had potentially rich surface curriculums.[5]

Preinstructional Planning by Teachers

An understanding of factors considered by teachers in their preinstructional planning can help curriculum workers design plans that are more apt to be implemented. Figure 6.2, a rational static model for linking a curriculum plan and instruction, shows the steps a teacher follows in preinstructional planning. This model assumes that the teacher's instruction will be based on the new curriculum plan. Of course this is not always the case and the teacher may be considering options that do not stem from the new plan. In the model represented by Figure 6.2 the teacher's values, knowledge, and skills influence every choice that is made. The teacher considers the curriculum plan: goals and objectives stated, curriculum design proposed, and instructional plans suggested. A teacher might envision several possible instructional plans emanating from the curriculum plan. These possible plans are "screened," and thus possibly reduced in number, by considering the values and educational expectations of the local community.

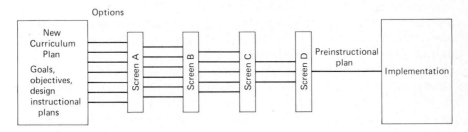

TEACHER AS A DECISION MAKER

(Influenced by personal commitments, professional knowledge, and repertoire of instructional models)

CONSIDERS

A: Community values and expectations

B: Pupil needs, interests, capabilities, role in planning

C: Educational environment—class organization, materials, administrative support and constraints

D: Teacher's final decision on an appropriate instructional plan

FIGURE 6.2 A rational static model for linking a curriculum plan and instruction

[5]Bussis, et al., p. 56.

The plans deemed acceptable within the community are considered in relation to the particular group of learners. Which of the possible plans are appropriate to the learners' needs and interests? Which plans are they capable of following? Will the learners participate in selecting possible plans? The feasible plans are then tested for their practicality in the educational environment. Which plans can be made to work given the environment of the educational institution, the materials available, the support of the administrators?

Relatively few options may remain open to the teacher. Note, however, that teacher judgment has been exercised at every step of the way. At this point, a teacher may reject possible instructional plans requiring new teaching strategies and develop an instructional plan he or she can "feel comfortable with."

This model illustrates why some curriculum plans are never implemented. For example, the study by Bussis and her colleagues, cited earlier, found that 12 percent of the teachers in "open schools" had not even adopted the surface curriculum—the outward appearance of an open classroom. The researchers found that for these teachers learning "grade-level facts and skills is clearly the dominant priority." The teachers had rejected the goals and objectives of the open education curriculum. The reasons may have included: interpretation of community values and expectations; perceptions of the needs, interests, and capabilities of students; lack of administrative support; the teacher's own commitments; and the teacher's feeling of insecurity in using an instructional mode or strategy appropriate to open education.

Few teachers would move consecutively through the steps suggested by the model in Figure 6.2. Further, the model implies a *de novo* approach by the teacher, who does not recognize the existence of an on-going program. Figure 6.3 presents the same factors for teacher consideration, but in a more realistic and dynamic fashion.

Figure 6.3 is a vector analysis in which the direction of an influence is shown by an arrow, with its strength indicated by the arrow's length. The model is dynamic in that it shows how a functioning instructional program is underway when a new curriculum plan is proposed. The length of the arrow representing the present instructional program shows the influence generated by the momentum of the existing program. Assume in the model that vector a represents a new curriculum plan, vector b represents students, vector c the teacher, vector d the educational environment, and vector e the community. To follow the new curriculum (vector a) requires a change in the instructional program. Students' needs, interests, and capabilities (vector b) would be influencing in the direction of this curriculum change. The teacher's commitments, professional knowledge, and repertoire (vector c) represents a strong influence, and, not supris-

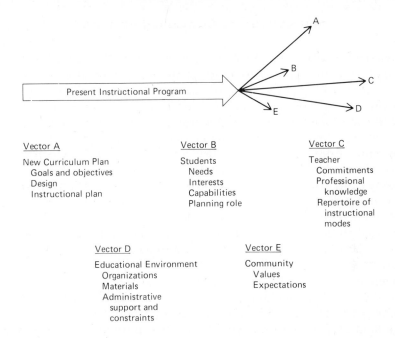

Vector A

New Curriculum Plan
   Goals and objectives
   Design
   Instructional plan

Vector B

Students
   Needs
   Interests
   Capabilities
   Planning role

Vector C

Teacher
   Commitments
   Professional
     knowledge
   Repertoire of
     instructional
     modes

Vector D

Educational Environment
   Organizations
   Materials
   Administrative
     support and
     constraints

Vector E

Community
   Values
   Expectations

FIGURE 6.3 A realistic dynamic model for linking a curriculum plan and instruction

ingly, in the same direction as present practice. The educational environment (vector d) is not particularly supportive of the new curriculum. For example, adequate materials may not be available. The community (vector e) is not perceived as supportive; although the vector is short, experienced educators know that community opposition to a new curriculum can grow rapidly. Vector analysis shows the direction of movement.

If the vector analysis represented in Figure 6.3 depicted an actual situation, one could predict that very little change would take place in classroom practice. If there were strong administrative support, that is if vector d paralleled vector a, there would probably be a "surface" change in the curriculum. However, if the administrator were to leave and the successor did not support the new curriculum plan, the veneer of the surface curriculum would soon disappear. Figure 6.3 demonstrates that adoption of a new curriculum plan requires the support of significant groups and the commitment of teachers. This is consistent with Miel's observation, cited earlier, that curriculum change is "a type of social change, change in people, not mere change on paper."[6]

[6]Alice Miel, *Changing the Curriculum* (New York: Appleton-Century-Crofts, 1946), p. 10.

Implications for Curriculum Planning

A curriculum plan is of no value unless it is used. The preceding discussion indicates why some curriculum plans gather dust. If they are to be used, some meshing of the suggestions made in the curriculum plan and the teacher's preinstructional plan is necessary. Talmage and Eash pointed out, "Ideally, curriculum, instruction, and instructional materials make different but essential contributions to an educational program."[7] They found from a series of studies that the most effective programs developed when there was a concerted effort to improve concurrently mutually supporting curriculum, instruction, and instructional materials.

Improving the linkage between curriculum plans and instruction results when curriculum planners pay attention to existing instructional practices. Hirst chided curriculum theorists who "have for too long given the quite false impression that rational decisions can be made on the basis of abstract, theoretical considerations and on purely external knowledge of the content." He concluded, "There is very good reason to think that detailed rational curriculum development can come only by modifying current practices from within, making them progressively more rational in the light of general principles."[8] Taba was using this idea successfully in the 1950s. In her inductive approach to curriculum development, described in Chapter 2, Taba helped individual teachers develop the best possible programs in their classrooms. From these good programs general principles were discovered inductively and were then used to build new curriculum plans.[9]

The surest way to have a curriculum plan implemented is to write a plan describing present practice. This is not what is meant when we say the plan should be rooted in present practice and research. Rather, the planner needs to recognize present practice and to design a curriculum to improve this practice.

Curriculum planners do not have to use an inductive approach to be sensitive to current practice. For example, research findings on teaching effectiveness provide valuable clues as to what to include—and what not to include—in a curriculum plan, particularly as regards implementation. A respectable body of research findings on teacher effectiveness is accumulating. *The Second Handbook of Research on Teaching* contains a summary of research completed through the early 1970s. The 1976 Yearbook

---

[7]Harriet Talmage and Maurice J. Eash, "Curriculum, Instruction, and Materials," in Penelope L. Peterson and Herbert J. Walberg (eds.), *Research on Teaching: Concepts, Findings, and Implications* (Berkeley, Calif.: McCutchan Publishing Corp., 1979), p. 161.
[8]Paul H. Hirst, "Reply to Jonas F. Soltis," *Teachers College Record,* 80, (May 1979): 788.
[9]Hilda Taba, *Curriculum Development: Theory and Practice* (New York: Harcourt Brace and World, Inc., 1962).

of the National Society for the Study of Education (NSSE), *The Psychology of Teaching Methods,* applies research findings to several different teaching methods. A 1979 publication of the National Society for the Study of Education, *Research on Teaching,* provides summaries of research by some of the most able researchers in the field.[10] We turn to some of this research in the next section.

Planning the implementation of a curriculum requires a knowledge of various teaching models. This chapter contains a catalog of some of the more common teaching models as well as a few new and promising models.

A knowledge of pervasive concerns in instructional practice enables curriculum planners to root implementation plans in reality. One of these continuing concerns is individualizing instruction. A new concern for teachers is the implementation of PL 94–142, mainstreaming. Curriculum plans need to be designed to enable teachers to meet the needs of handicapped children in the classroom. Another concern is the effect of the "unstudied curriculum" on students. This includes, but is more than, the hidden curriculum. Sections of this chapter are given over to each of these topics.

TEACHING AND INSTRUCTION

The title of this book, *Curriculum Planning for Better Teaching and Learning,* implies that more effective curriculum planning results in better teaching and learning. While there is research to support this conclusion,[11] we recognize that an effective curriculum does not assure better classroom teaching or learning. Thus, two teachers with contrasting teaching behaviors may produce different learning effects using the same curriculum. At the same time an individual teacher's effectiveness will vary with the quality of the curriculum used. This leads us to agree with Brophy's conclusion, "It seems intuitively obvious that educational outcomes will be determined by both what is taught (curriculum) and how well it is taught (method)."[12] As indicated in the next section, the context for teaching also is a major influence on educational outcomes.

Although this is not a textbook on teaching, some understanding of the

[10]Robert M. W. Travers (ed.), *Second Handbook of Research on Teaching* (Chicago: Rand McNally & Company, 1973); N. L. Gage (ed.), *The Psychology of Teaching Methods,* Seventy-fifth Yearbook, National Society for the Study of Education (Chicago: University of Chicago Press, 1976); Peterson and Walberg (eds.).

[11]See D. Walker and J. Schaffarzick, "Comparing Curricula," *Review of Educational Research,* 44 (1974): 83–111.

[12]Jere E. Brophy, "Teacher Behavior and Its Effects," *Journal of Educational Psychology,* 71 (1979): 734.

factors influencing teaching is desirable in planning curriculum, particularly since the curriculum plan itself is one of these factors. An understanding of the effect of teacher behavior on learning is also useful to the curriculum planner.

Hunter used a broad definition of teaching "as the process of making and implementing decisions, before, during, and after instruction, to increase the probability of learning."[13] Teaching decisions, according to Hunter, can be clustered into three categories: content to be learned, style of the learner, and behavior of the teacher. Hunter's definition and categories are particularly useful to curriculum planners. Her emphasis on decision making demonstrates that not only curriculum planning but teaching as well is a matter of making choices—choices based on the value commitments of teachers. Decisions regarding content to be learned are discussed in the previous section. Decisions related to the style of the learners are discussed in the section on individualizing instruction. This section deals with decisions related to behavior of the teacher.

Teaching Context and Learning

Out-of-classroom factors—including organization of the school, social forces, political influences—affect teachers' decisions regarding classroom behavior. For example, the bureaucratic needs of the school as an institution are served by placing approximately 30 students with one teacher. However, this structure may be inefficient and ineffective in achieving education.

Huebner reflected on his early recognition as a teacher that "helping an individual realize his or her own possibilities sometimes came in conflict with maintaining the order and routines of a classroom and school."[14] He continued, "Today I can see more clearly the school as a historical institution in which educational functions have been confused with noneducational functions." Huebner provided a particularly insightful explanation:

> The tension made manifest in the conflict between the possible education of the individual and the maintainance of the school is the tension between those who have an interest in a future emerging in the lives of children and young people, and those who have a future which now exists in their everydayness —the structures, orderliness, and meanings attached to the school and school related pursuits.[15]

[13]Madeline Hunter, "Teaching is Decision Making," *Educational Leadership, 37* (October 1979): 62. This issue of the journal contains a number of excellent articles on teacher effectiveness.
[14]Dwayne Huebner, "The Contradiction Between the Recreative and the Established," in James B. Macdonald and Esther Zaret (eds.), *Schools in Search of Meaning* (Washington, D. C.: Association for Supervision and Curriculum Development, 1975), p. 28.
[15]Huebner, p. 29.

Macdonald shared Huebner's view as he commented "It is possible to witness the displacem ent of the schools' goals for learning by the functioning of the organizational bureaucracy." He warned that "school bureaucracies may easily become self-serving. The arbitrariness of much bureaucracy means that contrary to the technological orientation, 'production' is not necessarily the major goal." When schools become politically oriented organizations, Macdonald observed they "may actually subvert the technical achievements of learning most efficiently and effectively."[16]

The concerns expressed by Huebner and Macdonald are representative of the thinking of a small but able group known as reconceptualists.[17] In addition to Huebner and Macdonald, Maxine Greene, William Pinar, and Michael Apple are often identified as reconceptualists. Many of these individuals have a background in the humanities and view curriculum as a moral enterprise rather than a technical one. They decry the political control of learners and work for their emancipation. For example, Pinar advocated "For movement to occur, we must shift our attention from the technical and the practical, and dwell on the notion of emancipation."[18]

The reconceptualists are to be encouraged in their work. As Huebner and Macdonald indicated, the goals of the school as a bureaucracy often displace the goals of education. This seriously limits the teaching methods from which the teachers may choose. Further, as indicated in a subsequent section, the school organization has a direct as well as an indirect effect on students.

While the reconceptualists work to develop new conceptions of education and curriculum, what can be done to improve the context of existing schools and thus encourage better teaching and learning? A number of studies have been conducted in an attempt to identify school characteristics that influence educational effects.[19] Most of these studies contrast the characteristics of exemplary or high performance schools with low performance schools. Exemplary schools have achievement test scores that are consistently and significantly above those of comparable schools.

Austin examined these studies and concluded, "There is no one single factor that accounts for a school being classified as exceptional." Rather,

[16]James B. Macdonald, "The Quality of Everyday Life in School," in James B. Macdonald and Esther Zaret (eds.), *Schools in Search of Meaning* (Washington, D. C.: Association for Supervision and Curriculum Development, 1975), p. 81.

[17]See William Pinar (ed.), *Curriculum Theorizing: The Reconceptualists* (Berkeley, Calif.: McCutchan Publishing Corp., 1975) for articles presenting viewpoints of reconceptualists.

[18]William F. Pinar, "Notes on the Curriculum Field, 1978," *Educational Researcher, 7* (September 1978): 11.

[19]See, for example, Herbert J. Walberg (ed.), *Educational Environments and Effects* (Berkeley, Calif.: McCutchan Publishing Corp., 1979) and Robert E. Klitgaard and George Hall, *A Statistical Search for Unusually Effective Schools* (Santa Monica, Calif.: The Rand Corp., 1973).

according to Austin, "These schools appear to have a critical mass of positive factors which, when put together make the difference."[20] Positive factors that contribute to this critical mass include:

1. Strong principal leadership;
2. Strong principal participation in the classroom instructional program and in actual teaching;
3. Higher expectations on the part of the principal for student and teacher performance advancement;
4. Principals felt that they had more control over the functioning of the school, the curriculum and program, and their staff;
5. Teachers were more satisfied with opportunities to try new things; they were free to choose teaching techniques in response to individual pupil needs;
6. Teachers expected more children to graduate from high school, to go to college, to become good readers, and to become good citizens;
7. More satisfactory parent–teacher relationships.

What emerges as exemplary schools are those staffed by professionals with high expectations for themselves and for their students and with freedom to shape educational experiences to realize their expectations.

Teacher Behavior and Learning

There is the beginning of a coherent body of knowledge linking the behavior of teachers and student achievement and, to a lesser extent, student attitudes.[21] Because of federal funding practices most of this research has been conducted in the first three grades using student achievement on basic skills tests as the product measure. The studies have been conducted primarily in classrooms serving children from homes of low socioeconomic status. It is hazardous and possibly misleading to generalize research findings beyond the context of the study. For example, teacher behaviors associated with cognitive outcomes may be different from, and even contradictory to, behaviors associated with affective outcomes.

One finding summarized by Brophy is that "in general students taught with a structured curriculum do better than those taught with more individualized or discovery learning approaches." An associated finding is that "those who receive much of their instruction directly from the teacher do

[20]Gilbert R. Austin, "Exemplary Schools and the Search for Effectiveness," *Educational Leadership, 37* (October 1979): 12.

[21]For summaries of this research see Jere E. Brophy, "Teacher Behavior and Its Effects," *Journal of Educational Psychology, 71* (December 1979): 733–750; Donald M. Medley, *Teacher Competence and Teacher Effectiveness: A Review of Process-Product Research* (Washington, D. C.: American Association of Colleges for Teacher Education, 1977); and Penelope L. Peterson and Herbert J. Walberg (eds.), *Research on Teaching: Concepts, Findings, and Implications* (Berkeley, Calif.: McCutchan Publishing Corp., 1979).

better than those expected to learn on their own or from one another."[22] This may suggest that some forms of open education and individualized instruction involve unrealistic expectations regarding the degree to which children in early grades can manage their own instruction.

Another of Brophy's conclusions from his review of research is that "students' opportunity to learn materials is a major determinant of their learning."[23] For example, Fischer and his colleagues reported on a study of academic learning time.[24] There are three components to academic learning time: allocated time, engaged time (that portion of allocated time when the student is on task), and student success rate. Academic learning time occurs when all three conditions apply simultaneously; "that is when time is allocated to a task, the student is engaged in the task, and the student has a high rate of success." As might be anticipated, the research showed that "students who accumulate more academic learning time generally have higher scores on achievement tests."[25] Other research studies reported similar findings.

Brophy cited studies showing that the more successful teachers are "those who are task oriented and business like in moving the class along at a brisk pace." He cautioned, however, that a distinction should be made "between (inappropriately) trying to teach students material that is too difficult for them and (appropriately) teaching material that is at the right level of difficulty but moving them through it at a brisk pace."[26] In summary, Brophy stated: "Learning gains are most impressive in classrooms in which students receive a great deal of instruction from and have a great deal of interaction with the teacher, especially in public lessons and recitations that are briskly paced but conducted at a difficulty level that allows consistent success."[27]

Some teacher behaviors have varying effects in different contexts. For example, reviews of research show that the use of indirect teaching (associated with such variables as student talk, use of student ideas, praise of good students) had an insignificant or even negative correlation with student achievement in the lower grades. However, such indirect teaching correlated positively with learning gains in seventh and eighth grade classes.

Brophy cited research demonstrating another context-related teacher behavior, "Teachers working with high-socioeconomic status/high-ability students generally are most successful if they move along at a rapid pace,

[22]Brophy, p. 735.
[23]Brophy, p. 735.
[24]Charles Fischer, Richard Marliave, and Nikola N. Filby, "Increasing Teaching by Increasing 'Academic Learning Time,'" *Educational Leadership, 37* (October 1979): 52–54.
[25]Fischer and others, p. 53.
[26]Brophy, p. 736.
[27]Brophy, p. 737.

continually demanding high expectations and enforcing high standards."[28] In contrast, "Teachers who are generally most successful in low-socioeconomic status/low-ability settings are equally determined to get the most out of the students, but they usually do so by being warm and encouraging rather than more businesslike and demanding."[29]

Soar and Soar found from their research that there was a "nonlinear relation between student gain in achievement and a measure of teacher behavior, which appeared to reflect teacher structuring and control of thinking and the development of subject matter."[30] They found that the shape of the curve was an inverted U since the greatest pupil gain was associated with an intermediate amount of teacher structure and control of behavior. They found that "there was an optimum level of this kind of teacher behavior, and the assumption that 'more is better' . . . did not appear to be valid."[31] A simple analogy is that the addition of a little salt enhances the flavor of a dish—too much salt ruins it.

Soar and Soar have done extensive research on emotional climate and management in elementary school classrooms.[32] Their findings raise questions regarding some of the "conventional wisdom" about teaching. For example, "The results of our studies provide no support for the widely held belief that it is necessary for a classroom to provide a warm emotional climate for learning. The results do suggest that an effectively neutral classroom can be functional. What is apparently crucial, however, is that the climate not be negative."[33] Their studies also raised questions regarding the universal prescriptions of giving students more freedom without specifying to what degree, or in what respect, or toward what objective. They found, "The amount of student freedom that is most functional for both learning tasks and thinking depends on the complexity of the learning task—for more complex tasks a somewhat greater degree of freedom is functional, but even then it may be too great."[34]

The research on teaching, valuable as it is, does not lead to universal prescriptions regarding effective teacher behavior. This led Brophy to observe that "elements of approaches to teaching must be orchestrated into systematic methods that fit the needs of students as seen by teachers or policy makers. Research on teaching can provide scientific support for

[28]Brophy, pp. 737, 738.
[29]Brophy, p. 738.
[30]Robert S. Soar and Ruth M. Soar, "An Attempt to Identify Measures of Teacher Effectiveness from Four Studies," *Journal of Teacher Education, 27* (Fall 1976): 261.
[31]Soar and Soar, p. 261.
[32]Robert S. Soar and Ruth M. Soar, "Emotional Climate and Management," in Penelope L. Peterson and Herbert J. Walberg (eds.), *Research on Teaching: Concepts, Findings and Implications* (Berkeley, Calif.: McCutchan Publishing Corp., 1979), pp. 97–119.
[33]Soar and Soar, p. 105.
[34]Soar and Soar, p. 118.

educational policy decisions, but it cannot dictate such decisions."[35] Brophy's observation is particularly important for those who develop curriculum plans. Research shows that the most effective teaching behaviors for a classroom teacher depend upon such variables as grade level, socioeconomic status of students, ability of students, and goals to be achieved. Curriculum plans, particularly suggestions for implementation, need to provide flexibility and encourage teachers to find and use their most effective behaviors.

CATALOG OF TEACHING MODELS

The term *teaching model* means a pattern of teaching made up of a number of discrete behaviors but with a specific focus. Joyce and Weil saw two ways in which a consideration of teaching models could improve the curriculum designing process: "1) to clarify and identify educational ends, and 2) to objectify and guide the selection of appropriate means for achieving those ends."[36] Teaching models can clarify educational ends by laying out a panorama of possible objectives to be achieved through their use thus possibly generating valid goals for the curriculum. The models probably make a greater contribution, however, as they suggest ideas for the achievement of goals of the curriculum. A consideration of teaching models expands the horizons of teaching possibilities for community agency educators who have not had the benefit of professional education, and provides a review and updating for individuals who have had methods courses.

Curriculum Designs and Models of Teaching

There is no agreement on the distinct models of teaching nor even on the major categories of models. This lack of agreement has handicapped researchers in improving teacher models. Nuthall and Snook identified three categories of models: behavior-control models, discovery-learning models, and rational models.[37] The categories have some similarity with the two identified by Rosenshine: "One kind of model might be labeled behavior-analytic, detail-specific, and structured in that the learner proceeds through small, prespecified steps toward each goal." Rosenshine labeled a second type of model "inquiry-oriented, learner-centered, and learner-choice in that the learner has greater choice of the means to be

---

[35]Brophy, p. 735.

[36]Bruce Joyce and Marsha Weil, *Models of Teaching* (Englewood Cliffs, N.J.: Prentice-Hall, Inc., 1972), p. 321.

[37]Graham Nuthall and Ivan Snook, "Contemporary Models of Teaching," in Travers (ed.), p. 49.

employed toward reaching the goal."[38] Weil and Joyce organized teaching models into four "families": 1) social interaction models, 2) information processing models, 3) personal models, and 4) behavior modification models.[39]

The 14 teaching models described in this chapter are organized according to the five curriculum designs discussed in Chapter 5 for the convenience of curriculum planners (Table 6.1). All possible teaching models are not included in Table 6.1; rather, representative models are listed and described. The ratings of "M" for most useful, "F" for fairly useful, and "L" for limited usefulness are approximations. The true contribution of a particular teaching model in a given curriculum design will depend upon the actual fit in a given situation. Thus, for example, if a group of students is interested in establishing a community volunteer service (interests and needs/activities curriculum design), the community activities teaching model would be "most useful," not just "fairly useful." With this qualification, we believe this classification will be helpful to curriculum planners as it describes the several models most clearly appropriate for each design.

Models Associated with Subject Matter/Disciplines

The subject matter/disciplines curriculum designs are used to transmit knowledge organized by disciplines. Newer approaches help learners

TABLE 6.1 Teaching Models Associated with Curriculum Designs

Various Models for Carrying on Instruction	Degree to which a Model Contributes to the Success of a Design as an Instructional Plan*				
	Subject Matter/ Discipline	Specific Competencies/ Technology	Human Traits/ Processes	Social Functions/ Activities	Interests and Needs/ Activities
Community activities	L	L	F	M	F
Discussion–questioning	M	L	F	F	L
Group investigation	L	L	M	M	F
Independent learning	F	F	L	F	M
Inquiry training	M	L	M	L	L
Instructional systems design	F	M	L	L	L
Jurisprudential	L	L	F	M	L
Lecture	M	L	L	L	L
Practice and drill	F	M	L	L	L
Programmed instruction	F	M	L	L	L
Role playing	L	M	M	M	L
Simulation and games	L	M	M	M	L
Synectics	L	L	F	F	M
Viewing–listening	M	M	L	F	F

*Codes: M–Most useful; F–Fairly useful; L–Limited usefulness

[38]Barak Rosenshine, "Classroom Instruction," in Gage (ed.), p. 338.
[39]Marsha Weil and Bruce Joyce, *Information Processing Models of Teaching* (Englewood Cliffs, N. J.: Prentice-Hall, Inc., 1978), p. 3.

understand the structure of the discipline and enable them to learn the methods of inquiry used in the discipline.

Lecture[40]

The lecture has been used for many centuries as a primary method of transmitting information. McLeish reviewed the research on lecturing at the university level and concluded that the lecture has its own specific virtues as a teaching method, but "that the lecture is open to serious criticism if used as an all-purpose teaching method."[41]

MAJOR CHARACTERISTICS.   A lecture can be a talk, address, or other type of verbal presentation to students by a teacher, guest speaker, or panel.

GROUPINGS.   A lecture may be used with any size class, but usually from 20 or 25 to 200 or 300 students. It is used primarily with students in high school and in general education courses at the postsecondary school level.

STUDENT ACTIVITY.   Students are passive and, it is to be hoped, are assimilating information through listening and note taking. There may be some viewing as a supplement.

TEACHER ACTIVITY.   Teachers engage in speaking, and reading, and often some visual illustration.

TEACHING RESOURCES.   The teacher may use a chalkboard, a model, transparencies, or other visual or auditory aids.

USES AND VALUE.   Uses include: creating interest in a topic or subject; transmitting knowledge to students; presenting students with new information or explanations of events or things, interpretations, and generalizations; helping students to clarify and gain a better understanding of a subject, topic, matter, or event; organizing and systematizing knowledge; reading or reciting poems, dramas, essays, and similar types of literature or performing a dance, musical selection, gymnastic acts, and the like; providing opportunity for other persons (guests or staff) to present information, views, or explanations or descriptions of events, phenomena, or issues.

[40]Useful references on these models include Ronald T. Hyman, *Ways of Teaching* (Philadelphia: J. B. Lippincott Company, 1970), Part Three; John McLeish, "The Lecture Method," in Gage (ed.), pp. 252–301.
[41]McLeish, pp. 296–297.

DRAWBACKS AND DEFECTS.   There is relatively little student activity and involvement.

Discussion—Questioning[42]

Often the traditional recitation method of teaching and a somewhat broader mode of participation that may be labeled as discussion are intermingled with the lecture mode in secondary schools today; these methods are also widely used at the middle and elementary school levels. A wide range of interactive processes could be submitted under this title, but we will reserve for later treatment the more participative group methods widely used by teachers today. Clear-cut categories are hard to identify, but here we are considering the more traditional modes of the recitation format.

MAJOR CHARACTERISTICS.   Discussion includes questions and answers about assigned material or related topics; discourse among members of the class and the teacher, largely on the topics under study but sometimes considering other matters introduced by the teacher or class members; working or presenting solutions to assigned problems, such as in mathematics and the sciences.

GROUPINGS.   Discussion is usually used in traditionally sized classes —20 to 35 students. It is used extensively at all levels of schooling. However, as Gall and Gall recommended, "While two to twenty students represents a reasonable lower and upper limit, the best group size appears to be approximately five members."[43]

STUDENT ACTIVITY.   Activity varies greatly among members of the class and from time to time, depending on the topic or subject. Some members of the class are quite passive most of the time. Teacher-pupil interaction is quite structured, except for occasional diversions to matters other than the planned lesson.

TEACHER ACTIVITY.   The teacher dominates the classroom situation; the lesson is often quite structured; the teacher usually talks much of the time, and may show film or use audio materials as supplement to recitation and discussion.

[42]References on these models include William C. Nutting, *Designing Classroom Spontaneity* (Englewood Cliffs, N.J.: Prentice-Hall, Inc., 1973); Meredith D. Gall and Joyce P. Gall, "The Discussion Method," in Gage (ed.), pp. 166–216; James R. Davis, *Teaching Strategies for the College Classroom* (Boulder, Colo.: Westview Press, 1976). Books on curriculum and teaching for a subject field usually have lengthy treatments of these models.
[43]Gall and Gall, p. 214.

TEACHING RESOURCES.   The teacher is usually the only resource. Some use may be made of open textbooks or other printed materials, chalkboards, and visual or auditory materials.

USES AND VALUES.   Uses include transmitting knowledge to students; assisting them in organizing knowledge and developing concepts and generalizations; testing students' achievement of objectives; identifying students interested in the subject and those with special ability; motivating students to carry out the assignment; answering students' questions; clarifying understanding; showing how to solve a problem or do something; giving students opportunities to interact with each other and with the teacher; improving students' ability to speak on a subject, to organize thoughts, and to communicate effectively; identifying difficulties in achieving objectives and helping students overcome them. These kinds of instructional methods may be used in carrying out any of the five types of designs, but they predominate in the subject matter/disciplines one.

DRAWBACKS AND DEFECTS.   Much too often discussion and questioning result in a regurgitative process with little real thought or reasoning apparent; too much teacher talk; may not expand knowledge or add to stock of information; may be too punitive in approach rather than developmental; students not involved actively learn little; often quite boring to students; low level of student participation of the kinds described in some models.

Viewing, Listening[44]

Every teacher today uses, to some extent at least, "educational technology" in carrying on instruction. It is an instructional model in its own right, but is also used as a part of the instructional process in almost all other models, even lecturing and recitation. Here we will analyze the use of instructional materials, machines, and equipment on the basis of their use as such, including use in conjunction with other models or as the sole or principal model.

The usual role of educational media is to convey cognitive information; thus it is often associated with the subject matter/disciplines approach.

[44]For an overview of educational media see David R. Olson (ed.), *Media and Symbols: The Forms of Expression, Communication, and Education,* Seventy-third Yearbook, National Society for the Study of Education (Chicago: University of Chicago Press, 1974); Aimée Dorr Leifer, "Teaching with Television and Film" in Gage (ed.), pp. 302–334. For projected new uses of electronic technology see Arthur J. Lewis, David Harrison, Paul Kajdan, Robert Soar, "Future Applications of Electronic Technology to Education" (Tallahassee, Fla.: Department of Education, 1978). For a review of research on effects of television viewing see Fred Emery and Merrelyn Emery, *A Choice of Futures: To Enlighten or Inform* (Canberra, Australia: Center for Continuing Education, The Australian National University, 1975).

However, greater use may be made of media in the specific competencies/technology design. Leifer concluded from reviewing studies that "on the average, television and film will impart information as well as the average live teacher does."[45] Television and film have also been demonstrated as effective in teaching social and emotional content and, thus, are valuable for several curriculum designs.

Rapid developments in electronic technology and the intermixing of telecommunications and computers could have as great an impact on education as did the invention by Gutenberg of movable type. Some of these developments are discussed in Chapter 8.

MAJOR CHARACTERISTICS. Uses of instructional media include printed material for reading and study by students individually or in small groups; materials for viewing and/or listening; materials or models for observing; materials solely for listening. Students may personally observe existing events, conditions, materials, processes, and habitats; use a computer that presents questions or problems and elicits answers or solutions; handle materials and use them in learning size, weight, color discrimination, and the like.

GROUPINGS. Media are used with regular sized classes to large groups; many ways in which individuals can use materials, equipment, or computers; some small-group use. Media are used at all school levels, including higher education.

STUDENT ACTIVITY. Activity ranges from very passive (as may be true in viewing television or film or listening to tapes or recordings) to very active (as in using computers or equipment, making a tape or recording, handling objects to be sorted or used for some purpose, or making field trips to observe and study actual things or situations). Passivity versus activity varies exceedingly according to kind of resource used and the purpose in using it.

TEACHER ACTIVITY. Activity of the teacher varies considerably although usually the teacher does not dominate the learning activity itself. The teacher arranges for use of equipment and materials, if necessary; plans showings, listenings, or observations; often explains or may demonstrate use of equipment; tells what students should do, see, or listen for; helps individual students who may have trouble in using equipment properly or in selecting or preparing correct answer; evaluates student competencies, especially in programmed learning activities; and may develop software for computer use.

[45]Leifer, p. 305.

TEACHING RESOURCES.   Resources include printed materials—books, pamphlets, magazines, newspapers, workbooks, manuals, encyclopedias, atlases; visual materials, often with listening—motion pictures, slides, filmstrips, videotapes, television, computers, charts, graphs, maps, globes, chalkboard, models, exhibits, specimens; auditory materials—recordings, tapes, radio; observing actual things—field trips of all sorts; manipulative materials—objects for handling, sorting, and using; instructional machines—teaching machines, electronically equipped teaching laboratories, such as for instruction in languages, reading skills, typing, and shorthand.

USES AND VALUES.   Educational technology contributes tremendously to teaching if used wisely and appropriately; some types are especially helpful in providing individual instruction; useful in providing remedial or catch-up work; especially useful in concept development among disadvantaged children. Media that require active participation by students may be highly valuable in motivating student activity; providing very meaningful experiences in developing the senses and concepts among the youngest children. Media are used in the implementation of all types of curriculum design.

DRAWBACKS AND DEFECTS.   Instructional media may be improperly or inappropriately used by teachers and hence ineffective in contributing to goals; teachers may overuse to the neglect of other desirable teaching models.

Inquiry Training[46]

A promising new development, particularly for the subject matter/disciplines curriculum design is to have students learn the method of inquiry appropriate to a discipline. Inquiry training requires that students develop skills in searching for and processing data and develop concepts of logic and causality. The ultimate goal is an autonomous learner. Thus the model is also very useful with human traits/processes designs. Two models of teaching related to inquiry training are Taba's inductive model[47] and Bruner's concept attainment model.[48] The laboratory model, also used with a subject matter/disciplines design, differs from the inquiry model in that far more direction is given to the student's activity.

MAJOR CHARACTERISTICS.   The procedures used relate directly to the way individuals expand their intellect "through three interacting and

[46]For further information on this model see J. Richard Suchman, *Inquiry Development Program: Developing Inquiry* (Chicago: Science Research Associates, 1966); Joyce and Weil, pp. 137–151; and Weil and Joyce, pp. 123–196.
[47]Joyce and Weil, pp. 123–136.
[48]Joyce and Weil, pp. 109–122.

complementary functions: 1) encountering the environment, 2) processing the data obtained, 3) reorganizing one's own knowledge."[49] Accordingly the inquiry training model uses a strategy where 1) materials of a puzzling nature are developed and presented to students; 2) students are encouraged to inquire into the puzzling situation through the collection and use of data; and 3) students are prompted to examine the processes they used in the inquiry.

GROUPINGS.   Groups for inquiry training are usually not larger than a normal class (22 to 35 students); often small-group and committee activity; individual study and investigation. Inquiry is used primarily in upper elementary, middle, or junior high school, and at high school levels, but many aspects used at an introductory level with younger children. Often inquiry is the primary method used in specialized courses at the post-secondary school level, such as seminars, research programs, and tutorials.

STUDENT ACTIVITY.   The students are confronted with an event which they cannot explain—a discrepant event. They have access to data through asking questions. At any time they can offer explanations or suggest theoretical formulations. The teacher neither explains the event nor offers judgments on the students' formulations. It is up to the students to test their theories through verbally mediated empirical tests or experiments.

TEACHER ACTIVITY.   The teacher identifies and presents the discrepant event. The nature of the event should be such as to interest and challenge the learner. The inquiry should be in a restricted domain with a relatively simple theory. The teacher should be able to supply the necessary data when questioned. Once the discrepant event has been explained and the explanation verified, the teacher should assist the students in tracing their steps in the inquiry process.

TEACHING RESOURCES.   A teacher needs to be able to present a puzzling situation, or a discrepant event. This can be presented through a physical object, a laboratory demonstration, or a description. A teacher also needs to have necessary data to respond to students' questions.

USES AND VALUES.   The inquiry approach enables students to learn concepts within a discipline through the method of inquiry appropriate to that discipline. The approach encourages students to become autonomous learners.

[49]J. Richard Suchman, *Inquiry Box : Teachers Handbook* (Chicago: Science Research Associates, 1967), p. 1.

DRAWBACKS AND DEFECTS. This approach requires a teacher with a thorough grasp of the method of inquiry and a knowledge of the data relevant to discrepant events.

Models Associated with Specific Competencies/Technology

The specific competencies/technology curriculum design, described in Chapter 5, uses a sequential analytic approach. Specific skills and knowledge that a student needs to learn in order to gain a competency are identified and organized into a hierarchy of difficulty. The most effective and efficient method of learning is employed. Three models of teaching associated primarily with specific competencies/technology curriculum design are described: instructional systems design, programmed instruction, and practice and drill. All of these models can be and are used with the subject matter/disciplines designs.

Instructional Systems Design[50]

The instructional systems design model of teaching is based on an information processing model of learning. Gagné related phases of instruction to these processes of learning: motivation, apprehending, acquisition, retention, recall, generalization, performance, and feedback.[51]

MAJOR CHARACTERISTICS. A linear system or flow-chart design is developed to provide the phases of instruction identified above. Although the language may differ somewhat, instructional systems designs generally include the steps outlined by Dick and Carey:

1. Identifying instructional goals
2. Conducting instructional analysis
3. Identifying entry behaviors, characteristics
4. Writing performance objectives
5. Developing criterion-referenced tests
6. Developing instructional strategy
7. Developing and selecting instruction
8. Designing and conducting formative evaluation
9. Revising instruction
10. Designing and conducting summative evaluation.[52]

[50]See Robert M. Gagné and Leslie J. Briggs, *Principles of Instructional Design,* 2d ed. (New York: Holt, Rinehart and Winston, Inc., 1979); Robert M. Gagné, "The Learning Basis of Teaching Methods," in N. L. Gage (ed.), pp. 21–43; Walter Dick, Lou Carey, *The Systematic Design of Instruction* (Glenview, Ill.: Scott, Foresman and Company, 1978); *Journal of Instructional Development* (A quarterly state of the art publication providing perspectives on the depth of use of instructional design, the variety of applications, and new techniques).
[51]Gagné, "The Learning Basis," pp. 28–30.
[52]Dick and Carey, p. 9.

GROUPINGS.   May be used with class groups or individuals. Strategies to be used depend upon the entry behavior characteristics of the learners (Step 3, above). When variations occur some adaptation is needed. A remedial program could be developed for students who lack the necessary prerequisite skills or knowledge. If too many students lack these prerequisites a modified program needs to be developed.

STUDENT ACTIVITY.   Student activity is determined by pretest results. Students with the prerequisite skills and knowledges are provided with a series of activities for learning, often utilizing a variety of media. Upon completion of the unit, students are tested and with satisfactory results continue to another unit or module; with unsatisfactory results, they engage in additional learning experiences.

TEACHER ACTIVITY.   Teachers who use a predeveloped system are primarily facilitators and monitors of student progress; while teachers who develop their own programs are instructional system designers.

TEACHING RESOURCES.   Predetermined units or modules may be available together with the necessary supportive materials. Teachers developing their own instructional systems may need consultative assistance and access to a variety of media.

USES AND VALUE.   Gagné identified five varieties of learning outcomes: 1) verbal information, 2) intellectual skills, 3) cognitive strategies, 4) attitudes, and 5) motor skills.[53] Of these five, instructional systems design is particularly effective with verbal information outcomes. Teachers can pinpoint their teaching to specific skills and knowledges and adapt instruction to individual needs of students. An effective instructional system uses a variety of instructional media.

DRAWBACKS AND DEFECTS.   Students may become bored with the constant use of such an approach; as one student put it, "There are no surprises." An instructional design strategy is not appropriate for all goals of education. Since students generally have little to say about their education, the model does not encourage the development of autonomous learners. These drawbacks can be overcome, or at least minimized, through the appropriate and judicious use of this teaching model.

[53]Gagné, "The Learning Basis," p. 31.

Programmed Instruction[54]

Skinner's theory of operant conditioning provides the basis for programmed instruction as well as behavior modification. The theory assumes that any process or activity can be behaviorally defined, that is, defined in terms of observable behavior. Two major operations are associated with the theory: reinforcement and stimulus control. The learner is motivated through the initial selection of a preferred activity. The appropriate response to this activity is given positive reinforcement.

MAJOR CHARACTERISTICS.   Joyce and Weil identified three essential characteristics for programmed instruction:

> 1) an ordered sequence of items, either questions or statements to which the student is asked to respond; 2) the student's response which may be in the form of filling in a blank, recalling the answer to a question, selecting from among a series of answers, or solving a problem; and 3) provision for immediate response confirmation sometimes within the program frame itself, but usually in a different location as on the next page in a programmed textbook or in a separate window in the teaching machine.[55] Linear programmed instruction allows students to progress at their own pace. Branching programs enable learners, unable to respond to a particular frame or sequence of frames, to have additional background material or more review material.

GROUPINGS.   Programmed instruction is an individualized activity. Whereas a group of students may be using the same program, they may progress through the program at different rates; or, if branching is available, students vary in the branches followed.

STUDENT ACTIVITY.   The student is responsible for responding to each stimulus through checking a response or writing a short answer and attending to the positive reinforcers provided by the correct answers.

TEACHER ACTIVITY.   Teachers are responsible for selecting programmed materials and monitoring student progress through the material. Computer usage can simplify the monitoring task.

[54]For discussions of programmed instruction see C. Victor Bunderson and Gerald W. Faust, "Programmed and Computer-Assisted Instruction," in N. L. Gage (ed.), pp. 44–90; Joyce and Weil, pp. 271–287; George F. Kneller and Steven L. Hackbarth, "An Analysis of Programmed Instruction," in *The Educational Forum, 41* (January 1977): 181–187. For background on behavior modification see Carl E. Thoresen (ed.), *Behavior Modification in Education,* Seventy-second Yearbook, National Society for the Study of Education (Chicago: University of Chicago Press, 1973).
[55]Joyce and Weil, p. 276.

TEACHING RESOURCES.   Programmed materials may be presented in printed forms or through a computer program. The computer has the advantage of maintaining a record of each student's progress (In Chapter 8 additional uses of the computer are described.)

USES AND VALUE.   Programmed instruction was heralded in the 1960s as an educational breakthrough. There followed the production of a great many programmed instruction packages of very uneven quality. Soon programmed material began to gather dust in classroom closets. However, industry and the military continued to use programmed instruction, having found that a carefully designed program, appropriately used, is effective.

DRAWBACKS AND DEFECTS.   Programmed learning promotes superficial activity—filling in blanks, turning pages—that has little to do with the content to be learned. Kneller and Hackbarth pointed out the "present programs give the student little or no opportunity to think for himself." Students are taught that every question has a single correct answer which the student must accept in order to get through the program. Because of these and other drawbacks, we agree with Kneller and Hackbarth, "Programmed instruction should be considered as a possible medium for presenting only that knowledge which already is highly organized and precisely formulated."[56]

Practice and Drill[57]

Models that rely on practice are used extensively when the purpose of instruction is to enable students to acquire a skill or a proficiency in doing some overt act. Often it is intermingled with recitation and discussion methods, such as in courses in foreign languages, mathematics, music, and art and in athletic programs of all kinds.

MAJOR CHARACTERISTICS.   There is a repeated performance of a learning act until a desired level of skill to do the act correctly is attained or the teacher and student settle for a lesser level of competency. The performance may be verbal, as in music, speaking a foreign language, and speech correction and therapy; written, as in mathematics, spelling, and shorthand; or manual as in industrial arts, art, athletics and physical education, and typing.

[56]Kneller and Hackbarth, pp. 185–186.
[57]For information related to practice and drill see Barak Rosenshine, "Classroom Instruction," in N. L. Gage (ed.), pp. 35–371; Barak V. Rosenshine, "Content, Time, and Direct Instruction," in Peterson and Walberg (eds.), pp. 28–56; Penelope L. Peterson, "Direct Instruction Reconsidered," in Peterson and Walberg (eds.), pp. 57–69.

GROUPINGS.   Practice and drill may be done in unison or by one or more individual members of a class of any size or by individuals in laboratories, teaching or resource centers, study halls, libraries, or audiovisual centers or at home.

STUDENT ACTIVITY.   There is complete student involvement with performance of overt acts; some witnessing of demonstration of the art of listening to explanation of what to do. The use of a computer or a machine necessary to the operation may be involved.

TEACHER ACTIVITY.   Teachers explain the nature of the act verbally, visually, or both; demonstrate proper ways of doing the act; explain to students, usually individually, errors in performance and show how to correct them; supervise students during practice periods; observe students in performance, such as athletic games, musical events, and sports exhibitions, and note success as basis for further teaching and practice; and evaluate performance, skills, and competencies.

TEACHING RESOURCES.   Models, equipment, chalkboard, films, videotapes, recordings, machines, tools, materials needed for the performance, computers, and communication systems are used.

USES AND VALUE.   May be used to develop a desirable skill to perform an act or to acquire a proficiency, especially one that may be habituated; to continue to repeat an act, to make something or to write or say something until it is fully understood; to accomplish something overtly that provides a student with a competency or sense of satisfaction, especially if it motivates further participation in learning activities; to develop an understanding of the principles underlying the operation of a machine, a tool, or object used in the performance of the skill; to be able to judge the quality of such an object; to individualize instruction, especially through use of teaching machines, computers, and audio-visual equipment. Rosenshine concluded from a review of the research that "controlled practice appears to be generally functional."[58] He cited studies showing that students made more progress when they spend time on work where they have a low error rate. Rosenshine also cited research showing that optimal patterns for drill and practice varied with the socioeconomic status of students.[59]

DRAWBACKS AND DEFECTS.   If overused, drill can become stultifying and boring, especially to students who readily learn such skills. Often

[58]Rosenshine, *Content*, p. 44.
[59]Rosenshine, *Classroom Instruction*, p. 363.

teachers fail to teach the principles underlying the skill or to develop concepts and understandings that extend the kinds of learning outcomes possible. Failure to individualize instruction in learning skills may waste the time of many students. If too much time is spent on skills, then other goals of learning are seriously neglected.

Models Associated with Human Traits/Processes

Human traits/processes curriculum designs, described in Chapter 5, have two features: the development of specified human traits is the goal; and educational processes are used to achieve the goals. Only two of several teaching models associated with human traits/processes designs are described: role playing and simulation. Other models include problem solving, inquiry training, and values clarification and moral development.

Role Playing[60]

Human traits develop through experience. Role playing provides a type of experience that enables students to explore human relations problems, including feelings, attitudes, values, and problem-solving strategies. Role playing can be a useful model to use with social functions/activities designs.

MAJOR CHARACTERISTICS.   At the simplest level, role playing is a process in which problems are dealt with through action. A problem is delineated, acted out, and discussed, with some students playing roles and others observing. At another level group members become so involved and experience so many of the same emotional reactions as in their own life situations that role playing becomes a part of their life. Role playing thus provides students with a life sample of human behavior that enables them to examine their feelings and gain insights into their attitudes, values, and perceptions. It also helps them develop problem-solving skills.

GROUPINGS.   Small groups or committess of a class can engage in role playing with the remainder of the class serving as observers. It may be used with all age groups that have achieved an appropriate level of maturity.

STUDENT ACTIVITY.   A sincere involvement of students in the roles being played is important. Students are encouraged to recognize and talk about their feelings.

[60]See Fannie Shaftel and George Shaftel, *Role-Playing for Social Values: Decision-Making in the Social Studies* (Englewood Cliffs, N.J.: Prentice-Hall, Inc., 1967); Marsha Weil and Bruce Joyce, *Social Models of Teaching: Expanding Your Teaching Repertoire* (Englewood Cliffs, N.J.: Prentice-Hall, Inc., 1978), pp. 25–108.

TEACHER ACTIVITY.   The traditional role of the teacher is deemphasized as students are encouraged to listen and learn from their colleagues. The teacher has the important responsibility of selecting and maintaining the focus throughout the role-playing activity by warming up the group, selecting participants, preparing observers, setting the stage, and leading in a discussion and evaluation as students share experiences and generalize.

TEACHING RESOURCES.   Usually few materials are needed, but sometimes a film, written description, videotape, or other media may be used to warm up the group or set the stage.

USES AND VALUE.   Weil and Joyce suggested four types of social problems that might be explored through role playing:

1. *Interpersonal conflicts.* "Reveal conflicts between people so that students can discover techniques for overcoming them."
2. *Intergroup relations.* Role playing may be used "to uncover stereotypes and prejudices or to encourage acceptance of the deviant."
3. *Individual dilemmas.* Help children deal with dilemmas when they are "caught between two contrasting values or between his or her own interests and the interests of others."
4. *Historical or contemporary problems.* "These include critical situations, past or present, in which policy makers, judges, political leaders, or statesmen had to confront a problem or person and make a decision."[61]

DRAWBACKS AND DEFECTS.   It takes time for students to get into the activity of role playing; new skills need to be learned and attitudes of openness developed. Skillful teachers are required to encourage free and honest expression of ideas and to help students deal with ideas they have expressed.

Simulation[62]

A simulated experience provides a learner with an opportunity to respond to a lifelike situation and through feedback of information to see the consequences of his or her action. For example, the student behind the wheel of a simulated driver trainer responds to a motion picture of a car moving down a highway by turning the steering wheel, braking, and accelerating. Failure to respond appropriately could result in a simulated accident.

[61]Weil and Joyce, *Social Models,* p. 33.
[62]For information regarding simulation see Constance J. Seidner, "Teaching with Simulations and Games," in N. L. Gage (ed.), pp. 217–251; Weil and Joyce, *Social Models,* pp. 181–242.

MAJOR CHARACTERISTICS.   A simulation is a representation of selected aspects of social and physical reality with which students may interact. Simulations involving the learner and a computer enable the learner to make decisions based on information supplied by the computer, feed these decisions into the computer, and observe their consequences from the computer output. Training airplane pilots on a simulated trainer is an illustration of a learner-computer simulation. Other simulations do not depend upon computers or other machines—the boundaries of the simulation are defined by specifications and rules regarding resources and behavior of participants; for example, the game of *Monopoly.*

GROUPINGS.   Some simulations are designed for individual use, others require a group response. For example, one airline trains pilots for flying jumbo jets in a multimillion dollar simulator that "crashes" when the crew of pilots makes a serious error. The "crash" is signaled by a loud sound, a sudden jolt of the cabin, followed by an ominous glow that turns the cabin into a fiery red.

STUDENT ACTIVITY.   The student becomes actively involved as he or she interacts with the simulation.

TEACHER ACTIVITY.   The teacher's role includes explaining the simulation and giving the learners only enough rules to get started. As in life, some rules are best discovered through the interaction. Once the simulation is underway, the teacher is responsible for refereeing or controlling the game to assure that the rules are followed. When students need coaching, the teacher may give players advice that enables them to play more effectively. After a simulation, the teacher may lead a group discussion exploring insights gained from the simulation.

TEACHING RESOURCES.   Resources vary from sophisticated machinery complete with computer software (such as in the jumbo jet airline trainer described previously), to a set of rules for a simulated game.

USES AND VALUE.   Students may learn directly as a result of their experiences in simulation. For example, a student learns "the feel" of a car by being at the controls of a driver trainer. Students may also learn from a discussion following a simulated experience as they compare their perceptions of the real world with that generated by the simulation. Through simulations it is possible to learn about such abstractions as competition, cooperation, empathy, social system, paying the penalty for poor judgment, and the role of change. It is also possible to learn new concepts and skills and to learn to think critically.

DRAWBACKS AND DEFECTS. The simulation teaching model is used extensively in military and industrial training programs. Its use in schools and colleges has been limited because of the cost of software and because teachers are often not trained to use simulations. The remarkable reduction in the cost of computer hardware should result in a rapid expansion of simulations in all of education.

Models Associated with Social Functions/Activities

The social functions/activities curriculum designs described in Chapter 5 enable learners to study social problems through engagements in social activities. Three teaching models appropriate to these designs are discussed in this section: community activities, group investigation, and jurisprudential. All of these models can also be used with the human traits/processes design.

Community Activities[63]

Throughout this book we have emphasized the desirability of a program of community-centered experiences for students, especially those enrolled in the middle and high schools. This aspect of the curriculum should loom large in instructional planning. In fact, community experiences should not and cannot be carried out unless there is a fully developed plan that states objectives for the entire program as well as each segment, the kinds of opportunities which will be made available for students, the conditions under which they will participate, the nature of supervision and control, and the responsibilities and obligations of the students participating. These community experiences, in turn, provide some of the most important opportunities offered in the entire instructional program.

MAJOR CHARACTERISTICS. Students participate in the work and activities of governmental agencies, social service and welfare agencies, civic organizations and programs, churches and synagogues, child-care centers, health clinics, nursing and convalescent homes, home-service programs, and similar service organizations, agencies, or groups; work in businesses, offices of professional persons, factories, construction firms, industrial firms on a nonpaying basis; participate on a paid basis in work-experience programs established by the school in cooperation with firms; participate in various types of campaigns, such as appeals for funds for community agencies, political campaigns, civic improvement programs,

[63]For information regarding community activities see Gary H. Deutschlander, "Action-Learning—The Curriculum Beyond the School," *NASSP Bulletin, 58* (November 1974); Edward G. Olsen and Philip A. Clark, *Life-Centering Education* (Midland, Mich.: Pendel Publishing Company, 1977); *NASSP Bulletin, 62* (September 1978): 1–40.

celebrations, and special events; engage in human development programs, often on a one-to-one basis.

GROUPINGS.　　　Participation is by individuals or small groups; usually at high school level, but some possibilities should be available for younger students.

STUDENT ACTIVITY.　　　There is complete involvement on a personal basis.

TEACHER ACTIVITY.　　　Teachers sponsor individuals or small groups; plan the program ascertaining opportunities available; supervise students in their work.

TEACHING RESOURCES.　　　The facilities and people of the entire community.

USES AND VALUES.　　　Community activities contribute significantly to attainment of goals of the school, especially in the affective domain; assist students in making career choices; develop good work habits; contribute to an understanding of the community—problems, future developments, needs, desirability as a place to live; develop leadership, self-assurance, self-discipline, and ingenuity; contribute to motivation for school work.

DRAWBACKS AND DEFECTS.　　　There may be difficulty in obtaining enough opportunities in community service for all students. Other difficulties include: extra cost and expense to the student; requires additional staff to provide supervision and administration, hence question of priorities in budget making; problem of safety and security; difficult to administer in terms of student schedules, other nonclass activities, bus schedules, lunch periods, outside-of-school duties; resistance of some taxpayers, parents, and employers of the community; opposition or lack of cooperation by employees in cooperating firms, offices, and agencies.

Group Investigation[64]

The group investigation teaching model enables students to inquire into a social problem and observe themselves as inquirers. Since social inquiry is basically a group process, the learner is aided in his inquiry role by an opportunity to interact with other solution-seeking people.

[64]For descriptions and applications of this teaching model see John U. Michaelis, *Social Studies for Children in a Democracy, Recent Trends and Developments,* 6th ed. (Englewood Cliffs, N.J.: Prentice-Hall, Inc., 1976): Herbert Thelen, *Education and the Human Quest* (New York: Harper & Row, 1960); Joyce and Weil, pp. 36–47.

MAJOR CHARACTERISTICS. The basis for a group investigation is an event which individuals react to and puzzle over. This event may be posed by the teacher, or identified by the learners. The presentation of a problem does not in itself generate the puzzlement that can come only as the learner adds "awareness of self and desire for personal meaning which will cause him to give attention to something and seek its reality."[65] A diagnostic process follows in which students identify and formulate the problem and pursue its solution. This inquiry calls for firsthand activity in a real situation that continually generates new information. Students collect data, associate and classify ideas, develop and test hypotheses, and study consequences. Finally, students reflect on their experiences.

GROUPING. The ideal size for group investigation is ten to fifteen students who possess a common level of sophistication and knowledge of the area to be investigated.

STUDENT ACTIVITY. Students are confronted with a stimulating problem. The students formulate the problem and then proceed to develop a strategy for working on the problem including analyzing the required roles they will play and organizing themselves accordingly. Then they act and share their results in order to arrive at a resolution of the problem. Finally, the group evaluates its solution in relation to the original problem.

TEACHER ACTIVITY. The teaching role is a sensitive one since inquiring into the problem is to be student initiated and formulated. The teacher serves as a counselor, consultant, and friendly critic. Joyce and Weil portrayed the teacher as guiding and reflecting group experience over three levels: "the problem-solving or task level (What is the nature of the problem? What are the factors involved?); the group management level (What information do we need now? How can we organize ourselves to get this?); and the level of individual meaning (How do you feel about these conclusions?)."[66]

TEACHING RESOURCES. Students need access to an adequate library, sources of information utilizing nonprint media, and access to community resources for information.

USES AND VALUES. In the hands of a skillful teacher, group investigation is highly versatile and comprehensive. It can be used to blend the goals of academic inquiry in all subject areas with social interaction and

[65]Joyce and Weil, p. 39.
[66]Joyce and Weil, p. 44.

social process learning. It enables the teacher to emphasize the formulation and problem-solving aspects of knowledge.

DRAWBACKS AND DEFECTS.   The typical classroom group of 20 to 30 students is too large to undertake a group investigation. A particularly sensitive and skillful teacher is required to perform a nontraditional role and a variety of reference materials are needed. An additional and critical drawback of "Group Investigation" may be community sensitivity or political repercussions from some topics. Teachers and students need to consider the pros and cons of areas of study before undertaking the study.

Jurisprudential[67]

The purpose of this model of teaching is to develop skillful citizens who can intelligently analyze and take positions on public policy issues. The method accomplishes this through the use of legal thinking and an open dialogue.

MAJOR CHARACTERISTICS.   Oliver and Shaver identified three areas of competence needed by persons who are skillful analyzers and discussers of public issues. First, they need to develop a values framework based on the values expressed in the principles of the Constitution and the Declaration of Independence. This value framework is used in judging controversial issues. Second, they need to have the skills required for clarifying and resolving issues. Finally, they need to know about contemporary political and public issues. The jurisprudential model helps students develop these three competencies as they take stands on policy issues that emerge when a specific situation becomes a legal case. "Thus, the Jurisprudential Model calls for a case study approach to curriculum. Students explore policy issues in terms of a specific legal case rather than in terms of a general study of values."[68]

GROUPINGS.   Although each student takes his or her own position, a group discussion of these positions is a part of the model. The model may be used with average size classes.

STUDENT ACTIVITY.   There are six phases to the jurisprudential model of teaching: 1) orientation to the case, 2) identifying the issues, 3) taking a position, 4) exploring the stances taken, 5) refining and qualifying the position, 6) testing the factual assumptions. In phase 2 the students are

[67]For a complete explanation see Donald W. Oliver and James P. Shaver, *Teaching Public Issues in the High School* (Boston: Houghton Mifflin, 1966); Weil and Joyce, *Social Models,* pp. 109–180.
[68]Weil and Joyce, *Social Models,* p. 116.

required to synthesize the facts of the case into a public policy issue and identify the underlying legal-ethical issue. Each student is then asked to take a position on the issue and state the basis for the position. These first three phases are analytical; the last three phases are argumentation and are discussed under teacher activity.

TEACHER ACTIVITY.   The teacher introduces the students to the activity and leads them as they synthesize the facts of the case into a public policy issue. In phase 4 the teacher uses a Socratic or confrontational model of discussion by questioning the relevance, consistency, and definitional clarity of the students' ideas (developed in phase 3). Teachers need to avoid reactions that could be interpreted as approving or disapproving students' comments. Teachers also need to guard against letting the Socratic dialogue degenerate into a threatening cross-examination or a game of "guess what the teacher wants you to say."

TEACHING RESOURCES.   Materials associated with the cases studied are needed.

USES AND VALUES.   Weil and Joyce pointed out that "by having to take a stand and defend a position, students become emotionally involved in the analysis." This forces them to clarify their values in order to come to a complex justification of policy issues. "Thus," according to Weil and Joyce, "the model, unlike many other teaching strategies, simultaneously integrates the personal and the intellectual."[69]

DRAWBACKS AND DEFECTS.   Both students and teachers need to learn new roles and relationships for the jurisprudential model to work.

Models Associated with Interests and Needs/Activities

Two models of teaching associated with curriculum designs based on interests and needs of learners are described: independent learning and self-instruction, and synectics. Two other models of teaching may be of special interest because of their distinctive nature: the nondirective model, based on the work of Carl Rogers,[70] and the awareness training model[71] which utilizes an encounter group. The nature of an individual's interests and needs might lead to the use of any of the models described in this book. For example, a student's interest might lead him or her to

[69]Weil and Joyce, *Social Models,* p. 119.
[70]Marsha Weil, Bruce Joyce, Bridget Kluwin, *Personal Models of Teaching* (Englewood Cliffs, N.J.: Prentice-Hall, Inc., 1978), pp. 103–165.
[71]See Joyce and Weil, pp. 253–264.

attend a lecture, interact with a computer on a simulation, engage in a programmed activity, and so on.

Independent Learning and Self-Instruction[72]

With all modes of instruction, students study—in the traditional sense of that term; much study is done on an individual basis. Learning is always an individual matter regardless of the nature of teaching. But here we single out for consideration what has become a very important dimension of education, and a readily identified process of instruction in recent years, especially in the secondary school. Traditionally, independent study is a major aspect of instruction in higher education.

The term *independent study* was used originally to designate a particular kind of instructional process and it has remained in the vernacular in that sense as an instructional method. We are not including here any method of individualizing instruction, but rather what Jourard defined as the "embodiment and implementation of imaginative fascination"[73] and what Macdonald has called self-selection—"student choice of activity as well as independent pursuit of tasks."[74]

MAJOR CHARACTERISTICS.   A student proposes a study project, investigation, research, or production of something which he or she will carry on largely independently of other class work or in lieu of class work in a course. If approved, the student carries out the activity under supervision of a staff member, if appropriate.

GROUPINGS.   Independent study is individual. Originally restricted to high school and postsecondary school students, it is increasingly available to middle school students and learners of all ages.

STUDENT ACTIVITY.   Individual students plan and carry out projects, usually with a minimum of supervision and direction.

TEACHER ACTIVITY.   Teachers stimulate qualified students to participate; advise and counsel on possible projects; grant approval if appropriate; supervise student as desirable; evaluate completed project.

[72]William M. Alexander, Vynce Hines, and associates, *Independent Study in Secondary Schools* (New York: Holt, Rinehart and Winston, Inc., 1967); Edgar Faure, *Learning To Be: The World of Education Today and Tomorrow* (Paris: UNESCO, 1972), pp. 160–165; Maurice Gibbons and Gary Phillips, "Helping Students Through the Self-Education Crisis," *Phi Delta Kappan, 60* (December 1978): 298–300.
[73]Sidney M. Jourard, "Fascination: A Phenomenological Perspective on Independent Learning," in Gerald T. Gleason (ed.), *The Theory and Nature of Independent Learning* (Scranton, Pa.: International Textbook Company, 1967), p. 85.
[74]James B. Macdonald, "Independent Learning: The Theme of the Conference," in Gleason (ed.), p. 2.

TEACHING RESOURCES.   Any appropriate learning resources are used whether in libraries, laboratories, studios, or shops.

USES AND VALUES.   Independent study provides a high level of cognitive and affective development. It may be used to develop competency in a specific field of study at a high level; develop self-directiveness and ability to further a student's own learning; enable particular students to develop a specialized talent or capability; prepare a student for advanced study in a field. Independent study can be used in the carrying out of any type of curriculum design.

DRAWBACKS AND DEFECTS.   Independent study may be misused for routine class work of little real challenge or homework under another name. It may be difficult to maintain student interest in a project over a long period of time. There may be a lack of facilities to accomodate all qualified students. Students may specialize too early in their education, neglecting other general goals.

Synectics[75]

Synectics is a strategy to increase the creativity of individuals working in groups. Based on the work of Gordon, synectics is built on two assumptions that run counter to the conventional wisdom: creativity, even though an essentially emotional process, can be learned; and creativity can be fostered through group activity.

MAJOR CHARACTERISTICS.   The basic activity of synectics, metaphor building, makes creativity a conscious process. Two strategies of teaching are based on synectics procedures: creating something new by using metaphors to see old problems, ideas, or products in a new light; making the strange familiar by using familiar analogies.

GROUPINGS.   Although creativity is an individual process, the dynamics of a classroom group can foster individual creativity. The synectics model is designed to develop a classroom atmosphere that encourages student creativity and the exploration of new ideas in science and the arts.

STUDENT ACTIVITY.   Five interrelated states of mind are necessary for a person to move through the creative process: detachment and involvement, deferment, speculation, autonomy, and hedonic response.[76] As students are working on a problem it is necessary to detach them from their present activity and involve them in a new problem. In synectics,

---

[75]For further information see William J. Gordon, *Synectics* (New York: Harper & Row, 1961); Weil, Joyce, and Kluwin, pp. 25–102.
[76]Weil, Joyce, and Kluwin, p. 33.

three types of metaphors are used to accomplish this: direct analogy; personal analogy—students involve themselves through empathetic identification with the objects or ideas under comparison; and compressed conflict—students create a description of an object or an idea using two words that are apparently in conflict.

TEACHER ACTIVITY.   The teacher asks open-ended, evocative questions that arouse student interest and draw all members of the class into the creative process; the teacher assists but does not manipulate students as they develop analogies. Students are encouraged to break out of conventional ways of thinking by indulging in such irrational states of mind as fantasy, irrelevance, and symbolism. Teachers encourage this approach by accepting the bizarre and unusual without judgment and by openly displaying some of the nonrational approaches to problem solving.

TEACHING RESOURCES.   In the realm of creative ideas, the teacher and the students are the primary resources.

USES AND VALUE.   The synectics teaching model can be used for the following purposes: creative writing; exploring social and discipline problems; solving problems concerned with social issues, interpersonal relations, and interpersonal conflicts; creating a design or product; broadening perspective of a concept. The synectics teaching model can be used in conjunction with many other models of teaching; for example, it could be used with the discussion method to help students grasp a difficult concept within a discipline.

DRAWBACKS AND DEFECTS.   In creativity the emotional component is more important than the unemotional and the nonrational more important than the rational. Since education has been oriented toward a rational and unemotional approach, students and teachers must engage in new ways of thinking.

BASES FOR SELECTING TEACHING MODELS

Illustrations of the various teaching models available are described in the previous section. Curriculum plans may either anticipate the use of one or more models or leave the selection up to the teacher. In either event, choices need to be made. All of the models described in the previous section have merit for accomplishing appropriate purposes; hence, all should be considered for use even by an individual teacher and certainly by a staff of teachers who will be utilizing the method during the school year. Just as we stated in Chapter 5 that it is desirable, even necessary, to use a number of methods of organizing the curriculum according to the purposes being served at a particular time for a specific group of students, so it is in the selection of teaching models. A variety of instructional methods is postulated for implementing something as broad and complex as a curriculum plan for the education of children, youth, and adults. In this section some important guides for the selection of teaching models are presented.

Goals and Objectives Being Sought

The first consideration in planning instruction is the purposes for which instruction is being undertaken. The objectives postulated for a course, activity, or unit of work—formulated to contribute maximally to the general goals of the school—should be a primary factor in planning. A general goal often may be attained by a wide range of routes, that is, units of work and teaching methods, but specific objectives for instruction once determined often narrow the choices considerably.

Training programs in business and industry have three specific and interrelated purposes: training new personnel, improving skills and performance of present employees, and accomodating employees to changes in knowledge and skills required in the business. Often a number of teaching models will be used in achieving a specific purpose. The nine-month training program Citicorp uses to train bank account managers provides an illustration.[77] Accounting and corporate finance are studied for the first 13 weeks using lectures and audio-visual materials. Trainees then learn to determine what risk is involved in lending to a particular company, how to structure a loan, and how to persuade the customer and the bank to accept those terms. Lectures and case study methods are used in this phase of training. In the case study trainees are given specific bank cases and are required to analyze the situation. After the classroom work, trainees are assigned to work with account managers in making analyses of real cases the bank is handling. Thus, lectures, simulations through case studies, and field experiences are all used.

Maximize Opportunities to Achieve Multiple Goals

An important consideration in planning instruction is to provide the richest opportunities feasible for achieving goals. Two facets of this aspect of selecting instructional models are apparent: any particular unit of instruction should be selected and planned so as to contribute maximally to the attainment of specified goals and corollary objectives; but, concomitant outcomes that may be realized should also be a factor in planning.

To illustrate these points, let us assume a general goal of one of the

[77]Stan Luxenberg, "AT&T and Citicorp: Prototypes in Job Training Among Large Corporations," *Phi Delta Kappan, 61* (January 1980): 314.

curriculum domains is: "To express ideas in speech, writing, or in some artistic form with increasing clarity and correctness." A multitude of instructional activities may be used to assist the student in achieving this goal. Hence a teacher or planning team in stating objectives and planning a unit of work, say at the upper elementary school level, that will contribute to the realization of this goal may choose among such activities as "writes a social letter that is correct in form and clear in expression," "speaks before the class in a pleasing manner and voice without being overcome by embarrassment or experiencing undue strain," "chooses the correct word, punctuation, or phrase for blank spaces in sentences in a workbook," or "uses correctly words in a list in sentences, referring to a dictionary if uncertain about the meaning," and so on.

The teacher might select the synectics teaching model to encourage creativity in the expression of ideas. Within this teaching model, what particular learning activity should be chosen? Additional factors to be considered follow, but here we suggest that it be one that enables students to achieve the goal and, at the same time, promises to provide the most in desirable concomitant learnings. Perhaps in the above list the suggestion of writing a letter may hold such a promise. The boy or girl may write grandmother to relate a recent experience. Perhaps, then, the concomitant is enhancement of friendship or of love.

Selecting instructional models for achieving objectives in the first category of the Bloom taxonomy in the cognitive domain, "knowledge," is quite different from choosing models that would be appropriate for the fifth category, "synthesis." In the affective domain choices would be more open-ended and less restricted by the purposes being served. However, it should be fully recognized that a choice of models is available in any instance. Hence, the goals and objectives being sought are directive but not definitive or decisive in planning teaching methods.

Moreover, in planning instruction for the realization of goals, teachers should take account of the effects of the hidden curriculum, to be discussed later, on the attainment or failure to attain goals. It often will be possible to enhance the contribution of this unofficial aspect of schooling, or, on the other hand, to counteract or eliminate what could be deterrents to goal achievements.

Student Motivation

The effectiveness of any teaching model depends upon the degree to which learners become engaged with learning opportunities. The continued use of the same teaching model day after day generally results in boredom on the part of the learners. Motivating learners has always been a challenge, but it is a greater challenge today because of the competition for learners' attention generated by the communications revolution of the last 30 years. Fadiman pointed out, "There is another, highly competitive educational system, opposed in almost every way to traditional schooling, that operates on the child and youth from the age of two. It takes up as much of his time as the school does, and it works on him with far greater effectiveness."[78] Fadiman identified the alternative educational system as a linked structure with television at the center and including radio, comic books, films, pop music, sports, and the life styles that this structure either supports or produces. Fadiman reported that "good teachers, when you question them inexorably, almost always admit that their difficulties stem from the competition of the alternative life."

Selecting the "right" teaching model is not going to put this competitive "educational system" out of business. However, some models hold greater potential for gaining student interest and getting them involved in meaningful learning experiences than do others. Compare for example, role playing, simulations, and synectics with lecture, discussion, and drill. Student interest is not the only criterion for selecting teaching models, but it is an important one.

Principles of Learning

The theories and principles of learning identified in Chapter 3 as an important data source for curriculum planning, should be drawn upon extensively in selecting models of teaching. Too often teachers rely on operant conditioning as the psychological base for teaching, neglecting the theories and principles enunciated by Jean Piaget, Carl Rogers, McVicker Hunt, Arthur Combs, Jerome Bruner, Erik Erikson, David Ausubel, Robert Gagné, David McClelland, Robert White, and others.

In spite of all that has been written and advocated by specialists in teaching methodology and psychologists, a rather severe indictment of teaching was made by Frederick McDonald, a well-known psychologist himself, in the first annual report of the Stanford Center for Research and Development in Teaching:

> Teaching style is probably the most static aspect of schooling. Teachers teach today in much the same way as they have for generations. The basic style is didactic, with the teacher dispensing information to passive pupils. At regular intervals, the teacher examines the children upon how much of this information they have absorbed and retained. It is the teacher who asks questions, rarely the pupil. The structure of the answers is predetermined by the context in which the questions are formulated; only infrequently does a child's schooling permit him to discover problems.[79]

[78]Clifton Fadiman, "Classroom's Rival: Pop Culture," *Gainesville Sun,* Aug. 5, 1979, p. 5A.
[79]Stanford Center for Research and Development in Teaching, "Second Annual Report" (Palo Alto, Calif.: The Center, April 1968, available as ERIC Document No. 024642), p. 146.

Psychologists and educators alike recognize the difficulty in translating psychological principles into practice, but much greater efforts to do so are apparent in recent years. The aspects of psychology that have the most to contribute to instructional planning are the nature of cognitive development, motivation, reinforcement, conceptualization, the development of attitudes and values, and the nature and growth of motor abilities and skills. The concept of basic human needs (Maslow, Prescott, Glasser, Erikson) is also important in planning instruction.

Facilities, Equipment, and Resources

Instructional planning, unfortunately, is often circumscribed by the facilities available, the equipment and teaching resources that may be used, and the administrative organization and structure of the school. The relation is evident in the use of educational technology, laboratories, shops, gymnasiums, outdoor or other life science centers, camps, and the like. Similarly, the use of games is restricted to those available or that can be contrived by teachers; field trips and community experiences, at least to some extent, are dependent on the availability of transportation. Creative work in some areas is limited by available materials; inquiry and discovery requires adequate library and other types of learning resources.

The whole administrative arrangements and structure also influence instructional planning. For example, if the time schedule is a rigid one set up in tightly prescribed blocks, independent study of the kind described above may be more difficult to arrange; if students are not permitted to work in laboratories or shops unless a teacher is present to supervise, inquiry and creative work may be curtailed; if students in secondary schools are rigidly scheduled in traditional classes for 25 to 28 of 30 available weekly periods, independent study, small-group work, use of learning resources on an individual basis, and similar student participation in self-learning is more difficult to arrange.

With respect to instructional planning, teachers should be as imaginative and resourceful as possible in a given situation in using models that involve students in a highly active role. Most observers point out that teachers can involve students much more than they do regardless of the restrictive factors considered above. Examples of how schools in both England and this country have been able to develop their programs of informal education in the most conventional and restricted settings point the way. In addition, teachers, individually and collectively, should be fully involved in budget-making and the selection and purchase of equipment, supplies, books, teaching materials, and the like. And, of course, teachers should be extensively involved in planning new buildings and renovations of existing buildings.

Training programs for executives and managers in business and industry face the problem of increasing costs to transport trainees to training sites. Accordingly, self-study programs are often developed. IBM, for example, has developed independent study programs (ISPs). The ISPs comprise different materials but generally include a student text and study guide. Dean reported that "the study guide contains unit assignments such as a self-evaluation quiz, a coding exercise, readings from formal support documentation, illustrations supporting audio tapes, or problems to be solved following the viewing of videotapes."[80]

Training programs in business and industry make extensive use of audiovisual technology. Ruark estimated that industry and business spent approximately $2.5 billion on audio-visual materials and equipment during 1978. He reported that the simple 35 mm slide is the most rapidly growing audio-visual format. By way of contrast, Ruark pointed out that total sales to educational institutions were about $1.7 billion in 1978.[81]

INDIVIDUALIZING INSTRUCTION AND CURRICULUM PLANNING

A variety of procedures for individualizing instruction have been developed and used. Predetermined plans for individualization influence the selection of a curriculum design and teaching models; similarly the curriculum plan and the teaching model selected will limit possible ways to individualize instruction. In this section, different bases for individualizing instruction are described and strategies of individualization are discussed.

Bases for Individualizing Instruction

A number of factors influence an individual's interest in and ability to learn. Theoretically, instruction could be individualized according to any one or combination of these factors. Practically, instruction should be individualized only when it enhances the learning potential of experiences offered to students.

Intelligence

A score on a standardized intelligence test was one of the first methods used to individualize instruction—it is also one of the most difficult to defend. It fails to take into account the motivation and interests of students and may result in a harmful segregation of students. Intelligence test scores are used to sort out learners at the extremes of intelligence and

[80]Peter M. Dean, "Education and Training at IBM," *Phi Delta Kappan, 61* (January 1980): 318.
[81]Henry Ruark, "A. V. News and Review," *Technical Photography, 11* (September 1979): 8, 9, 54–56.

assign them either to classes for the mentally retarded or for the gifted. These classes are generally smaller and may provide for individualized instruction. The practice of segregating mentally retarded learners has been challenged by PL 94–142—mainstreaming—which is discussed later in this chapter.

Achievement

The most common basis for individualizing instruction is the achievement level of the learner. The rationale is obvious—take the learner where he or she is and help him or her to progress. In practice, achievement level has been used as a basis for grouping students; differentiation and individualized instruction may or may not exist within these subgroups.

Educational stratification based on achievement may lead to teacher expectations that become self-fulfilling prophecies. Rosenthal and Jacobsen directed attention to this phenomenon through their investigation.[82] Although subsequent analyses of their data did not support their conclusions, their work triggered a number of subsequent studies.

West and Anderson summarized much of this research. They found that teachers' expectations are influenced by general information about a student (for example, socioeconomic status), student's achievement, and student's intelligence. From the studies reviewed, they concluded that day-by-day achievement of students was a more powerful influence on teacher behavior than general background information about the student.[83]

Teachers generally attempt to provide equal educational opportunity to each student in a class. However, classroom observations show that teachers unconsciously direct their teaching and expectations to some students at the expense of others. According to Bloom, "They give much positive reinforcement and encouragement to some students but not to others, and they encourage active participation in the classroom discussion and question and answer periods from some students and discourage it from others."[84] The achievement of students in the top third or fourth of the class, influences teachers to give them the greatest attention. This in turn influences the ways in which all students in a class view themselves as learners and their effectiveness as students, and thus prophecies become fulfilled.

It would be both impossible and impractical for teachers to ignore

[82]Robert Rosenthal and Lenore Jacobsen, *Pygmalion in the Classroom: Teacher Expectations and Pupils' Intellectual Development* (New York: Holt, Rinehart and Winston, Inc., 1968).
[83]Charles K. West and Thomas H. Anderson, "The Questions of Preponderant Causation in Teacher Expectancy Research," *Review of Educational Research, 46* (Fall 1976): 613–630.
[84]Benjamin S. Bloom, "New Views of the Learner: Implications for Instruction and Curriculum," *Educational Leadership, 35* (April 1978): 568.

differences in achievement among learners. There are ways, however, to recognize these differences in constructive individualized programs. For example, Bloom's mastery learning, to be discussed later, is one such way.

Cognitive Processes

Some curriculum designs and teaching models described in this book are based on the assumption that the environment, not the learner, determines the products of learning—for example, programmed instruction. Other designs and models are based on the assumption that learning from instruction should be viewed as an internally, cognitively mediated process—for example, inquiry training. Wittrock pointed out that a cognitive approach to instruction "involves understanding relations or interactions between the learner's cognitive processes or aptitudes, such as attribution, motivation, encoding, memory, cognitive styles and cognitive structures, and the characteristics of instructional treatments."[85] Since individuals differ in the strategies they use for information processing, these differences may serve as a basis for individualizing instruction.

"Cognitive styles," according to Wittrock, "are the stable ways people differ in perception, encoding, and storage of information."[86] Wittrock presented several ways in which researchers have contrasted cognitive styles. For example, Kagon and his associates contrasted a global information processing style with an articulated, analytic, and differentiated style. Another instance: "Pask and Scott classified learners as either serialists or holists. Curricula with organization that matched the cognitive styles of the learners sizably enhanced learning."[87] It is, of course, this latter finding that is of particular interest to curriculum planners.[88]

Strategies for Individualizing Instruction

A variety of strategies have been developed in order to match instruction to individual differences of learners. One of the earliest programs was developed in the 1920s by Carleton Washburne when he was Superintendent of the Winnetka (Illinois) schools. The similarities between the Winnetka Plan, as it was called, and those developed 60 years later are striking. The "common essentials" were organized in "parcels" and each child was encouraged to proceed at his or her own pace. Cremin commented on the plan, "Instead of a whole class proceeding at the same rate and achieving

[85]M. C. Wittrock, "The Cognitive Movement in Education," *Educational Researcher, 8* (February 1979): 5.
[86]Wittrock, p. 7.
[87]Wittrock, p. 8.
[88]For another classification of cognitive styles, see H. A. Witkin, C. A. Moore, D. R. Goodenough, and P. W. Cox, "Field-Dependent and Field-Independent Cognitive Styles and Their Educational Implications," *Review of Educational Research, 47* (Winter 1977): 1–64.

varying quality, each student proceeded at his own rate, thereby varying time in place of quality."[89] As children completed a parcel they asked for a test. If successful they went on to the next parcel, if not they continued to work on the parcel until they were successful.

Individual Packaged Programs

The parcels of the 1920s in Winnetka have become packages or modules in the schools of the 1980s. Programmed learning, described as one teaching model, provided the basis for some of the earlier packaged programs. The Individually Prescribed Instruction (IPI) program was developed in 1963 and was eventually used by over 300 elementary schools. This highly structured system of individualized instruction is organized around hundreds of behavioral objectives in the areas of mathematics, reading, science, handwriting, and spelling. Each subject is divided into several units and students are placed in the units depending upon their level of mastery. Students work their way through each unit by mastering the objectives. Teachers prepare written prescriptions, a type of daily lesson plan for each student. Individualization in the IPI system is in terms of the rate with which students progress through the system.[90]

A number of other individualized packaged programs have been developed subsequent to IPI. A few illustrations will be mentioned. Westinghouse Corporation developed PLAN (Program for Learning in Accordance with Needs) which provides students with many more options than did IPI. Nova High School (Broward County, Florida) developed a series of learning activity packages (LAPS) for use in all areas. Audiovisual Tutorial (AVT) packages combining programmed text, prerecorded audiotapes, and sets of slides are available to teach typing in community colleges in an instructor-monitored laboratory. Many current applications of packaged programs incorporate computers, which monitor student progress and supply feedback to teachers.[91]

Mastery Learning[92]

Bloom and his colleagues developed "mastery learning" as an approach that combines classroom instruction for a group supplemented by individ-

[89]Lawrence A. Cremin, *The Transformation of the School* (New York: Alfred A. Knopf, 1961), p. 297.

[90]For a description of IPI see Norman E. Gronlund, *Individualizing Classroom Instruction* (New York: Macmillan Publishing Company, Inc., 1974), pp. 21–31.

[91]For an example, see Frank Hunnes, "The Kelloggsville Story: Learning Management as a Means to More Effective Teaching of Reading," *Phi Delta Kappan, 60* (December 1978): 283–286.

[92]See J. H. Block (ed.), *Schools, Society, and Mastery Learning* (New York: Holt, Rinehart and Winston, 1974); Benjamin S. Bloom, *Human Characteristics and School Learning* (New York: McGraw-Hill Book Company, 1976); and Bloom, "New Views," pp. 563–576.

ualized instruction. They rejected the idea that there are good and there are poor learners; they recognized, however, that there are faster and there are slower learners. Bloom expressed the view, "What any person in the world can learn, almost all persons in the world can learn if provided with appropriate prior and current conditions of learning."[93] Mastery learning, by providing the "appropriate prior and current conditions of learning," enables about 80 percent of the students in a mastery class to reach the same final level of performance as approximately the top 20 percent in a traditional class.

In mastery learning the course is broken down into units of one to two weeks duration. Instructional objectives are clearly specified for each unit. The learning tasks within each unit are taught to the group. Formative tests, administered at the end of each unit, are used to diagnose needs for further instruction for those who have not mastered the unit. Individualized instruction is then provided to these students so that nearly all students (95 percent approximately) master the subject as they progress from unit to unit. Research evidence shows that this is an effective way to individualize instruction in a classroom using group methods when the goals and objectives are amenable to such an instructional model.

Aptitude-Treatment Interaction (ATI)

Learners differ according to such attributes as intelligence test scores, achievement levels, and cognitive processes used. Cronbach and Snow have demonstrated that students may learn more readily from one type of instructional approach than from another, that the best method or instructional approach will differ from student to student, and that such differences are related to the characteristics or aptitudes of learners.[94] In other words, there is an interaction between the aptitudes of the learners and the instructional treatment used. For example, Della-Piana and Endo reported a study in which first graders' aptitudes were measured by means of a visual motor sequential test. Different methods of teaching reading were then used with two comparable groups on this test; one group used a phonics treatment and the other used a look-say treatment. "The phonics method served poor visual sequencers best, perhaps because it provides a substitute for the poor sequencing ability and short memory in its analytical structured drill. The more able visual sequencers were better off under the look-say method."[95]

One application of ATI research results is to modify the treatment

[93]Bloom, "New Views," p. 564.
[94]L. J. Cronbach, R. E. Snow, *Aptitudes and Instructional Methods: A Handbook for Research on Interactions* (New York: Irvington, 1977).
[95]Gabriel M. Della-Piana and George T. Endo, "Reading Research" in N. L. Gage (ed.), p. 888.

(instructional method) in accord with the aptitude of the learners. Thus, following the example of the first graders, one should employ a phonics approach for some students and a look-say approach for others. Gehlbach suggested an alternative use when he proposed that ATI research results be used to improve the instructional treatment.[96] He pointed out that "AT regression[97] characterizes many of our best known instructional methods. If we could eradicate steep AT regressions, we would remove instructional processes from the list of social forces that maintain inequalities of opportunities and achievement in our society."[98] Gehlback proposed that through progressive modification and design of a treatment, the regression slope should be decreased without lowering the mean level of achievement.

Matching Cognitive Styles and Instruction

One approach to individualizing instruction is to match instruction or treatment to the aptitude of a learner. In an effort to relate cognitive styles directly to instructional strategies, Hill developed the construct of educational cognitive style—the way in which an individual acquires meaning. He then developed a procedure for mapping an individual's cognitive style.[99] Further, he developed a procedure for describing the ideal cognitive style for optimal learning from a given instructional strategy. A number of research studies have shown that matching ideal cognitive styles for instructional strategies to a student's cognitive style, as determined by cognitive mapping, enhances learning.

Other methods have been developed for determining learning as well as teaching styles.[100] Fischer and Fischer identified six types of teaching styles: the task-oriented, the cooperative planner, the child-centered, the subject-centered, the learning-centered, and the emotionally exciting.[101] The matching of learning and teaching styles has been proposed. We believe such a simplistic approach may be erroneous at this time for several reasons. First, the methods for determining learning styles and

[96]Roger D. Gehlbach, "Individual Differences: Implications for Instructional Theory, Research and Innovation," *Educational Researcher, 8* (April 1979): 8–14.
[97]AT regression refers to the interaction between the treatment and the aptitude. The steeper the AT regression curve, the greater the impact of the aptitude factor on the achievement.
[98]Gehlback, p. 12.
[99]Joseph E. Hill and D. N. Nunney, *Personalizing Educational Programs Utilizing Cognitive Style Mapping* (Oakland, Mich.: Oakland Community College Press, 1971).
[100]See, for example, Rita S. Dunn and Kenneth J. Dunn, "Learning Styles/Teaching Styles: Should They ... Can They ... Be Matched?" *Educational Leadership, 36* (January 1979): 238–244.
[101]Barbara Bree Fischer, and Louis Fischer, "Styles in Teaching and Learning," *Educational Leadership, 36* (January 1979):245–254.

teaching styles do not have sufficient research base to support their application in classrooms. Second, neither learning styles nor teaching styles cluster neatly into packages. Third, there may be advantages for students to be exposed to different teaching styles.

Implications for Curriculum Planning

Curriculum workers, as they plan implementation, need to consider how individual differences will be dealt with. There are some precautions to be observed with the individualization of instruction. First, it is not a universal good. For example, Johnson conducted a secondary analysis of applying an aggregate chi-square statistical analysis to 24 independent samples taken from 11 independent research studies. All of the studies compared self-paced individualized instruction at the high school level in mathematics-oriented subjects with traditional methods. He found "that self-paced individualized instruction practices were not superior to traditional instructional practices. In fact, the reverse could be implied: that traditional instructional practices were superior to self-paced individualized instructional practices" ($P < .002$).[102] Further analyses are needed at different grade levels and in different subjects before broad generalizations may be drawn. However, Johnson's study indicates that some individualized practices may be inferior to traditional teaching methods. For example, community colleges report that generally more students fail to complete a course using packaged programs than do those attending regular classes. A third precaution: an excessive use of individualized approaches can cause educational institutions to ignore goals best achieved through group approaches.

A judicious use of individualized instruction is called for. Generally, a better balance in the educational program can be maintained when individualized instruction is combined with group instruction. Bloom's mastery learning, for example, provides just such an approach.

MAINSTREAMING HANDICAPPED STUDENTS— PL 94–142

Public Law 94–142, the "Education for all Handicapped Children Act" was enacted in 1975 with an overwhelming majority vote of both houses of Congress. The act guarantees a free appropriate public education for all handicapped children in the least restrictive environment. Corrigan referred to this act as "the most important piece of educational legislation

---

[102]Paul Ivan Johnson, "The Relationship of Self-Paced Individualized Instruction to Pupil Achievement When Measured by Pooling the Probabilities of Several Independent Samples" (Gainesville, Fla.: University of Florida, unpublished doctoral dissertation, 1979), p. 64.

in this country's history."[103] Specific provisions of the act, to be explored in this section, have important implications for instruction and for curriculum development.

Provisions of PL 94–142

The intent of the act is best understood as a continuation of the Civil Rights movement of the 1960s. The same rationale that led to the 1954 Supreme Court Decision on integration was used by advocates for the rights of handicapped individuals. Since segregation has a harmful effect on those who are segregated, persons with handicaps should not be segregated but should have access to equal educational opportunity. Further, the quality of education gained through equal access should be guaranteed. Five themes inherent in the act are producing changes in education.[104]

1. *Education is a right.* Many seriously handicapped children are being deinstitutionalized, with enrollments in special schools and hospitals for retarded, deaf, blind, and emotionally handicapped being reduced by a half in some states. School exclusions, suspensions, and expulsions have been virtually eliminated except when due process requirements are met.
2. *Decisions on educational programming must be based on characteristics of the child.* Factors such as cost, administrative convenience, and physical access are of secondary importance. Handicapped individuals are educated in the least restrictive environment.
3. *A written accountability document is required.* Regular classroom teachers are participating in determining and writing Individualized Educational Plans (IEPs) for handicapped children.
4. *Parents have a role in determination of appropriate programs.* There is formal involvement of parents of exceptional students in assessment, placement, and planning activities with due process observed for all educational decisions.
5. *All personnel in a school system will participate in delivering educational and related services to handicapped persons.* The direct service of special education teachers is changing to indirect service through consultative and support functions. School psychologists, social workers, and other personnel are being redeployed to serve exceptional students in decentralized settings.

[103]Dean C. Corrigan, "Political and Moral Contents that Produced PL 94–142," *Journal of Teacher Education, 29* (November–December 1978): 10.
[104]See Edwin W. Martin, "Education of the Handicapped Act and Teacher Education," *Journal of Teacher Education, 29* (November–December 1978): 8; Maynard C. Reynolds, "Basic Issues in Restructuring Teacher Education," *Journal of Teacher Education, 29* (November–December 1978): 25–29.

Individualized Educational Programs (IEP)

The entire PL 94–142 Act has major significance for curriculum planners. Curriculum plans in the future need to be developed for all learners —not just the mythical average learners. The specific requirement [105] of an IEP could have a major impact. If the curriculum plan does not accomodate the use of the IEP, then the requirement of the IEP may shape the total curriculum.

The IEP is defined in the law as "... a written statement for each handicapped child developed in any meeting by a representative of the local education agency ... the teacher, the parents or guardian of such child, and, whenever appropriate such child ..."[106] Morrissey and Safer pointed out that "the IEP serves as a planning system for instructional service delivery and documentation ..."[107] The law stipulated that there shall be a planning conference in which educational decisions are made that result in an educational plan; that parents and sometimes learners shall participate in this planning; that the resulting plan shall be implemented, subject to periodic review and revision; and ultimately, the plan, as revised, will be used as a basis for evaluation.

The law states that the IEP "... shall include (A) a statement of the present levels of educational performance of such child, (B) a statement of annual goals, including short-term instructional objectives, (C) a statement of the specific educational services to be provided to such child ..., (D)... appropriate objective criteria and evaluation procedures and schedules for determining, on at least an annual basis, whether instructional objectives are being achieved."[108] The IEP employs the diagnostic/prescription system which is commonly used in special education. The content of the plan and the strategies inferred are consistent with the specific competencies/technology curriculum design and represent an application of the instructional systems design model of teaching.

Implications of PL 94–142 for Curriculum Development

The implementation of PL 94–142 dramatically affects the role of classroom teachers as well as the structure of schools and classrooms. This prospect led Reynolds to comment, "Never has it been more clear that change is a process, not an event, and that the schools face the work of a

---

[105]There are five direct references to the IEP in the legislation.
[106]Education for All Handicapped Children Act of 1975 (Public Law 94–142) Section 602 (19).
[107]Patricia A. Morrissey and Nancy Safer, "The Individualized Education Program," *Viewpoints, 53* (March 1977): 32.
[108]Education for All Handicapped Children Act of 1975 (Public Law 94–142) Section 602 (19).

decade, not an evening."[109] Schlecty and Turnbull posed two alternative consequences of implementing PL 94–142: a further bureaucratization of schools and classrooms with a consequent diminution of the classroom teacher's power and authority, or an enhancement of the professional status of teachers as they make pedagogical decisions that require specified performance from others.[110] Schlecty and Turnbull gave three reasons why the implementation of PL 94–142 may encourage "teachers and teacher educators to embrace pedagogical assumptions based on narrowly individualistic and behavioristic assumptions."

1. The requirements of IEP's, such as annual goals, short-term objectives, and evaluation criteria and procedures cause teachers to concentrate on individual achievement rather than broader social goals.
2. Narrowly conceived behavioral approaches to instruction and needs of bureaucratically oriented school administrators are mutually supportive.
3. The demands for individualization of handicapped students may lead to rigid bureaucratization for the many.[111]

The requirement of an IEP for all handicapped children, many of whom will be in the regular classroom, limits the options open to curriculum planners and classroom teachers. One option is to adopt an instructional system diagnostic/prescriptive approach for all students. But there are other teaching models more appropriate to some of the broader goals of education. For example, the role-playing, simulation, and jurisprudential teaching models can be very effective for achieving certain goals. A second option, then, would be to use some of these models but exclude handicapped students from participation as they work on their individualized plan. This option has two serious limitations; it ignores the importance of broad goals for handicapped children and it resegregates handicapped learners. A third option, and one we believe should be followed, is to incorporate into the IEP's broader goals and participation in total class activities. Parents and educators who value a total educational experience for handicapped children must encourage the use of the third option—even if it means revising the law regarding the nature of the IEP.

INSTRUCTION AND THE HIDDEN OR "UNSTUDIED CURRICULUM"

In Chapter 1 we described what some educational sociologists designate as the hidden curriculum and noted that students in school have purposes

[109]Reynolds, p. 28.
[110]Phillip C. Schlecty and Ann P. Turnbull, "Bureaucracy or Professionalism: Implications of PL 94–142," *Journal of Teacher Education, 29* (November–December 1978): 34.
[111]Schlecty and Turnbull, p. 36.

and objectives that may not be fully congruent with those of the school or the teacher. Moreover, they also set purposes for themselves that are usually unrecognized by the school officially or by teachers who interact with students in classroom or nonclassroom situations. Yet it is apparent to shrewd observers of student behavior in school and a few researchers who have studied the situation that this "unofficial curriculum" is an important aspect of the student's schooling. Although little research has been conducted on the effect of the hidden curriculum in nonschool settings, it is an important factor in any educational setting. For example, the reader may recall early experiences in a Sunday school, or other religious educational program, and identify a hidden curriculum that was in operation.

Research indicates that success in school is enhanced considerably when students develop and display certain personal interaction and task-related skills. Discovering and developing these skills become the goal of a student's hidden curriculum. Students receive cues as to the nature of a desirable personal hidden curriculum from the organizational structure of an educational institution, from its social climate, and from the nature of teacher-student interactions. Curriculum planners and all educators need to recognize the powerful effect of an educational institution's organization and social structure and teacher-student interactions on what and how students learn—these factors represent an "unstudied curriculum". An important function of curriculum planners is to analyze this "unstudied curriculum" and in effect make it a part of the recognized curriculum so that it contributes to the total effectiveness of an educational institution.

The hidden curriculum has influence because students and teachers learn to accept social norms, or principles of conduct, and act accordingly. Research studies show that: 1) the structured settings of educational environments determine the tasks, opportunities, and constraints available, 2) social norms are developed as individuals cope with the educational environments, and 3) the structured settings vary in nature.[112] The hidden curriculum that emerges as individuals learn to cope takes on added significance with the introduction of competency testing, the increase in the rate of change of morals and values, and the emergence of a "competitive educational system," as identified by Fadiman.

The hidden curriculum that students develop for themselves results

[112]See, for example, Philip W. Jackson, *Life in the Classroom* (New York: Holt, Rinehart and Winston, Inc., 1968); Benson Snyder, *The Hidden Curriculum* (New York: Alfred A. Knopf, 1970); Philip A. Cusick, *Inside High School: The Student's World* (New York: Holt, Rinehart and Winston, Inc., 1973); R. P. McDermott, "Social Relations as Contexts for Learning in School," *Harvard Educational Review*, 47 (May 1977): 198–213; Hugh Mehan, "Structuring School Structure," *Harvard Educational Review*, 48 (February 1978): 32–64; Herbert J. Walberg (ed.), *Educational Environments and Effects: Evaluation, Policy, and Productivity* (Berkeley, Calif.: McCutchan Publishing Corp., 1979).

from both the planned curriculum and from an unstudied, yet very real curriculum. Three kinds of unofficial sets of learning situations may be identified: the managerial and organizational apparatus and arrangements of the school; the sociology of the school—that is, the social climate and processes of group living and the interactions among the school family; and the images and situation-sets of students with regard to teachers and the school as an institution, and of teachers with regard to the students.

The three types of "unstudied curriculum" are intertwined, all being part of a philosophy of schooling that pervades any particular school. For purposes of discussion we will consider each briefly, yet acknowledging their interrelatedness.

Structure of the School

The administrative bureaucracy of the school often with its massive sets of rules, regulations, procedures, and managerial arrangements is a very significant element of the "unstudied curriculum." As pointed out earlier, the maintenance of this bureaucratic structure may become an end in itself. Many sociologists regard these aspects of the schooling process as a primary factor in the socialization of the child and the adolescent. Easily identifiable elements of this nature are the whole classification system employed in school (school grades, groupings, attendance areas, vertical organization of school levels, promotion practices, eligibility for activities); evaluation methods (tests, grading and marking, honor rolls, achievement awards); competency test requirements for graduation; rules for order (movement of students, attendance, toilet use, class seating arrangements, up and down staircases); sanctions and methods of punishment (scolding, ridicule, detention, suspension, dismissal, isolation, denial of privileges, chores); limitation and control of individual and group action (closed campus, censorship of publications, programs, presentations, and the like, selection of outside speakers, activities of clubs, student body committees, social affairs, behavior at school athletic events); and the authoritarianism of school officials and staff.

The structure of schools emphasizes competition and individual effort. Johnson and Johnson commented,

> For forty years competition among students has been promoted in most schools, and in the past ten years individual effort in the achievement of learning goals has been increasingly encouraged, in spite of the fact that research has indicated that the cooperative goal structure would be more productive than either the competive or individualistic one.[113]

[113]David W. Johnson and Roger T. Johnson, "Cooperation, Competition, and Individualization," in Walberg (ed.), p. 101.

Social Climate of the School

The social climate of the school is less readily characterized by overt actions, yet it too is a pervasive factor in schooling. In planning instruction, teachers should take cognizance of this whole set of informal arrangements and the nature of the interpersonal relationships that exist among and between students and the faculty. The peer-mediated culture, especially in the upper levels of schooling, is a significant factor in the education of the young. Kimball pointed out:

> the school itself ferments its own distinctive social patternings based upon the multiple similarities and differences of its population. Learning arises, is extended, and modified within these social settings. For this reason, we cannot separate the learning process from the social process. As a social and cultural context, learning must be examined in the context of social systems.[114]

A serious concern is the impact of the school climate and the socializing processes of the school on students from culturally disadvantaged and/or impoverished homes. Personnel in schools may attempt, often unconsciously, to convert students to their own way of life and thinking. As a result children from different subcultural groupings "face a difficult problem in adjusting."[115]

The effects of the school's social climate on ethnic and racial groups have been studied. Mehan analyzed studies of social counseling and concluded, "Black students who had average to high academic performance were consistently dissuaded from attending college, while white students with mediocre-to-low academic performance (but high socioeconomic status) were consistently encouraged to attend college."[116] Since some of the studies cited by Mehan were conducted in the early 1960s, one could hope that some improvement has been made. Yet, Mehan concluded,

> When the practical daily work of educators with students is examined closely and rigorously . . . it is clear that school, and to be more specific, the organized character of interaction in school, does make a difference in educational outcomes. Taken together, then, these . . . studies point to stratifying practices within schools that produce differential treatment and may result in differences in later life.[117]

Teacher and Student Interaction

The interaction of teachers and students in the classroom is affected by the structure of the school and the prevailing social organization. These

[114]Solon T. Kimball, *Culture and the Educative Process* (New York: Teachers College Press, 1974), p. 111.
[115]Kimball, p. 82.
[116]Mehan, p. 56.
[117]Mehan, p. 61.

relations, in turn, have a direct effect on the organizational context for presenting learning tasks. McDermott viewed teaching as a form of coercion, "All teachers, regardless of their orientation, are faced with the task of getting and directing the children's attention, directing it to a problem and leading them to some way of handling it."[118] McDermott believed that such coercion must be based on "working agreements wherein the children can trust the teacher's coercion to be in their best interests." Establishment of such trusting relationships may be a particular problem for minority-group children.

Student behavior in the classroom affects teachers' actions toward the student. Cartledge and Milburn reported, "The effect of student behavior on teacher responses has been demonstrated in a number of studies by systematically varying student behavior."[119] They identified two general categories of student social behaviors required for school success:

1. Personal interaction skills—for example, helping, sharing, smiling, greeting others, speaking positively to others, and controlling aggression.
2. Task-related skills—for example, attending, speaking positively about academic material, compliance with teacher requests, remaining on task.[120]

These skills represent important goals in the "unstudied curriculum." Students who adopt these goals as their hidden curriculum and master them are rewarded for their efforts and are achievers. Cartledge and Milburn proposed that this "unstudied curriculum" be made more visible and that children be taught to develop the necessary personal interaction and task-related skills. Some readers may object to such a blatant effort to make conformists out of children; they should object as vigorously to more subtle efforts to make children conform.

Implications for Curriculum Planning

What does this brief excursion into the realm of the unofficial instructional program imply for curriculum planning and instruction?

1. The existence, nature, and effect of this unofficial, unstudied aspect of the total program of schooling should be fully acknowledged and understood by administrators, teachers, students, parents, and citizens. Increasingly significant research and scholarly writings on the matter, citations to some of which have been made, should be examined by educators in graduate studies, institutes, workshops, and staff meetings. Parents and students should be involved in these programs of study.

[118]McDermott, p. 204.
[119]Gwendolyn Cartledge and JoAnne F. Milburn, "The Case for Teaching Social Skills in the Classroom: A Review," *Review of Educational Research, 48* (Winter 1978): 135.
[120]Cartledge and Milburn, p. 142.

2. A school staff, with students and parents as participants, should examine in depth the nature and character of the "unstudied curriculum" of their school.

3. Any formal efforts in planning should give attention to the whole matter of the "unstudied curriculum." This is especially desirable in defining goals and subgoals in the affective domain; plans for implementing any curriculum plan should take account of learning opportunities, planned or informally developed, that contribute significantly to the socialization process, especially with respect to moral and character development. Included in such programs of planning should be a deliberate examination of the organizational structure, administrative arrangements, and policies, rules, regulations, and procedures for the management of the school.

4. Human relationships are a significant aspect of the "unstudied curriculum"; the school staff, with students and parents, should examine the nature and character of these interactive processes, giving special attention to such matters as social class distinctions, cliques, favoritism and rejection, discrimination, and the like.

In essence, the hidden nature of the "unstudied curriculum" should be brought out in the open, be fully examined and evaluated, and then be deliberately made a part of a program of socialization and moral development.

ADDITIONAL SUGGESTIONS FOR FURTHER STUDY

Gage, Nathaniel L., *The Scientific Basis of the Art of Teaching.* New York: Teachers College Press, 1977. A leading authority and researcher on the art of teaching brings together a mass of research evidence on the nature of teaching, the variables that enter into teaching, and the bases for the improvement of the teachers' work.

Good, Thomas L., and Jere E. Brophy, *Looking in Classrooms,* 2d ed. New York: Harper & Row, Publishers, 1978. A practical guide to help teachers improve their instructional effectiveness through improving observational techniques in the classroom and becoming more aware of their personal expectations. Relevant research findings are applied.

Johnson, Mauritz, and Harry Brooks, "Conceptualizing Classroom Management," *Classroom Management,* Seventy-Eighth Yearbook of the National Society for the Study of Education, Daniel L. Duke (ed.). Chicago: University of Chicago Press, 1979. In this excellent analysis of the principles, roles, and methods for carrying on instruction, the authors review instructional methods historically, then present a model of the whole process of classroom management and explain it in detail.

Kozma, Robert B., Lawrence W. Belle, George W. Williams, *Instructional Techniques in Higher Education.* Englewood Cliffs, New Jersey: Educational Technology Publications, 1978. Written for the college classroom practitioner, this book presents a systematic model of instruction and offers practical suggestions for its use.

"Mastery Learning," *Educational Leadership, 37* (November 1979): 99–164. The major part of this issue is devoted to reports of research and practice regarding the use of mastery learning, as developed in the work of Benjamin Bloom. An interview of Bloom by the editor is included.

Moos, Rudolf H., *Evaluating Educational Environments: Procedures, Measures, Findings and Policy Decisions.* San Francisco: Jossey Bass, Inc., Publisher, 1979. Presents extensive findings on how college and high school students' learning and development are influenced by characteristics of their classroom and living group settings. Includes guides for determining how much emphasis should be placed in educational settings on competition, intellectuality, obedience to the rules, and other variables.

Training and Development Journal, Montclair, N.J.: American Society for Training and Development. The official magazine of the American Society for Training and Development. It contains articles on designing and implementing corporate training programs.

Trump, J. Lloyd, *A School for Everyone.* Reston, Va.: National Association of Secondary School Principals, 1977. Sums up a total program of school improvement, especially at the secondary school level. Aspects of this program had been developed in the original Trump Plan and the later Model Schools Project of NASSP. Suggestions regarding personalization, student motivation, human relations, and related factors are especially relevant to improving instruction.

Watson, Kathryn J. *The Going Places Classroom: A Community Involvement Program of Action Learning for Elementary Students.* Gainesville, Fla.: P. K. Yonge Laboratory School, University of Florida, Research Monograph #23, 1977. Study of the involvement of fourth and fifth grade students in community activities through field trips, work projects, and parent-teacher planning. Research data indicated school achievement positively affected by participation.

SEVEN

• • •

EVALUATING THE CURRICULUM

• •

Planning the evaluation of the curriculum and instruction, as was stated in Chapter 1 and shown in Figures 1.1 and 1.2 (pp. 29 and 30), is essential. Evaluation is implied in the very process of planning, for it is the act of placing a value on something, of determining its merits. Throughout this book we have emphasized that, at every stage, curriculum planning is a matter of making choices. This does not imply, however, that one choice is as good as another. Value judgments determine the appropriateness of each choice made, whether, for example, it is deciding on the goals for an educational institution or the instructional materials to use to achieve a particular objective. Curriculum evaluation is the process used in judging the appropriateness of curriculum choices.

New and important developments in the field of evaluation are described in the first part of this chapter, alternative models for evaluation in the second part. Recommendations regarding evaluation to be used at various phases of curriculum planning constitute a major portion of the chapter. The uses and abuses of evaluation for accountability are also discussed.

EVALUATION—NEW HORIZONS

If the word *evaluation* were used in an association test with educators, it would trigger such responses as: tests, marks, grades, and teacher ratings. This is not surprising since test results have historically provided the major data base for educational evaluation. However, this limited approach to evaluation focuses attention on the products or ends of education. Goodlad commented: "Because we have concentrated on ends, we have thousands of instruments for measuring the presumed effects of the race, but scarcely any for looking at the condition and nature of the track or of horse and rider." Goodlad called for an evaluation scheme that would help us to "answer the question as to whether this or that race should be run and, indeed, whether it is races we should be promoting."[1] New developments in curriculum evaluation help us move beyond considering only the ends —only who wins the race.

[1]John I. Goodlad, "On the Cultivation and Corruption of Education," *The Educational Forum, 22* (March 1978):277.

New Roles for Evaluation

Although evaluation has only one basic *goal*—the determination of the worth or value of something—it has many *roles*.[2] Appraisal of the outcomes of student learning in all of their ramifications is an example of one role. This type of evaluation is familiar to most teachers and administrators; it is accomplished through testing, measuring, and assessing pupil achievements, diagnosing individual progress, and comparing results with norms and scores of other members of the class or age group.

Another significant function of evaluation is determining the value of the curriculum itself. Is the curriculum fulfilling the purposes for which it was designed? Are the purposes themselves valid? Is the curriculum appropriate for the particular group of students with whom it is being used? Are the instructional models selected the best choices in light of the goals sought? Is the content the best that may be selected? Are the materials recommended for instructional purposes appropriate and the best available for the purposes envisioned? This role of evaluation is given much attention in the present chapter.

A third major role of evaluation in schools is to judge the merits of all the administrative and managerial arrangements and practices and the structures within which the educational institution itself operates. These aspects of the educational establishment are important determinants of curriculum and instruction, but this type of evaluation is beyond the scope of this book; references cited in this chapter provide assistance in making such comprehensive evaluations.

Formative and Summative Evaluation

Another way of looking at curriculum evaluation is in terms of the timing of the evaluation, the ways in which it is made and the instruments used, and the purpose for which the results are used. Scriven introduced into the literature of evaluation in recent years the concept of formative and summative evaluation.[3] Bloom, Hastings, and Madaus, in a useful handbook on evaluation, picked up Scriven's distinction and used it extensively in their treatment of the subject.[4] Formative evaluation, according to Anderson and colleagues, "is concerned with helping the developer of programs or products (curricula, books, television shows, etc.) through the

[2]For a definitive treatment of this point, see Michael Scriven, "The Methodology of Evaluation," in Robert E. Stake (ed.), *Perspectives of Curriculum Evaluation,* AERA Monograph Series on Curriculum Evaluation (Chicago: Rand McNally & Company, 1967), pp. 40–43.
[3]Scriven, pp. 40–43.
[4]Benjamin S. Bloom, J. Thomas Hastings, and George F. Madaus, *Handbook on Formative and Summative Evaluation of Student Learning* (New York: McGraw-Hill Book Company, Inc., 1971), especially Chapters 4–6.

use of empirical research methodology." By way of contrast, "summative evaluation is concerned with evaluating the over-all program after it is in operation."[5]

The merit of summative evaluation as a basis for revising curriculum plans has generally been recognized. Formative evaluation, however, provides a valuable and powerful new tool for helping curriculum planners reach rational and valid decisions. To capitalize on this tool requires a close collaborative relationship between the curriculum planners and a formative evaluation researcher. Morocco described how formative evaluation can be used at each of three stages of program development: planning/designing, implementing the program, and disseminating it to other users.[6] At the planning/designing stage, formative evaluation can help program developers gather information about alternative approaches to achieve the goal. Formative evaluation can provide information derived from a trial use of new plans, including views and attitudes of those trying out the plan. At the implementation stage, formative evaluation can "identify and conceptualize program factors or processes that are influencing the ultimate success of the program."[7] At the innovation stage, formative evaluation provides data regarding the actual use of the program as a basis for further modifications in program and strategies in implementation.[8] Planning and innovation work hand in hand.

The value of formative evaluation is illustrated by its use in the development of instructional television as described by Barbatsis.[9] In 1968 the Children's Television Workshop (CTW) began a test of the power of television as an educational tool. Previous tests were marked by inconsistent and statistically nonsignificant results. However, the program CTW produced *(Sesame Street)* "achieved significant and consistent results in measures of learning." *Sesame Street* succeeded where other programs had failed because the developers used a different evaluation approach. Whereas other television producers used summative evaluation to test the effectiveness of their programs after they were produced, CTW secured formative evaluation from the outset. Through the melding of production and constant formative evaluation they generated a single force working toward continuous improvement. Barbatsis attributed *Sesame Street's* success to this strategy.

[5]Scarvia B. Anderson, Samuel Ball, Richard T. Murphy and Associates, *Encyclopedia of Educational Evaluation* (San Francisco: Jossey-Bass Publishers, 1977), p. 175.
[6]Catherine Cobb Morocco, "The Role of Formative Evaluation in Developing and Assessing Educational Programs," *Curriculum Inquiry, 9* (Summer 1979):137–148.
[7]Morocco, p. 140.
[8]Morocco provides an illustration of formative evaluation applied to a new program, pp. 142–147.
[9]Gretchen Schoen Barbatsis, "The Nature of Inquiry and Analysis of Theoretical Progress in Instructional Television from 1950–1970," *Review of Educational Research, 48* (Summer 1978):399–414.

The value of formative evaluation should not blind curriculum planners to the utility of summative evaluation. In summative evaluation, we measure the results of instruction, presumably carried out according to a plan —either the plan previously developed as a part of the planning process or one improvised by the teacher on the spot. This type of evaluation is often based on tests of all sorts, student reaction to the instruction, teachers' views concerning the effectiveness of instruction, follow-up studies of students who have participated in a program of instruction, parents' reactions, employer ratings of graduates, reports from college examination bureaus, and similar types of evidence of varying degrees of validity. It should be evident, however, that any line of distinction between the two types of evaluation is rather nebulous. Certainly, summative evaluation also contributes highly significant data for revising curriculum plans, formulating new ones, adding or dropping courses of instruction, selecting new content, revising goals and objectives, and the like. The difference lies more in the purposes for which evaluation is used and when it is used than in methodology, analytical techniques, and the like. One value of formative evaluation has been to emphasize the importance of using evaluative processes as a part of planning itself.

EVALUATION MODELS

Expanded roles for evaluation and the development of formative evaluation opened up new possibilities for conducting and reporting curriculum evaluation. Concurrently there was an insistence by the federal government that programs and projects for which it provided funds be evaluated. This requirement is spelled out, for example, in the provisions of the Elementary and Secondary Education Act of 1965 and subsequent amendments, the Vocational Education Act and its later amendments of 1963 and 1968, and the Education Professions Development Act of 1967. There were demands for accountability by citizens, legislatures, Congress, students (the clients), and professional educators. In California, for example, the Stull Act, passed in 1971, requires a "uniform system of evaluation and assessment of the performance of certified personnel within each school district."

These conditions set the stage for a new emphasis on evaluation, with leadership being provided by a group of competent, vigorous professionals. New approaches, methods, analytical procedures, and conceptions of the place and role of evaluation are being developed. Evaluation, perhaps at long last, is fulfilling much more effectively its rightful place as a major factor in the process of curriculum and instructional planning.

The new evaluation models that have emerged reflect varied answers to the following questions:

1. Who conducts the evaluation?
2. What are the major audiences for the results?
3. What assumptions are made?
4. What methods are used?
5. What is the nature of the information used?
6. What are the hoped-for outcomes?

Five models, selected to represent a variety of approaches to evaluation, are described. The characteristics of these models are summarized in Table 7.1, a taxonomy of evaluation models. Note that evaluation models vary as to who conducts the evaluation, the major audiences for the evaluation results, the assumptions that are made as a part of the evaluation process, the methods used in collecting data, the nature of information used in the evaluation, and the expected outcomes of the evaluation.

Behavioral Objectives Model

The first great leap forward in the process of evaluation came with the work of Tyler in the 1930s in conjunction with his evaluation of the Progressive Education Association's Eight-Year Study program. Tyler defined education as changes in behavior; hence evaluation consisted of measuring the extent to which such changes had taken place, consistent with the previously defined objectives of the educational program being evaluated. This means that the goals and objectives of schooling are defined; instruction then seeks to bring about these changes in students; evaluation determines whether the desired changes have taken place.[10]

Evaluation in the Tyler model was largely summative, relying on testing, grading, classifying, marking, and measuring students' achievements. This was, and is even more so decades later, the day of the standardized test, teacher-made objective tests, college entrance examinations, performance standards, percentile ranks, and all of the rest. All too frequently this is about the only kind of formalized evaluation that takes place on a regular basis—even to this day. Little or no effort is made to determine why a unit of educational activities, a program, or an aspect of schooling is offered. Still less attention is given to determining the effectiveness of a program or its appropriateness in meeting the particular needs of the learners for whom it has been planned.

The behavioral objectives evaluation model has its roots in the scientific management movement and goes back to the work of Bobbitt and Charters. Because of the model's emphasis on product evaluation, it has been championed by advocates of teacher accountability. The drive for the use of behavioral objectives, led by Mager and Popham beginning in the 1960s (discussed in Chapter 4), emphasized the use of the behavioral objective

---

[10]This rationale is spelled out in a later publication of Tyler's, *Basic Principles of Curriculum and Instruction: Syllabus for Education 305* (Chicago: University of Chicago Press, 1950). Also see Bloom, Hastings, and Madaus, pp. 24–28, for a critical analysis of this approach.

TABLE 7.1 A Taxonomy of Evaluation Models

Model	Who Conducts	Major Audiences	Assumes Consensus on	Methods	Nature of Information	Outcome
Behavioral Objectives	Professionals	Managers Instructional systems designers	Prespecified objectives Quantified outcome variables	Achievement tests	Quantitative objectivity	Productivity Accountability
Decision Making	Program planners	Decision makers, esp. Administrators Curriculum planners	General goals Criteria	Surveys Questionnaires Interviews Natural variation	Quantitative objectivity	Effectiveness Quality control
Goal-Free	Unbiased observer	Consumers Curriculum planners	Consequences criteria	Bias control Logical analysis	Qualitative objectivity	Consumer choice Social utility
Accreditation	Professionals	Professionals Public	Criteria Panel Procedures	Review by panel Self-study	Expertise through experience	Professional acceptance
Responsive	Evaluator processing judgments	Clients Practitioners Curriculum planners	Negotiations Activities	Case studies Interviews Observations	Transactional knowing	Understanding Diversity

Adapted from House, Ernest R., "Assumptions Underlying Evaluation Models." *Educational Researcher*, March 1978, p. 12. Copyright 1978, American Educational Research Association, Washington, D. C.

model of evaluation.[11] Further, its objective measurement of prespecified goals fits nicely into a bureaucratic management style. Thus, applications for federal grant funds are required to include a statement of objectives to be achieved and procedures for measuring their achievement as a method of evaluating project effectiveness. This requirement and the press for product accountability have been major influences in maintaining the primacy of the behavioral objectives model of evaluation.

Decision-Making Model

The use of a behavioral objectives model provides a summative evaluation of products. In Tyler's words: "Evaluation is the process for determining the degree to which ... changes in behavior (of students) are actually taking place."[12] However, as indicated previously, formative evaluation is of particular interest and value to curriculum planners.

A national Phi Delta Kappa committee, chaired by Stufflebeam, developed a new approach that incorporates formative evaluation. The committee defined educational evaluation as "the process of delineating, obtaining, and providing useful information for judging decision alternatives."[13] The plan they developed fulfilled Cronbach's pioneering view of evaluation "as the collection and use of information to make decisions about an educational program."[14]

To provide information needed by decision makers, the decision-making model generates data regarding four stages of program operation: 1) context evaluation, which contributes to the definition of objectives; 2) input evaluation, which is necessary for decision making on matters of design; 3) process evaluation, which guides decision making on operations; and 4) product evaluation, which provides data for judging, attainments, and, hence, for revision, termination, or continuation.[15] For each of the four stages the following steps are taken in the process of evaluation:

1. The determination of what is to be evaluated; for what kinds of decisions is evaluative data needed?
2. The kinds of data needed in making these decisions.
3. The collection of these data.

[11]R. F. Mager, *Preparing Instructional Objectives* (Palo Alto, Calif.: Fearon Publishers, 1962); W. J. Popham, et al., *Instructional Objectives: An Analysis of Emerging Issues* (Chicago: Rand McNally and Co., 1969).
[12]Tyler, p. 69.
[13]Phi Delta Kappa National Study Committee on Evaluation, Daniel Stufflebeam, chairman, *Educational Evaluation and Decision Making* (Itasca, Ill.: R. E. Peacock Publishers, Inc., 1971), p. 40 Hereafter cited as Stufflebeam.
[14]Lee J. Cronbach, "Course Improvement through Evaluation," *Teachers College Record, 64* (May 1963):672.
[15]The gathering of evaluation data regarding Context, Input, Process, and Product led to the acronym CIPP for this model.

4. Defining criteria for determining the quality of the matter being evaluated.
5. Analysis of the data in terms of these criteria.
6. Providing information for decision-makers.

Note especially that decision making is not a part of the evaluative process itself. Evaluation provides the knowledge needed for decision making, and decision making involves making choices among alternatives. Of course, often—perhaps usually—the evaluator will make or certainly indicate a preference for a particular decision, but that is going beyond his role of evaluator and becoming a judge. The point of view of the Phi Delta Kappa Committee on this matter is that:

> The entire purpose of evaluation ... is to service the decision-making act— to identify the decision question that calls forth an answer; to identify alternative answers (decision alternatives) that might be given in response; to identify and refine the criteria (values) to be used in choosing among available decision alternatives; to identify, collect, and report information differentiating the decision alternatives; and, finally, to determine whether the chosen alternative did meet expectations for it.[16]

The decision-making evaluation model assumes that a consensus can be secured on the general goals for each stage of program development and on the criteria to be applied in assessing the achievement of the goals. For example, through context evaluation it might be agreed that a given program of education should meet the needs of a majority of students with special provisions made for other students. It would then be necessary to agree on criteria that would indicate that student needs were being met. These criteria could include, for example, attendance in school, attitudes toward school, and success of graduates. Data could then be collected from records, attitude surveys, and follow-up studies of graduates. Differences between the agreed-on goal of meeting student needs and the reality of meeting these needs, as evidenced by the data, represent a discrepancy. Overcoming discrepancies—that is differences between goals and reality —serves as a basis for program objectives.[17]

Discrepancy evaluation is used in several evaluation models.[18] Provus used the term "discrepancy evaluation" to refer to a model he developed for use in the Pittsburgh Public Schools.[19] The Provus model is a decision-making type of model somewhat related to Stufflebeam's model.

Provus stated that "program evaluation is the process of 1) defining program standards; 2) determining whether a discrepancy exists between

---

[16]Stufflebeam, p. 43.
[17]See Stufflebeam, Chapters 6 and 7 for an exceptionally clear and extensive discussion of the procedures followed.
[18]For a general description see Anderson, et al., pp. 127–129.
[19]Malcolm Provus, *Discrepancy Evaluation for Educational Program Improvement and Assessment* (Berkeley, Calif.: McCutchan Publishing Corp., 1971).

some aspect of program performance and the standards governing that aspect of the program; and 3) using discrepancy information either to change performance or to change program standards."[20] In his model, Provus regards four major developmental stages and four steps in each of the three content categories essential for the evaluation of an ongoing, single program. The fifth step, Program Comparison and Cost-Benefit Analysis, is an optional one, suggesting the possibility of comparing programs and defining the cost benefit of each in the total program.

The flow chart (Figure 7.1) illustrates Provus' process of evaluating an ongoing program. The evaluator starts with an ongoing program (step 1) in which standards (S) have been established as a part of the design process in initiating the program. Appropriate evidence is obtained on performance (P), and this compared (C) with the standard. Any discrepancy (D) is then evident. Discrepancy information always leads to a decision to either go on to the next stage, recycle the stage after there has been a change in the program's standards or operations, recycle to the first stage, or terminate the project. Provus described additional information gathered in successive stages of evaluating a project or program. All of these stages should be completed before any cost-benefit analysis is made.

It should be especially noted that Provus' model necessitates an evaluation of the goals and objectives themselves, something not many of the plans require as a part of the evaluation process. This occurs when program-performance data do not match standards. Provus pointed out that such a discrepancy requires the program planner either to revise the program's standards, modify the program, or discard the whole thing; if no significant discrepancy is found, the staff moves on to the next stage in the cycle until the whole program is acceptable and valid or has been discarded as undesirable.

We believe that a decision-making evaluation model, either that of Stufflebeam or of Provus, may be effectively used for curriculum development. Specific applications of this model are contained in the last part of this chapter.

Goal-Free Evaluation Model

Goal-free evaluation would appear to be a paradox. How can a value judgment be placed on an object or on an action without reference to a goal? Scriven, the originator of goal-free evaluation, had an overriding concern for bias in evaluation.[21] He proposed, therefore, that an evaluator

[20]Provus, p. 183.
[21]For an excellent summary of Scriven's writings on goal-free evaluation see David Hamilton, David Jenkins, Christine King, Barry MacDonald, and Malcolm Parlett (eds.), *Beyond the Numbers Game: A Reader in Educational Evaluation* (London: MACMILLAN EDUCATION LTD., 1977), pp. 123–142.

Stages	Content		
	Input	Process	Output
1. Design 2. Installation 3. Process 4. Product 5. Program Comparison	Design Adequacy Installation Fidelity Process Adjustment Product Assessment Cost-Benefit Analysis		

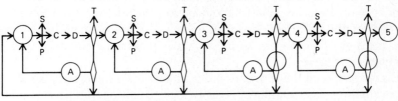

S - Standard
P - Program performance
C - Comparison
D - Discrepancy information

A - To change program
    performance or standards
T - To terminate program

FIGURE 7.1   Flow chart for Provus' discrepancy evaluation

should not be influenced, or biased, by the rhetoric of program developers' goal statements. Scriven summarized his position: "It seemed to me, in short, that consideration and evaluation of goals was an unnecessary but also a possibly contaminating step. I began to work on an alternative approach—simply, the evaluation of actual *effects* against a profile of *demonstrated* needs in this region of education. I call this Goal-Free Evaluation."[22]

The evaluator in goal-free evaluation is to be an unbiased observer. The nature of information used is qualitative objectivity (see Table 7.1) where "objectivity is equated with being free from bias or distortion."[23] The evaluator is free to collect whatever data appear to be pertinent in considering the total consequence of a program. These consequences then are evaluated against "demonstrated needs." The demonstrated needs, presumably determined by the evaluator, serve a function somewhat similar to goal statements in other models. In order for goal-free evaluation to have any impact on a program, there needs to be a consensus on the validity of the consequences reported by the evaluator, as well as on the definition of demonstrated needs used in the evaluation.

Scriven compared goal-free evaluation with the testing of drugs in medical research. The researcher, without knowing the intended purpose of the drug, evaluates its total consequences. The analogy is not lost on

[22]Michael Scriven, "Prose and Cons About Goal-Free Evaluation," *Evaluation Comment: The Journal of Educational Evaluation* 3 (1972):1. quoted in Hamilton et al., pp. 130–132.
[23]House, p. 8.

education. For example, what value is there in developing a new procedure for teaching a child to read if in the process he or she learns to dislike reading and everything associated with it?

Goal-free evaluation is essentially a summative type of evaluation oriented to the consumers (similar to a consumer report) and does not provide curriculum planners with useful formative data. However, in an age of growing consumerism and lack of confidence in educational institutions clients may press for goal-free evaluation. Educators, themselves, concerned for the unfortunate consequences of some educational programs and decisions may choose to incorporate goal-free evaluation in a total evaluation program.

Eisner proposed that educational connoisseurship and criticism be used for evaluating classroom life.[24] This type of enlightened criticism could be used with goal-free evaluation. Eisner compared a critic of classroom teaching to a critic of drama or art. Valid criticism, whether of drama, art, or teaching can come only from a connoisseur of the particular field. According to Eisner, "Connoisseurship . . . relates to any form of expertise in any area of human endeavor and is as germane to the problems involved in purse snatching as it is in the appreciation of fine needlepoint."[25] Lewis and Miel proposed a similar use of criticism of classroom teaching. However, they proposed that the critic "must have more than expertise. He must have lived perceptively and honestly within the field he critiques, and have loved and respected it, not be an outsider passing through if he is to have an effect on the work occurring within it."[26]

Teachers act as connoisseurs of teaching as they judge when students have "had enough" of one subject or one activity and sense that it is time to move on to another activity. Teachers often have gut-level feelings that some of the educational demands from outside the teaching profession are misguided or wrong. Many teachers have developed just enough connoisseurship to feel that something is wrong, but are unable to conceptualize just what it is. They need to be helped to develop their connoisseurship of teaching and living in the classroom.

The end of criticism is that of disclosure. "Criticism applied to classroom phenomena is the art of saying just what it is that is going on in that setting." To provide a vivid rendering of what transpires in the classroom, the educational critic employs "a form of linguistic artistry replete with metaphor, contrast, redundancy, and emphasis. . . ."[27] In the past "educational connoisseurship and criticism have not been encouraged. An ounce

---

[24]Elliot W. Eisner, "On the Uses of Educational Connoisseurship and Criticism for Evaluating Classroom Life," *Teachers College Record,* 78 (February 1977):345–358.
[25]Eisner, p. 346.
[26]Arthur J. Lewis, Alice Miel, *Supervision for Improved Instruction* (Belmont, Calif.: Wadsworth Publishing Company, Inc., 1972), p. 233.
[27]Eisner, p. 352.

of data, it seems, has been worth a pound of insight."[28] The development of the art of criticism of classroom teaching would provide an important additional dimension to evaluation.

Accreditation Model

Accreditation is one of the oldest educational evaluation procedures having been developed by the University of Michigan in 1871 through inviting high schools of that state to seek University approval of their academic programs. The graduates of the schools that were approved would then be admitted to the University without examination. Late in the nineteenth century voluntary regional accrediting associations for high schools were organized. Standards were set as a basis for membership, a practice that represented, in crude form at least, an appraisal system. In the past these two kinds of accreditation have always exercised a tremendous influence on high school programs throughout the country, shaping decision making on curriculum matters more significantly than all other factors except legal requirements. In recent decades, however, accreditation of high schools by universities has been virtually eliminated.

State departments of education have been a third agency exercising accreditation power over schools, and at the present time they constitute the primary factor in this form of program appraisal, for most of them are legally bound to make such evaluations. School systems must meet accreditation standards set by these departments or suffer severe penalties, which can be as serious as disestablishment or loss of state financial support.

Postsecondary institutions have united in accrediting associations, usually associated with secondary schools. Public and private universities, if members of accrediting associations, undergo the same type of accreditation activities as public schools. Accreditation of professional schools has been a particularly powerful influence on higher education.[29] Many a university budget has undergone serious strain to enable one of its professional schools to meet professional association standards and not lose accreditation.

The basic idea of accreditation is to utilize professional experience and knowledge to monitor and improve educational programs. House attributed another purpose: "The accreditation model began as a voluntary association to ward off government interference."[30]

The accreditation model utilizes a discrepancy type of evaluation. Stan-

---

[28]Eisner, p. 354.

[29]For a listing of institutions having one or more of 42 possible accredited programs see Arthur Podolsky, *Colleges and Universities Offering Accredited Programs by Accreditation Field, Including Selected Characteristics, 1977–1978* (Washington, D.C.: National Center for Educational Statistics, 1978).

[30]House, p. 10.

dards prepared by each association generally cover the four areas incorporated in Stufflebeam's decision-making model (context, input, process, and product) without using the terminology. For example, standards typically include items associated with context, such as statements of philosophy and goals, assessment of community needs, and descriptions of students to be served. Standards regarding inputs include: qualifications of staff, physical facilities, library resources, other instructional resources, and curriculum plans.

Two related approaches are used in determining discrepancies between the standards and practice. The institution seeking accreditation conducts a self-evaluation using the association standards or criteria. Usually a committee composed of staff members (and in some instances a few citizens, including parents) and students conducts the study for each aspect of the standards. The committee prepares a report that includes comments and recommendations concerning the particular field or aspect of education. Occasionally test data on achievement may be available, and surveys of student and/or parent opinion may be made. Follow-up studies of graduates may also be used in some instances.

The accrediting associations require that a "visiting committee" then spend one or more days—often three—in the institution to make its judgments about the program. Such committees may comprise as few as five to ten members or as many as 100 or more. In the latter instance, there usually is a small subcommittee for each area. The visiting committee prepares a report which comments on the evaluations prepared by the institution's committee and presents its recommendations, if any, for improvement of each area of the institution's program. If there is a discrepancy between any standard and actual practice as reflected in the visiting committee's report, the association decides whether or not accreditation shall be granted. Many associations provide time for the applying institution to correct any deficiencies before granting or withholding accreditation.

The effect of the "evaluative criteria" and such an accreditation program on the total program of an institution is often great. Anyone who has participated in the process knows the impact of such an evaluation on a school. Changes in curriculum, instruction, guidance services, availablity and use of instructional materials, the extrainstructional program—in fact, any area evaluated—are easy to identify. Accreditation is not permanent; associations require that reaccreditation take place within a specified number of years, usually between five and ten.

Accreditation's effectiveness as an evaluation procedure depends upon the quality of the standards; the validity of the judgments made by the faculty and the visiting team; and the procedures followed by the association in awarding and withholding accreditation. Standards, or criteria, are set by professionals within the association in order to define the best possible practice. However, these standards may reflect first class programs for the past and present but not the future. Thus the standards could actually contribute to making institutions obsolete in a rapidly changing society. At the same time, there is a danger that new standards may be adopted without sufficient evidence of their appropriateness. Glass concluded his analysis of the accreditation model by noting:

> Evaluation will not enhance the *value* of an educational program if it demands conformity to standards which themselves cannot be demonstrated to lead to valued goals. . . . The genetic flaw in the Accreditation model will probably never be corrected; thus it will not grow into the fully useful methodology of evaluation that is needed.[31]

How valid are the judgments made by the faculty in their self-evaluation and by the visiting team? This varies from association to association and from institution to institution. Some judgments are based on inadequate data. Visiting team members, themselves busy professionals and often inexperienced in evaluation, may be relying solely on subjective observation and interviews rather than seeking quantitative data. Accrediting associations are faced with the task of taking their visiting team's report and making a decision on accreditation. Associations work hard at being objective in making these decisions—a stance that becomes increasingly difficult in a politicized world.

We believe that even with its inherent problems, accreditation is a positive force in education and that it will continue to be a major factor in decision-making on curriculum matters; hence, it behooves those responsible for the program to upgrade the methods and procedure used, drawing on present knowledge of the evaluative process.

Responsive Model

According to Stake, originator of the responsive evaluation model, "An educational evaluation is *responsive evaluation* 1) if it orients more directly to program activities than to program intents, 2) if it responds to audience requirements for information and 3) if the different value-perspectives present are referred to in reporting the success and failure of the program."[32] In order to improve communication with audiences, responsive evaluators use issues rather than objectives or hypotheses as advance organizers. These issues or problems are identified by the evaluator after talking with students, teachers, parents, and administrators.

An evaluator using the responsive model arranges for various persons to observe the program. He or she then prepares brief narratives, portrayals, graph displays, or other types of information. The evaluator presents this information to determine what is of value to his or her audiences.

[31]Gene V. Glass, "The Growth of Evaluation Methodology" (mimeographed monograph available from the author, University of Colorado, Boulder, Colo.), p. 27.
[32]Robert Stake, "Responsive Evaluation," in Hamilton, et al., p. 163.

Hamilton described the procedure: "He gets program personnel to react to the accuracy of his portrayals. He gets authority figures to react to the importance of various findings. He gets audience members to react to the relevance of his findings."[33] According to Hamilton, "Stake sees the evaluator as processing judgments more than rendering them . . . refusing to set up the evaluator as a person uniquely qualified to offer criticism or endorsement."[34]

The reader should not view responsive evaluation as an amorphic activity. Stake proposed a specific model[35] to be used in the collection and analysis of information (see Figures 7.2 and 7.3).

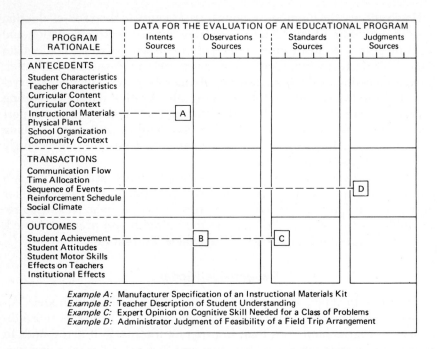

FIGURE 7.2   Stake's congruence-contingency model—data for evaluation.

From Robert E. Stake, "Language, Rationality and Assessment," in Walcott H. Beatty (ed.), *Improving Educational Assessment and an Inventory of Measures of Affective Behavior* (Washington, D.C.: Association for Supervision and Curriculum Development, 1969), p. 16.

[33]Stake, "Responsive Evaluation," p. 163.
[34]Hamilton, et al., p. 143.
[35]Robert E. Stake, "Language, Rationality, and Assessment," in Walcott H. Beatty (ed.), *Improving Educational Assessment and an Inventory of Measures of Affective Behavior* (Washington, D.C.: Association for Supervision and Curriculum Development, 1969). See also Robert E. Stake, "The Countenance of Educational Evaluation," *Teachers College Record, 68* (April 1967):523–540.

The rows in the first column of Figure 7.2 list categories of information or other data that an evaluator will need to collect: antecedents—"any condition existing prior to teaching and learning which may relate to outcomes"; transactions—"the countless encounters of students with teacher, student with student, author with reader, parent with counselor —the succession of engagements which comprise the process of education"; and outcomes—"abilities, achievements, attitudes, and aspirations of students resulting from an educational experience."

Data may be entered in each of the 12 cells for whatever items are under consideration in the antecedents, transactions, and outcomes. "Intents" are the "intended student outcomes," the goals and objectives; "observations" are the descriptive data—direct observations, test results, biographical data sheets, interviews, checklists, opinionnaires, follow-up reports, and the like. "Standards" are statements of what experts (teach-

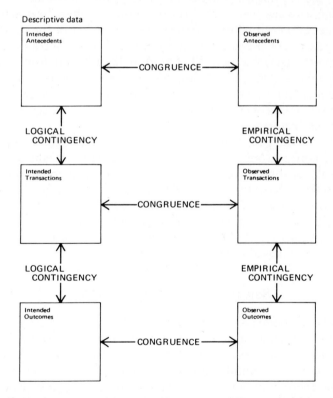

FIGURE 7.3   Stake's congruence-contingency model—processing of data.

From Robert E. Stake, "Language, Rationality and Assessment," in Walcott H. Beatty (ed.), *Improving Educational Assessment and an Inventory of Measures of Affective Behavior* (Washington, D.C.: Association for Supervision and Curriculum Development, 1969), p. 20.

ers, administrators, scholars, spokesmen for society, students themselves, and parents) believe should happen in the situation and, as Stake points out, what does happen in similar situations in other schools—"benchmarks of performance having widespread reference value." Stake insists that "standards vary from student to student, from instructor to instructor, and from reference group to reference group. . . . Part of the responsibility of evaluation is to make known which standards are held by whom."

The process of evaluation is depicted in Figure 7.3. This is a method of handling descriptive data, such as would be gathered for columns 1 and 2 of Figure 7.2. Congruence would be an identical match between what is intended and what is observed. Usually evaluation studies examine only the congruence between intended and observed outcomes, but Stake insists that one can judge the merits of a curriculum plan only if antecedents and transactions are also investigated. Congruence indicates only the degree of match, not the validity or value of the outcomes.

Contingencies are "relationships among the variables." An examination of contingencies is an effort to determine the "whys of the outcomes"— the particular set of antecedent conditions and the set of transactions that produce particular outcomes. What kinds of learning environments, what kinds of teaching methods and classroom procedures, what kinds of school arrangements and structures are causally related to the outcomes? These are the kinds of data or other information needed to make curriculum and instructional decisions.

Results of behavioral objectives evaluations or decision-making evaluations frequently go only to governmental authorities or educational managers; results of responsive evaluation go to the local community. House referred to Stake's evaluation as a democratic pluralism model. This presumes "a free market of ideas from which, ideally, consumers will select the best. Through a competition of ideas, truth will be strengthened and education improved."[36] Program planners committed to community involvement in education may find responsive evaluation a useful tool.

Selecting Models of Evaluation

A variety of models for evaluating curriculum plans have been presented. It is not necessary for curriculum planners to restrict themselves to one model; in fact they will probably use two or more models. For example, many curriculum planners will be in institutions that participate in periodic accreditation visits. Teachers may be using tests based on the behavioral objectives model and individual educational institutions may be using Stufflebeam's decision-making model to generate formative evaluation data.

[36]House, p. 11.

A coherent total plan for evaluation should be developed based on several considerations. One consideration is the type of curriculum designs and teaching models used. For example, the specific competencies/technology design and instructional systems teaching model are easily evaluated with a behavioral objective model.

Another consideration is the purpose of the evaluation. If the purpose is to measure the achievement of prestated objectives, the behavioral objective or decision-making models would be appropriate. However, if the purpose is to measure the total consequences of a program, Scriven's goal-free evaluation would be useful. If the purpose is to assist in program development, a model that incorporates formative evaluation, such as decision making or the responsive model, could be used.

Still another consideration is the audience to be served. The decision-making and behavioral objectives models serve bureaucratic needs of managers. Accreditation primarily serves professionals in the educational institution, while goal-free evaluation and responsive evaluation serve educational clients as well as practitioners.

Plans for curriculum evaluation should be comprehensive and multifaceted. Figure 7.4 illustrates the scope and nature of curriculum evaluation. It is an overview of the remainder of the chapter and will serve as a guide to the treatment of each part of the evaluation process. It comprehends both formative and summative types of evaluations and also Stake's concept of "preordinate" and "responsive" evaluations. As the figure shows, each aspect of evaluation is interrelated with other aspects; not only does the evaluator draw information and data obtained from other phases of the total program in making judgments about a particular segment, but that aspect contributes information and data in turn to other categories.

EVALUATION OF GOALS, SUBGOALS, AND OBJECTIVES

All plans for education—the total program, the curriculum, instruction, and evaluation—should be based on a definition of the purposes for which an educational institution is established. Hence, the first step in curriculum evaluation is determining whether these stated purposes are valid, appropriate, attainable, and acceptable. In terms of our discussion of purposes in Chapter 4, this means that the curriculum evaluator will provide information on the validity of the general goals, the subgoals, the curriculum domains, and instructional objectives.

Evaluation of General Goals

Stufflebeam emphasized the importance of evaluating general goals when he said, "We have to make sure that our goals are justified and

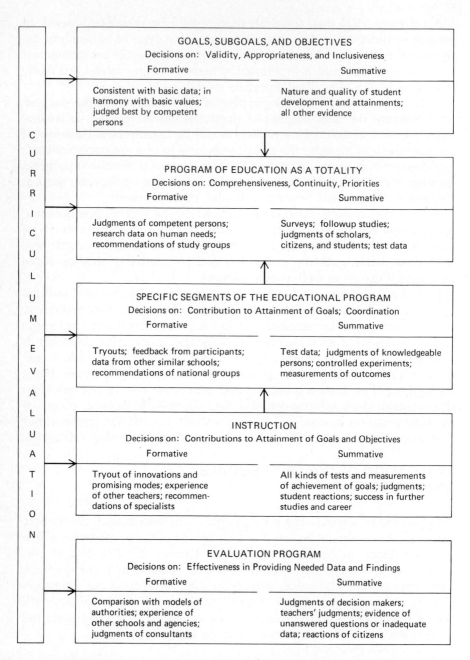

FIGURE 7.4 The scope and nature of curriculum evaluation

responsive to the needs of the people to be served."[37] Failure of educational institutions to conduct critical evaluations of their goals has resulted in a serious overloading of responsibilities. For example, schools have been mandated to take on more and more responsibilities. With no basis for evaluating the appropriateness of adding goals to an already crowded agenda, schools have been unable to refuse additional assignments. Evaluation of goals for any educational institution becomes particularly important in a learning society as described in Chapter 8. Within such a society goal determination involves two steps: first, determining the overall educational goals for citizens; second, determining goals for a specific educational institution within a network of learning systems. The goals adopted at both steps need to be evaluated.

How does one evaluate the purposes of an educational institution? At the outset, it should be recognized that this is an exceedingly difficult kind of evaluation to make. Evaluation of goals includes testing their consistency with basic data (see Figure 7.4). Stufflebeam recommended that data to be considered be collected "on a prospective, proactive basis. To me that means conducting an ongoing needs assessment of the people we are serving."[38] To be proactive, educational goals must grow out of expected changes—that is, they should be based on some image of the future. Thus educational goals need to be evaluated in relation to expected changes in society as well as existing cultural values and social forces within society.

Formative evaluation of general goals requires that competent persons judge the degree to which the goals are consistent with data and in harmony with basic values (Figure 7.4). The views of experts in social trends and students of cultural trends should be sought as well as judgments from competent people, including parents, citizens, students, and experts in the area of instruction. A further step, and a crucial one, in determining the validity of goals is to use the results of summative evaluations—the measurement of student outcomes—as feedback data. The evaluator analyzes the congruence, as Stake used that term, or discrepancies, as Provus states in his model, between outcomes and goals. Stake insists in all of his writings that antecedent conditions must be taken into account in any evaluation, and that especially would be true in evaluating goals. Subgoals and objectives also need to be evaluated as a part of summative evaluation.

Evaluation of Subgoals and Objectives

Formative evaluation of subgoals and objectives is important at the planning stage of curriculum development to assure that the subgoals and objectives will lead to the achievement of the general goals. The aim of evaluating objectives according to Lewy is to

---

[37]Ronald Brandt, "Our Evaluation: An Interview with Daniel L. Stufflebeam," *Educational Leadership, 35* (January 1978):250.
[38]Brandt, p. 250.

get some sort of agreement from others outside the curriculum team that the instructional objectives are:

1. Related to the objectives (and goals) of the program and likely to contribute cumulatively to the attainment of the program objectives.
2. Clearly stated.
3. Appropriate for, and attainable by, the pupils at the particular level of education and stage of mental development.
4. Important enough to encourage further learning by the pupils.[39]

Lewy proposed survey forms to be used to evaluate subgoals and objectives by individuals representing the following groups: subject specialists, curriculum specialists, educational psychologists, educational sociologists, teachers, and educational administrators.

The National Assessment of Educational Progress has prepared lengthy sets of what we designate as subgoals. They used the opinion and judgment of various groups of people in preparing and validating their lists. First, knowledgeable persons in a field prepared preliminary lists; these were then submitted to panels of interested persons—lay citizens, educators, and scholars—for review and revision. Later, in preparing for a second round of assessment, professional organizations of educators working in a field of study also participated in a revision of the goals.

The best test of the subgoals and objectives is to evaluate pupil achievement and other related pupil behavior after the curriculum plan has been implemented. These data will not be available to assist in the original planning but can be used in subsequent revisions. It is especially important when using summative evaluation to differentiate between "intended" treatment and "actual" treatment and take both into account in evaluation of objectives.

Taking these conditions into account, the evaluator—the planner would be involved here, too—must analyze congruency or discrepancy and recommend that either the program, the curriculum plan, or whatever is being evaluated be continued in its present form, which is tacit approval of the goals and objectives, that the goals be revised in light of these data, or that the program be revised so as to better serve the ends sought.

At this final stage of decision making the views and judgments of competent people should be obtained and they should assist in setting the criteria for judgment. Were the intended goals appropriate and sound or are changes desirable? Was what was actually done in seeking to achieve the goals a proper test of the goals? Thus goals are approved, at least for the time being, or revised.

Some help in assessing goals and objectives is currently available in the literature. Bloom, Hastings, and Madaus included a brief section in their

[39]Arieh Lewy, *Handbook of Curriculum Evaluation* (New York: Longman, Inc., 1977), p. 63.

handbook entitled "Evaluating Objectives."[40] It offers specific suggestions and cites two studies that attempted to make such appraisals. Stufflebeam and his committee included a short chapter on this matter.[41] Hulda Grobman, who was associated with the Biological Sciences Curriculum Study for some years, has provided two useful publications on curriculum evaluation.[42] In each book she described and discussed the formulation of goals and objectives from the standpoint of project development, but also gave some attention to their validation. A comprehensive treatment of assessing goals and objectives is provided in the UNESCO publication *Handbook of Curriculum Evaluation* edited by Arieh Lewy.

In summary, to evaluate a set of goals, subgoals, or objectives the evaluator subjects them logically to an examination of their appropriateness in light of all of the data that have been collected from primary sources; utilizes the opinions and recommendations of scholars, specialists in curriculum planning, teachers, parents, spokesmen for society at large, and students; makes a logical analysis of antecedent conditions that may affect the choice of goals; and then makes a judgment on the validity of the ends sought for a particular group of students in a particular situation. As summative evaluation of the program under consideration proceeds and moves to conclusions, congruences or discrepancies are analyzed, and in light of such evaluations the goals, subgoals, or objectives are reexamined.

In all candor, however, it must be acknowledged that a considerable degree of uncertainty exists in efforts to evaluate educational goals. The accumulation of many kinds of evidence, extending over years or decades, may be necessary before one may feel reasonably confident in the goals selected for educational institutions. Sociological, anthropological, historical, and comparative data among schools, states, and nations are essential sources in setting standards and making choices of goals. However, it is important to recognize the power of one's philosophical perspective in establishing the set of assumptions that operate in decision making even when common data are considered.

EVALUATION OF A TOTAL EDUCATIONAL PROGRAM

To evaluate a total educational program is to place a value judgment on all of the opportunities for educational engagements provided by a society for its citizens. This is a large undertaking since it requires finding satisfactory answers to the following questions:

[40]Bloom, Hastings, and Madaus, pp. 260–262.
[41]Stufflebeam, Chapter 4.
[42]Hulda Grobman, *Evaluation Activities of Curriculum Projects: A Starting Point*, AERA Monograph Series on Curriculum Evaluation, Robert E. Stake (ed.) (Chicago: Rand McNally & Company, 1968); and *Developmental Curriculum Projects: Decision Points and Processes* (Itasca, Ill.,: F. E. Peacock Publishers, Inc., 1970).

1. What does education intend to do? What knowledge will it transmit? What skills will it develop? What attitudes and values will it influence?
2. What are the results of education?
3. What values are assigned to these results?

The Macroeducational Level

Evaluation of a total educational program starts by looking at the big picture. Chapter 1 describes elements within society that provide education including: family, peer groups, formal educational institutions, community, and communication media. The influence of these elements varies over time. For example, in the last 20 years the communication media have become a powerful "alternative education."[43] Further, these elements interact in ways that either enhance or interfere with their individual and combined potency. The educational environment of the learner, Figure 7.5, is a static diagram of a highly complex and dynamic process.

Educational outcomes are much broader than academic achievement. Mushkin and Billings categorized outcomes as multidimensional and sequential. They are multidimensional since they relate to *personal development, quality of life,* and *societal development:* Objectives are sequential since there are *primary effects* in the course of education, *secondary*

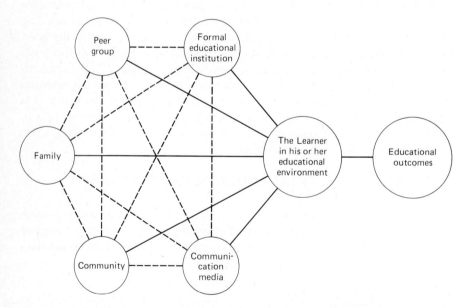

FIGURE 7.5 The educational environment of the learner.

[43]Clifton Fadiman, "Classroom's Rival: Pop Culture," *Gainesville Sun,* August 5, 1979, p. 5A.

effects, on completion of education, and *tertiary effects* that are intergenerational. Mushkin's and Billings's orientation as economists becomes apparent from their listing of educational outcomes in the dimension of societal development: primary effects (primary work skills); secondary effects (increased productivity, economic growth measured by employment and income, social and economic mobility); and tertiary effects (societal advance of children and migration patterns).[44] An examination of these educational outcomes, or any other list, demonstrates that the total environment of a learner influences his or her educational outcomes and reminds us of the futility of attempting to hold any one institution or element alone responsible for broad educational outcomes.

The Institutional Level of Education

Although it is difficult to trace educational outcomes back to specific institutions, evaluation of institutional programs is necessary if education is to be improved. However, to be effective, institutional evaluation should be conducted in the context of the total educational environment. A school system, composed of schools and various semiautonomous units, will be used to illustrate institutional evaluation. Similar principles may be adapted to other educational institutions such as religious groups.

The evaluation of a school system's complete program includes such things as: school offerings at each age level from prekindergarten children to senior citizens; provisions for out-of-school educational opportunities; special provisions for persons with exceptional needs; and opportunities provided outside the regular school-day program, such as summer programs, evening programs, camping, instruction by television and radio, and self-study programs. The programs of individual schools or school agencies also need to be evaluated. Suggestions for conducting these evaluations are offered later in this section.

Coordination between schools and community agencies should also be evaluated. The evaluating team should seek evidence regarding the relationship of various schools with other agencies of the community in planning and providing a total program of educational opportunities for the people of the community. One important item of this nature is the coordination and relations between schools and law-enforcement and correctional agencies, public welfare agencies, and health and mental health clinics.

Often it is difficult to obtain valid and reliable evidence that will be adequate for purposes of assessing a total educational program. But educators must make decisions based on such information, and thus it behooves professional evaluators to provide them with the best data possible. As in

[44]Selma J. Mushkin, Bradley R. Billings, *Types of Outcome Measurements* (Washington, D. C.: Public Services Laboratory, Georgetown University, 1975), p. 8.

the previous section, we will not provide a set of plans and procedures for making these kinds of evaluations, but rather will describe some methods now being used as well as consider problems and issues.

Professional Judgments

Evaluation of institutional educational programs is subjective, although it may be based on some empirical data. Procedures include securing judgments of educators both within and outside the institution. Other professionals, notably social scientists, can also make professional evaluative judgments.

ACCREDITATION.   The accreditation model, with all of its limitations, is discussed in an earlier portion of this chapter. As crude as accreditation may be in most instances, whether done under the auspices of a state department of education, a national or regional accrediting association, or a university, it nevertheless represents an effort to appraise the total program of an individual school or, in the instance of state accreditation, an entire school system. Actually, in many schools it is the only continuing effort to make at least some assessment of the total educational program. The accreditation reports made by the outside group have contributed to curriculum decision making and planning, often in a significant manner.

SURVEYS AND STUDIES.   Formal school surveys have long been used as a means of evaluating an educational program. Widely used in the 1920s and 1930s, their popularity has waned since World War II. Two significant ones conducted in the 1960s serve well as examples of this procedure for appraising a school program.[45] In some instances the studies have been state-wide, constituting an effort to appraise the educational program of a whole state without examining individual district and school programs.

Traditionally the school survey was as broad in scope as the present-day programs that use the "Evaluative Criteria," although it usually constituted a more intensive investigation of many aspects of the total program and used highly regarded specialists in curriculum and planning for each area of study in making judgments about the program. However, seldom were goals for a specific school situation stated, and the antecedent conditions or context input—essential ingredients in evaluation in the models cited—were largely ignored or scantily investigated.

SELF-STUDIES.   Faculty self-study of the educational program is required for most accreditation programs, but it is not limited to such programs. The use of self-study as part of the problem-solving approach to curriculum development is described in Chapter 3. One value of this

[45]A. Harry Passow, study director, *Toward Creating a Model Urban System: A Study of the Washington, D. C. Public Schools* (New York: Teachers College Press, 1967); Robert J. Havighurst, *The Public Schools of Chicago* (Chicago: Chicago Board of Education, 1964).

approach is that the findings from such evaluations may result in appropriate program changes. A systematic self-study program is being used in some New York City schools as well as in many smaller school districts.[46]

BEHAVIORAL SCIENCE STUDIES.   Behavioral science studies could be a valuable source of information for curriculum evaluation. Sociological and anthropological studies can be especially useful in understanding processes associated with curriculum development and instruction. One illustration is a social-psychological case study that focused on problems of educational change in one elementary school. The study produced considerable evaluative information.[47] Mehan provides another illustration. He used the term "constitutive ethnography" to refer to "studying the structuring activities that assemble the social structures of education."[48] Through "constitutive ethnography" it is possible to give attention to the processes of education as well as to the outcomes of structuring activities. Mehan concluded from reviewing several constitutive studies that "the organized character of interaction in school, does make a difference in educational outcomes."[49]

Citizen Judgments

Many school systems over the years have used citizens' studies to involve the people of the community and the members of the school staff in an assessment of the program of the schools. Staff members of colleges of education often serve as consultants or directors of these projects. A study guide or handbook for data collection is prepared. Opinion polls, follow-up studies, studies of community occupational patterns, and other data-collecting projects may be a part of the undertaking. Usually some publication is produced that reports the findings and recommendations of the group. State-wide study projects of this kind were carried on in years past in a number of states, including Texas, Florida, Georgia, Arkansas, and Kansas. State studies are usually directed more to planning the structure of schools, school financing, and the scope of a school program than evaluating the present program.

Task forces and study commissions have been used for many years as a method of appraising some specific aspect of the schools, such as finance, provisions for meeting the educational needs of particular groups of children and youth, governance, and the like, and recommending courses of action. Usually these commissions are concerned with schooling at the state or national level.

[46]Marc Bassin and Tom Gross, "Renewal: A Problem-Solving Model," *NASSP Bulletin* (May 1979), pp. 43–48.
[47]Louis M. Smith and Pat M. Keith, *Anatomy of Educational Innovation: An Organizational Analysis of An Elementary School* (New York: John Wiley and Sons, Inc., 1971).
[48]Hugh Mehan, "Structuring School Structure," *Harvard Educational Review, 49* (February 1978):32.
[49]Mehan, p. 61.

In some states, local citizen groups may make school studies. For example, in Florida, citizens' advisory councils are responsible for making an annual evaluative report to the community on each school. These reports often include the results of some type of community attitude survey.

The extent to which the public's expectations are satisfied is more important for a school's survival than its achievement. According to McNeil, "If teachers, parents, students, and community members are not satisfied that the school's program conforms to their definition of what education should be, then the school is in trouble, regardless of its success in affecting pupil achievement or socialization."[50]

The annual Gallup Poll on education provides a valuable source of information regarding the public's expectations and degree of satisfaction with its schools.[51] A publication providing suggestions for conducting local public opinion polls together with a summary of the Gallup Polls from 1969–1978 is available.[52]

Parents and students find ways to express dissatisfaction with schools. Withdrawal of students from school is one way parents signal a discrepancy between their expectations and their assessment of a school's accomplishments. High absentee records, drop-out rates, and school violence and vandalism reflect, in part, students' dissatisfaction with schools. Curriculum evaluators should pay attention to these "unobtrusive," but sometimes very painful, indicators of school quality.

Outcome Measures

Outcome measures provide summative evaluation data for total educational programs. The difficulty of relating educational outcomes to a particular educational institution's influence has been emphasized. Madaus and colleagues demonstrated the fallacy of comparing schools on the basis of standardized test scores,[53] a particularly pernicious practice when newspapers publish standardized test scores for each local school. Madaus and colleagues argued that school effectiveness should be measured by assessing student performance through tests that relate to information and skills covered in a specific course. This approach is used in the South American country of Paraguay. Each class is evaluated by a test constructed by the teacher and two representatives assigned by the Ministry of Education. The test is to measure the content of the course with the

[50]John D. McNeil, "Curriculum—A Field Shaped by Different Forces," *Educational Researcher, 7* (September 1978):21.

[51]George H. Gallup, "The Twelfth Annual Gallup Poll of the Public's Attitudes Toward the Public Schools" *Phi Delta Kappan, 62* (September 1980).

[52]Stanley M. Elam (ed.), *A Decade of Gallup Polls of Attitudes Toward Education: 1969–1978* (Bloomington, Ind., Phi Delta Kappa, 1979).

[53]George F. Madaus, Thomas Kellaghan, Ernest A. Rakow, and Dennis J. King, "The Sensitivity of Measures of School Effectiveness," *Harvard Educational Review, 49* (May 1979): 207–230.

proviso that 75 percent of the specified curriculum be covered in the test. The panel of three professionals administer the test and grade it the same day.

Outcome measures to be used as summative evaluation of a total educational program should not be restricted to tests. For example, follow-up studies of former students provide useful information for evaluating programs.

Implications for Curriculum Planners

Perhaps the types of information collected from professionals and non-professionals through surveys, studies, investigations, and appraisals would not be acknowledged by professional evaluators as full-fledged evaluations; however, such groups are recommending that evaluative decisions be made and that specific steps be taken to improve programs. If not acknowledged as true evaluation studies, they are certainly aspects of such a study, usually contributing significant data and judgments for a more inclusive program of evaluation. The principal questions from an evaluator's standpoint are these: Have the values, assumptions, and points of view about schooling of the members of the study group been identified? If so, or as implied from the report, are they valid in the judgment of other competent persons? What standards for judging quality were used or implied? Are they valid? Were valid and appropriate data obtained? To what kinds of systematic treatments have the data and the observations been subjected? And what evidence is there that the committee was competent to judge the quality of the program(s) under examination?

Too often in recent years decisions on the need for and effectiveness of existing programs have not utilized research and the writings of scholars on the nature of human growth and development and on the role of the schools in guiding the process. This is especially seen in some of the evaluations made of Head Start and other provisions for early schooling, day-care centers, nursery school programs for ameliorating the effects of deprivation and being disadvantaged, and, in fact, many phases of schooling.

In establishing standards for judging a community's provisions for schooling, the most authoritative works and research on the whole matter of human growth and development from birth to death should be fully utilized. Knowledge in these areas is accumulating rapidly, and anyone who evaluates programs or makes decisions concerning education should turn to such sources for the judgments of experts. The references cited in Chapter 3 may be useful.

In the next section the evaluation of specific aspects or segments of the curriculum will be treated; obviously, such program evaluations contribute fully and are necessary to the process of assessing the total educational program of an institution. Figure 7.4 (p. 334) portrays this relation. Formative evaluation of an educational program makes use of the findings from the same basic data that are gathered as a part of the planning process itself, but in addition data and recommendations from other competent sources are used. In summative evaluation additional data are collected from a number of sources, as shown in the figure, which, in turn, make use of data available from the evaluation of instruction.

EVALUATING SPECIFIC ASPECTS OF THE CURRICULUM

The ongoing, continuing evaluation of the numerous segments of the curriculum of an educational institution is one of the major responsibilities of the evaluator. Such evaluations are essential in the process of planning. Actually, the curriculum planner and the curriculum evaluator should work closely together in the development and improvement of the educational program; in many situations the same person may serve in both capacities. Formative evaluation is particularly valuable for program development.

Although a part of program evaluation, evaluation of the numerous aspects or segments of curriculum is a major undertaking, broad in scope and encompassing the many kinds of learning opportunities provided by the educational setting. Thus evaluation of the curriculum as a plan for providing sets of learning opportunities must include evaluation of the plan for organizing curriculum domains, the design or designs of the curriculum for each domain, courses offered, other kinds or sets of learning opportunities provided, extrainstructional activities sponsored, services provided students, and the kinds of informal relations that characterize the institutional climate. The five evaluation models presented earlier in this chapter may be fully used in the various aspects of curriculum evaluation.

Glass posed the all-important question in program evaluation: "Does the program under observation have greater value than its competitors or sufficient value of itself that it should be maintained?"[54] To answer this question it is necessary to determine what changes a program has produced. These changes range far beyond the achievement of goals to include attitudes, interests, career goals, and general understandings.

Steps in Evaluating Segments of the Curriculum

Evaluations of a unitary segment of the curriculum, or program, are based on the set of subgoals formulated within the general goals that apply to the program. A first step, therefore, is to list these subgoals—which should have already been validated. However, as Scriven points out in his

[54]Glass, p. 32.

plea for goal-free evaluation, an evaluator must look at the actual effects of a program of instruction, including the intended outcomes as stated in the goals or objectives, and also "side effects"—outcomes in addition to or in place of those anticipated in planning the program. To judge the merits of a product or effects of a program, an evaluator does not discard goals, but rather establishes standards for outcomes that should result from such instruction, product, or program that are free of the restricting influence of the predetermined goals, so that actual outcomes are judged as to validity, appropriateness, and essentiality.

Thus, while summative evaluation of the curriculum necessarily includes conclusions on the extent to which students attained the goals established for a course, segment, or set of opportunities, it should also include "goal-free evaluation." That is, it should seek to determine to what extent a particular segment of the curriculum is contributing to the education of a particular group of students. On the basis of such findings by the evaluation, the curriculum planner has data to aid in deciding, for example, whether a course in Latin is a better choice for a particular group of students at a particular point in their schooling than, say, a course in French, auto mechanics, or American Indian culture. Or as an alternative question, does the segment serve the educational needs of a group of students sufficiently to be included in the curriculum? Thus the evaluator contributes to determining priorities, developing cost analyses, and introducing accountability.

The second aspect of program evaluation is the determination of what Stake calls antecedents and what Stufflebeam and his associates label context input. Evaluators will need to have information regarding such items as: student characteristics, teacher characteristics, school organization, community values and needs, and a description of how the program relates to the total curriculum.

The third responsibility in curriculum evaluation is to determine standards by which outcomes will be judged in terms of what is good, what is acceptable, and what expectations are reasonable in a given situation. This is a difficult matter to decide, and none of the authorities cited previously offer much help. Certainly, standardized test results are no help, for they simply compare groups and do not offer evidence on what is desirable. Similarly, the National Assessment of Educational Progress simply reports percentages of students who choose each alternative answer to a test item. It is suggested evaluators may rely heavily on the opinions of scholars or experts in the field when setting the standards for knowledge and understandings of a subject area or field in which cognitive outcomes predominate. Similarly psychologists, sociologists, psychiatrists, and mental health experts may contribute in affective aspects of learning outcomes. Highly competent teachers certainly can assist in setting standards, as well as interested citizens. If comparative data from other educational settings are used, the evaluator must take full account of differences in antecedent conditions as well as the contingencies, or context conditions of which Stufflebeam and his coworkers wrote.

Minimum competency testing is viewed by some as a way to establish standards. The difficulties of using these tests to establish appropriate standards are discussed in Chapter 4. Standards set low enough to allow nearly all students to pass are criticized by the public; if they are set to provide some challenge to average students, many students are destined to fail.[55]

The fourth step is the collection of data on the outcomes of the program. Data obtained in the evaluation of instruction, considered in the next section, are, of course, essential for program evaluation. In fact, evaluation of the curriculum or any segment of it and evaluation of instruction are parts of the same undertaking. Methods of data collection should extend beyond examining student performance and attainment to include attitude measures, systematic observations, and follow-up studies of individuals who have been in the program. Miller proposed a number of unobtrusive measures that could be used for looking at total consequences of a program. These measures vary from determining the "number of situations in which students are evaluating their own progress with teacher assistance" and "percentage of students who are tardy each day"; to "number of teachers who are making positive remarks about students in the staff lounge."[56] A comparison of the recommended content of the program and the actual content used by the teacher is useful in interpreting the other data collected. The comparison may also be used to infer teacher views of the validity and usefulness of the program.

A fifth step is to make a technical analysis[57] of the program by answering such questions as:

1. Is the content related to the objectives?
2. Is the content valid and reliable?
3. Is the content relevant to the students?
4. Is there a logical organization of the program?
5. Do the learning tasks reflect a hierarchical structure and sequence?
6. Will the program develop understanding and critical thinking?
7. Is a multisensory approach used?
8. Does the program have transfer value?
9. How does the course relate to preceding courses?

[55]For a useful discussion of this point see Harry M. Brickell, "Seven Key Notes on Minimum Competency Testing," in Barbara Soloth Miller (ed.), *Minimum Competency Testing* (St. Louis, Mo.: CEMREL, Inc., 1978), pp. 46–58; Robert Frahm and Jimmie Covington, *What's Happening in Minimum Competency Testing* (Bloomington, Ind., Phi Delta Kappa, 1979).
[56]William C. Miller, "Unobtrusive Measures Can Help in Assessing Growth," *Educational Leadership, 35* (January 1978):264–269.
[57]For a useful discussion of technical analysis see Lewy, pp. 62–83.

Additional questions might be asked concerning such noninstructional considerations as cost, adaptability, and ease of use. Lewy proposed that answers to the various questions posed might be sought from subject matter experts, curriculum specialists, experienced teachers, and educational psychologists. A few of the characteristics could be evaluated by older students, for example, Is the content relevant to the students?

Another important aspect of the curriculum which should be included as a part of the technical analysis is the organization or design of the curriculum or of any segment of it. Usually attention is primarily directed to the organization of a domain, since, as was discussed in Chapter 5, the domains constitute the basis for organizing the school program. In addition, the organization of individual courses and other kinds of instructional segments should be scrutinized. The question to be faced in the evaluation of design is whether the design used for carrying on instruction contributed in and of itself to the realization of goals and the attainment of outcomes desired or whether it deterred or militated against effective goal attainment.

A final step in curriculum evaluation is for the evaluators and curriculum planners to make judgments based on all the data collected. The congruence between the outcomes produced by the program or segment of the curriculum and the intended outcomes will be tested. At the same time, evaluators will be alert to any outcomes identified by the evaluation, whether or not they were intended. The strength and weaknesses of the program as revealed through the technical analysis will be considered as evaluators decide whether to continue, modify, or abandon the program.

The designation of "steps" in evaluation suggests a sequential procedure that belies good practice. At any point in the evaluation it may be desirable to reconsider a procedure that has already been followed. For example, as a decision is being made regarding the future of the program, it may be desirable to seek further data.

The value and importance of formative evaluation becomes apparent. How much more effective it is to evaluate the program as it is being developed rather than to wait until it is in use to discover shortcomings. For example, it is not necessary to wait until a program has been used before it can be determined that the contents are neither valid nor reliable.

Examples of Program Evaluation

A valuable collection of excerpts from curriculum evaluation reports is included in the book by Hamilton and colleagues.[58] These illustrative evaluations include both formative and summative evaluations and utilize

[58]Hamilton, et al., pp. 229–355.

several of the models portrayed in Table 7.1 (p. 321). Programs evaluated include: a junior high school, a program for talented youth, Metro High School (Chicago), and the use of the PLATO computer system in a community college.

An evaluation of an upper elementary social studies program, *Man: A Course of Study,* was reported by Cort.[59] This evaluation considered input variables—students, teachers, and classrooms; process variables—activities, emphases, and procedural characteristics of classes; classroom climate; and outcomes. The evaluation "provided an opportunity to examine some relationships between students' perceptions of the social studies program, on the one hand, and measures of outcomes (achievement and attitude), on the other."[60]

A widely publicized evaluation of the federal Head Start, Follow Through program by Abt Associates has stirred considerable controversy and has impacted federal policy. House and three colleagues conducted an independent critique of the evaluation.[61] The Abt Associates evaluation compared the effects of 13 different Follow Through models. Each model had its own set of goals. House and his colleagues described the instruments used and raised the question: "How well and how fairly do these instruments measure the outcome domains indicated by the sponsors? Does the one viable instrument, the MAT (Metropolitian Achievement Test), adequately cover the outcomes of all the models?"[62] They concluded that "the classification of models and outcomes and the selection of measures favor models that emphasize rote learning of the mechanics of reading, writing, and arithmetic."[63]

The study just cited illustrates the problem, all too common, of a mismatch between the goals of a program and the evaluation instruments used. By way of contrast, the Ypsilanti (Michigan) Perry program for academically high-risk preschool-age children used several measurement instruments geared to the goals of the project.[64] Seven instruments were

[59]H. Russel Cort, Jr., "A Social Studies Evaluation," in Herbert J. Walberg (ed.), *Educational Environments and Effects* (Berkeley, Calif.: McCutchan Publishing Corp. .979), pp. 235–257.

[60]Cort, p. 235.

[61]Ernest R. House, Gene V. Glass, Leslie D. McLean, Decker F. Walker, "No Simple Answer: Critique of the Follow Through Evaluation," *Harvard Educational Review,* 48 (May 1978): 128–159. For responses to the critique see Richard B. Anderson, Robert G. St. Pierre, Elizabeth C. Proper, and Linda B. Stebbins, "Pardon Us, but What Was That Question Again?" A Response to the Critique of the Follow Through Evaluation, *Harvard Educational Review,* 48 (May 1978):161–170; Carl E. Wisler, Gerald P. Burns, Jr., and David Iwamoto, "Follow Through Redux: A Response to the Critique by House, Glass, McLean, and Walker," *Harvard Educational Review,* 48 (May 1978):171–185.

[62]House, et al., p. 142.

[63]House, et al., p. 145.

[64]D. P. Weikart, J. T. Bond, J. T. McNeil, *The Ypsilanti Perry Preschool Project* (Ypsilanti, Mich.: High Scope Educational Research Foundation, 1978).

used as indicators of academic aptitude and achievement, two instruments were used to assess children's social and emotional development, and two instruments were used to obtain information about the home environments of children. The evaluation study included the use of a control group.

Another feature of the Ypsilanti Perry evaluation program is that longitudinal data have been collected. A report released in 1978 included children who started in the preschool program and had completed fourth grade. The following findings were reported:

1. Children who attended preschool scored significantly and substantially higher than control-group children on standardized aptitude tests administered in the spring of their first and second preschool years.
2. On aptitude measures the magnitude of differences tended to decrease once treatment terminated and all children entered elementary school.
3. On achievement measures the magnitude of differences (in favor of the experimental group) tended to increase as the children experienced elementary education.
4. Children who attended preschool achieved significantly greater school success, that is, they were less likely to be retained in grade or placed in special education programs than control-group children.
5. Preliminary analyses of achievement test data obtained at eighth grade . . . indicate that the difference between the experimental and control groups continued to increase.[65]

Since the children were academically high risk their achievement levels were in general well below community and national norms. As the researchers said, "to conclude that experimental-group children were better able to cope with elementary school as a result of preschool is not to suggest that they flourished in that environment."[66]

An economic analysis was another feature of the evaluation of the Ypsilanti Perry Preschool Project.[67] The analysis showed three types of benefits:

1. Savings resulted because students who had preschool education required less costly forms of education as they progressed through school than comparable students who did not have preschool—they required less special education and no institutionalized care.
2. Students who had preschool education had higher projected lifetime earnings than students who did not have preschool education.
3. The parent's time released as a result of the child attending preschool has a value.[68]

[65]Weikart, et al., pp. 37–88 passim.
[66]Weikart, et al., p. 88.
[67]C. U. Weber, P. W. Foster, D. P. Weikart, *An Economic Analysis of the Ypsilanti Perry Preschool Project* (Ypsilanti, Mich.: High Scope Educational Research Foundation, 1978).
[68]Weber, et al., p. x.

The authors concluded from their economic analysis that "society could have borrowed money at 9.5 percent interest to finance the cost of the project, and would have been able to pay off both interest and the cost of the project from the benefits of the project during its life."[69] We recognize that the technical resources of High/Scope as a research organization exceed that of typical educational institutions. Nevertheless, it is instructive to see the type of program evaluation that is conducted under optimum conditions.

EVALUATING INSTRUCTION

If the "proof of the pudding is in the eating," then the ultimate test of a curriculum plan is in its implementation. Thus evaluation of instruction is a type of summative evaluation for a curriculum plan. In addition instruction as implementation of the curriculum must be evaluated in its own right, so that teachers and other decision makers may make the best choices of instructional objectives, modes, and content; teaching methods; and methods for evaluating outcomes.

The evaluation of instruction is also used for rating teachers, holding teachers accountable, and as a basis for helping teachers to improve. Although these purposes are not discussed in this section, some of the material presented may be useful for these other purposes. Because of its potential impact on curriculum, accountability is discussed in a separate section of this chapter.

Four of the five evaluation models described in this chapter (see Table 7.1, p. 321) can be used for instructional evaluation: behavioral objectives, decision making, goal-free, and responsive. Aspects of the responsive model are used in this section because it is oriented to program activities and responds to audience requirements for information. The section is organized around the data collection categories proposed by Stake (Figure 7.2, p. 330): antecedents, transactions, and outcomes.

Antecedents

The total educational environment of the learners needs to be considered in evaluating instruction. Environmental forces external to the school[70] —families, peer groups, other educational agencies, and communication media—have an impact on learners and their instruction (see Figure 7.5, p. 338). The school environment, including the organization of the school, support systems for students and teachers, and available materials, also influence instructional programs.

The curriculum plan is an important antecedent to instruction. A cur-

---

[69]Weber, et al., p. x.
[70]For an excellent analysis of these environments see Walberg (ed.), pp. 15–76.

riculum guide may list a number of objectives that sample the possibilities inherent in an instructional unit, leaving it to the teacher to further develop the list. A few more general objectives, comparable to subgoals, may be stated, or only subgoals for the entire course or unitary set of learning opportunities may be defined, leaving entirely to the teacher(s) the responsibility of formulating instructional objectives.

Thus, the evaluator often must take steps to have the teacher or director of an activity or service set down the intended outcomes; in some instances he may have to deduce them entirely from observing instruction or conferring with the teacher. Regardless, the evaluator must have a set of objectives or intended outcomes before he can complete the appraisal. This is not to repudiate goal-free evaluation, which was discussed previously, but rather to state that in the evaluation of instruction it is necessary to be fair to the teacher by taking account of his or her objectives.

The curriculum design to be followed, which may or may not be specified by the curriculum guide, is an antecedent. For example, procedures for evalating a specific competencies/technology-designed curriculum may be inappropriate for evaluating a social functions/activities-designed curriculum.

Of primary importance among the antecedents are the characteristics of the students in the institutional program. These data (the same kinds as described in Chapter 3) are essential for judging intended and actual outcomes, as well as for setting standards by which to judge the quality and appropriateness of instruction. Moreover, the data ought to be obtained personally from each student. This is a tremendous undertaking, as noted previously, but evaluation is inadequate, perhaps misleading, and seriously deficient as a basis for decision making and planning unless these characteristics are taken into account.

The kinds of student data of special importance in evaluating instruction include:

1. The capabilities, talents, and aptitudes of each student.
2. Appropriate aspects of the developmental status of each student at the time of the initiation of the segment of instruction being evaluated, particularly knowledge acquired, cognitive development, skills, attitudes, and ability to be self-directive and to direct and carry on his own learning activities.
3. Any evidence readily obtainable on learning styles, learning difficulties, and special learning aptitudes.
4. Nature and character of motivation for participating in the instruction, including personal interest, career plans, and supportive nature of the family and environmental situation.

The difficulty of obtaining reliable and useful data of these sorts is readily acknowledged; but school psychologists and highly trained evaluators are increasingly developing means of studying children and youth. Teachers themselves often have or can develop a considerable degree of competence in analyzing traits and characteristics of these kinds.

Characteristics of the teacher are another antecedent to be considered in evaluating instruction. How experienced is the teacher? Has the teacher used this curriculum plan previously? Does the teacher treat the curriculum plan as a recipe book? As a source of ideas? or As one more report filed in the bottom desk drawer? Does the teacher seek assistance in implementing the curriculum plan? And if he or she seeks help, is it forthcoming?

Transactions

A major aspect of instructional evaluation is concerned with the interactive process in the classroom. Stake labels this aspect of instruction as transactions and Stufflebeam and his committee as process evaluation (although both of these terms include additional matters). That such data are essential for instructional evaluation is, of course, recognized by all of the specialists in the new approaches to evaluation. Not only do data on classroom interactions enable the evaluator to make judgments about the classroom conditions under which the student outcomes were achieved and what these augur for decision making, but the interactive process itself is a major contributor to the achievement of many important instructional objectives. Hence, evaluating student outcomes must be done in the context of these classroom (broadly understood as the locale of instruction) transactions.

The teaching model selected by the teacher influences the nature of the classroom interactions. For example, consider the contrasting roles of teachers using a lecture model and an inquiry model. Teacher and student interactions appropriate in one model may be inappropriate in another.

Systems for analyzing and classifying the interactive process in classrooms have been described in recent professional literature.[71] The schemes most extensively used are the Flanders-Amidon, Bellack, and the Smith-Meux, although more recent versions of the Flanders method and

[71]For an exhaustive and exceedingly helpful description and analysis of systems and techniques see Barak Rosenshine and Norma Furst, "The Use of Direct Observation to Study Teaching," and Ira J. Gordon and R. Emile Jester, "Techniques of Observing Teaching in Early Childhood and Outcomes of Particular Procedures," in Robert M. W. Travers (ed.), *Second Handbook of Research on Teaching* (Chicago: Rand McNally & Company, 1973), pp. 122–183, 184–217. For descriptions of studies utilizing classroom observation techniques see Rudolph H. Moos, "A Typology of Junior High and High School Classrooms," *American Educational Research Journal, 15* (Winter 1978):53–66; Robert S. Soar, Ruth M. Soar, "Emotional Climate and Management," in Penelope L. Peterson and Herbert J. Walberg (eds.), *Research of Teaching: Concepts, Findings, and Implications* (Berkeley, Calif.: McCutchan Publishing Corp., 1979), pp. 97–119.

other approaches may be more appropriate. The use of videotaping machines greatly facilitates the gathering of such data. Much use is also made of the students' own reactions to the instructional process in a specific class. This form of data collecting has been widely used at the college level, and it certainly has value at the common school level, probably as early as the middle school. Reaction sheets, rating scales, and opinion polls are used to gather such data, but conferences and interviews are also useful. Parents' reactions are also used, especially those obtained by a neutral party.

Two aspects of classroom interaction are of particular importance in evaluating instruction as a part of a curriculum evaluation, use of time and social climate in the classroom. The amount of time a learner is actively engaged in direct academic instruction has been the subject of several studies. Rosenshine concluded after reviewing a number of these studies that "the educational implications of the results on content covered and time spent are that what is taught and how long it is taught are at least as powerful as how something is taught."[72] Corno pointed out that measures of engaged time are quantitative. "The crucial factors are the cognitive, behavioral, and organizational processes that *fill* that time, and the meaning those processes have for educational goals of high priority."[73] Thus the importance of "time on task" depends upon the relevance of the task. It follows that the curriculum cannot be evaluated by the achievement of students who have not spent "time on task" with learning experiences related to the curriculum.

Soar and Soar's work in assessing emotional climate was cited in Chapter 6. They studied selected classrooms in 156 elementary schools using six different observation instruments. They concluded from their studies, "For emotional climate, the conception of good teaching that emerges from this synthesis of results is that the avoidance of negative affect is important to pupil gain, but the expression of positive affect is not related." Since student achievement in classrooms with strong negative affect may be skewed it might be suspect as a basis for evaluating the curriculum. Another finding by Soar and Soar is pertinent to curriculum planners, "With respect to teacher management, rather than advocating freedom in all areas, as some educational theories seem to do, the results suggest that each area should be considered separately."[74]

Underlying patterns of social environment in junior and senior high

[72]Barak Rosenshine, "Classroom Instruction," in N. L. Gage (ed.), *The Psychology of Teaching Methods,* Seventy-fifth Yearbook, National Society for the Study of Education (Chicago: University of Chicago Press, 1976), p. 352.
[73]Lyn Corno, "Classroom Instruction and the Matter of Time," in Daniel L. Duke (ed.), *Classroom Management.* Seventy-eighth Yearbook, National Society for the Study of Education (Chicago: University of Chicago Press, 1979), pp. 267–268.
[74]Soar and Soar, p. 117.

school classrooms, as identified by Moos, include: involvement, affiliation, teacher support, task orientation, competition, order and organization, rule clarity, teacher control, and innovation.[75] Moos described procedures for observing these patterns of social environments and concluded after reviewing studies of these environments: "Students express greater satisfaction in classrooms characterized by high student involvement, by a personal student-teacher relationship, by innovative teaching methods, and by clarity of rules."[76] A knowledge of social interaction patterns in classrooms utilizing a curriculum plan assists the evaluator in weighing the outcomes of the plan. It is particularly important to consider any impact that the curriculum plan may be having on the social environment of the classroom.

The educational connoisseur skilled in the art of observing classroom living and writing criticism can provide valuable insights regarding the effect of a curriculum plan on the classroom environment.[77] The credence given to these insights depends upon the quality of the criticism and its acceptance by curriculum planners. Eisner pointed out, "In the world of the arts, critics have established themselves as inhabitants; art critics and art criticism are expected. Will teachers, school administrators, parents, educational theoreticians, and educational researchers accept educational criticism and educational critics?"[78] The danger is that a commitment to scientific objectivity will blind professionals to the value of qualitative judgments by critics who are connoisseurs of good teaching.

Outcomes

As professional evaluators of today point out, measuring student outcomes is about the only kind of formal instructional evaluation that was done in years past. It was the process of endless testing. Yet any plan for instructional evaluation even in the most up-to-date models relies extensively on formal test and measurement techniques. The difference between the two approaches lies in the very limited nature of the total plan of evaluation and the kinds of data collected in the traditional procedures contrasted to the plans for instructional evaluation recommended today. What also set present-day approaches apart are the scope and nature of the measurements used and the methods for treating and analyzing the data as a part of the total evaluation process. Four types of outcomes need to be considered in curriculum evaluation: achievement of students, attitudes of students, effects on teachers, and effects on community.

[75]Rudolf H. Moos, "Educational Climates," in Walberg (ed.), pp. 79–100.
[76]Moos, p. 90.
[77]For a discussion of this type of evaluation see Eisner pp. 345–358; Lewis and Miel, pp. 226–238.
[78]Eisner, p. 357.

Achievement of Students

A plethora of books, research reports, brochures, and articles on testing and measuring student achievement have been written, and the tests and other devices used to measure outcomes fill many file drawers. Hence, we will not here consider at length the whole field of testing, measurement, statistical analysis, and methods of appraising the achievement of individual students.[79] Rather, we will examine some problems and issues concerning their use.

Two relatively recent developments are of particular interest to curriculum planners and evaluators: the minimum competency testing movement and criterion-referenced testing. The minimum competency testing movement is discussed in detail in Chapter 4, "Defining Goals and Objectives." The placement in that chapter reflects our view that minimum competency testing has become a way to define goals and objectives rather than to evaluate their achievement.

Criterion-referenced tests are "used to ascertain an individual's status with respect to a well-defined behavioral domain."[80] Such tests enable a tester to determine whether or not specific objectives have been attained. Criterion-referenced tests are especially useful with the specific competencies/technology curriculum design (see Chapter 5) and are used extensively with the instructional system design model of teaching (see Chapter 6).

Criterion-referenced tests are often compared with the traditional norm-referenced tests that provide a comparison of the examinee's general level of achievement in some area of learning with the achievement within a norm group. Ebel made a number of distinctions between norm-referenced tests and criterion-referenced tests.[81] Norm-referenced tests indicate a wide range of achievement levels from excellence to serious deficiency. Criterion-referenced tests set a single standard for all—a pupil either meets it or fails. While criterion-referenced tests are more useful in formative evaluations, norm-referenced tests are more useful in summative evaluations.

The most important distinction, according to Ebel, is the conception of learning implied by the two tests.

If the primary goals of learning are to acquire a series of essential abilities, distinct enough from each other, few enough in number, and important

---

[79]A useful source book on measuring student achievement is Scarvia B. Anderson, Samuel Ball, Richard Murphy and Associates, *Encyclopedia of Educational Evaluation* 3d ed. (San Francisco, Calif.: Jossey-Bass, Inc., Publishers, 1977).
[80]W. James Popham, "The Case for Criterion-Referenced Measurements," *Educational Researcher,* 7 (December 1978):6.
[81]Robert L. Ebel, "The Case for Norm-Referenced Measurements," *Educational Researcher,* 7 (December 1978):3–5.

enough individually to be specified separately, studied separately, and measured separately, then a criterion-referenced test is clearly the test that ought to be used.

Ebel drew a sharp distinction in conceptions of learning when he said,

> But if the substance of learning is an infinity of particulars, too numerous to be specified separately, too interdependent to be studied or mastered separately; if the goal of learning lies beyond acquisition to understanding; and if understanding results from coming to know the multitude of relationships among these particulars, then a test that probes for these relationships at as many different points and from as many different angles as possible is the kind of test that ought to be used. Such a test is now commonly referred to as a norm-referenced test.[82]

Critics of norm-referenced tests would argue that Ebel has matched an unnecessary restriction of criterion-referenced tests with an unwarranted promise of norm-referenced tests. Popham, for example, asserted that "for purposes of instruction or evaluation, norm-referenced achievement tests are essentially worthless."[83] Popham's assertion may apply if the curriculum is restricted to a specific competencies/technology design. However, when other designs are used, such as subject matter/disciplines or social functions/activities, norm-referenced tests are more useful for summative evaluation. Curriculum planners and evaluators should not foreclose their options by restricting themselves to either criterion-referenced or norm-referenced tests.

One problem in assessing student achievement is the extreme difficulty, if not the impossibility, of measuring quantitatively through tests and other instruments many of the most significant outcomes desired, sought, and achieved. The authors of the Rand report, in summarizing their exhaustive analysis of research on school effectiveness, stated the situation:

> First, the data used by researchers are, at best, crude measures of what is really happening. Education is an extremely subtle phenomenon. Researchers in education are plagued by the virtual impossibility of measuring those aspects of education they wish to study. For example, a student's cognitive achievement is typically measured by his score on a standardized achievement test, despite the many serious problems involved in interpreting such scores.

But this is only part of the indictment:

> Second, educational outcomes are almost exclusively measured by cognitive achievement. Although no one would deny that non-cognitive outcomes and social outcomes beyond the individual student level are of major importance,

[82]Ebel, p. 4.
[83]Popham, p. 6.

research efforts that focus on these outcomes are sparse and largely inconclusive and offer little guidance with respect to what is effective.[84]

Many test-construction specialists, researchers, and staff members of test bureaus and colleges of education have endeavored to develop reliable and valid tests. Not only do these tests measure the higher levels of the cognitive processes, such as application, analysis, synthesis, and evaluation (so often neglected or minimized in the usual achievement tests used by schools) but they measure the development of the affective domain as well.[85] Nevertheless, such efforts, as the Rand people stated, still do not cover some of the most important aspects of schooling, and far too many schools simply do not use the instruments that are available. Equally serious is the fact that most parents have little interest in measures of student achievement except those that produce comparative norms or percentile scores denoting the extent to which factual knowledge and communicative and computational skills have been acquired.

In addition to tests, many other methods may be used to gather information about student outcomes. Admittedly, the evaluator faces a much more difficult problem in obtaining reliable data from these methods, although in many instances the data may be more valid; moreover, the analysis and treatment of the data presents even greater hurdles. As Combs insisted, however, judgmental and other methods of assessment must be used: "Judgment frees us to go beyond mere observation. To reject it as a tool for assessment is to limit ourselves to the least important aspects of our educational efforts and so to assure the increasing irrelevance of a system already desperately ill of that disease."[86]

Attitude of Students

Important outcomes of an instructional program and the curriculum plan it represents extend beyond student achievement to include student attitudes and interests. Moos stated, "Several investigators have recently emphasized the importance of focusing on educational outcomes . . . such as cognitive preferences, satisfaction with school, and continuing interest and motivation to learn."[87] These outcomes can be studied.

Cognitive preference tests, instead of measuring the information a student has absorbed, measure what the student does with the information. Tamir reviewed research on cognitive preferences, described an instru-

[84]Harvey A. Averch and others, *How Effective Is Schooling? A Critical Review and Synthesis of Research Findings,* Final Report to the President's Commission on School Finance (Santa Monica, Calif.: The Rand Corporation, December 1971), available from the Government Printing Office, Washington, D.C., Catalog No. Pr. 37 Sch6/2, p. ix.
[85]The authoritative handbook edited by Oscar K. Buros, *The Mental Measurements Yearbook* (Highland Park, N.J.: Gryphon Press, periodic editions), is an essential tool for any evaluator.
[86]Arthur W. Combs, *Educational Accountability: Beyond Behavioral Objectives* (Washington, D.C.: Association for Supervision and Curriculum Development, 1972), p. 14.
[87]Moos, p. 90.

ment for measuring the preferences, and reported a study measuring cognitive preferences of students using the Biological Sciences Curriculum Study (BSCS) materials.[88] He stated as one of the major conclusions, "Studying a BSCS type curriculum from BSCS oriented teachers for several years results in a remarkable effect in terms of the acquisition of inquiry oriented cognitive styles by the students."[89] Such a finding is of considerable importance in evaluating a curriculum with a goal of helping students use methods of inquiry.

Student attitudes toward school are of concern regardless of the curriculum goals. Epstein and McPartland developed an instrument to assess students' reaction to their school life in three dimensions: "1) satisfaction with school in general, 2) commitment to school work, and 3) attitudes toward teachers."[90] The use of this validated instrument could provide important data for curriculum evaluation. Regardless of its merits, a curriculum plan that results in a decline in the quality of school life would in the long run be dysfunctional.

Another important educational outcome is continuing motivation. Maehr defined continuing motivation "as the tendency to return to and continue working on tasks away from the instructional context in which they were initially confronted."[91] Maehr illustrated continuing motivation by the ten-year-old who checks a book out of the library on Indians after a social studies unit. Continuing motivation is necessary for the type of lifelong learning required in a rapidly changing society. Maehr argued, "It may not be amiss to view the school in its ideal as a place where learning is *initiated* and the *interest in learning* fostered rather than exclusively (or even primarily!) as a place where it occurs. In other words, continuing motivation may well be the critical outcome of any learning experience."[92] Continuing motivation is not a new idea; teachers have always felt rewarded when one of their students gets "turned on." Parents may be enlisted to observe continuing motivation in a systematic way, and so provide valuable data for curriculum evaluation.

Effects on Teachers

The effect on teachers of the implementation of a curriculum plan will influence its future use. Numerous curriculum plans have failed because

---

[88]P. Tamir, "The Relationship among Cognitive Preference, School Environment, Teachers' Curricular Bias, Curriculum, and Subject Matter," *American Educational Research Journal, 12* (Summer 1975):236.

[89]Tamir, p. 262.

[90]Joyce L. Epstein, James M. McPartland, "The Concept and Measurement of the Quality of School Life," *American Educational Research Journal, 13* (Winter 1976):15.

[91]Martin L. Maehr, "Continuing Motivation: An Analysis of a Seldom Considered Educational Outcome," *Review of Educational Research, 46* (Fall 1976):443.

[92]Maehr, p. 444.

teachers neither understood nor accepted the underlying principles. Sarason documented this in his case study of the introduction of "new math" into an elementary school.[93] Bussis and colleagues, in a study cited in Chapter 6, found that teachers without a commitment to open education made only a surface change in the curriculum—or no change at all.[94] In Tamir's study, cited earlier, it was students in classes with BSCS-oriented teachers who acquired inquiry-oriented cognitive styles.[95]

The implementation of a curriculum plan may affect the social climate within the classroom. For example, an effective open classroom requires freedom and movement on the part of students. Changes in social climate that are inconsistent with the values held by teachers or that cause teachers to feel they are losing control of the classroom have a negative effect on teachers and eventually on students. Implementation of curriculum plans should not cause teachers to lose their self-respect.

Formal instruments—surveys and questionnaires—should be supplemented by informal procedures in assessing the effects of an instructional program on teachers. Information can be gained through visits to classrooms, interviews, and listening to informal comments in the teachers' lounge. However, the information is too important to leave its collection to chance.

Effects on Community

Long-range effects of an educational program should be reflected in the quality of living. An effective curriculum should result in better-educated individuals and a better society. Important as these long-range effects are, they are extremely complex to evaluate and are so closely interwoven with many other influences on community life that they almost defy evaluation.

Short-range effects, particularly community attitudes toward the curriculum, are easier to evaluate. These attitudes influence whether or not the curriculum will be continued and whether the general community will support education. When a community is in tune with an educational program, the teaching is more likely to be supported and enhanced by other agencies. Community discontent with an educational program in a voluntary agency can result in a "drying up" of the program. Discontent with a publicly supported program can spawn campaigns to censor materials and reduce funds.

Instruments for evaluating the community effects of educational pro-

[93]Seymour B. Sarason, *The Culture of the School and the Problem of Change* (Boston: Allyn and Bacon, Inc., 1971), pp. 29–48.
[94]Anne M. Bussis, Edward A. Chittenden, Marianne Amarel, *Beyond Surface Curriculum* (Boulder, Colo.: Westview Press, 1976).
[95]Tamir, p. 562.

grams include public opinion polls, questionnaires to parents of children, and personal interviews. Citizen advisory councils can be a source of information. Less formal techniques of evaluation may also be valuable. These would include summarizing telephone inquires received by teachers, administrators, and school board members; questions asked by citizens in school board meetings; and letters to the editor of the local paper.

Judgments

Drawing on all the information generated by studying antecedents, transaction, and outcomes, judgments need to be made regarding the instructional program and the curriculum plan it represents. Stake's responsive model of evaluation, which was followed in the collection of data, may be used in the analysis of data and the making of judgments. The evaluator who applies this model would have arranged for various persons to observe the program and assist in data collection. Issues identified by students, teachers, parents, or administrators would have provided focal points for the collection of additional data.

The evaluator would then synthesize the collected information into brief reports, using scenarios, displays, graphs, and the like. These reports would be shared with faculty and parents. As Moos pointed out, "The reactions of staff to data gathering and feedback are valuable clues to the functioning of an institution."[96] Thus, sharing information generates new data. Sharing also makes it possible to correct inaccurate information and identify the need for more information.

An evaluator using the responsive model is more involved in processing judgments than in rendering them. As well as the views of professional staff, the views of parents, the students themselves, specialists in an area of study, and concerned citizens should be used in judging the quality of the instruction. Of course, the evaluators may elect not to use a responsive model and may assume full responsibility for processing the data. In any event, the final responsibility of the evaluator is to report findings to the decision makers and other planners. Again, this task requires ingenuity and a keen understanding of the purposes of evaluation. An examination of almost any educational evaluation report, especially in relation to instruction, reveals the ineptness and shallowness of the document. Much of this weakness is due to the inadequacy of the evaluation itself, but even in the more commendable projects the reports leave much to be desired.

In concluding this section on curriculum evaluation, we note again that the entire program of educational opportunities made available for the children, youth, and adults of a community must be evaluated. The evalu-

[96]Moos, p. 96.

ation of a course, a set of learning opportunities, or any segment of the curriculum is an aspect of and contributes to the evaluation of the total educational program, and thus the total curriculum plan for a school system or an individual school. Similarly, evaluation of instruction is an integral part of the process, contributing essential data to the other, broader, aspects of curriculum evaluation.

EVALUATION OF TRAINING PROGRAMS IN BUSINESS AND INDUSTRY

Woodington observed that "evaluation of training in industry is like the weather. Everyone talks about it but few are willing to spend the time or money to do anything about it, at least not until a program comes under attack."[97] Woodington indicated that effective evaluation is often missing because there is no clear understanding of the training program as an instructional system. In some instances, he said, "There is a lack of a clear perception of what constitutes the evaluation of training."[98] There are, however, exceptions to Woodington's generalizations.

The purposes of training programs in business and industry include directing and orienting new personnel, improving the performance of present employees, and enabling employees to gain new knowledge and skills required by changes in operations. Since these purposes are generally shared with in-service or continuing education programs in the professions, similar evaluation models may be used. Since the purpose of training programs is usually the development of specific competencies, either the behavioral objectives model or the decision-making model of evaluation is appropriate.

Goldstein proposed an instructional model for training programs.[99] The evaluation phase of this model includes the following steps: develop criteria, pretest trainees, monitor training, evaluate training, and evaluate transfer. Note the provision "monitor training," which is one way to evaluate process as included in the decision-making model of evaluation.

Kirkpatrick identified a series of logical steps of evaluation to determine the effectiveness of a training program:

Step 1— Reaction. How well did the conferees like the program?
Step 2— Learning. What principles, facts, and techniques were learned?

[97]Donald Woodington, "Some Impressions of the Evaluation of Training in Industry." *Phi Delta Kappan, 61* (January 1980):326.
[98]Woodington, p. 327.
[99]Irwin I. Goldstein, *Training: Program Development and Evaluation* (Monterey, Calif.: Brooks/Cole, 1974), p. 18.

Step 3— Behavior. What changes in job behavior resulted from the program?

Step 4— Results. What were the tangible results of the program in terms of reduced cost, improved quality, improved quantity, etc.?[100]

The reaction sheet is a popular means of gathering evidence on training or continuing education programs. Effective reaction sheets provide questions that may be tabulated and analyzed. Open-ended questions should also be provided. Reaction sheets indicate only the degree of acceptance of the training or continuing education program; they do not show whether or not the objectives have been achieved.

Measuring the learning—that is the knowledge gained or the skills acquired—may require the preparation of a paper-and-pencil test. Another type of test may require a demonstration of performance. For example, AT&T in their training programs include tests that "consist of a student's being required to fix an artfully broken or fouled-up piece of equipment or to solve a difficult engineering problem."[101]

Measures proposed by Kirkpatrick—behavior and results—can be used to evaluate transfer as proposed by Goldstein. Behavior evaluation measures the change in job performance based on a training program. Woodington reported that "it is not used extensively in business and industry, principally because it is difficult and time-consuming."[102] Often it is the training directors who must develop procedures for observing, recording, and analyzing on-the-job performance.

Results evaluation has to do with the total consequences of a training program. Business and industry executives are looking for increased productivity and profits as the bottom line. Whether training is actually profitable is often difficult to evaluate objectively because of the many compounding factors that enter into profit and loss for a corporation. However, the continued growth of corporate training programs is evidence that executives and managers see positive results from their educational efforts.

ACCOUNTABILITY

The drive to hold schools accountable for pupil progress picked up momentum in the late 1960s. The pressure on school administrators to be accountable for the management of their institutions has continued. Deming commented that this pressure "has been funneled in turn to supervi-

[100]Donald L. Kirkpatrick, "Evaluation of Training," in Robert L. Craig and Lester R. Bittel (eds.), *Training and Development Handbook* (New York: McGraw-Hill, 1967), pp. 87–110.
[101]Stan Luxenberg, "AT&T and Citicorp: Protypes in Job Training among Large Corporations," *Phi Delta Kappan, 61* (January 1980):315.
[102]Woodington, p. 327.

sory and staff personnel and to the classroom teacher." He added, "At the level of classroom teaching, accountability has often been made operational through the performance approach to instruction. We now find teachers being encouraged, persuaded, exhorted, and even threatened into selecting or formulating behavioral or performance objectives for their students."[103] To the extent that this is happening, it is affecting curriculum.

The Florida Educational Accountability Act of 1976 provides one illustration of how the rhetoric for accountability is being followed by action. The act provides a system of accountability which intends to guarantee that each student is afforded similar opportunities for educational advancement. It provides for basic skills tests in grades three, five, and eight; a minimum competency test (or literacy test) at grade eleven, which must be passed if a student is to graduate; and a plan for reporting to the public. Tyler headed a panel which reviewed the Florida Accountability Legislation.[104] They concluded that "one serious potential abuse . . . is the use of students' scores on the basic skills and functional literacy [eleventh grade test] tests as the major criterion for evaluating a teacher's effectiveness in the classroom."[105] They cited a school superintendent who had proposed that test results be used to evaluate teachers.

National attention, however, was focused on Florida's use of the minimum competency test for graduation because of the national trend to such a requirement (see Chapter 4). The minimum competency testing movement was generally supported by advocates of teacher accountability as a way to hold schools and teachers accountable. There may be a subtle difference, however, as illustrated by a brief history of accountability.

At the turn of the century, children who failed in school were blamed for their failure. However, by midcentury, studies of social classes led to the conclusion that a child's school failure could be attributed in large part to cultural conditions in the home and community. Thus the home, community, and society in general were held responsible for failures. The emphasis shifted again in 1970 as critics placed the blame on teachers and schools for lack of basic skills in children. The minimum competency testing program seems to shift the onus for failure back to the learner. Critics of minimum competency testing say, "You are punishing the victim." What will come next? Are we moving to the time when students, schools, teachers, homes, and communities will share in accountability?

DeNovellis and Lewis pointed out in 1975 that "current applications of

[103]Basil S. Deming, "The Performance Approach: Limitations and Alternatives," *The Educational Forum, 61* (January 1977):213.
[104]Ralph W. Tyler, et al., *The Florida Accountability Program: An Evaluation of Its Educational Soundness and Implementation* (Washington, D.C.: National Education Association, 1978).
[105]Tyler, p. 13.

accountability to schools have run into difficult and complex problems. Many of these problems relate to political and philosophical issues. . . . The political issues revolve around the question of who makes what decisions about accountability. The philosophical issues are related to fundamental ideas about education including basic values, standards, and individual and national goals."[106] Recommendations for overcoming these problems were presented by DeNovellis and Lewis in the form of guidelines:

1. The purpose of maintaining an educational accountability program is to improve the quality of education.
2. Any person or group sharing responsibilities for the quality or nature of educational experiences should be accountable to the affected children, parents, community, and to the larger society.
3. Schools, teachers, and others should be held accountable for objectives in the affective and psychomotor realms as well as in the cognitive realm.
4. Accountability should be measured in terms of the input and process, as well as the product of education.[107]

Deming said that "process accountability holds the teacher responsible for knowing his subject matter, knowing his students, knowing the factors that influence learning, and using professionally sound instructional procedures."[108] If this type of process accountability and guidelines proposed by DeNovellis and Lewis were followed accountability could be a positive force for good education.

EVALUATING THE EVALUATION PLAN

Curriculum planning involves a series of choices. Curriculum evaluation is used to judge the appropriateness of these choices. But since the selection and use of an evaluation plan is itself a choice, the plan needs to be evaluated.

This chapter can be summarized by a series of questions that may be used in judging a curriculum evaluation plan.

1. Were various possible models considered in developing the plan?
2. Is the plan appropriate to the curriculum design followed, the teaching models suggested, and the purposes of the evaluation?
3. Does the plan use subjective as well as objective data? When possible, are validated instruments used for collecting data?
4. Does the plan recognize the need for compatibility between means and ends, between processes and purposes?

[106]Richard L. DeNovellis, Arthur J. Lewis, *Schools Become Accountable: A PACT Approach* (Washington, D.C.: Association for Supervision and Curriculum Development, 1974), p. 12.
[107]DeNovellis, Lewis, pp. 12–16 passim.
[108]Deming p. 217.

5. Does the evaluation plan recognize the importance of unanticipated consequences and emerging goals rather than being limited to anticipated goals and objectives?
6. Does the plan provide for the evaluation of goals, subgoals, and objectives?
7. Is the total program of education evaluated?
8. Are specific aspects of the program evaluated?
9. Is the implementation of the curriculum (instruction) evaluated?
10. Are there provisions for sharing findings with faculty, parents, and students, and securing their reactions?
11. Have plans been made to use the evaluation results?
12. Are teachers and administrators committed to the evaluation plan and its use?

Under the best of circumstances, it will be difficult to have a positive response to every question. For example, it may not be possible to secure a commitment to the evaluation plan by teachers and administrators before they examine it. In which case, securing their commitment becomes a major priority for the evaluator. For the final and ultimate judgment of any evaluation plan is based on whether or not it results in improvement in the program of education.

ADDITIONAL SUGGESTIONS FOR FURTHER STUDY

Center for the Study of Evaluation, *Evaluation Comment.* Los Angeles, Calif.: University of California. A periodical published by the only organized, federally supported agency devoting its total scope of work to the exploration and refinement of strategies in evaluation. Articles in the periodical deal with evaluation theory, procedures, methodologies, and practices.

Educational Evaluation and Policy Analysis. Washington, D.C.: AERA Central Office. A bimonthly publication of the American Educational Research Association. Contains articles regarding evaluation models, application of evaluation models, and research utilizing evaluation.

Hodgkinson, Harold, "What's Right with Education?" *Phi Delta Kappan, 61* (November 1979):159–162. Provocative analysis of opinion polls and other data indicating that schools and colleges have done very well except in communicating their success to citizens.

Goodlad, John I., Kenneth A. Sirotnik, and Bette C. Overman, "An Overview of 'A Study of Schooling,'" *Phi Delta Kappan, 61* (November 1979):174–178. The team that spent more than six years in analyzing the nature and character of American schooling in a major national study describes the types of data obtained for the evaluation and methods of collecting them.

Willis, George (ed.), *Qualitative Evaluation: Concepts and Cases in Curriculum Criticism.* Berkeley, Calif.: McCutchan Publishing Corp., 1978. A collection of essays and papers from a variety of writers who analyze and recommend more extensive use of esthetics and private reflection as a means of evaluating educational programs.

Wolf, Richard L., *Evaluation in Education: Foundations of Competency Assessment and Program Review*. New York: Praeger Publishers, 1979. Wolf presents a framework for evaluation based on Ralph Tyler's characterization of the education process, which involves the intertwining of three elements: objectives, learning experiences, and learner appraisal. The tasks necessary for conducting a comprehensive evaluation are defined and described.

EIGHT

...
CURRICULUM
PLANNING AND
THE FUTURE
▪ ▪

Previous chapters have had a futuristic orientation; for example, the importance of self-directed learners who can solve future and as yet unknown problems is emphasized. This chapter demonstrates the need for all aspects of curriculum planning to have a future orientation and offers suggestions for achieving this goal. Possible societal changes are described and their implications for the curriculum are explored. Future changes affecting the organization of education, and thus in turn influencing curriculum and instruction, are discussed. The final section looks to the future of a learning society.

Future changes within society will result in new educational content and configurations of educational programs. Changes in program configurations should be based solidly on curriculum considerations. That is, the form of education should follow the functions to be served.

There are, we believe, some basic assumptions that should serve as guides to educational planning in the concluding decades of the twentieth century:

1. Education should meet society's needs for socialization and citizens' needs for personal development.
2. All citizens should have access to quality education.
3. Opportunities for lifelong learning should be available to all individuals.
4. Society must make maximum use of all available resources for education.
5. Those responsible for education should help in planning the curriculum.

This chapter shows how curriculum planners may use future forecasts within the framework of these guidelines.

The effectiveness of the chapter should not be gauged by the extent to which readers agree with the forecasts and their implications. Rather, its effectiveness should be judged by the degree to which readers develop an interest and concern about the use of future forecasting in curriculum planning and the extent to which this influences their practice.

THE FUTURE AND CURRICULUM CHOICES

Future forecasting, although a relative newcomer to education, has been used for some time in other sectors of society. Burdin noted that "futurism is a much-used tool for decision making, enabling elitist power brokers to prepare for change and to benefit from it."[1] Our complex and rapidly changing society requires that we plan in advance to be ready for new events. Failure to do this results in unfortunate breakdowns in society.

Futurism can play an important role in the management of education, but it is even more important in curriculum development. As Scanlon said, "It is our image of the future that largely will determine what kind of curriculum is planned."[2] However, humanity's enduring values and accumulated knowledge provide for stability and continuity in curriculum planning. Therefore, we believe it is more accurate to say that our image of the future will guide us in making appropriate changes in curriculum.

An effective way to visualize the use of future forecasting in curriculum planning is to refer to Figure 1.1 (p. 29), Elements of the Curriculum System. A static use of the system portrayed would be to consider only *existing data* regarding society, learners, knowledge, and legal requirements. A dynamic use would be to employ *forecasts* regarding society, learners, knowledge, and legal requirements.

Curriculum planners who restrict their data to existing conditions are assuming that the future will be like the present. This approach may appear to be adequate since there are relatively few changes over a short span of time. Weather forecasters say that on the average, today's weather is the best forecast of tomorrow's weather. That plan may work for short-term forecasts, but anyone who has lived in Minnesota from a summer through a winter knows that it does not apply to long-range forecasts.

Need for Future Forecasting in Curriculum Development

To plan education as though the future will be similar to the present may have been appropriate in 1918, when Bobbitt studied adult society to identify those things children and youth must do and experience to function effectively as adults.[3] But Bobbitt lived just at the beginning of a period of rapid change. As a result, Socrates returning some 2300 years after his death to visit Bobbitt's world of 1918 would likely have had fewer surprises regarding technological developments than Bobbitt would have if he were to visit today's world! Socrates would have been impressed with progress in transportation—with automobiles, steamships, railroads, and the beginning of air travel—as well as with the use of electricity and radio. However, consider the new developments confronting Bobbitt: super-

[1] Joel Burdin, "The Changing World and Its Implications for Teacher Education," in Kevin Ryan (ed.), *Teacher Education,* The Seventy-fourth Yearbook of the National Society for the Study of Education (Chicago: University of Chicago Press, 1975), p. 296.
[2] Robert G. Scanlon, "Policy and Planning for the Future," in Louis Rubin (ed.), *The Future of Education,* p. 87.
[3] Franklin Bobbitt, *The Curriculum* (Boston: Houghton Mifflin Company, 1918).

sonic air transport, space travel to the moon, a voyager spacecraft traveling for several years and over a billion miles in space and sending back radio signals that produce remarkable pictures of various planets, instantaneous worldwide television communication via satellites, and computers capable of storing and manipulating vast amounts of data and challenging all but the best of human chess players. Bobbitt would be pleased to see the remarkable progress in medicine, including the transplantation of human organs; he might not be as pleased to learn that we have unlocked the secret of the atom and hold in our power the ability to wipe the human race off the face of the earth. Many people alive today have witnessed all of these changes.

Because tomorrow almost always is similar to today, we may lose sight of the pace of change. Orwell's book, *1984*,[4] was greeted with skepticism when it was published in 1949 because the events portrayed seemed so unlikely to occur. A scientist, Goodman, made a careful study of *1984*.[5] To read his analysis and realize how rapidly we are approaching the world of *1984* is a chilling experience. Goodman identified 137 predictions in *1984* and found that over 100 had already come true. He concluded: "All of Orwell's scientific and technological predictions have either come true or could soon come true."[6] Although it is less certain that the grim social and political predictions will come true, Goodman stated, "Not one of Orwell's predictions is beyond the range of possibility, and almost any of the social and political trends . . . could be brought to a head by just a single triggering incident."[7]

Mead called attention to the generation gap caused by rapid change.[8] Engle and Longstreet extended the idea of a generation gap to include "intra-generational disjuncture," which arises because "the experiences of our youth, that come to be an intimate part of the way we think, of what we are, are increasingly less relevant to our adult lives. The things we grow to love and believe in as youngsters are distant from the realities of our maturity."[9]

Students in school today will spend most of their lives in the twenty-first century. The purpose of futurism in education is to help today's youth

[4]George Orwell, *1984* (London: Lecker and Warburg, 1949).
[5]David Goodman, "Countdown to 1984: Big Brother May Be Right On Schedule," *The Futurist*, 12 (December 1978): 345–355.
[6]Goodman, p. 351.
[7]Goodman, p. 352. In a subsequent issue of *The Futurist*, readers suggested ways to avoid *1984*. "Can We Escape 1984?" *The Futurist*, 139 (August 1979): 291–296.
[8]Margaret Mead, *Culture and Commitment: A Study of the Generation Gap* (Garden City, N.Y.: Doubleday and Company, Inc., 1970).
[9]Shirley H. Engle and Wilma S. Longstreet, "Education for a Changing Society," in James John Jelinek, *Improving the Human Condition: A Curricular Response to Critical Realities* (Washington, D. C.: Association for Supervision and Curriculum Development, 1978), p. 229.

cope with crises they will face and grasp opportunities that will emerge in a changing world. Burdin urged educators to "use futurism—an intellectual and imaginative projection of emerging phenomena and conditions—to keep schools in the mainstream of life."[10]

Utilization of Future Forecasting in Curriculum Planning

The procedure for using future forecasting in needs assessment, described in Chapter 4,[11] could be used by a curriculum planning group. Another approach to future forecasting and curriculum planning is summarized in Figure 8.1. This approach treats forecasts as conjectures, asks for tests of their credibility, allows participants to assign weights to the probability of their occurence and to identify possible implications. The work sheet in Figure 8.1 provides a guide to the process and a record of

1. Event:

2. Source(s):

3. Credibility tests:

4. Probability that the event will occur:

Never   Certain

.0	.1	.2	.3	.4	.5	.6	.7	.8	.9	1.0

5. Probable that event will occur by:

Never	1985	1990	1995	2000	2005	Beyond 2005

6. What will be the impact if the event occurs?

7. What other events will this influence?

8. What are the implications for curriculum?

9. Procedures for monitoring the event:

FIGURE 8.1   Future forecasting and curriculum planning work sheet

[10]Joel L. Burdin, "Futurism as the Focus in Instructional Planning," *Journal of Teacher Education*, 25 (Summer 1974): 141.
[11]See Lois Jerry Blanchard, "Creating a Climate of Rapid Response to Needs for Change," *Educational Leadership*, 36 (October 1978): 37–40.

the results. A faculty or a community planning group using this work sheet, or a variation, could start by brainstorming a list of possible forecasts. The forecasts listed in the next section, or in other lists, could be used as a starting point. From the resulting list of forecasts they would select five to ten for further study. Each of the selected forecasts would be assigned to teams of two or three members, who would be responsible for gathering information regarding the forecast, including its source(s).

Although it is difficult, groups will need to decide whether each forecast considered is credible. To assist the group in making these decisions, the team would seek answers to the following questions:

1. Who is making the forecast? Some research groups and institutions have full-time staff working on forecasting, often for private industry or business. The success of these groups depends upon the credibility they establish and maintain. They often use advanced forecasting techniques. Generally, more confidence can be placed in a forecast emanating from a recognized forecaster or one associated with a major research institute.
2. What value assumptions were made by the forecaster? Are they implicit or explicit? Values affect forecasts. For example, the variation in forecasts regarding energy supplies reflects, to some extent, different value orientations.
3. What procedures were used in making the forecast? Is the forecast an extrapolation of a time series trend line? How valid is the trend line which was extrapolated? Is the forecast based on the Delphi technique? If so, what qualifications did the reacting panel have? Is the forecast the result of scenario writing? If so, who wrote the scenarios and with what assumptions?[12]
4. Does the forecast take into consideration any interacting forecasts? For example, does an enrollment forecast consider both birthrate and migration patterns? For another example, does the fertility rate used in population forecasts take into account the trend toward increased numbers of married women working?

At a subsequent meeting of such a planning group, teams would report their findings. An entire meeting may be devoted to one or two forecasts. After a discussion of the team report, each individual in the group estimates the probability that the event will occur and the probable date. This may be done by having each person mark a transparency sheet showing their estimation on the probablility scale and the probable date of occurrence (items 4 and 5 on Figure 8.1). If the group is relatively small, it is possible to stack the transparencies on an overhead projector and have an instant "read out" of the group's views. After observing and discussing the

---

[12]For descriptions of forecasting techniques including trend line extrapolation, Delphi technique, and scenario writing see Stephen P. Hencley and James R. Yates, *Futurism in Education, Methodologies* (Berkeley, Calif.: McCutchan Publishing Corp., 1974).

group views, individuals are given the opportunity to change their estimates. The resulting scores are averaged to find the mean probability and date of occurrence. With the information before it, the group decides whether or not to give further consideration to the forecast. A forecast with good credibility and with an estimated probability of .6 or better to occur by 1990 would appear to be worthy of further consideration. Once it has been agreed to work on a forecast, the remaining questions on the work sheet need to be answered. This requires a spatial, holistic type of thinking (largely associated with the right half of the brain). Members of the group need to be encouraged to be creative in their thinking.

An example will show the types of ideas that might be generated. Joseph forecast that by the middle 1980s portable personal computers for student use would be available costing in the range of hundreds of dollars and eventually tens of dollars. These personalized computers would soon "know" their owner's knowledge base as well as styles of preferred learning.[13] In checking on the credibility of this forecast it is noted that Earl Joseph is a recognized futurist who has published widely and that he is employed by Sperry Univac, a manufacturer of computer components. Joseph's forecast is supported by 1) trend data showing reduction in size and cost of computers, and 2) the statement by various authorities that the technology to achieve personal computers has already been developed. Assume that a planning group assigned a probability of .8 to this forecast and estimated 1985 as the most likely date. Based on the data available, they decide to explore the implications of this forecast.

Analogy building provides one approach to use in anticipating the impact of a forecast, in this case of personal computers on education (see discussion of synectics in Chapter 6). One analogy that comes to mind readily is that giving students personal computers might be compared with giving students books to carry around. What impact did the availability of books have on education? Did it change the role of the teacher from the repository of information to be dictated to students to that of a motivator, an assigner of material to be read, a leader of discussions, a tester of students' knowledge? It provided for diversification of education according to student interests. It made information available to anyone who could read and had access to books. For the first several decades, however, printed material, under the control of an authoritarian church, was used to indoctrinate people. Church leaders had the ability to read to the masses from church-printed materials. It was not until people had the ability to read for themselves and additional material (at first, produced surreptitiously) was available that reading led to liberation of the minds

[13]Earl C. Joseph, "Long-Term Electronic Technology Trends: Forecasted Impacts on Education," *Foresight Hearings on Future Trends in Elementary and Secondary Education* (Washington, D. C.: U.S. Government Printing Office, 1979), pp. 25–43.

of men and women. Was there concern that learning from print, as contrasted with learning through interaction with another human being, would result in a depersonalized and inhuman education? A planning group, having noted these points, could consider how personal books and personal computers are alike and different. They could then begin to consider creatively, the impact of personal computers on education.

A different analogy might be drawn between personal computers and another electronic development, television. At one time it was thought that television would have a major impact on teaching in the classroom. Although direct television instruction is used in very few classrooms, the medium has had a profound impact on schools, on education, and on all of society. This happened largely because television's ability to entertain was capitalized on by advertising agencies. Could commercial interests produce software for personal computers that contained their advertisements, or in more subtle ways, promoted their own interests? There are major differences in the degree of learner involvement in television and computers. How does this influence the analogy? Again, the purpose of this, or any other analogy, is to help people gain a new perspective and thus free their thinking about the possible impact of personal computers on education.

To continue our illustration, after the group has identified several impacts of personal computers on education, they would consider the interaction of these impacts with other areas. For example, if the use of computers requires new roles and new skills from teachers, what are the implications for their preservice and in-service education? Another example, with the cost of energy increasing for travel to schools and for heating and cooling schools, will personal computers make it possible for students to carry their "school" with them? If personal computers provide many learning experiences, should schools become responsible, primarily, for socialization activities and serve as monitoring agencies? Could student progress be monitored more efficiently and effectively by "read-outs" from personal computers rather than from tests? These are illustrative of the questions to be considered.

Finally the group needs to decide what are the implications of the forecast of personal computers for the curriculum. For example, a group might decide to help their students develop computer literacy. In addition, a study might be instituted to see how computers could be used in various instructional programs.

Some procedure is needed to monitor progress toward an event that has been forecast, particularly if the event has caused a change in the educational institution's program. As a hypothetical example, if a major technological shift made computers obsolete, to continue to develop computer literacy would be as useless as teaching fish-grabbing in Professor Peddiwell's satire on the saber-tooth curriculum.[14] Some forecasts may be temporarily "shelved" by a group pending further developments. These forecasts should also be monitored.

ILLUSTRATIVE CHANGES THAT COULD AFFECT THE CURRICULUM

Curriculum planners need access to forecasts of possible futures. Chapter 3 contains a number of such forecasts that are summarized here for easy reference. These are forecasts, not predictions. That is, the probability that they will occur is above .5; in no case does the probability reach or even approach 1.0.

Learners

Two types of forecasts about learners are pertinent to curriculum planners—demographic data and developmental characteristics.

Demographic Data

- Secondary school enrollments will drop by approximately 25 percent from the 1976 high to 1990.
- Elementary school enrollments could increase in the 1980s as "baby-boom" people have their own children.
- The median age of the population will continue to increase by about two years in each decade.

Changes in Developmental Characteristics
If present trends continue:

- The height and weight of young adults will increase.
- There will be an increasing pattern of alternating work and education—a system of educational interludes.

Social

A number of changes taking place within society have implications for curriculum. These forecasts relate to such areas as family, community, work and leisure, mass communication, and health and welfare.

[14]Harold R. W. Benjamin (alias J. Abner Peddiwell), *The Saber Tooth Curriculum* (New York: McGraw-Hill Book Company, Memorial Ed., 1972).

Family

- The number of families with both parents working will continue to increase.
- The percentage of children living in one-parent families will continue to increase.
- The present percentage of children born out of wedlock will continue.

Community

- High mobility of families will continue.
- The influence of community groups on education will increase.

Work and Leisure

- The percentage of women working will continue to increase.
- The percentage of jobs in the service industries will increase.
- There will be major growth in occupations related to the processing and storing of information.
- Leisure time will increase.

Mass Communication

- An increase in cable television will provide greater variety in programming.
- Satellite interconnections will facilitate broadcasting of international programs.
- Quality of programs for in-school viewing will improve.
- The use of videotapes and videodiscs will increase.
- The interconnection of computers and telecommunications will increase the information available and make it more accessible.

Health and Welfare

- The cost of health care will continue to increase.
- As the number of elderly increases, there will be increased costs for social security, social services, health care, and geriatrics.

Environment and Energy

In Chapter 3 the delicate relationship between environment, energy, and life style is discussed. Many plans for an energy increase would have a negative impact on the environment. As one environmentalist put it, "Coal may be the answer—so long as you don't mine it or don't burn it."

Future forecasts indicate a reduction of fossil fuel. This has slowed industrial production and reduced the standard of living in many countries. The most desirable substitutes appear to be solar energy and nuclear fusion. However, neither has been developed to the extent that it can assume any appreciable share of the energy load.

Knowledge and Technology

The knowledge explosion is discussed in Chapter 3. Forecasters are not in agreement that the amount of information available will continue to increase at the same rate as in the recent past.

With the exceptions of genetic engineering (where knowledge is doubling every two years!) and electronics, the growth of technology is slowing down. Davis attributed this slow-down to three interrelated factors: declining support of basic research, increasing difficulty of developing new breakthroughs, and shortage of energy.[15] He pointed out that "from 1970 to 1976, federal expenditures for basic research in the U.S. declined in real terms by 22 percent, and the trend is expected to continue in the coming decade." Davis also indicated that what is easily discovered is found first and what remains is harder and more expensive to find.

Davis's third reason for forecasting a declining increase in technology is the economic downturn caused by the energy shortage. "In times of economic decline . . . technology is among the first of human enterprises to be afflicted." Davis added, "Writers who base their hope for the continuation of industrialism on the steeply exponential growth of knowledge do not take into account that the knowledge curve ultimately owes its shape to the energy curve, and the energy curve must soon peak."[16]

The forecast of a slowdown of technological development by Davis is supported by other futurists.[17] It serves to remind us of the interrelated nature of events. For example, the preceding forecasts on family and social life are essentially "surprise-free" forecasts. That is, they are based on a continuation of past trend lines. However, if a continuing shortage of energy exacerbates the decline in technological development, the consequences could affect a number of the forecasts; they would no longer be "surprise free."

Sources of Information on Futures

Curriculum planners will find many resources for expanding their understanding of future forecasts. The best single source is *The Futurist* magazine, which accompanies membership in the World Future Society.[18] There are local, state, and regional chapters of the World Future Society. The Educational Section of the World Future Society sponsors an annual conference and publishes a newsletter, *Education Tomorrow*. The

---

[15]W. Jackson Davis, "Energy: How Dwindling Supplies Will Change Our Lives," *The Futurist, XIII* (August 1979): 261.

[16]Davis, p. 261.

[17]See Orio Giarini and Henri Louberge, *The Diminishing Returns of Technology: An Essay on the Crisis in Economic Growth* (New York: Pergamon Press, Inc., 1978).

[18]World Future Society, 4916 St. Elmo Avenue, Washington, D. C., 20014.

World Future Society operates a book service that provides annotated announcements of recent publications on futures.

The number of publications on the study of the future is growing rapidly. Some of the better-known books that will provide a general background include:

Daniel Bell, *The Coming of Post-Industrial Society* (New York: Basic Books, Inc., 1976).
Andrew A. Spekke (ed.), *The Next 25 Years: Crisis and Opportunity* (Washington, D.C.: World Future Society, 1975).
Alvin Toffler, *Future Shock* (New York: Bantam Books, 1970).

A number of books on education and the future have been written. The following are representative of some of the more useful books:

Louis Rubin (ed.), *Education Reform for a Changing Society: Anticipating Tomorrow's Schools* (Boston: Allyn and Bacon, Inc., 1978).
Harold G. Shane, *Curriculum Change Toward the 21st Century* (Washington, D. C.: National Education Association, 1977).
Alvin Toffler (ed.), *Learning for Tomorrow: The Role of the Future in Education* (New York: Vintage Books, 1974).

The books listed above will help you build general background and become oriented to the field of futurism. However, because forecasts change rapidly, it is important to read periodicals such as *The Futurist*. Occasionally articles on the future appear in professional journals.[19] Many educators find that reading and studying about the future provides an effective and pleasant way to stimulate their thinking and expand their personal horizons. Further, as educators begin to understand possible futures they can help to shape them.

IMPLICATIONS OF FUTURE FORECASTS FOR THE CURRICULUM

As indicated in Chapter 5, there are two futures—the one we are drifting into and the one we want. The dour forecasts of social trends reported in the previous section suggest a considerable variation between the future we are drifting into and the one we want. Forecasts are useful as they help us see the shape of the future we are drifting into and enable us to move toward a future we prefer. It is unwise to navigate in unknown and un-

[19]See, for example, Harold G. Shane, "Forecast for the 80's," in *Today's Education, 68* (April-May 1979): 62–65.

charted waters without a sailor at the watch to spot indications of shoals and rocks ahead; it is foolish to ignore the sailor's warnings.

Can anything be done to prevent drifting into an undesirable future? Lasswell answered the question: *"Over the long pull, no specific outcome, especially if repugnant to human dignity, is 'inevitable.'* If we mobilize our resources of knowledge and motivation, we can pass beyond the status of passive instruments of history and become its most effective principals." Lasswell assigned an important role to education: "It is this mobilization . . . that I believe should principally preoccupy public education."[20] Anyone who helps to plan education is helping to decide how to steer the ship when the watch calls out, "Rocks ahead!"

The nautical analogy oversimplifies the complexity of our world. Not everyone agrees with a warning of rocks ahead. Even when they do agree on a problem, they may not agree on procedures to follow to avoid the problem. For example, consider the advice given by economists regarding the solution of problems of inflation. The analogy also implies that immediate remedies can be taken with nearly immediate and observable results. Such is not the case. The analogy, however, is accurate in demonstrating the importance of using forecasts as early warning devices and of responding to the warnings.

Curriculum planners have in their grasp the possibility of using future forecasts and directing their power of education to achieve the best possible future. One approach suggests Bobbitt revisited (see Chapter 1), but with two important differences. First, instead of selecting goals and objectives from the existing society, they are selected from the most accurate available picture of the future world in which learners will live. Second, the goals and objectives selected must transcend specific competencies to be learned and include human traits to be developed. Curriculum planners may design specific programs in response to future forecasts. They may also use future forecasts to rethink general goals and objectives. A third approach is to engage learners directly in a study of their own futures. All of these approaches should enable students to function more effectively in the future.

Specific Curriculum Responses to Future Forecasts

Figure 8.1 shows a future forecasting and curriculum planning work sheet that any planning group may use, as it relates future forecasts to specific curriculum responses. The illustration used in the preceding section indicates the ways in which a group might respond to a forecast regarding availability of personal computers.

[20]Harold D. Lasswell, "The Future of Government and Politics in the United States," in Louis Rubin (ed.), p. 21.

The implications of some forecasts may be relatively straightforward. For example, the forecast that the number of children born out of wedlock will continue at the present high level could be changed through appropriate sex education. In a recent study, Zabin, Kantner, and Zelnik found that half of all initial premarital pregnancies in teen-agers occur during the first six months of sexual activity, with one fifth of these first pregnancies occurring during the first month of premarital sexual activity. "Within two years after commencing sexual activity, two thirds of those who have never used contraception became pregnant." The researchers found that "because of the relatively greater likelihood of nonuse of contraception at early ages, young age at initiation of intercourse has a profound effect on the risk of pregnancy."[21]

There would appear to be a direct connection between the forecast and curriculum changes: institute education on birth control for youngsters before they become sexually active. Zabin and her colleagues concluded "that neither education nor service can await the initiation of intercourse. Timing is crucial." However, "some way must be found to resolve the ambivalence of a society which seeks to prevent adolescent pregnancy but fears the effects of early reproductive education."[22] After society resolves its ambivalence, the question remains: What agencies should assume responsibility? Should it be the home? a health clinic? a religious organization? the school? The present ad hoc method of birth control education is not working—too many youngsters are learning after unwanted pregnancies. Could some plan be developed whereby the parent has the option of how a youngster will receive birth control information, but at the same time society is assured that every young person has such information before he or she becomes sexually active? If so, the ascending curve showing the number of births to unwed mothers would become a descending curve.

The two illustrations, personalized computers and birth out of wedlock, show how future forecasts may be related to education. A serious study of future forecasts produces questions regarding possible roles of education.[23] In studying the illustrative list in Table 8.1, the reader should keep in mind that education takes place in a number of settings and through a variety of delivery systems. Schools are one part, a very important part, of a total educational system. The questions are not asking what can schools do, rather what can education do?

[21]Laurie Schwab Zabin, John F. Kantner, and Melvin Zelnik, "The Risk of Adolescent Pregnancy in the First Months of Intercourse," *Family Planning Perspectives, 11* (July/August 1979): 215.

[22]Zabin, Kantner, and Zelnik, p. 222.

[23]These questions were generated by studying forecasts in Arthur J. Lewis and associates, "Social and Economic Trends Influencing Education." Prepared through a grant from the Florida Department of Education, Tallahassee, Fla., May, 1979.

TABLE 8.1 Illustrative Questions Generated from Studying Future Forecasts

How Can Education

1. Strengthen family units?
2. Become more responsible for the social, ethical, and moral development of children and adolescents?
3. Increase contact between people of different age groups?
4. Make better use of television as a learning tool?
5. Utilize computers as learning tools?
6. Prepare learners who can anticipate change and cultivate needed flexibility?
7. Prepare learners who are tolerant and can accept reasonable alternatives?
8. Avoid oppressive atmospheres in educational institutions?
9. Help learners develop outlets to channel personal pressures?
10. Prepare students for productivity in general but with an emphasis on independent living?
11. Enable citizens to make effective use of leisure time?
12. Prepare individuals for lifelong learning?
13. Make citizens aware and aggressive in the areas of environment and energy?
14. Prepare citizens for possible new life styles?
15. Prepare citizens to live in an age based on computers and communications technology?
16. Enable citizens to deal with the moral and ethical issues surrounding the increased use of computers and information technology?
17. Help citizens avoid a computer-managed society and move toward a society marked by participatory democracy where humanity controls destiny?
18. Help learners develop and clarify their own beliefs and values?

General Goals and Future Forecasts

Considering future forecasts in a one-by-one serial fashion may not reveal some of the broader fundamental curriculum concerns that need attention. An examination of several trends and their interconnections may lead to reconsiderations of general goals of education. Four such goals or themes and their related future forecasts are illustrated.

The first two goals are interrelated and are an integral part of this book. Consider the following forecasts:

- Most skilled workers will need to be completely retrained between three and five times in the course of their careers.
- Many children in elementary schools today will hold midcareer jobs that have not been thought of as yet.
- The amount of knowledge available will continue to grow.
- Personal awards will be based more on education and skill and less on inheritance and property.
- There will be an increase in leisure time.

When these forecasts are viewed together, the clear need for lifelong education emerges.

This resulting forecast of a need for lifelong education may be combined with the forecast that mankind will continue to be faced with social, economic, and technological changes, probably of an unprecedented nature (see Chapter 1). In a world where survival becomes dependent upon the ability to influence and direct rapid changes, and adapt to those that cannot be changed, the ability to learn becomes a primordial need. The combination of these two forecasts leads to the conclusion that individuals need to take increasing responsibility for their own education. Thus to help individuals become self-directed learners becomes a major goal of education. Because of the extreme importance of this goal it is discussed in Chapter 1 and used for illustrative purposes in Chapter 4.

A third set of forecasts leads to another goal. Consider these forecasts:

- Satellite interconnections will facilitate broadcasting of international programs.
- There will be worldwide shortages of energy.
- The danger of worldwide pollution and ecological breakdown will continue.
- The need for international agreements in such areas as pollution control, fishing limitations, and disease control will increase.
- Many of humanity's present and future problems can only be addressed at the global level.

Mead described the emergence of a world community: "For the first time beings throughout the world, in their information about one another and responses to one another, have become a community that is united by shared knowledge and danger."[24] Mead's description, coupled with the preceding forecasts, leads to the conclusion that education should help people become effective citizens in a world community.

Reischauer identified three categories of educational needs for global understanding. A few highly trained specialists need to be developed who would have expert knowledge and high skills in communication related to specific parts of the world. A somewhat lesser degree of knowledge and perhaps some skills in communication will be needed among the millions of people who will be concerned in some ways with international contracts and cooperation. These first two types of needs would be primarily the responsibility of postsecondary institutions. The third, and most crucial need according to Reischauer, "exists at the level of elementary and secondary education. A generalized understanding of world problems and a sense of world citizenship obviously have to be developed here." Reischauer pointed out, "Something as basic as a sense of world citizenship is probably formed either early in life or not at all."[25]

One other general concern is illustrated by a consideration of the following forecasts:

[24]Mead, p. 69.
[25]Edwin O. Reischauer, *Toward the 21st Century: Education for a Changing World* (New York: Alfred A. Knopf, 1974), pp. 138, 139.

- Instantaneous worldwide communications and supersonic transport will increasingly expose societies to abrasive, clashing values.
- The peer group and "pop" culture will become increasingly important in transmitting values.
- Conflicts between centralized and decentralized controls will continue.
- The world will witness steadily greater and more widespread sophistication in terrorist activities.

These forecasts, and others that could be added, indicate that individuals in our society will probably have increasing difficulty in dealing with the value questions they will confront. What role can and should education serve in the sensitive and yet important area of helping people learn to deal with value questions? A satisfactory answer to this question will require cooperation between various educative agencies.[26]

Teaching about the Future

The importance of teaching students about the future was emphasized by Toffler when he argued:

"The concept of the future is closely bound up with the maturation of the learner. . . . How children or young adults see their future is directly connected with their academic performance and, more important, with their "experiential performance"—their ability to live, cope and grow in a high-change society. Future-conscious education is a key to adaptivity."[27]

Toffler pointed out that a focus on the future was relevant to learners of all ages and indicated "that the future is not merely a 'subject' but a perspective as well."[28]

Burdin believed, "The ultimate purpose of futurism in education is not to create elegantly complex, well-ordered, accurate images of the future, but to help learners cope with real-life crises, opportunities, and perils."[29] To achieve this purpose a study of the future needs to permeate the curriculum. Ideally every teacher in every subject and at all grade levels brings concepts and information from future forecasts into the teaching as appropriate. Thus, for example, the biology teacher might introduce the possibility of cloning humans and ask the class to think of the social and economic implications.

McDanield described materials that would be useful in teaching about the future as those

[26]For a valuable discussion of the school's role see R. Freeman Butts, Donald H. Peckenpaugh, and Howard Kirschenbaum, *The School's Role as Moral Authority* (Washington, D. C.: Association for Supervision and Curriculum Development, 1977).

[27]Alvin Toffler (ed.), *Learning for Tomorrow: The Role of the Future in Education* (New York: Vintage Books, 1974), p. xxiv.

[28]Toffler, p. xxv.

[29]Burdin, p. 143.

that will help maturing individuals—

1. cope with their society,
2. understand themselves,
3. understand their investment in the future,
4. not to feel powerless or impotent,
5. identify with the society they will inherit,
6. understand the nature of change,
7. see the means of affecting the direction of change,
8. understand key social-science concepts and their relation to change,
9. identify roles they can take in the change process,
10. avoid ethnocentrism,
11. incorporate classroom learning into their immediate environments,
12. transfer classroom learning to future responsibilities.[30]

This list might be extended in two ways. First, it can apply to all learners whether mature or maturing. Second, it could be expanded to include materials and *experiences* that will help individuals cope with their society, and so on.

One valuable tool for acquainting students with alternative futures is science fiction. Livingston outlined a number of characteristics of science fiction that facilitate its use in teaching about the future:

- provides a psychic preparation for a world of accelerating change,
- presents important social attitudes toward social change that may be representative of the general public,
- portrays some possible future events,
- permits students to understand that forecasting itself is a social act with social consequences.[31]

Livingston also pointed out the value of science fiction in stimulating the imagination and in developing attitudes and values.[32]

A number of high schools and colleges have formal courses on the future. Rojas and Eldredge compiled valuable information regarding curriculum materials, resources, sample syllabi, and a directory of future studies.[33] Courses they reported included such goals as: understand forecasting methods, recognize the continuing impact of technology on society, develop alternative scenarios of the future, learn to anticipate change as a basis for career choices, develop ability to evaluate forecasts, study

[30]Michael A. McDanield, "Tomorrow's Curriculum Today," in Toffler (ed.), p. 104.
[31]Dennis Livingston, "Science Fiction as an Educational Tool," in Toffler (ed.), pp. 237–242.
[32]For a useful anthology of science fiction for junior high school students see Theodore W. Hipple and Robert G. Wright, *The Worlds of Science Fiction* (Boston: Allyn and Bacon, Inc., 1979).
[33]Billy Rojas and H. Wentworth Eldredge, "Status Report: Sample Syllabi and Directory of Future Studies," Appendix in Toffler (ed.), pp. 345–399.

major trends shaping the future. The most common background topics in future courses include: "population, ecology and environment, education, international relations, historic conceptions of the future, urbanization, privacy, automation, computers, cybernetics, systems thinking, science fantasies and utopias, creativity, and concepts of time."[34]

The World Future Society has prepared a book on the study of the future with a student handbook and instructor's manual.[35] This material is developed primarily for postsecondary students. Information regarding materials at all levels is available from the Center for Futuristic Studies at the University of Massachusetts, Amherst, Massachusetts.

A major curriculum change utilizing future forecasting is proposed by Engle and Longstreet.[36] Their curriculum is based on the assumption that "the present historical circumstances of accelerating change, multiplying information, and runaway technological production have escaped the control of our democratically oriented society, threatening its survival." They concluded that "regaining control via systematic use of logical analyses, reflective reasoning, and an increased independence from enculturating processes must take precedence over all other possible functions of schooling."[37]

A lack of space prohibits a description of their well-reasoned proposal for achieving this goal. However, their use of a "bilevel scenario" in their "values strand" (one of four strands) illustrates the nature of their approach. Students are asked to write a scenario forecasting the future of society based on the use of data. Once these scenarios are completed and the probabilities of their occurrence are estimated, students redevelop the scenarios in terms of their own lives; "What might this mean for my life, for what I cherish, for what I hope to be? etc. Subsequently, value questions, applied societally and personally, to the change predicted are explored by students."[38] The use of such bilevel scenarios would overcome a problem often identified with studies of the future. Individuals may recognize intellectually that an event may occur in the future but fail to relate this possibility to their own lives. As a result there is little motivation to either encourage or discourage the occurrence of the possible event. Students need to be not passive observers, but active participants through future studies.

The implications for preservice and in-service education are clear. Teachers need to be involved in future studies—need to understand possi-

[34]Rojas and Eldredge, p. 352.
[35]Edward Cornish with members and staff at the World Future Society, *The Study of the Future: An Introduction to the Art and Science of Understanding and Shaping Tomorrow's World* (Washington, D. C.: World Future Society, 1977).
[36]Engle and Longstreet, "Education for a Changing Society."
[37]Engle and Longstreet, pp. 234–235.
[38]Engle and Longstreet, p. 255.

ble futures and believe they can help to shape that future—if they are to help students to gain from studies of the future.

THE FUTURE AND THE ORGANIZATION OF EDUCATION

Future forecasts portend changes in the organization of education that would affect curriculum planning. A combination of events regarding demands on education, resources available for education, and educational technology could result in new conceptions and configurations of education.

Demands for Education

Forecasts regarding a need to retrain skilled workers three or four times, an increase in knowledge available, and the coming of a new information-technology age indicate the need for lifelong education. Forecasts that the number of employed women will increase indicate an increased need for early childhood education, or at least care. Legislative groups and courts have recognized that every person is entitled to a quality education. These forecasts indicate that the need for an education encompassing all ages will increase and that the demand for education will probably continue.

Resources of Education

Will additional resources be available to meet increased needs and demands for education? Forecasts indicate that inflation will continue. Increases in educational budgets have failed to keep pace with inflation. Should this condition prevail, the "real dollars" available for education will continue to decline.

Forecasts of increasing costs for energy will have two effects on education. First, additional money spent on energy by educational institutions for heating and cooling buildings and for transportation of students will divert funds from the educational program. Second, the growth in national productivity will slow down as energy becomes increasingly scarce, thus reducing the potential funds for education.

Will education's share of the tax dollar increase? Forecasts of increased costs for health care, social security, and social services indicate that the competition for tax funds will become more intense. This competition would be exacerbated by a continuation of a "taxpayers revolt." Total expenditures for education in the United States were 2.8 percent of the Gross National Product (GNP) in 1947 and increased to 7.8 percent for the 1971–1972 school year. However, five years later this percentage had decreased to 7.7 percent, suggesting we may be reaching a limit of the percentage of GNP that can go to education.[39] Miller forecast: "High-quality education programs will be required and expected by our more highly educated and articulate citizenry, but expenditures will remain the same as today in proportion to GNP."[40] It appears that additional finances will not be available to meet the increased needs and demands for education.

In education, people play an all-important role. A shortage of money will make it difficult to employ the needed personnel. Accordingly it will be important to make the most effective use of available personnel, to extend the use of voluntary personnel, including retirees, and to make more effective use of peer tutoring. Miller observed, "Much more effective use will be made of educational technology and community resources in instruction, so as to maximize pupil interest and learning time."[41]

Future Uses of Educational Technology

Developments in electronic technology and telecommunications hold the potential for important changes in education.[42] A major development in educational technology has been the micro-computer. The development of integrated circuits in the 1960s made it possible to reduce the size, cost, and energy requirements for computers. The number of components on an integrated circuit has increased by several orders of magnitudes. It is estimated that by 1990 it will be possible to process six million bits of information on a chip only 1,000 times as wide as an atom. At the same time data storage capability or computer memory is increasing in efficiency and decreasing in size. For example, a "bubble memory" cylinder .0001 inches tall and .0001 inches in diameter can store 287,000 pieces of data. It is such developments that lead to the forecast of portable personal computers.

Videodiscs, plastic or vinyl "floppy" disks, provide a significant advance in the storage of information. It is possible to store up to 300 books of 250 pages each or 50 hours of high fidelity music on one side of a 12-inch "floppy" disk.

Another technological development of value to education is holography. Through the use of laser beams it is now possible to project a three-dimensional hologram in space. Laser beams are used in transmitting light

[39]W. Vance Grant and C. George Lind, *Digest of Education Statistics, 1977 Edition* (Washington, D. C.: U.S. Government Printing Office, 1978), p. 23.
[40]William C. Miller, "What Will the Future Bring for Education?" *Phi Delta Kappan, 60* (December 1978): 288.
[41]Miller, p. 288.
[42]For a description of new developments and their implications for education see Arthur J. Lewis, David Harrison, Paul Kajdan, and Robert Soar, "Future Applications of Electronic Technology to Education" (Tallahassee, Fla.: Department of Education, 1978).

along nonlinear pathways through optic fibers. Such transmissions are already used for telephone communications. Fibers carry many more messages than the same size copper wire, and with greater fidelity.

The development of computers and telecommunications improves the amount and quality of information available. Lewis and colleagues proposed that access to this information might be through a learning center that would "have a communications console consisting of a high resolution color video monitor and camera, a computer keyboard, and data communications arrangements." They visualized that this communications console "could be used for picturephone communication and as a computer terminal. Vast amounts of information could be stored in the users console."[43] The communications console would make it possible to couple videodisc images and sound track to an interactive computer. Through such an arrangement filmed material could be coupled with audio transmission and computer data output. The possibilities for individual instruction based on learning styles, interests, and knowledge of the learner are limited only by the available software. This may, however, prove to be a major limitation.

A less sophisticated system could use student interaction with personal computers. These interactions could include:

1. Computer presenting information and checking to see if student has assimilated, correcting any misunderstandings.
2. Computer responding to questions asked by students with complex answers.
3. Computer presenting a simulated problem for the student's response.

The power and efficiency of these programs could be enhanced by connecting the computer to a central terminal.

Although computers do not allow human, one-to-one interaction, an individual's microcomputer could be hooked up to an educational telephone system to permit communication at specific times with teachers and other pupils. Eventually image phone lines could be used to provide visual imagery.

There is great potential for self-directed learning by means of computers and the more sophisticated communications consoles. However, technology's limitations should be recognized. In this regard, the distinction between information and knowledge needs to be understood. Computers can store vast amounts of information; however, it is humans who develop knowledge as they use this information to solve problems. Thus, in the future the emphasis in education should shift from gaining large amounts of information to learning how to process and use it.

[43]Lewis, et al., "Future Applications," p. 13.

Lewis and colleagues warned, "If we are to avoid Orwell's thought control world of 1984, citizens of all ages need to maintain a balanced view of technology."[44] Such a view would recognize that technology will probably not overpower us, neither will it save the world. Technology, including computers, is a collection of tools. They have no power by themselves; they only amplify the power of those who use them. Therein lies the danger of technology—it can give individuals and groups power over others and ultimately over their own consciousness.

Huebner cautioned, "Technology becomes dangerous when it no longer works together with the imagination of the people who use it, but acts instead as a substitute for their imagination."[45] Lewis and colleagues summarized, "The technology to be feared the most in our society is the one that is understood the least. In ignorance, we live in danger of being dominated by technology and those who control it."[46] The potential of educational technology as a resource will increase. Curriculum planners need to understand that technology and make it work for the benefit of humanity.

PROPOSALS FOR A BETTER FUTURE

The educational future we appear to be drifting into will not meet society's needs. Determining a preferable future and finding ways to achieve it presents a complex problem. It has been said that for every complex problem there is a solution that is direct, that is simple, and that is wrong. Education has its share of illustrations.

A Conception of Education

Solutions are often ineffective because they deal with only a part of the problem. An examination of the interactions between society's expectations of education, the various groups that provide education, and the learners, provides a base for considering alternative solutions.

Society's Needs for Education

Any society's survival requires socialization of its citizens. Survival of the U.S. society requires civic cohesion based on 1) a belief that in a free society people are capable of governing themselves through community effort, and 2) a commitment to work for the community good. In addition to encouraging civic cohesion, education for socialization includes the

[44]Lewis, et al., "Future Applications," p. 21.
[45]Dwayne Huebner, "Technology vs. Man: What Will Be the Outcome?" *Educational Leadership, 31* (February 1974): 393–396.
[46]Lewis, et al., "Future Applications," p. 22.

development of ethical and moral values and the ability to work with other people.

The U.S. society also expects education to foster personal development. Through education its citizens are expected to develop: the skills and attitudes necessary for continued learning; a knowledge base enabling them to utilize existing knowledge and develop new knowledge; the skills needed to function effectively in society; and the specialized preparation necessary for meaningful employment.

Society's third expectation applies only to schools: to provide supervised care for children and youth. Although this responsibility is often not listed as one of the functions of schools, it is a reason many parents send their children to school. The need for supervised care of children and youth will probably increase as more children grow up in single-parent families and as more mothers in two-parent families are employed outside the home.

In reviewing society's needs for education, one area of weakness is the development of civic cohesion. Butts proposed that this weakness was because the "belief that the prime goal of public education is to promote a sense of civic community and obligation for the public good has precipitously declined. The catchwords today are personalized learning, individualized instruction, and above all alternatives," Butts observed that "the decline in faith in public education is partly cause and partly result of the diminished sense of community in the nation as a whole."[47]

Institutions that Support Education

Historically the family and the community have been important educational influences in U.S. society. Their actions as educational agencies have been supported by societal norms and expectations.

Citizens have taxed themselves to support formal educational institutions including schools, colleges, extension services, and libraries. Tax funds are also used to support educational activities in other governmental agencies such as military establishments. Partially supported by tax funds are a number of educational institutions, including public television and radio networks, museums, zoos, and symphony orchestras.

Many private organizations provide educational activities related to their own interests, such as private schools, churches, newspapers, magazine and book publishers, and radio and television networks. Other private groups, supported through public contributions, provide educational opportunities. These include such activities as Girl Scouts, Boy Scouts, Campfire Girls, and Little League athletic teams.

Out of this array of educational institutions, schools have been given or have assumed more and more of society's responsibilities for education. As the traditional educational influence of many homes and communities weakened, school people responded to the need with additional programs.

[47]Butts, p. 25.

Some needs were related only indirectly to education; for example, school breakfast programs were started in some schools.

Many additional responsibilities were assigned to schools because the general public failed to distinguish between education and schooling. Thus as social problems required educational solutions, schools were given the responsibility. For example, driver education, formerly the family's responsibility, was assigned to schools rather than to insurance agencies, or police departments, or to automobile dealers. For a variety of reasons schools have assumed more responsibilities than they can possibly fulfill and their failure has resulted in a diminution of moral and financial support.[48] The possibility that some other agencies could more reasonably and efficiently meet some of these responsibilities needs to be explored.

Learners and Education

Educational categories, such as socialization and personal development, have no meaning for learners. They are responding to some educative influences because of society's requirements and to some from their own volition. Where learners have an option, they respond to educational influences based on their perceived needs, their interests, and the attractiveness of the activity. For many learners there is a sharp break between society's educational requirements and their own interests; for them there is "the real world" and then there is the school.

An area of increasing need is education for recreation and leisure. This increased need is related to, but not limited to, the increase in adult age population. Adults do more than work or retool for work. Actually much adult education is in areas only tangential to work, for example, the housewife taking quilting, cooking, or exercise classes. The phenomenal growth in the number of "how-to-do-it" books is testimony of citizens' needs to fill leisure time with meaningful activities.

Alternative Proposals

Against this brief background of society's needs for education, society's institutions for education, and the learners' needs for education, it is possible to consider illustrative proposals that have been developed in an attempt to find a better future for education.

Deschooling Society

The proposal of Illich to deschool society was a logical extension of criticisms heard during the 1960s. In Illich's view, schools have lost their unquestioned claim to educational legitimacy. He argued that "the hidden

---

[48]For a cogent argument that schools restrict their special responsibilities to intellectual development and citizenship see John Henry Martin, "Reconsidering the Goals of High School Education," *Educational Leadership, 37* (January 1980): 278–285.

curriculum of school requires—whether by law or by fact—that a citizen accumulate a minimum quantum of school years in order to obtain his civil rights."[49] He also charged that schools have alienated persons from their learning and that, as a result, they do not trust their own judgment. Illich's deschooled society would have no compulsory attendance, no discrimination on the basis of prior school attendance, and would be accomplished by the transfer of school funds from institutions to people.

Although the proposal to deschool society has not been adopted, some of the elements of the proposal and its basic rationale have influenced subsequent reform proposals. For example, community control of education, freedom schools, alternative schools, and elimination of compulsory education were all responses to criticism similar to those Illich had responded to.

What would be the consequences of adopting Illich's proposal? This can only be conjectured, for no modern society has been deschooled. Illich assumed that alternative networks would emerge to provide the needed education. One way to consider the impact would be to imagine the concerns to be addressed if it were announced that all public schools in the U.S. would close at the end of the month. One obvious concern would relate to the provision of equality of educational opportunity. Affluent and well-educated parents would find ways to educate their children. But what about the children of the poor? The area of education that might be most vulnerable would be socialization, particularly the promotion of a sense of civic community and obligation for public good. It may be argued that our present educational system is inadequate in providing equal educational opportunity and building civic cohesion. But would deschooling society improve these conditions?

In a deschooled society, how will children and youth spend their time? During the 1970s several national panels studied the reform of secondary education. A recurring theme was changing school attendance laws to lower the school-leaving age. Passow analyzed these recommendations and found, "Presently, there is a dearth of alternatives for youth, with exploitation of youth in unskilled work experience hardly a real option. There is a frightening prospect of large numbers of youth not enrolled in school, and unable to find jobs that will be personally satisfying and start them on career ladders."[50] Passow added that children of the poor and those from ethnic and racial minority groups are most likely to suffer. Passow concluded: "Lowering the age of compulsory education without

---

[49]Ivan Illich, "After Deschooling, What?" in Alan Gartner, Colin Greer, and Frank Riessman (eds.), *After Deschooling What?* (New York: Harper & Row, Publishers, 1973), p. 8.
[50]A. Harry Passow, "Early School Leaving—An Invitation to Disaster," *Educational Leadership, 35* (December 1977): 214.

providing viable options for youths' self-realization and social development is to invite disaster for youth and for society in general."[51] And all
Passow was describing was lowering compulsory school age—not deschooling society.

Family Choice in Education

Proposals have been made to increase family choice regarding their
children's education. The use of optional schools, magnet schools, and
educational vouchers to increase parental choices is described in Chapter
2. A strong advocate for family choice, Coons, was the architect and chief
proponent of California's "Initiative for Family Choice."[52] The proposed
initiative provided for two new types of schools, independent public
schools and family choice schools. Independent public schools would be
established by boards of education but would free educators from "state
mandates about class size, teacher hiring, and curriculum."[53] The family
choice schools would be formed as individual nonprofit schools by private
individuals or groups. "The new schools would generate income by at-
tracting families, each of whom would be entitled to a state certificate
redeemable for the full cost of education; its value would be set at 90
percent of the amount spent upon a similar child in a similar public
school."[54]

Families would probably seek schools that would provide the most personal development for their children and the maximum amount of quality
supervised care. Would parents be less concerned for socialization and the
development of civic cohesion? In fact, would a type of natural selection
segregate children by racial, ethnic, or socioeconomic groups, thus leading
to less civic cohesion? Butts questioned the wisdom of giving up "a common school system devoted primarily to the task of building civic community among the vast majority of citizens . . . in favor of public choice."[55]
He urged the profession to recognize the legitimacy of parental participation, but argued that this participation would be most effective in the
public arena rather than in private contracting.

Restricted Responsibilities of Schools

If schools are hampered because they have been assigned and agreed
to assume too many educational responsibilities, why not reduce the num-

[51]Passow, p. 209.
[52]John E. Coons, "Of Family Choice and 'Public' Education," *Phi Delta Kappan, 61* (September 1979): 10–13.
[53]Coons, p. 11.
[54]Coons, p. 12. As of October, 1980, this proposition has not been submitted to the California
voters.
[55]R. Freeman Butts, "Educational Vouchers: The Private Pursuit of the Public Purse," *Phi
Delta Kappan, 61* (September 1979): 8.

ber of responsibilities? This is a rationale given for the "back-to-basics" drive. Unfortunately, even as the "back-to-basics" drive continues, new mandates are being placed on schools, usually through legislative action.

The proposal to restrict the school's responsibilities has merit provided it is carried to its logical conclusion. Society cannot afford to limit the school's function to narrow goals without making provision for other goals to be met elsewhere in society. Thus, for example, if schools are told to ignore the development of human traits related to moral and ethical values, other arrangements should be made so that this important aspect of education is not ignored. Further, some type of monitoring is needed to assure that effective experiences are provided wherever the responsibilities are assigned.

TOWARD A LEARNING SOCIETY

There is no panacea for the overarching problems of providing more and better education to a greater number of people with the same or even a reduced financial base. And yet society cannot afford to settle for the alternative of a gradual deterioration of its programs of education accompanied by a loss of skills, loss of effectiveness and, most of all, a loss of spirit. While there is no one answer to the problems ahead, a major change in the direction in which we are now drifting is necessary. One possible change could lead in the direction of what might be called a learning society.

A number of themes permeating this book provide, we believe, a basis for a learning society. After summarizing some of these themes, we propose an agenda for the future that could lead toward a learning society. This is but one possible agenda and is offered to stimulate thinking about alternatives.

Basic Beliefs that Undergird a Learning Society

As indicated previously any proposal for new directions in education needs to be clear on its underlying assumptions. The proposal then can be judged on the validity of its assumptions and the extent to which it reflects the assumptions. The following assumptions should guide in the development of a learning society.

Purposes of Education

A learning society must assure that educational needs associated with both socialization and personal development are met. Socialization includes the need to advance civic cohesion through developing a belief in the democratic process of governance and a commitment to work for the public good. Goals for personal development include achievement in subject fields and learning necessary skills. The development of human traits is as necesary as the learning of behaviors. The most basic goal is to help individuals become self-directed learners.

Equality of Educational Opportunity

The ancient Athenians had the goal of a learning society. However, this society was open only to boys who were citizens. Any educational system in our future needs to assure access to equal educational opportunity for all citizens.

Lifelong Learning

A plan for lifelong learning will be needed to meet the demands for retraining of skilled workers and continuing education of professionals. All citizens will require continuing education to play a part in directing their own destiny and to cope with societal changes beyond their control. Individuals of all ages should have the opportunity for the personal growth and satisfaction that accompanies learning.

Utilization of Resources for Education

Successful programs of education must capitalize on every resource for learning. Formal educational institutions will continue to play a major role. However, the structure and function of these institutions may be altered. Other agencies within the community will play increasingly important roles. Virtually all citizens can teach something to other citizens, including peer tutoring by children and youth in school. The extent to which any proposed plan for education will be successful will be associated with the degree to which the proposal utilizes all available educational resources.

Curriculum Planning

Those responsible for education should help in planning the curriculum. There is a truism that "the curriculum teachers choose is the curriculum teachers use." Educators recognize the value of teacher involvement in curriculum planning; but in a society that utilizes all educational resources many others are also responsible for education. Constructive and useful roles need to be found for various individuals and groups as they join educators in planning. Curriculum plans should not be narrowly conceived to fit into one pattern but rather should select as appropriate from among the variety of available curriculum designs (Chapter 5), teaching models (Chapter 6), and evaluation procedures (Chapter 7).

An Agenda for the Future

It is one thing to assert that moving toward a learning society is desirable; it is quite another thing to prescribe procedures to be followed.

There are no models to follow since there are no learning societies we can turn to for illustrations. At this stage of development there simply are a series of questions:

1. How can we secure community-wide planning?
2. How can learners become responsible for their own education?
3. How can educational resources be made available to learners?
4. What uses can be made of human resources and of technological resources?
5. How can education be made responsive to learners?

We have converted these questions into six agenda items that suggest a course of action that could lead to a learning society. At this stage we need demonstrations of this plan in action so we can study its total consequences and make appropriate modifications.

The agenda items listed cannot be prioritized and attacked in a serial piecemeal manner. The completion of one agenda item may have little impact in isolation. For example, making a variety of resources available will have little meaning if learners are not self-directed. Thus it is necessary to move on all fronts concurrently. This does not mean that the planning cannot be undertaken item by item. But even then, the whole picture needs to be kept in mind.

Use Community-Wide Curriculum Planning

The locus for curriculum planning needs to be broadened to include all of the community, not just schools, colleges, and universities; and to include an assessment of current and future educational needs of all citizens. Purposes of education need to be stated to assure that the needs of individuals as well as of society are met. A central planning group, representative of various community agencies, needs to be established to do this work. See Figure 4.1 (p. 165) for one approach to defining the goals and objectives for all educational institutions.

The planning group should assess various educational resources within the community and educational plans developed to encompass such groups as the following: formal educational institutions; business and industry; institutions such as libraries, museums, parks, and zoos; religious organizations; youth groups such as Boy Scouts, Girl Scouts, Campfire Girls, 4-H clubs; governmental agencies such as military, health services, and police; social service agencies such as those concerned with family planning, parent education, and alcohol and drug abuse; media outlets such as newspapers, radio, and television; and, of utmost importance, the home. Representatives of these groups need to be involved in the planning.

To involve such a large number of people from such varied groups is complex. It can only happen if the individuals and groups see some "pay-off" in terms of their own interests. For example, participation in the planning might be a prerequisite to being included in the resource list (to be discussed later) or to being assigned an educational responsibility. Groups that do not originally participate can be asked to come in at a later date.

Given the needs assessment and the resources available, the planning group would negotiate educational responsibilities. Financial support might accompany some assignments. In the event that an agency needs strengthening in order to carry a logical role, the planning group might consider ways to strengthen that agency. For example, the family unit may need to be strengthened if it is to play its appropriate role. The community group might wish to assign primary and secondary responsibilities for some functions. For example, the primary responsibility for driver education might be placed with the automobile agencies, but with the home playing a secondary role.

In some instances several agencies might offer an educational service and the learner, or the learner's parents, would select the agency they would use. The example of sex education, described earlier, suggested that youngsters could learn about birth control methods from their family, their church, their school, or a social or health agency.

The planning group needs to guarantee that appropriate opportunities are available for all learners and to monitor the total educational program to assure that goals are being achieved.

Help Learners Assume Responsibility

The success of a future learning society hinges on changing the attitudes of both learners and teachers toward education. In formal educational institutions teachers are responsible for teaching and learners are obliged to learn. However, in nonformal education the learner becomes responsible for his or her own learning, and teachers are obliged to help the learner. The responsibility for learning needs to shift from teachers to learners in all aspects of the learning society.

Learners cannot assume responsibility for their own learning until they become self-directed. A number of suggestions for achieving this goal are offered in this book. A major block may be the difficulty teachers have in changing their roles from directing learning to helping learners become self-directed.

Make Educational Resources Available
to Learners

Self-directed learners need access to available learning resources. To facilitate learner access, a master list of resources needs to be compiled by the planning group. In addition to resource groups, this list would include people in the community willing to share a talent or skill with a learner. Ideally this list of resources would be placed on a computer for ease of access.

The planning group will need to make judgments as to what is placed on the resource file. As a general rule the planning group would include all on the list but the obviously inappropriate. A procedure would then be established to have learners report the degree to which a particular resource helped them to achieve their goals. These assessments would be available to prospective resource users. Some obviously poor resources would not be used and could be dropped from the list.

In order for learners to utilize learning resources most effectively, they need the assistance of a counselor. This individual would help learners assess their own strengths and weaknesses, put them in touch with possible learning resources, and aid them as they assess the experience.

There are three important questions to be asked by the planning group as it works with the list of learning resources. First, are there adequate provisions for learners to study and learn subject matter that is organized by disciplines? There will doubtless be many resources to help students learn particular skills and competencies, but are there opportunities for them to learn the structure of the various disciplines? Such a foundation is necessary not only as a base for their own further development but in order that new knowledge may be generated. The future of our society is directly related to this need. A primary function of the schools of the future, particularly secondary schools, colleges, and universities may continue to be intellectual development through the study of subject matter.

A second question a planning committee should ask is, will specific resources be overloaded in their use? The nature and the extent of this problem was revealed by Saylor through an analysis of proposals for the reform of secondary education.[56] He found that the principal import of the recent proposals for reform "is that secondary education must be a community-wide program, centered in the high schools but involving parents, citizens, and community and public agencies of all kinds."[57] Saylor pointed out some of the practical problems of providing just one semester of community experience for a high school student on a full or part-time basis. To achieve this goal Saylor estimated that in a city of 150,000 population from 2,000 to 2,500 students would be enrolled in each grade. He then asked, "Will the community agencies of a city of 150,000 be willing to absorb more than 1,000 students each successive semester in a worthwhile program of educative experiences ... ?"[58]

[56]Galen Saylor, "Reform in Secondary Education: The Continuing Efforts to Reform Secondary Education, and a Modest Proposal," *Curriculum Bulletin, 32* (May 1978): 1–25.
[57]Saylor, p. 20.
[58]Saylor, p. 20.

This leads to a third question the planning group needs to consider. What provisions are to be made for the supervision of children and youth during a major part of the day? Historically, parents have depended upon schools for this supervision. Are there more effective and efficient ways to supervise individuals?

Make Better Use of Educational Technology

The future uses of electronic technology and telecommunications are explored in an earlier section of this chapter. This technology is already having a profound impact on training in business and industry. Educational technology can be used to enhance learning in the school, the home, libraries, museums, and other such places. With the use of educational technology, a vacant store can by converted into a learning center; and by connecting the computers to a central terminal and using interactive telecommunications, this learning center can become a sophisticated educational environment. Educational technology will play an important role in the future learning society.

Make Better Use of Human Resources

A learning society will require that learners become resource personnel as they assume responsibility for their own education and as they "teach" other learners. Many additional individuals, often volunteers, will play important roles as teachers and planners; although many of the roles of teachers will change, they will not lose importance. A number of instructional tasks, particularly in subject fields, will continue to be the teacher's responsibility augmented by educational technology. Skilled teachers will provide activities leading to socialization. A major task of teachers will be to assist learners to become self-directed. As children and youth become self-directed, teachers can serve as guides and counselors. There will be no shortage of need for human resources in a learning society; the challenge will be to make the best use of human talents.

Make Education Responsive to Learners

One characteristic of a learning society will be that the total educational system is responsive to the learners. Monitoring procedures must be established to assure that the system is meeting the needs of the learners. At the same time the planning group will need to be certain that all of the purposes within our society are being achieved.

A responsive system is a flexible system. Whether or not education moves in the direction of a learning society through the agenda sketched here, or some other one, there will be changes ahead. If these changes are to be sound they will be based on curriculum considerations—it is the educational program that should determine the future shape and nature of education. Curriculum planners, therefore, will be in the vanguard as educational programs are reshaped. Effective curriculum planners will have a knowledge of future forecasts, will be cognizant of good curriculum and teaching principles and practices, and will be personally open to new ideas. With these attributes, curriculum planners can confidently join their fellow professionals in what may well turn out to be the most important enterprise of the last decades of the twentieth century in helping to shape the future of education and thus of the nation.

ADDITIONAL SUGGESTIONS FOR FURTHER STUDY

Becker, James M., *Schooling for a Global Age.* New York: McGraw-Hill, 1979. A handbook to enable teachers to introduce a global perspective into contemporary and future schooling patterns.

Dickson, Paul, *The Future File.* New York: Rawson Associates, 1978. A summary of forecasts gleaned from the writings of respected futurists is included in the first five chapters. Part II is a combined almanac and directory of developments in future studies and resource materials.

Goodlad, John I., *What Schools Are For.* Bloomington, Ind.: Phi Delta Kappa Educational Foundation, 1979. In Chapters 5 and 6 a leading authority draws on an extensive study of American schools in the late 1970s to present plans and ideas for the improvement of our educational system now and in the decades ahead.

Harman, Willis W., *Citizen Education and the Future.* Washington, D. C.: U.S. Office of Education, HEW Publication No. (OE). 78–07006. The main essay projects alternative futures of our society and the kind of citizen activity likely to characterize the major alternatives, as viewed by the author. Five commentaries are included as footnotes on relevant issues and also as appendices.

Hummel, Charles, *Education Today for the World of Tomorrow.* Paris: UNESCO, 1977. Based on the 1975 International Conference on Education, this UNESCO report summarized problems and trends of education under four captions: Reforms and Innovation, Lifelong Education, Democratization of Education, and Education and Society. A final chapter makes projections for "Education tomorrow"; there is a full bibliography of international sources.

Kerr, Clark (chr.), *Giving Youth a Better Chance: Options for Education, Work, and Service.* A Report of the Carnegie Council on Policy Studies in Higher Education. San Francisco: Jossey-Bass Publishers, 1979. This very important study concludes that one third of American youth are "ill-educated, ill-employed and ill-equipped to make their way in American society." It proposes a radical restructuring of American high schools with much greater opportunities for noncollege-bound students to participate in apprenticeships and acquire job skills.

Overly, Norman V. (chr.), *Lifelong Learning: A Human Agenda.* 1979 Yearbook, Association for Supervision and Curriculum Development. Alexandria, Va.: The Association, 1979. The needs and the problems in establishing a lifetime program of continuous learning are presented in episodic sketches and analytical essays in the first two sections; principles, concepts, and ideas for developing such a program are given in Part III.

Toffler, Alvin, *The Third Wave.* New York: William Morrow and Company, Inc., 1980. According to this book, today we are viewing the impact of the third tidal wave of change in history. (The first wave accompanied the agricultural revolution—the second, the industrial revolution.) The many ways in which this third wave is creating a new civilization in our midst are described.

Wagschal, Peter H. (ed.), *Learning Tomorrows: Commentaries on the Future of Education.* New York: Praeger Special Studies, 1979. A collection of essays by a number of educators who have advocated major reforms in the schools during the 1960s and 1970s in which they offer plans and ideas for developments during the 1980s. The most important essays call for much greater diversity among the plans for schooling and a greater degree of educational pluralism.

NAME INDEX

van Geel, T., 114
Vars, G. F., 238
von Moschzisker, M., 239

W

Wagschal, P. H., 401
Walberg, H. J., 132, 264, 265, 267, 268,
  270, 282, 309, 350, 352
Walker, D. F., 57, 70, 265, 348
Washburne, C., 15, 301
Watson, G. B., 93
Watson, K. J., 314
Wax, M. L., 150
Weaver, R. A., 105
Weber, C. U., 349
Weikart, D. P., 348, 349
Weil, M., 228–229, 271, 272, 277, 281, 284,
  285, 288, 289, 290, 291
Weinstein, G., 236–237
Weller, R. H., 255
West, C. K., 300
White, R., 297

Whitehead, A. N., 141, 142, 174, 212, 213,
  214, 227
Wiles, K., 224, 228
Williams, G. W., 313
Willis, G., 365
Winne, P. H., 220
Wisenbaker, J. M., 27
Wisler, C. E., 348
Witkin, H. A., 301
Wittrock, M. C., 152, 153, 301
Wolf, R. I., 366
Wollett, D. H., 101–102
Woodington, D., 361, 362
Wright, J. E., 50
Wright, R. G., 228, 384
Wynne, E. A., 127

Y–Z

Yates, J. R., 372
Zabin, L. S., 380
Zahorik, J. A., 7, 12, 13, 175, 237
Zaret, E., 266, 267
Zelnik, M., 380

SUBJECT INDEX